Resigned as Prime Minister 4/5/55 –

    80 years of age –

Anthony Eden, successor.

Knighted by Queen Elizabeth

*Winston Churchill*

## BOOKS BY ROBERT LEWIS TAYLOR

WINSTON LEONARD SPENCER CHURCHILL

*Robert Lewis Taylor*

# WINSTON CHURCHILL

*An Informal Study of Greatness*

GARDEN CITY, N.Y.

*Doubleday & Company, Inc. 1952*

*Library of Congress Catalog Card Number: 52–7606*

# *Illustrations*

*Part*

I

# Chapter 1

THE LAST of the great statesmen, Winston Churchill, a man of multiple genius, will be devotedly remembered as one of the most exasperating figures of history. For seventy-seven years he has flashed over the public scene, a beckoning, outsized diamond in a trumpery world. Before moments of British crisis, he has been so uniformly right that his incandescent prescience has itself become a burden to his colleagues and to his countrymen at large. Though frequently tossed aside, Churchill has never permitted himself the luxury of humility. He inherited superior gifts of impatience. His father, Lord Randolph Churchill, a brilliant, impetuous fellow, once established a high-water mark of nonchalance by hiring a waiter to listen to the end of an anecdote by a club bore. The son is no less reluctant to be harried by prolixity. During one interminable debate in the House of Commons, when a speaker was presenting a dramatic list of statistics on Brussels sprouts, Churchill observed an aged member, toward the rear, desperately leaning forward with an old-fashioned ear trumpet. In a voice clearly audible over the House, Churchill said to Anthony Eden, "Who is that idiot denying himself his natural advantages?" He was chided by the Speaker, but without visible effect.

By now, Churchill has developed an immunity to censure. Indeed, some of his acquaintances feel that the times when he has been assailed by self-doubt might be counted on the fingers of one hand. His clothing is a case in point. Churchill's cos-

tumes have provoked reactions ranging from shock to indignation nearly everywhere in the world. Visiting an anti-aircraft
gunnery display, in 1940, he wore a pair of gum boots, a naval
topcoat, and a yachting cap. The unit, logging his tour and
gamely attempting a military description of his dress, finally
wrote in, "No uniform other than Churchillian." At a shoot
arranged by the Duke of Westminster, Churchill's hat, in the
words of a British correspondent, "attracted a great deal of unfavorable comment." It was a homburg of his own design, in
a sickly green, with a pork-pie crown and with a sort of flapping brim turned up all around. It was remarked that the duke,
though sportingly silent, was very considerably off his aim
throughout the afternoon. Churchill also went contrary to
ritual at an upper-class boar hunt in Normandy, in 1927: he
smoked a cigar without removing the band, one of the deadliest sins of the chase. The French were mollified when they had
a close-up look at his garb, which consisted of a scarlet coat
with a green collar, fawn breeches, top boots, and a peaked
black velvet cap. He also had on a fur-trimmed greatcoat and
carried a gold-headed cane. On one of his transatlantic cross-
ings, on the old *Berengaria,* the other passengers, after a succession of Churchillian sartorial tableaux, made up a pool on
his probable headpiece at the ship's fancy dress ball. The money
was redistributed when the subject turned up in a red fez, a
gift of several years previous from an admiring Turk.

The Churchills have a family tailor, on Savile Row, in
London, whose establishment has for years swathed the
normally impeccable line. It is only under extreme prompting
by his wife, however, that Churchill will consent to step in for
a new outfit. He considers that, creatively, he is the equal of
any tailor on record, and besides, he cares very little one way
or another. His gabardine "siren suit," which he concocted in
the early part of the last war, was a familiar sight to the thousands who saw him in person and to the millions who knew him
as a heartening staple of the newsreels. When one of his
friends, pressed for an opinion, commented that the siren suit,

to him, seemed "pretty damned dull," Churchill made one of his rare bows to criticism; he ordered a pin-striped siren suit. The friend was unmoved by the improvement. The Russians in particular were dismayed by the siren suit and eyed it with deep Slavic suspicion, which is believed to be one of the deepest kinds known. Upon his celebrated return from Moscow, in August 1942, Churchill remarked to greeters, with immense good cheer, that his ensemble "didn't go down very well." His tone lacked contrition and even indicated that he would probably wear the siren suit if he went back.

As a rule, when Churchill needs new attire he sends his butler-valet, William Greenshields, who has been with him for years, down the street, any street, to buy something off a rack. According to Brendan Bracken, his closest friend and adviser, Churchill never inquires whether these spot acquisitions cost five pounds or fifty but slips them on with abstracted docility and proceeds to whatever function is at hand. Happily, so unerring is Greenshields' judgment that the master thus outfitted always looks faultlessly groomed. But, as indicated, there have been critical times when, proceeding on his own, he has failed to give unanimous pleasure. In 1908, when Churchill married the beautiful Clementine Hozier, a granddaughter of the Scottish Countess of Airlie, the usually fair-minded British journal, *Tailor and Cutter,* recorded an aggrieved comment on the groom: "We cannot congratulate Mr. Churchill on his wedding outfit; it was not a success. It did not fit him, neither did it suit him. The sleeves were too short and too backward hanging and consequently creased badly when the arms were brought forward. It was too long and heavy for a morning coat and too short and skimpy for a 'frock.' It was neither fish, flesh nor fowl."

*Tailor and Cutter,* in 1908, was only taking early note of what later would be adjudged the most notably independent spirit of modern times. By a simple process of giving full credence to his own opinions, Churchill has attained immortality as conservative statesman, liberal statesman, orator, historian, biographer, wit, war correspondent, and brandy drinker, and has established somewhat lesser records as artist, bricklayer, novelist, aviator, polo player, soldier, and race-horse owner. A comparison of him to the multifaceted hustlers of the Renaissance is inevitable. Leonardo da Vinci painted masterpieces, designed war machines, and built an airplane that flew several dozen feet off a rooftop before crashing. Later history has also had its men of incongruous gifts. Raleigh, the elegant pirate, wrote masterly verses, and Paderewski, perhaps the greatest pianist after Lizst, served very successfully as President of the essentially discordant Poland. But it is in Churchill that the triumphal accomplishments of the well-rounded celebrity have found their most felicitous meeting. It is wholly possible that he is the liveliest personality yet produced by the upper vertebrates.

In any study of a foremost man it is of vital interest to ponder the probable causes of his rise above the mediocre and the merely talented. The people who know Churchill best believe that his motive-power derives from a blend of three main ingredients: matchless energy, a combination of intelligence and memory, and the pushiest ambition since Alexander's wistful complaint about the scarcity of worlds to conquer. Eminent physicians have decreed that energy is born and not made, that humans, through the secret formulas of heredity, receive an impetus at birth which sets the pace for their bumpy journey across the mortal span. In a general way, then, the life-force is influenced more by ancestors than by vitamins. Churchill has been fortunate in both departments; his ancestors could hardly have been selected with greater profit, and his successes with nourishment have been a source of international amity. The Russians in the late war, while disgruntled at his funny suit, were enormously impressed by Churchill at the board. The impunity with which he absorbed caviar and vodka convinced the Soviet leaders that they were fighting on the right side. Hitler, a bilious ascetic, had drunk next to nothing and picked at his food like an anxious raccoon. As wartime Prime Minister, Churchill displayed bursts of energy that occasionally gave rise to modest snarls. During the London blitzes he was usually persuaded to stay downstairs in his headquarters, where he continued working. It was a difficult station for him to maintain; all too often, in the wardens' view, he would clamber up to the roof and watch the show. One night in the midst of an especially savage raid, he went up and took a seat on a tile and thrust a dead cigar into his mouth. Ten minutes later, a worried A.R.P. officer appeared through the trap door, then retired when Churchill glared at him. He reappeared in a few minutes and was stared down again. Meanwhile, the Prime Minister was concentrating on the fiery spectacle, though he was puzzled by what sounded like a flock of geese honking somewhere down below. He had just shrugged this off as impossible when the A.R.P. officer popped through the trap door for the third time and cried out, "Excuse me, sir."

"Young man," said Churchill, "what the deuce is the matter with you?"

"Excuse me, sir," said the officer, "but you are sitting on the smoke vent and the people downstairs are suffocating."

The fathomless wellsprings of energy that drive Churchill have led to interesting alterations in his home of Chartwell, a red brick, nineteen-bedroom farm establishment he acquired in 1923, near the village of Westerham, in the county of Kent. Not long after he bought the place, with his literary earnings, he went down to watch some bricklayers patch things up here and there. He quickly conceived the notion, not entirely foreign to him in other connections, that here was an enterprise at which he could readily excel. He got a trowel and a barrowful of bricks and set to work on a crumbling outhouse. The head bricklayer thereupon advised him that laying brick was not something one went around doing promiscuously but involved joining a union. With a little help, Churchill practiced up in secret, to the point where he was laying, as he said, "two bricks a minute," then he applied for membership in the Southern Counties Division Building Union. The application provoked

a genuinely heart-warming row. One local branch went on
record as considering the gesture a piece of "dangerous and
degrading buffoonery," and another suggested that all bricklayers desist from drinking beer, so as to withhold beer-tax
funds from the Exchequer, of which Churchill was then Chancellor. In the face of this picturesque resistance, it was expected
by many that the highborn amateur would retire, leaving the
field to professionals. But they had reckoned without their
man; Churchill imperturbably pushed his membership through,
paid his first week's fee of nine shillings, and returned to the
outhouse, from which he soon advised that he had accelerated
his tempo to three bricks a minute—no mean figure, if accurate.

His work with the bricks convinced Churchill that he was a
stonemason as well, and he started building his own swimming
pool, in 1929. Wearing waders and other extravagant pieces
of apparel, he supervised the digging of a sizable hole, then
laid the concrete floor himself. He rocked up the sides and devised an ingenious but only partly successful system of heating
the water by natural means. To fill the pool, the water trickles
down over a long series of shallow rock steps, acquiring, it is
always hoped, sufficient warmth from the sun to make it suitable for swimming on any uncloudy day. But England is a
northern land, made habitable mainly by a thoughtful Gulf
Stream, and swimming there is a brisk exercise at the best.
Churchill later installed a mechanical aid to the laggard sun-
shine—an outbuilding containing a furnace and a boiler. Between the two systems, the pool in the swimming months is
kept at a temperature which increases slowly each year, since
Churchill has given out that he prefers to swim in water whose
temperature is precisely the same figure as his age. "Actually,
it isn't a very good pool," says one of his neighbors, John
Pudney, the well-known British poet, who was invited with his
family to enjoy it one afternoon a couple of years ago, or when
the water was at seventy-five degrees. "The bottom is irregular,
being homemade, as it were, and one is forever stepping into

pits and declivities." On this particular afternoon, Churchill arrived on the scene wearing a Roman toga and a sombrero, which he removed and hung on a bush. "All of a sudden, he mounted a board and rather *flung* himself into the water, it seemed to me," recalls Pudney. "My young daughter was in the pool at the time, and I thought for a moment he'd dashed her up on the ledge. But then I saw her—she was quite frightened but swimming strongly for the ladder." Once in the water, Churchill executed what Pudney describes as "a series of perfectly inexplicable front and back somersaults. Then he got out, took up his toga and hat and disappeared toward the house. I fancied he was busy whacking out one of those books of his."

Chartwell was thrown open briefly to the public in 1950, for the first time. It was a busy and gala day, only slightly marred by several of those minor slip-ups that are the bugaboos of famous-house showings. To start off, some resurrected special buses were run down the twenty miles or so from London, and a number of them gave up en route. The weather turned uncommonly cold, rather considerably too cold for the heating provisions made at Chartwell. Mrs. Churchill, badly embarrassed and in no way at fault, spent most of the day apologizing for the clammy conditions inside the house. The English are a hardy race, inured to inadequate defenses against a hostile climate, and the crowds trundled joyously through the residence in which their war leader was preparing his memoirs. It had been decided to levy a fee of two shillings inside the house for those who wished to view the master's paintings, which were exhibited on the ground floor. So immediate was the interest in these that the queues, knotting up, proved too bulky for the toilet arrangements upstairs. One of the secretaries suggested that some of the art crowd be diverted to a downstairs toilet. But by bad luck, the secretary in charge of the downstairs overflow thought he had been assigned to sell tickets, and he charged the excited throng two shillings a head to use the toilet. When it came time to check up, at the end of

the day, it was found that the secretary at the toilet queue had
taken in almost as much as the chaps upstairs, but a few of the
visitors were mildly piqued; they pointed out that they had
never paid more than a penny, or tuppence at the best, in the
subway and that two shillings was a little steeper than they
would care to go, for the most part.

Nearly all visitors to Chartwell exclaim over the ambitious
handiwork of its owner, in the related divisions of painting and
bricklaying and in other fields of his catholic selection. Churchill is incapable of approaching any new enterprise at half
throttle. He is the prime exponent of the restless philosophy of
"whole hog or nothing." At the age of twenty-three he produced an ornate novel called *Savrola, a Tale of the Revolution
in Laurania.* Of the central character, he wrote, with a disarm-
ing lack of self-consciousness, "Ambition was the motive force,
and Savrola was powerless to resist it." After fifty years, the
thought can be taken as a true and valid motto of Churchill's
own career. He has always known where he was going, and he
has forged on without that false modesty which acts to the
detriment of so many lesser men. On the occasion of his first
public address, at a Conservative rally at Bath, shortly after
the novel, the London *Morning Post* permitted him to correct
the story of the speech as reported by one of its veteran correspondents. The editor thought it augured well for the young
man's future when he crossed out the parenthetical word
"cheers." A moment later, the editor realized that the young
man was marked for stardom when he wrote in, over the
elision, *"loud* and *prolonged* cheers." One of the best examples
of Churchill's dutiful attention to the long objective was his
famous and well-authenticated utterance during England's war
in the Egyptian Sudan, which he joined as a young and thrustful soldier-correspondent. "Keep cool, men," he cried to his
troops, who were being hotly pressed by the Dervishes. "This
will make excellent copy for my paper."

An anonymous reporter for the London *Daily Mail* (lately
revealed as G. W. Steevens, himself a noted war correspond-

ent) wrote a stunningly clairvoyant eulogy of Churchill in 1898, after his Sudan exploits and before he had actually entered politics. "In years he is a boy"; wrote Mr. Steevens, "in temperament he is also a boy; but in intention, in deliberate plan, purpose, adaptation of means to ends, he is already a man. In any other generation but this he would be a child. Any other than he, being a junior subaltern of Hussars, would be a boisterous, simple, full-hearted, empty-headed boy. But Mr. Churchill is a man, with ambitions fixed, with the steps toward their attainment clearly defined, with a precocious, almost uncanny judgment as to the efficacy of the means to the end.

"At the present moment he happens to be a soldier, but that has nothing whatever to do with his interest in the public eye. He may and may not possess the qualities which make a great general, but the question is of no sort of importance. In any case, they will never be developed, for, if they exist, they are overshadowed by qualities which might make him, almost at will, a great popular leader, a great journalist, or the founder of a great advertising business.

"He is ambitious and he is calculating; yet he is not cold—and that saves him. His ambition is sanguine, runs in a torrent, and the calculation is hardly more than the rock or the stump which the torrent strikes for a second, yet which suffices to direct its course. It is not so much that he calculates *how* he is to make his career a success—how, frankly, he is to boom—but that he has a queer, shrewd power of introspection, which tells him his gifts and character are such as *will* make him boom.

"What he will become, who shall say? At the rate he goes there will hardly be room for him in Parliament at thirty, or in England at forty."

Mr. Steevens' paragraphs stand up after half a century as an almost unique piece of divination, comparable to the forward-looking flashes of Churchill himself. When the latter was twenty-six, and making his first considerable speech in the

House of Commons, he said, in a general discussion of a national defense bill, "In former days, when wars arose from individual causes, from the policy of a Minister or the passion of a King, when they were fought by small regular armies of professional soldiers, and when their course was retarded by the difficulties of communication and supply, it was possible to limit the liabilities of the combatants. But now, when mighty populations are impelled against each other, each individual embittered and inflamed—when the resources of science and civilization sweep away everything that might mitigate their fury, a European war can only end in the ruin of the vanquished and the scarcely less fatal commercial dislocation and exhaustion of the conquerors. Democracy is more vindictive than Cabinets. The wars of peoples will be more terrible than those of kings."

This precocious warning, in 1901, or more than a decade before the sad, opening salvos of the first great "people's war," set a level of prediction beneath which Churchill has never fallen. His has been the voice of intelligent criticism, imperial Britain's conscience, the court of last appeal in time of danger. His friends feel that he was born with an urge to improve and protect. At Harrow, the select boys' school from which he was graduated well toward the bottom, he was regarded as interesting but a monumental nuisance. He was forever criticizing whatever fell within his view. In the biblical phrase of one of his contemporaries there, "Winston sat in the seat of the scornful." Among the musty records of the institution is to be found a letter of Churchill's, rather evasively signed "Junius Junior," to the *Harrovian*, the school newspaper, in which he took up the cudgel against a correspondent known as "Aequitas Junior." The bone of contention was the (to Churchill) inexcusable decay of the gymnasium. He wrote of the unhappy Aequitas, "I will not pause to criticise his style nor comment on his probable motives, though I am inclined to think that both are equally poor," and he went on with such warmth that the dispatch ended on an editor's note: "(We have omitted a portion of our correspondent's letter, which seemed to us to exceed the limits of fair criticism—Eds. *Harrovian*.)"

It is not too much to say that, down the years, Churchill's critical warning voice, whether mild or intemperate, has often accomplished the salvation of an England seemingly bent on self-destruction. In August of 1939, nearly forty years after that wise, fledgling speech in the House of Commons, he was again hearing the alarms of war in the ill wind from across the Channel. In this he stood almost alone among the weak and deluded leaders of the world. Responding to a Government statement by Sir Thomas Inskip, who said that "War today is not only not inevitable but is unlikely," he described the queer hush that had fallen over Europe:

"What kind of hush is it? Alas! it is the hush of suspense, and in many lands it is the hush of fear. Listen! No, listen carefully; I think I hear something—yes, there it was quite clear. Don't you hear it? It is the tramp of armies crunching the gravel of the parade grounds, splashing through rain-soaked fields, the tramp of two-million German soldiers and more than a million Italians—'going on maneuvers'—yes, only on maneuvers! Of course it's only maneuvers—just like last year. After all the Dictators must train their soldiers. They could scarcely do less in common prudence, when the Danes, the Dutch, the Swiss, the Albanians—and of course the Jews— may leap out upon them at any moment and rob them of their living space, and make them sign another paper to say who began it. Besides, these German and Italian armies may have another work of Liberation to perform. It was only last year they liberated Austria from the horrors of self-government. It was only in March they freed the Czechoslovak Republic from the misery of independent existence. It is only two years ago that Signor Mussolini gave the ancient kingdom of Abyssinia its Magna Charta. It is only two months ago that little Albania got its writ of Habeas Corpus, and Mussolini sent in his Bill of Rights for King Zog to pay. . . . No wonder the armies are tramping on when there is so much liberation to be done, and

no wonder there is a hush among all the neighbors of Germany
and Italy where they are wondering which one is going to be
'liberated' next."

Churchill's high intelligence is coupled to a memory of uncanny brilliance. The two qualities, so neatly supplementary,
make it possible for him to adjudge the probable shape of the
future in the light of what he remembers, and interprets, of the
past. Whereas intellect is a gift from the gods, memory can be
trained; however, Churchill's powers of recollection, like his
father's, approach the abnormal. On a bet one time at the
Carlton Club, Lord Randolph read a whole page of Gibbon's
*Decline and Fall of the Roman Empire* and recited it verbatim.
His son is no less endowed. As a schoolboy, Churchill once
memorized 1200 lines of Macaulay's *Lays of Ancient Rome*
and rattled them off at a brisk gallop in class, to the amazement
of his instructor and to the exhausted boredom of his fellows.
(The Roman vinculum between father and son is incidentally
without significance; memory knows no geographic limits.)
One of his principal amusements in school was to memorize
entire scenes of Shakespeare and catch up his teachers, with
scathing comments. Nothing can be more dampening to a
Shakespeare-fevered master, in the hot clutch of declaiming,
say, "Is this a dagger which I see before me, the handle toward
my head?" than to have a small child pipe up with "—'toward
my hand,' if you don't mind." Churchill's devotion to off-center
learning earned him frequent canings, but he continued, and
continues, to exercise his peculiar skill.

Certainly he remembers his old friends. In 1949 he heard
that the bricklayer who had tutored him years before in that
first, frenzied struggle with the outhouse had become ill and
fallen upon hard luck. Churchill, who loves money, made him
the beneficiary of a tax-free pension of eight pounds, thirteen
shillings, fourpence per month and wrote him the following
note: "I hope this will help you in the difficult times. I look
forward to some more bricklaying with you soon."

# Chapter 2

THE London *Times* of December 3, 1874, included in its list of births for the week the modest announcement, "On the 30th November at Blenheim Palace, the Lady Randolph Churchill, prematurely, of a son." From this brief newspaper debut, the son, named Winston Leonard Spencer Churchill, was to go ahead and attract more space in the *Times* than that cautious journal has ever devoted to any other person.

A good deal has been made, principally by his enemies, of the fact that Churchill was born prematurely. Because of his early ambition, and the accelerated character of his birth, he was given the name "Young man in a hurry" by a no doubt indolent writer of the late 1800s, and the phrase stuck. A magazine article at the beginning of the recent war described him as "Old Man in a Hurry." Between these two pieces of composition, and since, the subject has indeed appeared to be in a fearful rush, in a general way, although he has seldom been known to turn up on time for any specific engagement, large or small. As a very young subaltern, he once kept the Prince of Wales and a dinner party of twelve waiting for nearly an hour. The prince, a grand eater and in the blackest kind of mood, refused to go in until the chancy number of thirteen was made fourteen by the dilatory guest. When Churchill arrived, he was asked the meaning of this unseemly breach of good manners. "Do you have an excuse, young man?" inquired the prince, before a drawing room full of starved nobility. "Indeed I have, sire," explained the unusual boy. "I started too late."

Very few of Churchill's ancestors ever wasted much time. On both sides the lines have been busy, dedicated to toil, quick advancement, and high living. On his father's side, he is descended directly from the first Duke of Marlborough, England's greatest soldier, who showed such genius for incurring royal favor that he survived several changes of crown and wound up with huge estates, vast wealth, and a fame that has only recently been surpassed, in England, by that of his latter-day kinsman, the infant mentioned in the *Times* dispatch. On Churchill's mother's side he is American; she was Jennie Jerome, of New York, the reigning international beauty of her day. Many years ago, when he was on a speaking tour in the United States, Churchill was introduced by Mark Twain, who said, simply, "Ladies and gentlemen, the lecturer tonight is Mr. Winston Churchill. By his father he is an Englishman, by his mother an American. Behold the perfect man!" An English journalist, attempting to assay Churchill's inherited traits, wrote, "from his father he derives the hereditary aptitude for affairs and the grand style of entering upon them, which are not the less hereditary in an English family because they skip nine generations out of ten. . . . From his American strain he adds to this a keenness, a shrewdness, a half-cynical personal ambition for advertisement, and, happily, a sense of humor."

Old British records yield up an abundance of material pertinent to the Churchills. It is of interest not only because of its relevancy to the present statesman, but also because it throws light on the business of how great families are founded. In America, the forebears of today's impeccable aristocrats achieved the color of their blood by hawking tinware and furs; in England, men became noble by inventing pretty sayings and powdering the King's wig. A few others added to these useful amusements a conspicuous enterprise at arms. Churchill's formidable ancestor, the first Marlborough, may be counted among the latter group. It is conjectured that the line sprang from the Barons of Courcil, or Courselle, in Normandy and that one or another of them drifted over with that hungry nuisance, William the Conqueror. But the first Churchill of which history takes much note was an early Winston Churchill, whom a seventeenth-century historian described as "a brilliant but erratic Cavalier." The historian Macaulay, presumably in the light of later news, modified this view by calling him "a poor Cavalier who haunted Whitehall and made himself ridiculous by publishing a dull and affecting folio." Still a third historian, the pseudonymous "Ephesian," rather unkindly wrote in 1927 that both of these characterizations "were not altogether inapplicable to his modern namesake."

The first Winston married a Miss Drake, who was related to Sir Francis Drake, the navigator and gentleman of fortune, and also to George Villiers, the Duke of Buckingham. When the English Civil War of 1642 broke out, he stoutly took up arms for the King, and was soon chagrined to see that he had backed the wrong side. The winners, the Roundheads, fined him the somewhat curious sum of £4446, which he was able to meet only by forfeiting his estate to the Commonwealth. As the present Winston Churchill has so frequently done, he found himself unhorsed but not discouraged. He went to live with his wife's family, at Axminster, and awaited developments, which were not long in coming. The Restoration of 1660 returned him to high favor with the authorities, got him back his property, and saw him knighted, no petty accomplishment in those days. The system of honors has undergone some changes, not entirely for the better. The royal sword lays about with indiscriminate gusto, prodded into action by whichever politicians happen to be in power. Men are knighted for capering on the stage, for accumulating more butterflies than their neighbors, and for encouraging coal miners to dig at an improved tempo.

The first Winston, receiving the title, took as his heraldic motto the Spanish phrase, *"Fiel pero desdichado,"* or "Faithful but unfortunate." The gloomy inscription was handed on down, long after it had become richly incongruous on the shield of the triumphant Marlborough, and remains today the official family slogan. It may be seen emblazoned on the arms at Blenheim Palace, the massive ancestral seat of the Churchills, where the subject of this biography was born, as stated in the *Times*. The present proprietor, the tenth Duke of Marlborough, Winston Leonard Spencer Churchill's obscure and unambitious cousin, may in justice be said to claim some slight merit in the motto, living as he has done for several decades in the shade of his illustrious but untitled kinsman.

The mighty Marlborough, the first duke, was the second son of that early Winston, or Sir Winston Churchill. With him began the real fame of a notable English family. His name was John Churchill and he was born in 1650 in the manor house of Ashe, in Devonshire; his rise to a position of power and command was a triumph of honest skill and sly bravado. At the age of fifteen he talked himself into a job as pageboy to the Duke of York, while his sister, Arabella, a very toothsome girl, became maid of honor to the duchess. Arabella was admired exceedingly by the males of the court and added a fresh stroke of beauty to an otherwise hard-faced collection, if we are to credit the surviving portraits of the period. In those days, as at present, the countries of Europe were periodically going to war against one another, to liven up the dull times and keep the nobility from getting rusty. In 1672, Holland was declared to have become commercially aggressive, and the British sent 6000 troops to join the French in crushing the land of tulips. The Duke of York went along and took young Churchill, who soon became a captain of foot soldiers and appeared in the forefront of every battle, fighting like a maniac. Among other exploits, he saved the life of the Duke of Monmouth, recaptured with a handful of men a position lost by a noted French colonel, and personally killed great numbers of Dutchmen, helping to put a speedy end to the war.

The former pageboy was now covered with glory and he returned home to marry Sarah Jennings, the favorite lady in waiting to Princess Anne, daughter of the Duke of York. It was one of the best-calculated matches in English history. When the duke, as James II, succeeded to the throne, in 1685, the Churchills emerged as court pets, as much through the wire-pulling of Sarah as through the political endeavors of John. Like all kings, James shortly found himself in hot water, besieged by his old friend and ally, the Duke of Monmouth, who stated that he was anxious to sit on the throne himself. Churchill had only recently saved Monmouth's life, and now he was asked to go out and extinguish it. Nothing loath, he took the field, second in command to a general named Feversham, to whom the King owed an old debt. In a praiseworthy action, Churchill proved the foolishness of this alignment when he got up very early one morning and trounced Monmouth while Feversham was being shaved. King James, quickly seeing that his old pageboy was a strategist who placed victory ahead of a clean chin, elevated him to be generalissimo. But what was the poor King's confusion, in 1688, when Churchill deserted to the banner of William of Orange, another nosy continental, who was coming over to stamp out the growing Catholicism in England. William only partially succeeded in stamping out Catholicism, but he did kick out James, and Churchill was made Earl of Marlborough. And then, because he kept in touch with the deposed monarch, naturally wishing to copper every bet, he got himself thrown into the rather social Tower of London, where nearly all Englishmen of any account spent some time at one point or another.

The present-day Winston Churchill has written brilliantly about the energetic feats of his famous ancestor, in an epic four-volume biography published between 1933 and 1938. His *Marlborough, His Life and Times,* is filled with detail gleaned from the family papers and is altogether one of the most exhaustive and affectionate works ever turned out. A great many of Churchill's friends believe that he has always identified himself with the first duke. To be sure, the two have much in common—a passionate curiosity about the military, political ambition, a keen regard for money, and a tendency to switch parties now and again. To write the big biography, Churchill designed and built with his own hands a special workroom in the attic of his house at Chartwell. It included a broad inclined shelf that ran all along one side, so that he could lay out his multitudinous references. Then he hired a zestful bunch of secretaries and began to write, working them until three and four each morning. Churchill fortified himself repeatedly during these ordeals by nipping at some handy beverage, but many of the secretaries didn't drink. They began to fall by the wayside and, at length, were walking off in groups. The biographer, undismayed, bought a newfangled dictaphone and announced to his family that he would probably be stepping up his output. He came down the next day very jubilant, holding a disc and saying, "I got a whole chapter finished." Everybody was anxious to hear it, so he put it on the machine, and they all took chairs, hoping to get some information about William of Orange and those early troubles. Nothing came out of the machine but a sort of scratchy whir, unsuitable for biographical use. They tried several times, but it wasn't any good—the record was entirely blank. Churchill had forgotten to switch on the button. He put on his hat and coat and went out to look for some more secretaries.

By the time he finished the biography, which took several years, Churchill was thoroughly saturated with ancestral lore. He had raised the ghost of Marlborough; those similar kinsmen had walked together night and day. The famous soldier and his equally famous descendant had indeed become almost inseparable. Churchill began to insert harkbacks to his subject in many of his speeches. "As the great Marlborough did—" or "As the great Marlborough said—" became familiar allusions in the House of Commons, and are still frequently heard there. It is a kind of retroactive nepotism, healthy and inoffensive since nothing much can ever come of it, outside of promoting the sale of the book.

Churchill's work does not dwell on the duke's chafing existence in the Tower—no family enjoys discoursing on its members' incarceration in jails, as lively and instructive as those episodes are likely to be. The Life of Marlborough goes on to chronicle the great victories, the tribulations, the final ascension to power of that colorful man. While Churchill stresses the battles, other histories bear down on intrigue. The duke (at that time the earl) was eventually released from the Tower by William of Orange, but he never actually came into his own until Anne, the daughter of the Duchess of York, became Queen Anne, in 1702. With her succession to the throne began the golden period of Marlborough. His excellent wife, Sarah, was privy to the inmost secrets of the Queen, whom she ran pretty much as an American manager runs a prize fighter.

Sarah all but overmatched the Queen in the very first year of her rule, by allowing her, with Holland and Austria, to declare war on France. Suitably enough it was Marlborough who saved the day. The opening trumpet blasts of the coronation had scarcely faded away before he had been named commander-in-chief of the English armies and made a Knight of the Garter to boot. In a superb invasion of France, he won important battles at Venlo, Liége, and Kaiserswerth, and when he came home Queen Anne promoted him to duke and granted him a handsome gratuity of £5000 a year (around $25,000 dollars on the old exchange and worth about $14,000 now). Treatment of this sort would stimulate any man and it stimulated the new duke to get right back to France. In his absence, Louis XIV had conceived the odd notion of trying to capture Vienna. This turned out to be one of the poorest ideas that unfortunate monarch ever had, and he was notable, even among kings, for making mediocre decisions. On August 13, 1704, a prime date in the Churchill family history, Marlborough drew up his forces before the outlying village of Blenheim, a beautiful place on the bank of the Danube, or had been until the several armies arrived and began throwing refuse around. Ordering the charge, Marlborough advanced on Blenheim with a gorgeous panoply of caparisoned horses and brightly uniformed soldiers. He was hurled back unceremoniously, los-

ing about a third of his men. However, in a second try he made
a few feints and crashed right through the center of the French
line. The enemy, routed everywhere, delivered up 11,000 prisoners. An interesting footnote to Marlborough's French campaigns has to do with his sister Arabella, who had begun her
court career back when he had become a pageboy. That
shapely girl (her figure was notorious) had so warmly served
James II and his family that she bore him four sons, one of
whom later became a Marshal of France. As the Duke of Ber-
wick, he was among the ablest leaders lined up against his
Uncle Marlborough on the Continent.

Not long after Blenheim, Louis XIV, a slow man but
capable of being convinced, saw that the jig was up; he went
on home and tried to forget about Vienna. The great days of
French military power were temporarily over. England ruled
supreme.

The Battle of Blenheim became a popular British watch-
word, savored for a while by nearly everybody except a few
chronic malcontents, like the poet Southey, who penned some
fairly sour verses on the event:

> "It was the English," Kaspar cried,
>   "Who put the French to rout;
> But what they fought each other for,
> I could not well make out;
> But everybody said," quoth he,
> "That 'twas a famous victory."

No matter how hard generals get out and work to make
things look good, somebody always comes along and tries to
knock it all down. And besides, poets are by nature hardheaded
and overly practical-minded. A grateful nation saw only the
glorious, jingoistic aspect of the victory and heaped honors
and wealth on the triumphant duke.

Easily outstanding among these expressions of good cheer
was Blenheim Palace, which Queen Anne ran up for Marlborough on the crown property of Woodstock, with the hearti-

est kind of backing from the tireless Sarah. England had a Parliament now, and it voted £240,000, or about $1,200,000, in public money to be used on the buildings alone. There was no trouble in deciding on the name; "Blenheim" epitomized Marlborough's services to the nation. No pains were spared to outfit a proper dwelling in which to house the duke and wherein the future Winston Churchill could be born. The Queen hired an architect, a strong-headed fellow named Sir John Vanbrugh, and almost immediately the racket began. Sarah wanted the palace one way, and Sir John preferred it another. Her complaint, oddly enough, was that the estate was shaping up as too magnificent. To a certain bridge on the grounds she took exception as being "pompous." But for once in her life, Sarah had met her match. Sir John continued stolidly at work, drawing things just as pompous as he pleased, and as a clincher he even put his name to the bridge, which bears it to this day. The finished product, *tout ensemble,* was indeed magnificent, though the residence was a little on the gelid side, as houses go in America.

Winston Leonard Spencer Churchill's birth, in 1874, was under auspices about as regal as may be imagined at any time anywhere in the world. It is difficult to convey to citizens of a republic, even a moneyed republic, the incredible splendor of life in the ducal castles of Victorian and Edwardian Britain. Blenheim is a gigantic stone pile, not dissimilar in size and shape to Buckingham Palace. It has 320 rooms and is surrounded by rolling lawns, gardens and parks, ponds and streams and forests and grassy hillocks—2700 acres of them altogether. Here and there amongst the grounds are hunting lodges, picturesque cottages, gatehouses and other outbuildings necessary to maintain an establishment of such grandeur. Turner's famous painting of Blenheim shows the walls and turrets of the vast and lofty edifice in the far left background, overlooking the tree-ringed lake, handsomely spanned by the pompous Vanbrugh Bridge, and in the foreground a scattering of scarlet-coated gentry gathering with their horses and hounds to make things miserable for the local foxes, who were perhaps the only tenants of Blenheim with anything valid to complain about.

Validly or invalidly, a good many poets seemed to take umbrage at Blenheim, both the house and the battle. Alexander Pope, a man of such critical persuasion that he eventually wrote a snarling poem about criticism itself, was terribly upset by Blenheim Palace:

> See, sir, here's the grand approach;
> This way is for his grace's coach:
> There lies the bridge, and here's the clock;
> Observe the lion and the cock,
> The spacious court, the colonnade,
> And mark how wide the hall is made!
> The chimneys are so well designed
> They never smoke in any wind.
> This gallery's contrived for walking,
> The windows to retire and talk in;
> The council chamber for debate,
> And all the rest are rooms of state.
> "Thanks, sir," cried I, " 'tis very fine,
> But where d'ye sleep, or where d'ye dine?
> I find by all you have been telling,
> That 'tis a house, but not a dwelling."

In a later section, he vilified the much-discussed bridge, exactly as Sarah had done, but another poet, forgoing the bridge, laid viciously into Sarah:

> Who with herself, or others, from her birth
> Finds all her life one warfare upon earth.

Eventually, not only poets yapped at the couple's heels. Marlborough found his civilian existence frequently more troublesome than the old days in the field. By all accounts, he was an extraordinarily mercenary man, as well as being a military genius. At one point it was contended that he had pilfered $300,000 from army contractors and that he had knocked down, as the saying goes, 2½ per cent on the pay of all foreign troops subsidized by England. He was censured by the House of Commons, and the Queen directed the Attorney General to proceed against him. But it all blew over. One is moved to admiration in reading the musty old lists of his "preferments," or salaries: he had $35,000 as Plenipotentiary, $50,000 as General of the English Forces, $15,000 as Master of Ordnance, $10,000 as Colonel of the Guards, $50,000 from the States-General, $25,000 as Pension, $9125 for Traveling, and $5000 for his Table. This adds up to $199,125 annually and is a pretty neat haul, even for a victorious duke. Moreover, he received $45,000 in the percentages mentioned, but he was obliged to spend this on "secret service." Or so he told the Attorney General.

It was to be expected that Sarah would participate in the general grab. She was in the public bin to the tune of $15,000 as Groom of the Stole and $7500 each as Ranger of Windsor Park, Mistress of the Robes, and Keeper of the Privy Purse. There is no record of her actual cleanup activities in Windsor Park, but it seems likely that she kept a vigilant eye on the Privy Purse.

Down the years, Blenheim and its owners admirably withstood the slings and arrows of the bards, and of the other critics, and the ceremonies in the palace were very grand and stately in the time of Churchill's childhood. His grandfather, the seventh duke, was a formal man, who clearly enjoyed playing the *grand seigneur*. Meals were stiff-necked and solemn, and, it is presumed, as vapid and indigestive as English cooking is in the present day. Puddings were then as now among the chief staples of the diet, and their all-around resemblance to wet cement has been remarked by many. Experts have wondered how a perfectly sound pheasant or woodcock can run the gamut of a British kitchen and come to the table tasting like a ski boot boiled in shampoo. It is a curious riddle; nobody seems able to solve it. Astoundingly enough, the English appear immensely well satisfied with their food and can hardly get along on any other. Churchill himself has choked over some of the tenderest viands of the American cuisine, which is matchless (as every American knows). During a tour he made in this country he found the big, meaty Blue Point oysters "quite an undertaking" and regarded Southern fried chicken as "interesting." For only one dish, Maine lobster, was he able to muster any enthusiasm.

During his boyhood times at Blenheim, the luncheon table was crowded with as many as a dozen entrees, each on a solid silver platter. It was the shortsighted custom of the duke to carve for everybody, an assignment of crippling size, since the family was a large one and there were numerous tutors, governesses and other attendants. Lady Randolph Churchill, Winston Churchill's American mother, set down her memoirs many years after her accouchement at Blenheim and added richly to the extant lore of the establishment. The duke ran a taut ship, as they say in the Navy. He was disinclined to see anybody loaf. Throughout the day he had set aside various Hours, as being propitious intervals for self-improvement. Perhaps the most uncommon of these was the Newspaper Hour, in which the household were obliged to bone up on things like hangings, market quotations, the two brothers reunited after a separation of 68 years, and the state of the government. In one way or another, everybody was hard at it from dawn to dusk, and if grumbling may be taken as a sign, there were those among them who would just as soon have been connected with an earl, or a baronet, or even a commoner, as long as he could relax. "So assiduously did I practice my piano, read, or paint," wrote Lady Randolph, "that I began to imagine myself back in the schoolhouse."

Blenheim had been stocked with treasures, one of the costliest arrays in existence. Some of the world's familiar masterpieces—paintings and tapestries—adorned its walls, and there were vast collections of gems, Oriental, Sèvres and Saxe china, jewel cases, statuary, rare old books and carpets and furniture, and miscellaneous objects of art. Much of this had been presented to Marlborough by the heads and notables of nations grateful for his having fixed up France. It is always pleasant to see a powerful neighbor bite the dust, and France was now in a position of humble exhaustion, her stinger drawn, her best men slain. The King of Prussia, for one, was so buoyed up by this state of affairs that he sent Marlborough a first-class Raphael, and other rulers came through as handsomely. No doubt both Marlborough and the King of Prussia cheerfully understood that, had the Battle of Blenheim gone the other way, the Raphael would have been mailed to France, with exactly the same protestations of felicity. While the treasures were gifts in the main, the first duke had a sharp eye for beauty and he himself made a priceless collection of gems, intaglios, and cameos, easily the finest in England.

It should be recorded that by the time of Winston Churchill the Blenheim treasure was cruelly dissipated. Like ordinary mortals, dukes can get hard up, and between the first duke and the seventh duke, Churchill's grandfather, there had been some champion spenders. It was not uncommon, after an unsuccessful Goodwood or Ascot, for a member of the family to snatch down a Rubens, clap on his hat, and head for the front gate, perhaps followed by a second cousin whose pockets were bulging with snuffboxes. London's National Gallery got the King of Prussia's old gift, the "Ansidei Madonna" by Raphael, for $350,000, as well as a Vandyke portrait of Charles I for $250,000. The Baron Alphonse de Rothschild bought two others for a similar sum. Altogether, 450 pictures had been sold, including Rubens' entertainingly naked "Lot and His Daughters" and "Progress of Silenus," which had hung, for some reason inexplicable to Lady Randolph, in the dining room. In fairness to the dukes, it might be remarked that they each spent a fortune looking after the Woodstock villagers, in true feudal fashion. The day's routine at the palace included trips to the poor and needy by the children, who carried baskets of assorted goodies, cov-

ered over with imported linen and damask. As the poor and
needy were cared for, they became poorer and needier, and
others dropped their jobs and joined in, so that eventually the
dukes were supporting almost the entire countryside, which
entailed a heavy strain on the budget.

While living or visiting at Blenheim in his childhood,
Churchill often helped distribute the immemorial alms. Occasionally he joined the village boys in games at one of the
neighborhood playing fields. A villager, now grown very old,
remembers that he borrowed pads in which to play cricket
and "bowled one for six." He is also remembered as having
been absolutely fearless. When a member of his opposing
team once asked who he was, somebody replied, "Oh, his
name is Winston Churchill and he's something to do with
the people up at Blenheim Palace." The remaining snuffboxes at Blenheim must have made a strong impression on
Churchill, for he began dipping at a pretty early age and
has continued briskly to do so ever since. In the House of
Commons, snuff is thoughtfully provided by His Majesty's
Government. The head attendant, who sits in a high basket
chair at the entrance to the Chamber, keeps a boxful for any
Members who have forgotten their own supply and might
demand an emergency snuff at some hot point in the debate.
Churchill always holds out his hand for the box as he enters,
preferring to cleave to the old adage of "a stitch in time."
During the last war, the attendant's ritual snuffbox was destroyed, and Churchill replaced it with a beautiful silver
one from the Marlborough collection. He still goes back to
Blenheim from time to time. People who know him think he
is in some way renewed and thrust on by walking among
the monuments to the family's past and present glory—the
escutcheons, the grim-faced portraits of the dukes, the giant
tapestry of the Battle of Blenheim. Not long ago he returned
to make a major speech to crowds gathered on the palace
grounds. More than 60,000 turned out for an all-afternoon's
outing. In the party accompanying Churchill was Gerald

O'Brien, the Conservative Party's public relations officer, who strode back into the palace with him when the speech was concluded. The statesman moved through the great halls as majestically as if he had been the first duke himself. O'Brien could not help but wonder if the two leaders of the high and mighty clan were in some subtle communication. It was a thought to make the blood stir. "O'Brien," said Churchill, swinging around fiercely, "has this old ruin got bathroom facilities for all those people?"

# Chapter 3

WHEN Winston Churchill was two years old, the Prime Minister, Disraeli, persuaded the duke to become Viceroy of Ireland, and the family at Blenheim picked up and moved to Dublin. Churchill has always maintained that his first memories are of Ireland, of life in a house called "The Little Lodge," which lay near to and complemented the Viceregal Lodge, the main residence of the King's Lieutenant. His father, Lord Randolph, went along in the capacity of unpaid secretary to the duke. The Lady Randolph, in her sprightly memoirs (for decades out of print), has described the family's entrance into town, in itself a memorable event:

"The Duke in uniform rode with a glittering Staff around him. The rest of the family, in carriages with postilions and outriders, drove through the crowded streets to the black and grimy old Castle, which for centuries had witnessed these processions come and go." Precisely what the Irish thought of this ornate invasion is not recorded in the memoirs, but Lady Randolph makes it plain that she considered the whole ambassadorship useless: "The Lord Lieutenant, however intelligent and ambitious he may be, who is not in the Cabinet, is but a figure-head, a purveyor of amusements for the Irish officials and the Dublin tradespeople, on whom he is obliged to lavish his hospitality and his money, with no return and no thanks. The wives of the Viceroys labour in good works, each in turn vying with the other in charitable ardour. However popular the Lord Lieutenant and his wife may have been, however successful their attempts to cajole, conciliate, and entertain—though out of their private means they may have spent money like water—in a week all is forgotten."

As others have noted, the Irish have ever been wanting in gratitude for the many fine things England has tried to do for them. They have taken, and still take, the baffling view that they would prefer to do things for themselves. The duke's skill at cajolery, conciliation, and entertainment must have been transmitted in some degree to his precocious grandson, who was often to shine at soothing the Irish in later years. When he was twenty-six, and had just concluded his famous experiences in the Boer War, Churchill made a lecture tour of America. English-Irish relations were at one of their frequent record-low ebbs, and in Chicago Irish workmen filled the balcony of his lecture hall to heckle. Each time the speaker got well started on a lively anecdote, the workmen would commence a systematic braying that halted the show. ". . . and in this desperate situation," shouted the grandson of the duke, "the Dublin Fusiliers arrived, trumpeters sounded the charge, and the enemy were swept from the field!" The heckling broke off, and the galleries burst into wild cheering. Thereafter, whenever the workmen became restless, perhaps at an incautious suggestion that Englishmen were also on the field, Churchill would ring in the Fusiliers again. He called for them at some amazing places in his South African narrative, at points when they were reputed to have been several hundreds of miles distant, and altogether he made them appear one of the most overtaxed regiments in military history. But the workmen went home satisfied, convinced (as they had suspected all along) that the Irish had won the war.

The Irish question was to play an important part in the life of Churchill's father, a few years after the secretariat in Dublin. Lord Randolph was an immensely gifted man, with a few limiting frailties. Despite the latter, he was to rise to prominence and flash briefly but brilliantly across the British political scene. Important among his frailties was the fact that he was a *bon vivant* on a grand scale, a man of convivial triumphs. In the England of the late 1800s there was not much employment for the sons of dukes; these unfortunates had to improve the hours as best they could. Some took to the Army, others to growing petunias; still others, such as Lord Randolph, started a career of the clubs and salons. Augmenting the latter, he successfully stood for Parliament soon after his marriage, but his real participation was not to begin until later. Speaking of his post with the new Viceroy, Lady Randolph said that "it proved to be of the greatest interest and value to him, diverting his mind from the frivolous society to which he had till then been rather addicted, and which now had ceased to smile on him." The demolished smiles were not the result of his marriage to an American but involved his championship of his brother, who had got into a uniquely gaudy scrape. Boiled down, it centered on his importunate wooing of a married lady toward whom the Prince of Wales was directing his equally rakish glances. The situation embraced a fine point of protocol; the lady's husband objected to being made ridiculous by anything less than royalty. The Prince of Wales, a man of judicial genius, took the side of the husband; as a result, the brothers were banned from court society for a period of eight years.

Lord Randolph and the American beauty, Jennie Jerome, had met at the fashionable English yachting center of Cowes, a spa that has more or less gone to seed in recent years and is now supplanted by Riviera fleshpots like Cannes and Eden Roc. Theirs was a romance to quicken the heart of every true lover of Victorian fiction. In the late 1800s, it was considered routine for all American heiresses to go abroad in search of a title, and for all marriageable European nobility to fix their sights on an American fortune. The arrangement was a sensible one, bringing some badly needed but faintly disreputable culture to American shores and providing a critical transfusion for the Old World gentry, many of whom were living in gigantic entailed palaces but with scarcely a dollar to call their own. Despite the businesslike aspect of these matches—the hint of Cupid firing with a gold-tipped arrow—they enraptured the weary and downtrodden, and furnished the theme of some spectacularly painful novels.

Cowes was a popular covert for the two packs of hunters, but Lord Randolph and Miss Jerome, whatever drew them there originally, had an authentic romance. This is easily demonstrated by the fact that both families opposed a wedding. The duke felt that his son should get elected to Parliament before entering into any entangling foreign alliances, and Miss Jerome's father displayed a monumental apathy toward the suitor. Just how close the American father and his future son-in-law were may be seen from a description the latter gave of the former to the suspicious duke, as reported around the London clubs. "Mr. Jerome," said Lord Randolph, "is a gentleman who is obliged to live in New York to look after his business. I do not know what it is." Notwithstanding this offhand précis, Leonard W. Jerome, the indeterminate businessman, was an American of substance, himself a high liver of cyclonic competence. Besides being the father of Miss Jerome, he was also known as the Father of the American Turf. His diversified parenthood made no difference to the duke, who finally decreed that, if the match must indeed go through, a fat dowry was in order. After the two families had cooled down a trifle, this matter was settled to the satisfaction of all. Jerome's reasons for feeling able to snoot with the frostiest clans in Britain were perfectly in order. Although he had sprung from humble farming stock, in upper New York State, he had risen to glory. One of ten children, he had worked his way through Union College (generally given out as Princeton afterward), married a neighbor, studied law at Albany and gone into the newspaper business, soon acquiring control of the Rochester (New York) *Native American*. At some point along the way he had picked up a raging disapproval of slavery, and he filled his paper with such

malevolent editorials on the subject that somebody, probably
a Southern senator, conceived the idea of paying him honor
by appointing him American consul to Trieste. Jerome had
a growing family, but he agreed, wrote three or four quick
editorials that made *Uncle Tom's Cabin* look like the work
of a secessionist, and set off for a three-year incarceration in
diplomacy. He was miserable. There were no slaves in Trieste,
and besides, the place was too quiet. Winston Churchill's
mother, spending her earliest childhood abroad, spoke Italian
before she spoke English.

When Jerome returned home he had a great deal of pent-up
energy. He settled his family in New York City and went
into Wall Street, where he made an immediate million dollars,
after the style of the period. He himself acquired style by
leaps and bounds and was soon known as one of the brightest
lights along the Rialto. Branching out rapidly, he bought a
sizable share of the New York *Times* and began to build race
tracks, in the first flush of his Turf-fathering phase. Among
the tracks for which he is responsible, for better or worse,
were those at Jerome Park, Sheepshead Bay, and Morris
Park. Also, he and August Belmont were the principal organ-
izers of the American Jockey Club. Jerome's horses lost him
a fortune, and the New York *Times* almost lost him his life.
Slavery again. In the draft riots of 1862, an armed mob
gathered to smash the paper, which had blasted the Copper-
heads, or Southern sympathizers. Jerome was compelled to
rush around the corner and buy some guns. His rewrite men
and copy-trimmers took up an uneasy stand at the windows,
no doubt peering out mistily through bifocals, and a nasty
crisis was averted. A show of strength had kept the peace, as
it is always likely to do.

In the following years the Jeromes lived at fashionable
addresses—in New York's Madison Square in the winter and
at Newport in the summer. They went out much in society.
The Father of the American Turf cut a very gay figure around
town, famous for owning the never beaten Kentucky and,

later, the Pacific Mail Line. He drove the first "four-in-hand" seen on the streets of New York. Jerome, a robust man, liked to be in the vanguard of events, and when the laughable Cyrus Field finally put to sea with his rickety transatlantic cable, he strode the deck beside him, spurring him on with turfy shouts and promises of financial support. Jerome's steam yacht, the *Clara Clarita,* trailed along behind in case of accidents. In 1867 he took his family to Paris, where his ailing wife consulted the celebrated Dr. Sims, confusingly enough an expatriate American. Mrs. Jerome and her two daughters, Jennie and Clare, were to stay on for years, while the husband traveled back and forth at the dictates of his business, whatever it happened to be at the moment. He continued to make and lose fortunes as his family, in the gaudy French capital, rang up social triumphs never before equaled by Americans in Europe. Jerome's eventual death, at the age of seventy-four, was of more than routine interest. He had attended a circus, in London, and listened indignantly to the strong man's offer of fifty pounds to anybody in the house who could stay five minutes with him in the ring. Jerome was walking with a cane at the time, but he hobbled up, removed his cutaway, hung his cane on the ropes, and beat the giant senseless. Not long afterward he fell dead of a heart attack. The doctors suggested that he might have strained himself.

His daughter Jennie's introduction to Lord Randolph Churchill, at a ball aboard a cruiser anchored off Cowes in August 1873, was no new sort of experience for the girl. She had only recently been taken boating by Napoleon III. Like most Americans, she had democratic instincts, and she made the descent from emperor to lord gracefully. Lord Randolph was said to have remarked to a friend directly after the meeting, "There is my future wife." She was greatly sought after, the confidante of such notables as the Princess Metternich, the Duc de Persigny, and the Duc de Praslin, whose father had caused a mild stir in French court circles by throttling his wife, thus providing the basis for an American novel

and movie of later years, *All This, and Heaven Too*. The
late, hasty duc's much-maligned but innocent nurse had gone
to America and married the Rev. Henry M. Field, brother of
Leonard Jerome's old friend Cyrus, the Atlantic cable addict.

After her own marriage, Lady Randolph found considerable fault with England and complained of the traditional
view the English took of Americans. "The innumerable caricatures supposed to represent the typical American girl depicted her always of one type," she said. "Beautiful and
refined in appearance, but dressed in exaggerated style, and
speaking—with a nasal twang—the most impossible language.
The young lady who, in refusing anything to eat, says, 'I'm
pretty crowded just now,' or in explaining why she is traveling alone, remarks that 'Poppa don't voyage, he's too fleshy,'
was thought to be representative of the national type and
manners." Accustomed to the freedom of France, Lady Randolph thought England strait-laced and dull: "The strict
observance of Sunday filled me with awe and amazement. I
had lived most of my life in Paris, where everything gay and
bright was reserved for that day, and could not understand
the voluntary, nay, deliberate, gloom and depression in which
everyone indulged."

A young lady never went driving by herself, and feminine
smoking was entirely out of bounds. A certain Lord ———,
visiting at Windsor, was so hard pressed for nicotine that he
was found in his bedroom lying on his back and smoking
up the chimney. When Queen Victoria (herself a non-smoker)
heard of this desperate situation, she installed a smoking
room in the castle, one of the first in England. The English
masked balls were an especial bane to Lady Randolph, who
believed that such frolics warranted a slight relaxation of
austerity. She found that, even if a dancing partner were
costumed as a Siberian wolfhound, he still insisted on behaving like an Englishman. When she essayed a harmless piece
of coquetry with one fellow, he uttered a few strangled cries,
in a public school accent, and fled out into the night. "De-

ficient in humor and not overburdened with brains," said Lady Randolph, "he could not take the joke, and left the house a miserable man." Summing up, she added, "Generally speaking, there is no doubt that English people are dull-witted at a masked ball, and do not understand or enter into the spirit of intrigue which is all-important on such occasions."

All in all, Lady Randolph was vastly pleased when the duke accepted his appointment in Ireland and the family moved to Dublin. Later she came to love England and lived on there the rest of her life, or many years after her husband had died. She was, in those Irish years, a glittering beauty, with a keen wit and a mischievous sense of humor. Like her father, she had little or no awe of the British, despite their sturdily superior manner, and enjoyed treating them as ordinary mortals. She and her husband once went to a Sunday dinner at the Prince of Wales' in a dilapidated hack, not wishing to interrupt their servants' holiday. When they left, the prince handed her in and said, "Madam, your conscience is better than your carriage." "Is it not, Sir, the Queen's carriage?" she replied, remembering that public conveyances were known as the Queen's carriages. "How can I have a better?" The prince took it sportingly. The Viscount d'Abernon penned a brief sketch of Lady Randolph in this period. "I have [he wrote] the clearest recollection of seeing her for the first time. It was at the Viceregal Lodge at Dublin. She stood on one side, to the left of the entrance. The Viceroy (the Duke of Marlborough) was on a dais at the further end of the room surrounded by a brilliant staff, but eyes were not turned on him or on his consort, but on a dark, lithe figure, standing somewhat apart and appearing to be of another texture to those around her, radiant, translucent, intense. A diamond star in her hair, her favorite ornament—its lustre dimmed by the flashing glory of her eyes. More of the panther than of the woman in her look, but with a cultivated intelligence unknown to the jungle. Her desire to please, her delight in life, and the genuine wish that all should share her joyous faith in it, made her the centre of a devoted circle."

A life-sized, tinted photograph of Lady Randolph now
hangs in an antechamber of Winston Churchill's home. It is
one of the first things visitors to the house see as they enter.
He was to write of her, years after Viscount d'Abernon composed his sketch, "My mother made a brilliant impression
upon my childhood life. She shone for me like the evening
star, I loved her dearly but at a distance. She always seemed
to me a fairy princess." The Britons' attitude toward their
young is far less gluey than that of Americans. It is the tribal
practice, in England, to pack children off to boarding school
as soon as they can be transported without actually endanger-
ing their lives, and even at home they are seldom underfoot,
the management being given over to a domestic. Perhaps
as a result, the English beyond doubt have the best nervous
structures of all the civilized races. Churchill, as a child,
rarely saw his mother. In this regard, she took easily to the
English ways, having been in the first place socially energetic
and disposed toward her own amusements.

The best early sources concur that the boy Winston Churchill was marked by an almost unique intransigence. He was
mule-headed to a degree. His appearance left no doubt of
the smoldering fires within: he was small, red-haired, pep-
pered with freckles, had a slightly pug nose and a mouth that
signaled competition as plainly as a signpost. His eyes were
blue and gazed out with unflinching calm, and a touch of
impatience, on children and grownups alike. The composite
message of his countenance was strongly reminiscent of South
Carolina's unpacific slogan: "Don't tread on me." Even at
his tender age in Ireland he was too much for the average
nanny. One of the richest compliments to his young life
was paid him years afterward by a woman who had contracted to teach him some rudiments of good behavior. "I
used to think him the naughtiest little boy in the whole world,"
she wrote, with a strong suggestion of relief that the ordeal
was behind her. Authority acted on Churchill like magnesium
on water. Nannies, governesses, and nurses followed one

another in pretty rapid succession. One day, learning that a
new warden—somewhat younger and stronger—was expected,
he followed the only course possible to a boy of such spirit:
he borrowed a donkey and ran away. It was bad judgment,
however, for he had not taken the precaution of learning
to ride. He fell off on his head and suffered a concussion,
which healed.

Happily, both for Churchill and the countryside, he was
at last provided with a nurse of real ability, a Mrs. Everest,
who took him in hand with great tact. It was the beginning
of a relationship that was to play an influential part in his
life. Mrs. Everest encouraged him at innocuous pursuits,
such as collecting lead soldiers. The military passion of the
first Marlborough, long latent in the line, suddenly sprang
to life in the child. He was attracted immediately to the fascinating game of war, and has had a good deal to do with
it ever since. Altogether, he rounded up fifteen hundred
beautifully made toy figures, which he formed into an infantry
division with a cavalry brigade. He also got some toy cannon
and other fighting equipment. So elaborate and ingenious
were his maneuvers with this array of miniature might that
his father, ordinarily aloof, one day consented to visit the
battlefield. Lord Randolph stood solemnly studying the
terrain, asking questions and watching his son. He said at
length, "Would you like to go into the Army?" Churchill replied affirmatively, and the father said the matter would be
arranged. Some years afterward, Lord Randolph confided to
a friend that he had considered his son a little retarded and
thought that the Army might be an easy solution all around.

Life passed pleasantly enough in those days in Ireland.
Churchill has retained memories of a social bustle around
the Viceregal Lodge, of Mrs. Everest talking endlessly about
a wonderland called Kent (where he was later to establish
his house of Chartwell), and of his grandfather unveiling
a statue to Lord Gough, saying, "and with a withering volley
he shattered the enemy's line." The whole family enjoyed

the place. Lady Randolph later said that she had never met
a dull Irishman. She apparently never met a dull Irish fox,
either, for her memoirs are crammed with rhapsodies to
the local sport. In perhaps no other country of the world
does the urge to get out and chivvy foxes so closely approach
a mania. The average upper-class Irishman finds it impossible
to live in the same county with a contented fox; he has to
round up some hounds and show it who's boss. Taken all
around, if foxes were as smart as they're traditionally supposed to be, the ones in Ireland would have joined the snakes
in the general walkout at the time of Patrick's tantrum. "Hunting became our ruling passion," wrote Lady Randolph. "Many
were the tosses I took," she added gaily. Probably the worst
rider in the neighborhood, and possibly in the world, was
the Empress Elizabeth of Austria, who had come over for
the express purpose of fox hunting and taken a house nearby.
The Empress may safely be written down as a devotee on
a par with the slavering Irish. In arriving, she had changed to
the ritual garb on the train, pulled up at a suburb, and slid
onto a horse's back from the vestibule. Voicing the horrid
cry of the chase, she had lit out down the road, holding the
reins in one hand and carrying a fan in the other. The horse
then rounded a sharp curve and the Empress sailed on straight,
landing on the imperial behind in a ditch. Nothing like it
had ever been seen around Dublin, but she was greatly applauded for having a congenial anti-fox bias. The Empress
ordered a gymnasium built onto her house and worked out
with bar bells every morning to condition herself for the
crunching spills she took. She was very popular. The only
disparaging comments heard about her involved her use of
rice paper instead of handkerchiefs. She littered the countryside like a billposter. The Empress was finally assassinated,
but the tragedy had nothing to do with foxes.

On the young and impressionable Winston Churchill this
zealous attention to the great outdoors left its stamp. Until
his adulthood he always thought of The Little Lodge as

being situated in a vast game-ridden forest, miles from the main house, or Viceregal Lodge. When he became famous, at a comparatively early age, he revisited the Lodge in connection with making a speech at Dublin. "When I saw it again," he wrote afterward, "I was astonished to find that the lawn was only about sixty yards across, that the forests were little more than bushes, and that it only took a minute to ride to it from the Viceregal where I was staying." The spirit of the hunt was solidly bred into Churchill, who for years performed creditably as a pigsticker in India, a boar hunter in France, a fox hunter in several countries, and a nemesis of small animals and birds generally. He developed a reverential feeling for the saddle, and worked hard to become expert. When he was a young soldier, and scheduled to take part in a steeplechase, he was sleepless for several nights beforehand. Sometime before dawn of the day in question, he arose, shook up his startled groom, and said, "We'd better have a secret rehearsal." As the early mists rose from the course, he went over the entire route, fences, water jumps and walls. Then he turned in for a nap. That afternoon he finished third in a field of four, to the dismay of the groom, who felt that he had shot his bolt before the other contestants had eaten breakfast. Churchill was perfectly satisfied; he told his comrades he'd done better than he expected on an entirely strange course. George Bernard Shaw, to whom a fox hunter was something that ought to be placed under observation, was relieved when Churchill eventually took up other hobbies. "Churchill's recreations are now civilized—painting and bricklaying rather than hunting and shooting," he said in 1950, not long before he died. Churchill and Shaw maintained a curious friendship, on a basis of high cerebral sparring. Before one of his opening nights, Shaw sent Churchill a pair of tickets, with a note saying, "Come to my play and bring a friend, if you have a friend." Churchill returned the tickets with the message, "I'm busy for the opening, but I'll come on the second night, if there is a second night."

# Chapter 4

IN 1880 the Churchill family's political world took a great
fall. Disraeli, the English-Jewish Prime Minister, the
leader of the Tory Party, was defeated by Gladstone, the
Liberal, of whom Winston Churchill was later to write, "[He]
was a very dangerous man who went about rousing people
up, lashing them into fury so that they voted against the
Conservatives and turned my grandfather out of his place as
Lord Lieutenant of Ireland." The Churchills had affection
and respect for Disraeli, but they cared nothing at all for
Gladstone. "Lord Beaconsfield, then Mr. Disraeli, sometimes
dined with us," Lady Randolph remarked of that general
period. "On one occasion Randolph and I were discussing
the evening after our guests had departed, and he commented
on Mr. Disraeli's flowery and exaggerated language, saying,
'When I offered him more wine, he replied, "My dear Randolph, I have sipped your excellent champagne, I have drunk
your good claret, I have tasted your delicious port, I will
have no more." ' This greatly amused me, as having sat next
to him at dinner I had particularly noticed that he drank
nothing but a little weak brandy and water. Mr. Disraeli was
always kind and talked to me at length, which occasioned
much chaff among my friends. . . ."

Disraeli, out of office, was able to return to his political
novels, in which his perhaps exaggerated and flowery language was put to sharp effect, but the duke was obliged to
go back to being a duke. He trooped home to Blenheim,

with his shiny retinue, and his grandson accompanied Mrs. Everest, the nurse, to her family's at Ventnor, on the Isle of Wight. This was a delightful time for Churchill, whose existence amid the pageantry and social hubbub of the Vice-regal Lodge had been desperately lonely. Mrs. Everest played a role in his young life not unlike that of Peggotty in David Copperfield's. She was devoted and faithful and had anecdotal relatives in interesting places. Whereas Copperfield journeyed to Yarmouth to hear Peggotty's brother talk of the sea, Churchill went to Ventnor to hear Mrs. Everest's brother-in-law talk about jail. He had been a prison warden and had a collection of first-class material on his charges. Churchill listened carefully and, again like Copperfield, grew up to be a writer. Besides the doings in the Big House, the brother-in-law was also posted on the Zulu War, which was then being fought in South Africa. In this prosperous phase of her empire development, England was obliged to wage a series of small wars dedicated to keeping various colonial tribesmen in line. The skirmishes were mostly on a nuisance scale and, in fact, contributed to the national health, since they provided a patriotic spark and kept people's minds on the dangerous tribesmen and off their own troubles. Churchill's companion related how the Zulus, in their war of aggression, had struck a number of Englishmen with ugly spears called "assagais," and he even made some assagais for the boy out of fern stems. "I was very angry with the Zulus," Churchill has written, "and glad to hear they were being killed; and so was my friend, the old prison warden. After a while it seemed that they were all killed, because this particular war came to an end and there were no more pictures of Zulus in the papers and nobody worried any more about them."

Churchill's visit to Ventnor had been occasioned chiefly by the birth of a brother, John (called Jack), who was named for the first duke. The year 1880 was an eventful one for the family in several ways. In addition to seeing the Tory collapse and the arrival of John, it marked the real beginning of

Lord Randolph's vivid but ill-fated political career. Woodstock (the village near Blenheim) had returned him to Parliament, but his duties as secretary to the duke, who sat in
the House of Lords, had curtailed his parliamentary activity.
Now all was changed. To secure his seat in Commons, Lord
Randolph had defeated the Liberal candidate, W. Hall. It
was a fairly narrow squeak; the people at Woodstock had been
chafed by the family's long absence. It was felt that a duke,
if he was any kind of duke at all, had better stay home and
look after his parish. But the villagers, a fair-minded lot, eased
up sufficiently to give his son another try. They were not
disappointed; the Woodstock M.P. was to provide political
fireworks that kept the nation richly entertained for nearly
a decade.

Lord Randolph became the most beloved man in England,
far better known than his father. Although a Tory, he differed
with the leaders of his party and led a faction of his own,
called the Fourth Party and devoted to a platform of what
he described as social reform. Even those of his contemporaries who liked him best agreed that he was a marvelously
peculiar man. Lord Rosebery, the Tory minister, with whom
he had grown up, wrote, "From the first moment that I can
remember him there was a tinge in him of the eccentric, the
petulant and the unexpected." Winston Churchill, who was
to write his father's biography, said of him in another book,
"I have heard that on neutral ground [unsocial occasions]
he was incredibly fierce, and affronted people by saying the
most blunt or even savage things. Certainly those who did
not know him well approached him with caution or heavily
armed." In appearance, Lord Randolph was bald, slight,
sallow, drawn, popeyed and had a gigantic walrus mustache.
Despite this essentially ungorgeous inventory, he was curiously
dapper and prepossessing. The protrusive eyes were an inherited characteristic. At Blenheim, which was periodically
opened to the public, Lady Randolph and two or three other
girls of the family used to join the gaping queues incognito

and make the rounds, now and then offering up acidulous comments on the décor. They once broke into merriment and fled when a frank visitor, gazing at the frowning gallery of portraits, cried out, "What popeyes these Churchills have!"

Shortly after Ireland, Lord Randolph moved his family to London and rented a small house in St. James's Place; then he bore down on politics in earnest. "I met at my father's house many of the leading figures of the Parliamentary conflict," Winston Churchill has written, "and was often at luncheon or dinner when across the table not only colleagues, but opponents, amicably interchanged opinions on the burning topics of the hour. It was then that I first met Mr. Balfour, Mr. Chamberlain, Mr. Edward Carson and also Lord Rosebery, Mr. Asquith, Mr. John Morley and other fascinating ministerial figures. It seemed a very great world in which these men lived; a world where high rules reigned and every trifle in public conduct counted; a duelling ground where although the business might be ruthless, and the weapons loaded with ball, there was ceremonious personal courtesy and mutual respect."

In the main, Lord Randolph established his reputation by cursing out Gladstone. Theretofore, the eloquent and sulphurous Prime Minister had raged inviolate over a trembling House, few members of the Opposition daring to come within range of his guns. In Randolph, the great Liberal leader found a foeman disturbingly worthy. The newcomer had a vast and available vocabulary of billingsgate, a genius for denunciation. He was happy in the role of giant killer. Gladstone began to find himself hounded and harried throughout England. Of his mercurial father, Winston Churchill later wrote, "Although he was only a private member, and quite isolated, everything he said even at the tiniest bazaar was reported verbatim in all the newspapers, and every phrase was scrutinized and weighed." The public weighed, and found diverting, such appraisals of Gladstone as: "The Prime Minister, his colleagues and his party—these children of revolution, these

robbers of churches, these plunderers of classes, these destroyers of property, these friends of the lawless, these foes of
the loyal."

The culmination of Lord Randolph's tirades, in 1885, was
an address which, said Lord Rosebery, "as a specimen of
political invective is not likely soon to be outdone. It was
justly censured for violence and extravagance. But coming
from Randolph, whose seasoning was always high, and issued
at a moment of fierce and seething excitement, it was, I
thought, not ill-calculated for its purpose." The Government
of Gladstone came tumbling down, and Lord Randolph, with
his wild but popular eccentricities, was awarded a Cabinet post
as Minister to India and a year later succeeded to leadership of
the House of Commons. When a friend asked him how long
he thought his tenure might endure, he replied flippantly, "Oh,
about six months."

"And then?"

"And then? Why, Westminster Abbey."

At this bright point in his career, when his face and name
were familiar to everybody in Europe, Randolph made a
remarkable decision. He elected to take a long walking trip
under the name of "Mr. Spencer." He wanted quiet, he said,
choosing a method certain to result in notoriety. "His holiday
consisted of a passage from one hornet's nest to another,"
observed Lord Rosebery, who added that the English papers
were hard-pressed for an explanation. For three days the
management of a Vienna hotel addressed him determinedly
as "Lord Randolph" but he made a correction each time by
saying, "Mr. Spencer, a *private* citizen." ". . . the incident
illustrates a certain perversity of character, not unlike that
popularly attributed to the ostrich," wrote Lord Rosebery.
"He was determined to be incognito, therefore he persuaded
himself that he would be incognito."

In the history of Winston Churchill, Lord Randolph's
traits and actions are of pointed significance. Throughout this
period of the father's ascendancy, the son came to be a close

observer of politics. Only infrequently was he encouraged to play with other children; his manners, tastes, recreations, his thinking in general were shaped by his scrutiny of the thrilling adult drama being performed so close at hand. For most children this would have meant a disastrous start in life, and even Churchill was often miserable. "All the great men of my acquaintance are the products of unhappy childhoods," he was to remark long afterward. In his own case, though, he was peculiarly well adapted to a boyhood of partial neglect. His competitiveness, his indifference to authority, and the especially robust constitution with which he seemed to have been blessed at birth combined to give him an extraordinary determination to succeed over everything. He was seldom abashed. As he watched his father's progress, with its frequent small setbacks, he felt a surge of filial sympathy. He offered to help write Lord Randolph's speeches. The offer was refused. For the most part, his father was unapproachable. On one occasion, quite early in the morning, Churchill fired off a double-barreled shotgun beneath Lord Randolph's bedroom window. The boy was astounded, and uplifted, by the brilliant torrent of abuse which promptly issued from the room. Randolph under full steam was a rich and rewarding entertainment, no matter what the circumstances. Churchill stood silently, reloading his shotgun and committing to memory various crushers in the high-sounding blasphemy. A short while later, his father unexpectedly descended to apologize. "Do remember things do not always go right with me," he told his son. "My every action is misjudged and every word distorted. So make some allowances." Then, for a great change, he talked in what Churchill has described in his book *A Roving Commission* as a "wonderful and captivating manner" about school, the Army, "and the grown-up life which lay beyond." It was to prove virtually the sole occasion when the boy and Lord Randolph ever chatted on terms of father-and-son intimacy.

The diligence with which Churchill studied his father's

public and private blasts paid dividends in after years. His own style was influenced by the fine early training. "This boneless wonder," he was to say in Commons, waving toward Ramsay MacDonald, and again (to friends), eulogizing a jubilant Neville Chamberlain, who was waving a paper signed by Adolf Hitler, "See that old town clerk looking at European affairs through the wrong end of a municipal drainpipe." During the last war, Churchill, as Prime Minister, asked Sir Duff Cooper to find a good man to place in charge of his News Division. Cooper selected a former director of London transportation, and took him along to No. 10 Downing Street. The director was considered to be an outstandingly sharp dresser and a man of vocal staying power. Wearing flawless morning attire and carrying a newly shined topper, he arranged himself in front of the Prime Minister and delivered an impassioned twenty-minute statement of intentions, touching on Freedom of the Press, the Honorable Name of British Journalism, and other hogwash. Churchill, who is one of the world's poorest listeners, writhed in agony, chewing to bits two expensive cigars. The door had scarcely closed behind the visitor when he cried out to Cooper, "Never send that impeccable bus conductor to see me again!"

Lord Randolph was named Secretary of State for India in 1885 and rose to the second highest political eminence in England in 1886, when he was made Chancellor of the Exchequer, a post his son was to fill some years later. Under his first stewardship, Burma was annexed to the Empire and relations between India and England were tolerably calm, with a few modest uprisings but nothing compared to the rows that India could, and would, produce as an autonomous state. He became known as a fierce champion of the Indians and spoke out bitterly when he thought Parliament was neglecting them. He called on the House to watch "with the most sedulous attention, to develop with the most anxious care, to guard with the most united and undying resolution the land and the people of Hindostan." Of the situation generally he said that "Our rule in India is, as it were, a sheet of oil spread out over a surface of, and keeping calm and quiet and unruffled by storms, an immense and profound ocean of diverse humanity." The quotation is important, since it represents almost identically the view which Winston Churchill adopted, and still retains, of the reciprocal benefits from an Anglo-Indian connection.

Randolph had hit on an uncommon device for getting his own way within the broad confines of the Tory Party. Whenever he was opposed, he resigned. He resigned one political post in 1884, another in 1885, and a third in 1886. For a while his system worked admirably; his popularity was such that he was regarded as essential to the party's stability, and besides, he had ousted Gladstone and the Liberals almost singlehanded. But he finally became so boisterous that Lord Salisbury, the Tory Prime Minister, could stand it no longer. Lord Randolph was declaring in favor of such startling reforms, all grouped under his new term of "Tory Democracy," that the old-line conservatives were horrified. In essence, he advocated a staunch maintenance of the class system together with a program of improving living conditions in the lower brackets. Asked his views on Temperance, he said that "As long as we allow such an immense portion of our population to live in pigsties, the warmth and false cheerfulness of the public-house will be largely sought after. The two questions appear to me to be inseparable." Some of his colleagues believed that Randolph, despite his aristocratic nature, would have switched to the Liberal Party had it not been for the problem of Irish Home Rule, which the Liberals supported and he opposed, coining the famous slogan of "Ulster will fight, and Ulster will be right!" In any case, instead of working patiently within the party for his reforms, he behaved with such intractable violence that he accomplished nothing, a common failing of reformers everywhere. Upon the occasion of his third resignation, over a trivial point of budget economy, Lord Salisbury accepted with record dispatch. At the ripe age of thirty-seven, Lord Randolph found his political career finished and himself, in the words of a contemporary, "the chief mourner at his own protracted funeral."

In some ways, Randolph made an unusually gay mourner. He became subject to wild and unexpected whims. Sometimes these took the form of travel. He appeared before his family one day wearing a slouch hat, a pair of high leather boots, and a belt to which was affixed a frying pan. When he was (not unnaturally) asked where he was bound, he replied, "To South Africa to dig for gold." The incredible fact is that he made the trip, joined the crowds at Johannesburg, and came up with seven thousand pounds, which he spent on a sight-seeing tour of Japan. Back home in England, he turned to horses. He bought up a large string and went at the sport with the same zest that had made things so brisk for the Irish foxes. His application bore fruit; he began to win races. But he was seldom on hand to receive the prizes. When his horse won the important Oaks, the stewards searched the crowd for Lord Randolph and learned, at length, that he had gone to Norway "for the spring canoeing." To the end of his days, he was seen at the meetings at Epsom and elsewhere, often happy and debonair, again brooding, shaky, and silent. At rare intervals he attempted a public speech, but a kind of paralysis that was draining him of physical and mental vigor prevented his articulating clearly. He died in 1895, forty-six years old; his star had risen, and fallen, with a rapidity unprecedented in British politics. "It is a black moment when the heralds proclaim the passing of the dead, and the great officers break their staves," said Lord Rosebery. "But it is sadder still when it is the victim's own hands that break the staff in public. I wonder if generations to come will understand the pity of it, will comprehend the full tragedy of Randolph's marred life."

Of the traits that he passed along to Winston Churchill, perhaps the tendency toward boyishness, or impishness, is the most readily identifiable. "For Randolph could not grow up," wrote the British historian Guedalla; "and in default of a more solid destiny he became the Peter Pan of politics." The son's enduring youth has fortunately been coupled to balance and self-control, but it has familiar facets. A few years ago, H. G. Wells wrote, of Winston, "There are times when the evil spirit comes upon him, and then I can only think of him as an intractable little boy, a mischievous, dangerous little boy, a knee-worthy little boy. Only by thinking of him in that way can I go on liking him." In the view of another British writer, "as a criticism of a responsible statesman this has scant importance," but it makes an interesting tribute to Lord Randolph's son. In addition to his inheritance, Churchill's unsatisfactory childhood doubtless gave him an urge to cling to exceptionally youthful ways. Several seasons past, at the height of the English mah-jongg craze, he attended the opening of the play *Saint Joan*. At a point when the character Dunois stood on the riverbank intoning "West Wind, West Wind, West Wind!" the audience was amazed to hear a hoarse, carrying "Pong!" issue from the dark recesses of the Churchill box. Even the Prime Minister's appearance seems to remain little changed today. Not long ago, when he made one of his infrequent appearances at the swank but sleepy Carlton Club, to which he belongs, an aged member seated near a window turned to a friend and said, "Isn't that young Churchill? I haven't seen him since the Boer War."

# Chapter 5

CHURCHILL'S early school days have no counterpart in the annals of great men. Neither in fact nor in fiction is there to be found precisely that quality of volcanic rebellion which characterized nearly all his actions. Penrod Schofield's departures were the accidental by-products of abstraction, and Tom Sawyer was a serious researchist. Whatever Churchill did (and he accomplished wonders) he did on purpose. His first consignment was to an expensive and fashionable seminary at Ascot, an institution that was critically shaken by the experience.

His mother took him to the train and gave him three half crowns for spending money. His humor has not been recorded for posterity, although intelligent guesses are possible. He had already declared against learning, a decision based on a fleeting brush he'd had with a tutor, who had essayed to teach him mathematics and then gone off for a rest cure. ". . . The figures were tied into all sorts of tangles and did things to one another which it was extremely difficult to forecast with complete accuracy," Churchill later wrote in his memoirs. Like many another, he complained that it was not any use being "nearly right." "In some cases these figures got into debt with one another; you had to borrow one or carry one, and afterwards you had to pay back the one you had borrowed. These complications cast a steadily gathering shadow over my daily life. They took away from one all the interesting things one wanted to do in the nursery or in the

garden. They made increasing inroads upon one's leisure.
One could hardly get time to do any of the things one wanted
to do. They became a general worry and preoccupation. More
especially was this true when we descended into a dismal bog
called 'sums.' There appeared to be no limit to these. When
one sum was done, there was always another. Just as soon
as I managed to tackle a particular class of these afflictions,
some other much more variegated type was thrust upon me."

It was expected by Churchill's parents that Ascot would
mend all this. Their expectations were not fulfilled. The boy
arrived, stole a pocketful of sugar, was soundly birched, and,
catching a moment free, kicked to pieces the headmaster's hat,
a straw boater he had bought only the previous week in London. Altogether, the faculty regarded the episode as an in-
auspicious start, even for a son of the titled gentry. We are
indebted to Churchill for his first impressions of Ascot, and to
other sources for his accomplishments there. "It [the school]
modelled itself upon Eton and aimed at being preparatory for
that Public School above all others," he has written. "It was
supposed to be the very last thing in schools. Only ten boys in
a class; electric light (then a wonder); a swimming pond;
spacious football and cricket grounds; two or three school
treats, or expeditions as they were called, every term; the
masters all M.A.'s in gowns and mortar boards; a chapel of its
own; no hampers allowed; everything provided by the authorities."

Besides these comforts, Ascot also had a "caning room," not
mentioned in Churchill's memoirs. From the very beginning
he was one of the most faithful pilgrims to this shrine. He
quickly became notable for argument, and for marathon discourse in general. In the newcomer's second month at the
establishment, a visitor to the school, at recess, noticed a small
red-haired boy running at full tilt in wide circles, spurred on by
an under-instructor. "Who on earth is that?" inquired the
visitor, and the headmaster replied, "Why, that's young
Churchill—it's the only way we can keep him quiet." The

child took an abnormal dislike to Latin, viewing the subject as a piece of calculated persecution on the part of the authorities. He has preserved minutes of a session in which he catechized his unfortunate Latin teacher. The point under discussion was the vocative case of the noun *mensa,* meaning table, or "O table," in this case.

"What does O table mean?" inquired Churchill.

*"Mensa,* O table, is the vocative case," said the teacher.

"But why O table?"

"O table—you would use that in addressing a table, in invoking a table. You would use it in speaking to a table."

"But I never do," replied Churchill.

"If you are impertinent, you will be punished, and punished, let me tell you, very severely," said the teacher, taking the usual last resort in the school's dealing with the boy.

Churchill steadily refused to learn Latin, or to have anything much to do with it at all, not only at Ascot but in later schooling, and he grew up with this dubious blank spot in his education. However, when he began making speeches he saw that the distribution of a few high-sounding Latin phrases was a prime asset, and kept most people sufficiently aggravated not to take exception to the speech as a whole. In true Churchillian fashion, never stumped for an expedient, he sat down and memorized an entire dictionary of Latin quotations. From then on he excelled in this department. *"Ecce signum,"* he would cry. "Look at the proof." Or, in discussing the closed minds of the Labor Party, " *'Fas est ab hoste doceri*—it is right to be taught even by the enemy,' as the great Marlborough used to say."

On November 12, 1936, he made a speech in the House of Commons that is interesting both quotationwise and for unerring prescience: "Let us now examine our own position," he said. "No one can refuse sympathy to the Minister for the Coordination of Defense. From time to time my Right Hon. Friend lets fall phrases or facts which show that he realizes more than anybody else on [the Treasury] Bench the danger

in which we stand. One such phrase came from his lips the
other night [when he said nothing can restore us the years that
are past].

" *'Eheu! fugaces, Posthume, Posthume,*
    Where are the years that are lost to me, lost to me?'

"From the year 1932 and certainly from the beginning of
1933 when Herr Hitler came into power, it was general public
knowledge in this country that serious rearmament had begun
in Germany. There was the change in the situation."

Later in this same session, Stanley Baldwin, the Prime Minister, commented gratefully on Churchill's erudition, saying,
"[Mr. Churchill] seldom speaks nowadays without a quotation
from the Latin tongue and I rejoice that it should be so."

The fault at Ascot was not all on one side. The headmaster
was a sadist of a sort not uncommon in schools of that period,
a man with whom flogging reached a religious fervor. He felt
that he was scourging out devils, and he sang at his work. A
former student at the place tells an illustrative anecdote about
the "caning room." Churchill and a group of boys were sent
there one morning without explanation. A subordinate master,
seeing them and wishing to keep things moving, seized up a
rod and gave them all a routine flogging. When the Head appeared, a few minutes later, the master said, "I've saved you
the trouble, sir. I've dealt with them properly." "It's of no importance, Eubanks," said the Head, "but this was my confirmation class. Good show!"

The headmaster's meeting with Lord Randolph's son represented an important setback for both of them. It was a
collision of two inexorable forces. Unluckily for Churchill, the
headmaster had a weight advantage of more than a hundred
pounds. The canings became so numerous and spirited that
the boy began to think in terms of long-range revenge. As
previously mentioned, Churchill's memory is phenomenally
sound, and he clung to his project tenaciously. Biding his time,
he hardened his muscles. Some years later, when he was a

cadet at the nearby military academy at Sandhurst, he felt that the hour had struck. He was trained to a fighting edge. Accordingly, he mounted his horse and rode to Ascot, rehearsing in his mind several successful stratagems of the late Marlborough. The day was brilliantly fine, the turf had just that degree of sponginess which can spell victory for an athlete to whom footwork is paramount, and the breeze was fresh but not disturbing. Churchill reined up before the headmaster's study, dismounted, and banged rudely on the door. A pale, begoggled stranger opened it timorously.

"Where's old So-and-so?" asked the boy.

"Mr. ——— passed on to his reward a year ago the fourth of June," replied the stranger, assuming a look of official prostration.

It was a stunning blow. Churchill reflected that the headmaster had taken typical unfair advantage, but there was nothing further to do. He thought briefly of thrashing the stranger, just for the record, but he dismissed the idea as unworthy.

In less than two years at Ascot, Churchill's health had declined so alarmingly that his family thought it prudent to remove him. Arrangements were made to enroll him at a gentler establishment, one conducted by a pair of elderly ladies at the healthful seaside resort of Brighton. Neither of the proprietors being in especially good trim, canings were played down at Brighton. The emphasis was placed on getting educated. Before entering, Churchill was taken for a few weeks to the German spa of Gastein; it was his first visit to a people whose truculent habits he was to be called on frequently to curb in the years ahead.

From the very beginning, his school life at Brighton was a picturesque improvement on Ascot. He had not been on hand a week before the elderly ladies were thinking wistfully about engaging a caning-master. "Few days pass at Brighton when Churchill is not in trouble," writes one of his biographers who had agents close to the school. All sources, including two or three of his schoolmates who are still living, agree that he constituted a plague spot at an otherwise serene institution. The dancing instructor, Miss Eva Moore, offered to resign and return to the stage if she was kicked once more on either shin. The football coach had him on the carpet for the use of questionable epithets. During a match in which Churchill participated, he had ranged up and down the field shouting a mysterious slogan of his own coinage: "St. George, St. Dunstan, and the Devil!" He was not a particularly good player, said the coach, but his frightful cries demoralized not only the opposing side but his own teammates, together with the spectators.

Observing the school's experiments with a newspaper, Churchill began one of his own, not very surprisingly called *The Critic*. Its first issue was devoted to an imaginary yacht race, symbolized by a drawing intended to seed the most important people on the campus. The proprietors were shown in the lead, with Churchill close behind; the rest of the school was an indistinguishable jumble far to the rear. Perhaps the high light of his three years at Brighton was his appearance as Dick Dowlas in the school play, Colman's *Heir at Law*. Churchill was authentically regarded as the best actor in the student body, his performance being marred only by his misreading of the repeated line, "I will send my carriage." He had seen the last word as "carrot," and since his hair was flaming red, the effect of his error was to produce uproarious laughter throughout the house. He was unmoved.

Churchill's conduct was never dishonest, but it was frequently artful. It was the custom at Brighton, during roll call each evening, for a student to step forward when he heard his name and report his harvest of demerits for the day. Pretty generally, Churchill was in the forefront of this competition. One evening he responded with "Nine," an unusual tally even for him. It then appeared that disciplinary action was being considered, since he was summoned next day by the authorities.

"Nine?" asked one of the ladies.

"The word I used was *nein*," replied Churchill—"German for no."

"Well, that's different," said the headmistress. "Dismissed."

Churchill saluted smartly and returned to his room, where he had been engaged in opening a can of contraband sardines. Since his visit to the learned jailer of Ventnor, he had been inordinately interested in smuggling. Soon after his success with Dick Dowlas and carrots, he rewrote a play called *The Smuggler* and tried to produce it himself, with indifferent results. His mechanical ideas were so elaborate that nothing short of a professional company of great resources could have brought the production off. In this period, he had begun to read a good many plays, as well as novels and poetry. While Churchill reacted rather dangerously to the efforts of other people to educate him, he was not averse to undertaking the assignment himself. He read *King Solomon's Mines* and found it entertaining, though no more expert than his rewrite job on *The Smuggler*. During a school vacation, one of his relatives, Lady Leslie, wrote on his behalf to the author, H. Rider Haggard, saying, "The little boy Winston came here yesterday morning, beseeching me to take him to see you before he returns to school at the end of the month. I don't wish to bore so busy a man as yourself, but will you, when you have time, please tell me, shall I bring him on Wednesday next, when Mrs. Haggard said she would be at home? Or do you prefer settling to come here some afternoon when I could have the boy to meet you. He really is a very interesting being, though temporarily *uppish* from the restraining parental hand being in Russia."

Haggard came over, and Churchill quizzed him about various obscure passages in the book. "Now what do you mean by this business?" demanded the child at one point, laying the book open. Haggard, very rattled, read it over and was obliged to confess, "Really, you know, I haven't the slightest idea." Churchill's expression suggested that he'd suspected so all the time. Later on he wrote Haggard, "Thank you so much for sending me 'Allan Quatermain'; it was so good of you. I like

A.Q. better than 'King Solomon's Mines'; it is more amusing. I hope you will write a great many more books." He read *Treasure Island* and was enchanted; he has gone through it nearly every year since then. In 1950, while making a critical speaking tour by train, he sequestered himself in one of the private coaches and left word he was not to be disturbed; he was preparing to "polish up" his remarks. When an important cablegram was delivered to the train, Gerald O'Brien, the Conservative public relations officer, tiptoed in to Churchill's compartment. The great man was preparing for the political crisis by reading *Treasure Island;* the book was opened to the inspiriting fight at the stockade, when Silver's group is routed. O'Brien dropped the cablegram and fled, while Churchill glared crossly, looking a little like a frustrated pirate himself.

In 1888, the future Prime Minister finished his far from exemplary preparatory tuition at Brighton. The school, though shaken, was still intact; the boy himself felt in splendid shape. There is a story that when Churchill had cleared the campus for the last time the lady proprietors declared a half holiday and ordered the janitor to break out the British ensign. Certainly it was one of the few authentically restful days at the school in several years. It was an uplifting time for Churchill, too. He was ready for the best, and worst, experience of every upper-class English boy's young life—the ambiguous stint at Public School. He was headed for home, and Harrow, and adventures in education that will not soon be forgotten.

# Chapter 6

BEFORE Winston, the male Churchills had traditionally gone to Eton, the symbolic pinnacle of the English public school system. Nearly all the members were troublesome. Lord Randolph's fledgling air at that romantic establishment has been immortalized by a schoolmate, who remembered him as "a small boy in an extremely disreputable hat. Now the hat was at Eton in those days almost as notable a sign of condition as among the Spanish nobility. Moreover, his appearance was reckless—his companions seemed much the same; he was, in a word, but a pregnant word at Eton, a Scug. His elder brother had left Eton before I came, because, I think, of some difference with the authorities as to the use of a catapult. Randolph looked as if he too might differ with the authorities on any similar issue."

Winston's general air, when he first arrived at Harrow, made his father's and uncle's Etonian behavior seem effeminate by contrast. In a word, he took exception to everything. His family had selected Harrow because of its location. The child was supposed to have weak lungs (this was later proved sensationally fallacious), and the doctors advised that he be kept on high ground. Harrow is situated on a hill, while Eton is situated in a bog. Despite their difference in elevation, the two schools are on a basis of near-parity in a social way. They are the leaders, where the sons of dukes, the obscure relatives of kings, the young moneyed and the wellborn are trimmed and polished into that ineffable enigma, the English gentleman. The term "public school," as nearly all Americans know, is somewhat misleading, meaning, in fact, precisely the reverse. A public school in England is a private school, far too expensive for the children of the lower classes, who must go to state-run schools, where they doubtless have a better time. Among the best reasons advanced for the extra-human good spirits of the English gentleman is the fact that he has put public school behind him. Once the ordeal is over, nothing in his future life can seem really irritating. Being caught in a cloudburst, having a bucket of paint fall on him from a scaffold, walking into a manhole—these strike him as but the normal contretemps of a perfectly ripping day.

Writing of Harrow in Churchill's day, the present chaplain of the school has said, ". . . there still existed the age-old feud between masters and boys, for boys looked upon masters as their natural enemies; a master was seldom seen talking to a boy in the street, and in form he spoke with the air of a magistrate rather than of a friend." Every sort of classism was encouraged: the boys in the upper forms detested the boys in the lower forms, the older boys beat the younger boys, various cliques rose in opposition to other cliques, and a general and merry warfare reigned. The accommodations at both Harrow and Eton, and at most public schools, offered the usual comforts of the average Trappist monastery. In an inmate's room there was a wooden bunk, often equipped with springs and mattress, a chair, a kind of desk, and little else. The chamber itself was of no great size, providing only sufficient arm-room to swing a board, or a spike, or a mace, depending on the traditions of the school in question.

The impact of these conditions on Churchill was jarring, but not as jarring as his impact on Harrow. Upon his arrival, he consented ungenially to an examination in Latin. He was handed a piece of paper, and some Latin paragraphs, and told to cough up a suitable translation within two hours. At the end of that period he turned in his results, which consisted, *in toto,* of a large blot, a classical smudge, a pair of brackets, and his name, printed in block letters. Dr. Welldon, the head-master, studied the report, harking back frequently to the para-graphs, and found it inadequate. To his everlasting credit, he sat silently appraising the boy and then for some reason de-cided that he was eligible to pass into Harrow, notwithstanding the Latin fiasco. Churchill was assigned to a housemaster, H. O. D. Davidson, who took him in tow much as one might pick up a snake with a pair of tongs. What was Davidson's astonishment, as they proceeded to the boy's quarters, to hear him ask chattily, "And what did you think of the House of Commons vote on the last military bill?" Churchill was placed in the lowest form and never rose far above it in four and a half years. When he started, two boys were listed below him in scholastic capacity, but as he warmed to his work, he easily supplanted them, then for a space held supreme sway as school clown. "His lack of progress put him at least once in danger of compulsory removal," an English journalist wrote.

Since Ascot, Churchill had been opposed to education in general, but at Harrow he got his back up in earnest. As before, his pique centered on Latin. Somewhat later, he wrote down a few "general observations about Latin which probably have their application to Greek as well. In a sensible language like English important words are connected and related to one an-other by other little words. The Romans in that stern antiquity considered such a method weak and unworthy. Nothing would satisfy them but that the structure of every word should be reacted on by its neighbors in accordance with elaborate rules to meet the different conditions in which it might be used. There is no doubt that this method both sounds and looks more impressive than our own. The sentence fits together like a piece of polished machinery. Every phrase can be tensely charged with meaning. It must have been very laborious, even if you were brought up to it; but no doubt it gave the Romans, and the Greeks too, a fine and easy way of establishing their posthumous fame."

Even when he was told that Gladstone read Homer for fun,

the boy made no improvement, but only commented that it "serves him right." Altogether, his condition was so static that Dr. Welldon, a conscientious man, volunteered to tutor him. Three times a week, despite his heavy schedule, the headmaster fired Ovid and Caesar at an obdurate Churchill, and three times a week he retired from the field not having scored a single hit. As commonly happens, though, Churchill eventually found a way to absorb a minimum amount of Latin with which to satisfy the authorities. He dug up a wonder child to whom the reading of Latin was no more vexing than reading a paper-backed novel in English. He filled the bill exactly. After a little persuasion, and a few threats, he agreed to drop around and run over each day's lesson. It was no trouble for Churchill, with his dazzling memory, to fix the translations in mind for twenty-four hours and thus get by. In return, he provided essays for the linguist, cranking them out on any subject at half an hour's notice. One of these struck the fancy of Dr. Welldon, who summoned the panic-stricken youth to his study. "This is a splendid effort," said the doctor. "I was especially interested in your point here, though I think you didn't carry it far enough. Precisely what did you have in mind?"

"No more than that, really," said the boy. "That just about states the case, in my view."

"You wouldn't want to elaborate on it?" asked Welldon.

"Not just at this time," said the boy.

He was allowed to return to his room, but he told Churchill he'd have to play down the ideas in the future. "Write them mediocre," he said.

The few remaining authorities have differing versions of this story. Sir Cyril Norwood, the former president of St. John's College, Oxford, writes, "In the form in which the tradition came to my ears, it is related that Mr. Welldon summoned the Sixth Former, and pointing out that the essay was obviously beyond his unaided standards, demanded the source of his in-spiration. There was as a result produced from the School's under-world Winston Churchill as the only begetter. Mr.

Churchill did not deny this story when I put it to him, but merely said that knowing these things Harrow did nothing about it, but left him where he was. It is only fair to say that the story as related by himself in his 'My Early Life' is somewhat different, and perhaps the authorities knew nothing about this early precocity. . . . The little Churchill was a pretty tough proposition for an organized system of education."

On his first Sunday at Chapel, the boy was instructed to sit on a bench in front of the monitors, the house being full. When the service was ended, the monitors, august and privileged, arose to file out by themselves, in accordance with ritual usage. Churchill got up and, yawning, filed out with them. The gasp heard over the room made no impression on him; he waved in very democratic style to two or three fellow sufferers and walked on down to the village to lay in some sweets.

As a general thing, the village was proscribed territory to the boys of Harrow. At certain times they were permitted to visit shops and attend to necessary business. Churchill was well known in the village, and used it freely. A week after his arrival at school, he learned that it was forbidden to keep dogs. As soon as he could get two dogs, an hour or so later, he arranged to have them quartered at a house on West Street. He and his best friend in town, the local detective, enjoyed walking the dogs and talking about current events, which Churchill considered to be over the heads of both masters and students up on "the hill."

In 1941, E. D. W. Chaplin, one of the most ardent Harrovians in the history of the school, drew up a collection of anecdotes and reminiscences about Churchill. His excellent little book, called *Winston Churchill and Harrow,* was published by the school Book Shop "in aid of the hospital on the Hill" and adds famously to the outstanding lore about this phase of the statesman's tutelage. Several townspeople were then living who remembered the mischievous red-haired son of Lord Randolph. Wright Cooper, whose family lived over a sweet shop (called a "Tuck Shop" by the boys), saw him as "honest and generous in a day when robust appetites were not always accompanied by well-lined pockets. . . . When Churchill was downstairs we all knew it. Boys always crowded round his table. He talked loudly and usually led the conversation. He knew, too, what he was talking about, and nothing came amiss to him. He was witty and critical and kept the other boys in roars of laughter. He was exceedingly popular and even the seniors sought his company."

J. F. Moore, who retired as manager of the Harrow Book Shop after fifty-three years of service, recalled that Stanley Baldwin, another Harrovian of that period, "was a boy of retiring disposition and was in great contrast to Mr. Churchill. The latter in his schooldays already showed evidences of his unusual command of words. He would argue in the shop on any subject, and, as a result of this, he was, I am afraid, often left in sole possession of the floor. Mr. John Galsworthy was a thoughtful boy. He walked about looking at the ground, as if thinking deeply. Was he, one wonders, even then meditating upon the novels and plays which have since made him so famous? Mr. Amery (a senior boy in Mr. Churchill's time), small and alert, was a brilliant scholar, and was well known at the Book Shop.

"Visitors were always interested in the old Book Shop, and well they might be, for it was in this house, then tenanted by the Rev. Mark Drury, that the great Sir Robert Peel spent his terms at Harrow, and in which Byron lived.

"The room which Peel occupied was long kept in its original state, and a brick on which he had carved his name was taken from the outer wall and preserved for a time, but it is now lost. Among visitors, I remember Lord Randolph Churchill, and Mr. Horace Annesley Vachell, the author of 'The Hill,' who had left before my time at the Book Shop, but who often came to see his son Richard, who was a boy in the School."

Of the great men whose footprints are left in the drafty corridors of Harrow, Churchill is the only one who refused categorically to conform. Peel, Byron, Baldwin, Galsworthy —these were children who bent to their studies, were in awe of their masters, obeyed the rules, and hoarded their energies for the circumstantial days ahead. Overendowed with energy and hostile to education, Churchill had ample resources for mischief of an unbelievable variety. He was known as "Carrot Top" to the boys of Harrow, who quickly learned that he had the explosive qualities thought to accompany red hair. An instructor's son made the mistake of selling him, for a shilling, a sparrow's egg advertised as a "cuckoo's egg." When Churchill discovered the fraud, by checking his purchase with a local bird-walker, he gave the instructor's son a brisk drubbing, and took his shilling back. He frequently went off half cocked, and as frequently made amends. One day while dickering for some peas for his peashooter, with which he hoped to immobilize a particularly offensive member of the faculty, he got into a row with a woman shopkeeper. He suddenly dashed a handful of peas over the front room of her tiny establishment and ran. A male bystander overtook him and gave him a shaking up. Far from being resentful, Churchill went up to the woman and apologized handsomely. She forgave him, and they became good friends.

"Churchill as a schoolboy was always of an inquiring mind," says E. D. W. Chaplin, with Harrovian restraint. The lad's inquiries about a haunted house nearly got him killed. A massive residence called Roxeth House, empty since 1861, stood at the junction of West Street and Bessborough Road, near the school, and was reputed to be a popular hangout of ghosts. Several recognizable ghosts had been spotted in the upper rooms by men going home from taverns, and there was much rattling of chains, groaning, winking of sickly lights, and other activity typical of high spirits. Churchill determined to get at the truth. In the bottom of an old trash-filled well on the grounds, there was said to be a secret tunnel to the house, a suitable starting point for his investigations. He quickly saw that the trash could be removed only by a good-sized bomb, upon which he set to work. He spent all his allowance on chemicals and additional materials and finally, after several false starts, assembled a genuinely formidable-looking machine, about the size of a pumpkin and with a foot or two of fuse sticking out. Tucking it under one arm without any attempt at concealment, he made off toward the house. It is a peculiarity of Harrow villagers that they stare when they see a child on the street with a bomb, and a good many stared nervously at Churchill. His old friend the detective nodded and said laughingly, "That's quite a parcel you have there—looks like a bomb."

"Oh, it's a bomb right enough."

"Quite so, a bomb, to be sure," said the detective, and he waved absently as Churchill hurried on his way.

An aunt of one Mr. Harry Woodbridge, a former Harrow resident, had just finished hanging out her laundry and was looking over a fence to the grounds of Roxeth House. She takes up the narrative. "I was gazing out at nothing in particular," she said, "when all of a sudden there was a deafening explosion and a big pall of black smoke, and one of the Harrow boys seemed to come flying up out of the old well. I rushed over and helped him to his feet. His face looked badly scorched and his clothing was a ruin. I got him into my home and bathed his face, which was not greatly damaged after all. He seemed in a splendid humor and said only, 'I expect this will get me the bag.'"

The trouble was, Churchill had lit the fuse; then, when nothing happened, had begun to lower himself into the well. At that moment, the pumpkin disintegrated brilliantly, easily justifying all of his trouble. The authorities took a sour but resigned view of the case, and he failed to raise any ghosts, but he wrote down the explosion as a successful adventure, despite everything.

Churchill's best friend at Harrow was Jack Milbanke, a pleasant and pliant but courageous boy, the son of a baronet of ancient family. His life previous to Harrow had been normally restricted; he had never seen anything even remotely like Churchill before. The association was a stimulating one, and kept Milbanke continually in hot water. One week his restless companion came into his room and said, "I've been digging into the old rules and have found a way to avoid playing compulsory football."

"Good-oh," replied Milbanke, who loved football but who loved Churchill more. Churchill also rather enjoyed playing football, but he was opposed to playing, or doing, anything by command. He had discovered an elderly Harrow regulation stating that there should be no compulsory football during "trial," or examination week. He instructed the agreeable Milbanke to refuse to play and, in fact, to climb into his bunk with a good book and enjoy himself. Churchill did likewise. "By doing so we courted a severe caning from the monitors," he said later. The school was thrown into an uproar, the issue being, as he wrote, "gravely debated in the highest circles." In the end it was decided that technically the miscreants were in the right, but the incident by no means solidified their popularity in high echelons. As usual, the son of Lord Randolph was undisturbed by public opinion. "I trust the precedent thus boldly established has not been lost in later generations," he remarked blandly afterward.

Churchill was at Harrow from April 1888 to December 1892, a period that embraced fourteen school terms. During three of these he was in H. O. D. Davidson's Small House and for the rest he was in the headmaster's. His last three years were devoted to Army Class, that is, he took the course aimed to prepare him for Sandhurst, the English equivalent of the American West Point and the French St. Cyr. Since the day of the toy-soldier review for his father, and Lord Randolph's query about the Army, he had accepted it as decisive that he was headed for a career in the military. A. W. Siddons, a former master at Harrow, has written that he "never rose very high in the School, and consequently some people have thought that at that time he was stupid; but that is a mistaken idea. One of my correspondents writes of his school days, 'he was not an easy boy to deal with. Of course he had always a brilliant brain, but he would only work when he chose to and for the masters he approved of.' Another writes, 'He was plainly uninterested in the academic subjects.' Yet a third correspondent writes, 'As a boy, I formed the highest opinion of his abilities and never ceased to wonder why he did not rise higher in the School. But he hated the Classics, and in his time that kept him down.'"

In his book, *My Early Life*, Churchill has been wonderfully articulate on this subject: "By being so long in the lowest form I gained an immense advantage over the cleverer boys. They all went on learning Latin and Greek and splendid things like that. But I was taught English. Mr. Somervell—a delightful man, to whom my debt is great—was charged with the duty of teaching the stupidest boys the most disregarded thing—namely, to write mere English. He knew how to do it. He taught it as no one else has ever taught it. . . . As I remained in the Third Form three times as long as anyone else, I had three times as much of it. I learnt it thoroughly. Thus I got into my bones the essential structure of the ordinary British sentence—which is a noble thing. And when in after years my school fellows who had won prizes and distinction for writing such beautiful Latin poetry and pithy Greek epigrams had to come down again to common English to earn their living or make their way, I did not feel at any disadvantage. . . . I would make them all learn English: and then I would let the clever ones learn Latin as an honour, and Greek as a treat. But the only thing I would whip them for would be for not knowing English. I would whip them hard for that."

In addition to Somervell, Churchill was devoted to two other masters at Harrow—C. H. P. Mayo, who taught him mathematics, and L. W. Moriarty, who headed the Army Class. Mayo performed the stupendous feat of giving the boy a respectable mathematical grounding in six months, a job that the people at Ascot might have sworn would take upwards of fifteen years. He later wrote of Mayo, "he convinced me that Mathematics was not a hopeless bog of nonsense, and that there were meanings and rhythms behind the comical hieroglyphics; and that I was not incapable of catching glimpses of some of these. Of course what I call Mathematics is only what the Civil Service Commissioners expected you to know to pass a very rudimentary examination." Moriarty was greatly beloved by the whole school; he more than anyone else was responsible for easing the traditional class tensions. In the words of a man who knew him then, he had "such charm of manner and remarkable powers of conversation that the glacial distinctions melted away, and the springs of friendliness were soon apparent, the friendliness between masters and boys which is such a feature of Harrow life at the present day."

Churchill used to go to Moriarty's house in the evenings to discuss essays and history; also, the two fenced at the gymnasium. "Probably Mr. Moriarty was the master who had the greatest influence on Winston Churchill's future career," says Siddons, the housemaster. In the years after Harrow, Churchill and Moriarty kept up a regular correspondence; the former's letters were all signed, "Your affectionate pupil." Moriarty wrote a congratulatory note when Churchill was named Under-Secretary for the Colonies, in 1905, and Churchill replied, saying, "Almost the only valuable and pleasant part of my instruction there was received at your hands, and though I fear I am sadly lacking in scholarly education, the taste for history which I acquired or developed in your Army Class has been very pleasantly indulged by me in the years that are past."

His qualifying for Moriarty's Army Class in the first place involved a stroke of high fortune, as Churchill has admitted. It was among the few examinations he ever passed without difficulty at Harrow. Furthermore, many boys of high scholastic standing had failed it. To begin with, Churchill was in top spiritual condition for the ordeal. Offsetting his several incapacities, he had just learned 1200 lines of Macaulay's *Lays of Ancient Rome* (as mentioned in Chapter 1) and recited them without a single error, winning a prize. For the Army test, he and the others knew they would be required to draw from memory a map of some country. The night before, he put all the maps of his atlas into a hat, then he withdrew one, which proved to be New Zealand, and set about learning it. The next day, the first question asked him was to draw a map of New Zealand. His memory was in well-oiled shape; he filled it in with such specificity, including streams of a dozen yards' breadth and whistle stops on the narrow-gauge railroads, that Moriarty never quite got over it. "This was what is called at Monte Carlo an *en plein,* and I ought to have been paid thirty-five times my stake," Churchill said afterward.

One of the most curious aspects of his rampage through Harrow was the extraordinary interest taken in him by the headmaster, Dr. Welldon. There can be no doubt that the boy was permitted breaches of conduct that were denied to anybody else. Besides tutoring him and taking him into his house, Welldon kept a sharp personal eye on Churchill's general progress and development. The doctor's forbearance is the more admirable in view of Churchill's attitude toward him, which was, charitably, offhand. At one time, haled in to the headmaster's study, the boy was told, "Churchill, I have very grave reason to be displeased with you." The unpenitent reply was, according to excellent sources, "And I, sir, have very grave reason to be displeased with you." Welldon, himself an Etonian, was a religious man, noted for his powerful sermons in Chapel, and the theory has been advanced that he accepted his brush with Churchill as on the order of Joshua's wrestle in the Wilderness. In any event, he buckled to his duty like a Christian martyr, and did his best in the face of stunning odds. The rumor got around that Churchill's vocabulary included a number of words not ordinarily recommended for public school use. Welldon wearily sent out another summons. "Now, my lad," he said, "when was the last time you used bad language?" "Well, as I entered this room, I tripped over the door mat and I'm afraid I said 'damn,' " Churchill replied.

Despite his cavalier behavior, he evidently had a lasting affection for Welldon. Much later, when Churchill was stationed as a young soldier in India, Welldon, then Bishop of Calcutta, fell dangerously ill. His old pupil made a long and hazardous trip in a period of civil strife to look him up and give comfort. At many points in his life, seemingly oblivious of past favors done him, Churchill has made generous and unexpected gestures of appreciation. A taxi driver who had often served him at Westerham, the village near Churchill's house of Chartwell, tells of an interesting trip they once made. Proceeding down the road—fairly rapidly because Churchill was late for an engagement—the driver was suddenly quizzed from the rear seat.

"Did I not hear that your wife was ill?"

"She's in the hospital and will be operated on this afternoon, sir."

"Stop the car!" cried Churchill, leaning forward and brandishing a stick. "Turn around and drive to the hospital and don't leave until she's out of danger."

While some of the Harrow boys found him a nuisance, all of them left with vivid impressions of him and have been competing with Churchill anecdotes ever since. L. C. M. S. Amery, who later rose to be one of the highest servants of the Crown, suffered a characteristic introduction to Churchill. Amery was standing beside the school pool, called "Ducker," when "I suddenly felt myself propelled into the water by a foot in the small of my back, while unseen hands reft me of my towel. I emerged spluttering to see which of my friends had done this, only to meet the gleeful grin of a small, freckled, red-haired boy whom I had never seen before." This act of Churchill's turned out to be very rash indeed, since Amery was a member of an upper form, was one of the best athletes at Harrow, and was altogether disinclined to accept duckings from upstarts. He scrambled out of the pool, took after Churchill, who was now energetically alarmed, caught him, and carried him back to the pool, where he gave him a businesslike dousing. But it was

notorious in the school that nobody could stay peeved at
Churchill long. "Next day at Bill [roll call] Winston came up
to me," says Amery, "and with the same ingenuous frankness
that has so often disarmed an angry opposition in the House,
explained that he had not realized that I was in the Sixth Form,
but only that I was small enough to be the most suitable victim
to hand, adding: 'My father, too, is small and he also is a great
man.' "

It might be noted concerning "Bill" that roll call at Eton
and at Harrow are conducted on somewhat different lines. At
Eton, it is the custom for the boys to line up and, as their names
are called, to lift the top hats which are such a well-known part
of their school dress. At Harrow, the boys walk past the authorities in single file and themselves announce their names. At
Churchill's first roll call, his family and a number of other
visitors were present. For reasons of scholastic deficiency and
other considerations, he had been placed last in line. The
visitors were astonished to see the son of Lord Randolph pacing along in this ignominious position, but his demeanor effectively took the curse off it. "He was totally unconcerned and in
fact seemed to suggest that it was the post of honor," said a
man who was there.

Like school children today, the boys at Harrow were reluctant to have even the members of their immediate family
visit them. "Boys at that time were very nervous about being
seen walking with a lady in the street," says the present vicar,
Edgar Stogdon. "If your mother wrote to ask if she could come
down to see you, you told her what hat to wear, and if her
figure was beyond the accepted standard, you suggested post-
ponement; and above all, there should be no form of endear-
ment." Churchill invited his old nurse, Mrs. Everest, down for
the day. Grown rather fat but intensely happy, she arrived
wearing an old poke bonnet, to be effusively greeted by Churchill at the station. He showed her around the school, pointing
out students in their rooms much as a zoo keeper might exhibit
some interesting but unimportant animals, and spent most of

the day walking arm in arm with her on the street. "It is about the nicest thing a Harrow boy has ever done," says Mr. Stogdon.

Another source recalls that Churchill once shocked the entire school by darting up during a house debate to refute one of the seniors and then to "carry all before him with a magnificent speech." His heritage of easy presumption expanded significantly at Harrow. He became surer of himself with each scholastic disaster. Twice during vacations he accompanied Monsieur Minssen, the French and fencing master, to his home at Versailles, where he met many officers in the French Army. On one occasion, as the officers and Minssen were discussing military history, a certain battle of antiquity was brought into the conversation.

"I know very little about it," said one of the officers, and the others confessed that they, while they could name the victor, could add little more.

"Why, I think I can fill you in on that," said Churchill, arising with good-natured condescension from a chair some distance apart. Taking the center of the floor, he asked a couple of lieutenants to step up a little closer and then began with, "You see, the Babylonians had fifteen hundred bowmen arranged in a semicircle over the north brow of a small mountain thirty-two kilometers from the village of Mogul. The day was warm, with a mild breeze from the southeast——" and he went on to present the struggle in stupefying detail.

Later that night, Monsieur Minssen said, "Churchill, wherever did you get all that material on the battle? Did you make it up?"

"Oh, no," said Churchill. "Mr. Moriarty explained it last term, and I was able to remember bits and pieces. My memory is rather good that way."

Fortunately for Churchill, Amery, the boy he ducked, had an equable and forgiving disposition. He was a power in the school and exercised a strong influence over many departments of campus life. Notably, he was editor of the *Harrovian,* the

student paper, which received from one to ten carping letters
from Churchill per week. Amery read them carefully, toler-
antly, much entertained, and ran as many as he could without
being removed from his position. The truth is that Amery, a
remarkable boy who could speak Russian and several other
languages, was thoroughly amused by Churchill, and egged
him on in various subtle ways. "He [Churchill] submitted a
trilogy of articles on Ducker, Gym, and the school workshop,
breezy, entertaining and frankly critical of the existing administration of these departments," says Amery. "I can still see the
look of misery on his face as, in spite of his impassioned protests, I blue-pencilled out some of his best jibes. However, even
my pedantic zeal for the Victorian respectability of the *Harrovian* did not altogether save the expurgated text from criticism by the authorities concerned." In after years, Dr. Welldon
himself told friends that he had been obliged to call Churchill
up on the carpet in this connection. His account of his statement to the suspect went as follows: "My boy, I have observed
certain articles which have recently appeared in the *Harrovian*,
of a character not calculated to increase the respect of the boys
for the constituted authorities of the School. As the *Harrovian*
is anonymous I shall not dream of inquiring who wrote those
articles, but if any more of the same sort appear, it might become my painful duty to swish you."

Sure enough, more of the articles appeared, and Dr. Welldon
performed his painful duty. Churchill had heard him out respectfully, made a slight bow, and, demonstrating a fleetness of
foot for which he was acquiring a name, sprinted back to compose a howling beef about the recent Assault-at-Arms, an
athletic exhibition. "All these things that I have enumerated,"
he said at length, "serve to suggest that there is 'something
rotten in the State of Denmark.' I have merely stated facts—it
is not for me to offer an explanation of them. To you, sirs, as
directors of public opinion, it belongs to lay bare the weakness.
Could I not propose that some of your unemployed correspondents might be set to work to unravel the mystery, and to

collect material wherewith these questions may be answered?

"The School itself has an ancient history; even the Gymnasium dates back to a Tudor. In those days they were not wont to Risk [this was a pun of Churchill's—Tudor Risk was the first superintendent of the gymnasium] the success of the School Assault-at-Arms in the manner in which it was done on Saturday last. For three years the Assaults have been getting worse and worse. First the Midgets, then the Board School, and, finally, the Aldershot Staff have been called in to supplement the scanty programme. It is time there should be a change, and I rely on your influential columns to work that change."

The effect of Dr. Welldon's swishing was, however, temporarily chastening. Balked at complaints, Churchill poured his literary energies into a commemorative ode to Influenza. Essentially, the poem, which had twelve stanzas, was derogatory; he did not relieve Influenza of responsibility but he paid homage to its ubiquitous journeying through the world. From every standpoint, the work is an arresting effort for a boy of his years. From his opening theme in Stanza One—"Oh how shall I its deeds recount, or measure the untold amount of ills that it has done?"—he goes on in Stanza Two to take a knock at czarist Russia: "O'er miles of bleak Siberia's plains, where Russian exiles toil in chains."

Churchill displays his knowledge of political geography, always profound, in Stanza Six:

> Fair Alsace and forlorn Lorraine,
> The cause of bitterness and pain
> In many a Gallic breast,
> Receive the vile, insatiate scourge,
> And from their towns with it emerge
> And never stay or rest.

The faint but unmistakable drums of jingoism are heard in Stanza Nine, as Influenza reaches France:

> In Calais port the illness stays,
> As did the French in former days,
>     To threaten Freedom's isle:
> But now no Nelson could o'erthrow
> This cruel, unconquerable foe,
> Nor, save us from its guile.

The scourge did, in fact, penetrate England, but "it came with broken force."

> For though it ravaged far and wide
> Both village, town and countryside,
>     Its power to kill was o'er;
> And with the favoring winds of Spring
> (Blest is the time of which I sing)
> It left our native shore.

And in peroration, the voice of the future Prime Minister:

> God shield our Empire from the might
> Of War or famine, plague or blight
>     And all the power of Hell,
> And keep it ever in the hands
> Of those who fought 'gainst other lands,
> Who fought and conquered well.
>                     WINSTON S. CHURCHILL (1890)

Amery's blue pencil was busy during Churchill's correspondence to the *Harrovian,* but he also salvaged and printed much that was worth while. The two boys established a friendship that endures to the present. In the several decades since their Harrow days, their political views have frequently diverged, but their personal relationship has been steadfastly affectionate. Amery, who became at different times First Lord of the Admiralty, Secretary of State for the Colonies, Secretary of State for Dominion Affairs, and Secretary of State for India, continues to be amused by his old contributor, who will always interest him as much for his fiery impetuosity as for his matchless talents. After Harrow, their paths crossed again in a few

years, while they were mountain climbing in the Alps. Amery
was relieved to find absolutely no change in Churchill, who
"determined to outdo us by ascending the highest mountain
within reach of Zermatt." He had picked out the difficult Monte
Rosa and stuck at the job, as Amery says, "in spite of mountain sickness and a face grievously flayed by the scorching snow
glare. But I do not think the sport appealed to him, and anyhow
his interests and career soon led him elsewhere."

And they were to meet again before long—sharing a tent
in the Boer War, from which one morning, as Amery overslept,
Churchill crept forth to beg a ride on an armored train, and
to project himself into an adventure that captured the imagination of the entire civilized world. He was to find himself
famous at twenty-six, and his career properly under way.

Churchill often goes back to Harrow. He has a curious loyalty for his old school, in view of his unscintillant activities
there. The sole distinction he gathered in the course of his fourteen terms was the winning of the public school fencing championship at Aldershot, in 1892. His gymnasium sessions with
Moriarty and his friendship with Minssen the fencing master
had borne fruit. Some of his acquaintances felt that, while he
despised the classics, he considered swordplay an enterprise
that might have been endorsed by the unscholastic Marlborough, whose shade was already beginning to be influential
in his life. He made a memorable visit to Harrow in the early
part of the recent war, not long after he had succeeded to the
highest governmental post in England. What his feelings were,
as he trudged around the establishment in which he had once
occupied the lowest post, he did not divulge, but he seemed in
triumphant spirits. In Chapel, he called for the singing of some
of his favorite Harrow songs, and he bawled out the words,
keeping time with a stick, with faultless recollection. In his
party was Mr. L. C. M. S. Amery, now Secretary of State for
India in Churchill's Cabinet, who kept watching his former
correspondent as if he expected him to dash out a window with
a slingshot. Nothing untoward happened. The mischievous

schoolboy had given way to the controlled but always smoldering diplomat and statesman.

*Stet Fortuna Domus,* the song that praises Harrow's men of state, had been enhanced with a special verse for the occasion:

> Nor less we praise in darker days
>    The leader of our nation,
> And Churchill's name shall win acclaim
> From each new generation.
> For you have power in danger's hour
>    Our freedom to defend, Sir.
> Though long the fight, we know the right
> Will triumph in the end, Sir.

It must have been a great satisfaction for Churchill to hear himself thus eulogized after such a rackety and unfruitful career at Harrow. Despite his flippant attitude there, he was hurt by his failures, and has alluded to them bitterly many times. "I was on the whole considerably discouraged by my school days," he wrote in *My Early Life.* And again, "It is not pleasant to feel oneself so completely outclassed and left behind at the very beginning of the race. . . . I am all for the Public Schools but I do not want to go there again."

Even so, Harrow performed a great service for Churchill and for the unregimented world. In turning him aside, in rolling on unheeding, it gave him an insatiate urge to rise up and make Harrow sorry. His hot ambition, his doggedness, his restless search for command, are perhaps in good part the result of Harrow and its slights. "Never give in," he told the students on that visit in 1941. "Never, never, never, never!" smashing his stick against the floor. "Never yield in any way, great or small, large or petty, except to convictions of honour and good sense. Never yield to force and the apparently overwhelming might of the enemy."

*Part*

**II**

# Chapter 7

A PUZZLING metamorphosis took place in Churchill's manner when he left Harrow. The old stubbornness, the resolution, the bold and unabashed spirit remained unchanged, but the mood of capricious dissent began to fade. Something purposeful was evolving from his gift for willful mischief. No doubt the imminence of the stern and spartan Sandhurst had a sobering effect, but it is likely, too, that the precocious child felt himself ready to engage the not very formidable problems of an adult world.

For some little time after his graduation, the threat of Sandhurst was only theoretically bothersome. Churchill's first examination for the college resulted in ignoble failure. He had made a mark, of a sort, at Harrow, but he had neglected to prepare himself for life in a classical age. Battles were won with bullets, as Sandhurst freely admitted, but epithets were hurled more effectively in Latin. The long-dead but always dangerous Caesar had downed another aspiring soldier. Setbacks to Churchill have ever been nothing more than an incitement to total war; with an air of deadly determination, he took the examination again, and was not much edified to note that several of his marks were rather considerably lower than on the first round. After this, his family agreeing, he arranged to tutor for the unrelenting Sandhurst. One Captain James, a military man of academic persuasion, agreed to take the job on. He and a group of sous-officiers, also suitably learned, kept an establishment in the Cromwell Road, and had a high reputation for creating order out of mental chaos. "It was said that no one who was not a congenital idiot could avoid passing thence into the Army," Churchill wrote of the place.

Things were looking very good—his parents were laying modest bets that, since he was *not* a congenital idiot, he would wind up in the military after all—when Churchill fell victim to his native inquisitiveness. On the eve of his departure for the captain's, he and his brother Jack and a young cousin went exploring. The family were living at the Bournemouth estate of his aunt, Lady Wimborne. It was a beautiful place, wild, with a fir forest, and sloping down to the sea. Among its attractions for children was a sort of canyon, called a "chine," that was spanned by a rustic bridge fifty yards long. The three boys had organized a lively game of chase, with the candidate for Sandhurst as the quarry. All three being descendants of the canny Marlborough, it was touch and go for hours. At length, however, the pursuers having divided forces, they trapped Churchill in the middle of the bridge. Never at a loss, he assayed his chances rapidly. What would Marlborough do? The answer came clearly; he would leap into the tops of some fir trees growing up from the chasm, slide down from limb to limb, make his getaway, and apply for several additional pensions. Churchill calculated the method and the risks as coolly as an experienced general, then gave a derisive cry, and leaped. He recovered consciousness three days later.

For three months the boy was bedfast, and for nearly a year he was ailing, suffering from a variety of injuries, including a ruptured kidney. Of his tactics, and the message from Marlborough, he said afterward, "The argument was correct; the data were absolutely wrong." Had he lit in the fir trees, the evasion might have been completed brilliantly, but he had missed the trees and flung himself down twenty-nine feet to the earth and rocks below. The best specialists in England were summoned to save his life, and their efforts were rewarded only after a long period of indecision. Churchill reported that he had lain in bed and listened with satisfaction to accounts of the enormous fees they were charging. He had never previously realized his full importance, though he had intuitive flashes about it from time to time. The fall gave rise to an inaccurate joke, alluding to Lord Randolph's independent spirit, that had quite a little vogue in the London clubs. "I hear Randolph's son met with a serious accident." "Yes, playing a game of follow-my-leader." "Well, Randolph is not likely to come to grief in that way."

When Churchill was up and around, he was sent with his brother and a tutor to take a therapeutic walking tour in Switzerland. They were provided with a moderate amount of pocket money, which they spent in riding on trains. They climbed two medium-sized mountains. When they returned home, Churchill placed himself in the hands of Captain James, who tackled the job cheerfully and with military thoroughness. He found that he had bitten off about all he could chew. James was reputed to have remarked, when he finished with Churchill, "That lad couldn't have gone through Harrow, he must have gone under it." In any event, the tutoring paid dividends: on the third try the boy actually passed the examination for Sandhurst, although with marks about as low as he could get and still qualify. Informing his old school of his modified success, he wrote sourly, "I would have done better from Harrow." There was no indication then or later that Harrow was inclined to shoulder the blame, notwithstanding his note. Churchill's examination paper was regarded as so pronouncedly feeble that he was assigned to the horse cavalry, which was somehow classed as a corps fit only for dolts.

Lord Randolph was furious, for several reasons. First, because he had set his heart on lodging Winston with an old family friend, the Duke of Cambridge, who was colonel-in-chief of the 60th Rifles, a famous infantry regiment. Randolph, whose faith in Captain James was childlike, had already been so precipitate as to write the duke making inquiries about a berth for his son. The duke's reply had been accommodating and all was arranged, except for the examination, which

snarled everything up. Churchill's father was obliged to report
to the duke that the boy had struck a clinker, Captain James
or no Captain James, and that he would be seen, in a military
way, in the saddle or not at all. Another irritating aspect of
the situation from Lord Randolph's standpoint was the fact
that to join the cavalry one must buy a horse. He had been
prepared eventually to stand his son a batman, after the
fashion of upper-class British soldiering, but now he would be
taxed with a batman *and* a horse. He viewed the extra, outsized
mouth as excessive, and said so, in a strongly worded letter to
his son. "Little did he foresee," wrote Churchill gleefully later,
"not only one horse, but two official chargers and one or two
hunters besides—to say nothing of the indispensable string of
polo ponies!"

The year was 1893, a time of quiet and prosperity for the
British Empire, and the place of young Winston Churchill's
last formal education was the Sandhurst Royal Military College, an establishment to train officers for the fiercely aristocratic British Army. A cadet's pay was three shillings a day
(about seventy-five cents), and his expenses were burdensome.
It was never even considered that the Queen might make up
this deficit; the fathers of young gentlemen of the leisure class
were expected to pay in large part for the military preparation
of their sons, as a patriotic duty. Upon Churchill's family this
blow fell heavily, happening to coincide with Lord Randolph's
intermittent and unexpected tours of such beauty spots as
Johannesburg, Japan, and Norway. A good deal of scraping
was done to keep the boy horsed and learning. And by good
fortune, he rallied to his responsibilities; from the very beginning he found the school a romantic spur to an ambitious
nature. He dug in and worked, and tried to make the most of
his opportunities. These were not glittering. Like most military
posts, Sandhurst was unfrivolous, and even chafing. It still is.
The school consists of a solemn-looking group of functional
buildings in a setting of typical English country splendor,
thirty-three miles southwest of London. A yearbook of Church-

ill's time described things as follows: "In the foreground are to be seen smooth lakes—a vast expanse of water—fringed with dark fir trees and silvery birches, and dotted with evergreen-planted islets; beyond their margins the eye rests on solemn pine forests, which extend for miles, clothing the shallow valleys and low hills; while here and there sparkling streams flow down through woods of birch and alder. Black mosses, overrun with bog-myrtle and willow scrub, form in the hollows, and beach woods or ark plantations ring the changes. Beyond these forest lands lie the open, heather-covered moors, presenting as wild a scene as can be well imagined—as bleak and silent a stretch of country as any to be found in the uttermost parts of Scotland or on the high fjelds of Norway."

The village of Camberley, named for some dim forebear of the Duke of Cambridge, lies outside its gates, and another ducal touch is provided by the Duke of York tavern, which looks across the highroad and into the grounds, whence the thirsty cadets can watch with envy the comings and goings of the unrestricted public. The school got its name from an unusual geological formation: "the Bagshot sands," a hardpan of sand and gravel that lies eighteen inches under the surface of the ground thereabouts. Water never seeps through the pan, but has to drain off into one of the sparkling streams mentioned in the elderly yearbook. When farmers wish to plant trees, they must take a pickax and hack through the crust, at a cost of hard labor. In the winter, when the freezes come, all is a swamp; dammed by the ice, the waters pile up and form glassy and ungeometric lakes for as far as the eye can see.

It was a great lark in Churchill's day for the cadets to go abroad and dig for relics. It is easy for Americans to forget that nearly anywhere one disturbs the earth in England he is apt to turn up mementos of the ancients. The spring plows are forever uncovering Roman coins, and even in London excavating workmen find valuable art objects that date back for centuries, across the consecutive spans of dead civilizations. The area of Sandhurst was a prime hunting ground. In the very gardens of

the college an occasional flint instrument of the Celts was to be
found, and at nearby Chobham Ridges, Easthampstead and
the Hartford Bridge Flats the barrows of those dark and frightened people, who flourished around the fifth century before
Christ, were on view. Churchill was frequently a leader of expeditions to these subterranean graves and dwellings, whose
counterparts, after twenty-five hundred years, are now everywhere building against the Atomic Age, a similarly unraveling
civilization. It was excellent training for the future Prime Minister, who, in the Second Great War, was called upon to start
the long-delayed movement back to the earth. Having studied
the barrows, he understood the first, and last, sanctuaries of
man.

Near the Wickham Bushes faint traces of stone huts told
where the Belgic invasion took over from the tiring Celts, and
at Nine Mile Ride, Churchill's old nemesis, Caesar, was once
encamped with his ravening legions. The strong evidences of
that notable visit—a citadel, fosses, entrenchments, numerous
pieces of pottery, pavement and rusted-out weapons—presumably made an unfavorable impression on the youth, for he
embarked upon a series of carping comments about the Italians, and has been at it pretty faithfully ever since, coming to a
climax with his House of Commons snarl of year before last to
"go talk to the Italians—that's all you're fit for."

His new curriculum kept Churchill busy, but it was more
sustaining than the awed preoccupation with deceased tongues,
poets, and generals at Harrow. The principal subjects were
now Tactics, Fortifications, Topography (mapmaking), Military Law, and Military Administration. There was also a great
deal of drill. He was put under the supervision of an excellent
horseman, senior cadet Prince Alexander of Teck, who
watched the happy Harrovian wheel and maneuver, and
promptly clapped him into the awkward squad. At Sandhurst
there was always—and still is—a handful of foreign nobility,
sent over to learn the systems of training that had led to the
accumulation of a world empire by a tiny, frostbitten island.

Among these around Churchill's time, besides Prince Alexander, were the future Alfonso XIII of Spain, the Egyptian Prince Ibrahim Hassan, Alamayn of Abyssinia, and the Crown Prince of Siam. For the most part, the foreigners fitted in nicely to Sandhurst life and were popular, though occasional adjustments were necessary to dovetail the widely differing cultures. It was remarked that the Egyptian, a descendant of the Pharaohs, was apathetic about digging for Roman pottery. Pressed for an explanation, he was reputed to have said that he was "not much interested in modern art."

In addition to the academic side at Sandhurst, a day's routine included outdoor work that was regarded as a practical application of the lessons indoors. In some cases, this was questionable. Lay experts have noted that military tuition everywhere seems to lag from a decade to three hundred years behind the actual current methods of fighting. In the last war, naval officers at American indoctrination schools were amazed at the total absence of talk about airplanes, the Bureau of Personnel still pinning its faith on ironclads, and at Sandhurst, in 1893, it was felt that the newfangled bomb was on its way out. It was incorrect that, as one graduate later stated, the instruction revolved around hot pitch and defenses against the stone catapult, but even Churchill, content with his new vocation, took exception in some measure. He wrote afterward that the hand grenade was believed to have passed its peak in the eighteenth century "and would be quite useless in modern war."

The cadets "dug trenches, constructed breastworks, reveted parapets with sandbags, with heather, with fascines, or with 'Jones iron band gabion.'" They put up chevaux-de-frise and made fougasses (a kind of primitive land mine), cut railway lines with slabs of guncotton, learned how to blow up masonry bridges, drew contour maps of the hills round Camberley, and made road reconnaissances in every direction. Churchill's inventory of his college work represented military activities, as he said, "no doubt very elementary," and he padded out his knowledge by wangling invitations to dinners at the Staff Col-

lege, about a mile away. There he heard officers who were being trained for the high command talk of those glamorous
adjuncts to human progress—logistics, interior and exterior
lines of communications, supply, personnel, attrition, flanking
maneuvers, and other matters so dear to the soldier's heart. He
and his fellow cadets complained bitterly that they had been
born out of their time. The British Army, Churchill observed
with scorn, "had not fired on white soldiers since the Crimea,"
forty years before. It was felt that this was a pretty shabby
record for any self-respecting army, which ought to fire on
white soldiers at least once a week, if simply to keep up a
decent standard of marksmanship. "If it had only been a hundred years earlier," wrote Churchill thirty years later, "what
splendid times we should have had! Fancy being nineteen in
1793 with more than twenty years of war with Napoleon in
front of one!"

Dreams of another such situation, with its almost limitless
opportunities for shooting white soldiers, kept the cadets at
Sandhurst alive. And lest it might be imagined that the British
Army, through some kind of bias, was organized to shoot *only*
white soldiers, it should be pointed out that, in this period, it
was equitably shooting as many black, brown, and tan soldiers
as it could manage. As Churchill himself remarked, "Luckily,
however, there were still savages and barbarous peoples."
These laggards were being eliminated in South Africa, in
Afghanistan, and in the Egyptian Sudan, in small, unrewarding
skirmishes. Among the more farsighted cadets, it was hoped
that the Indians might get sufficiently irritated to revolt. "At
that time the natives had adopted a mysterious practice of
smearing the mango trees," wrote Churchill, "and we all fastened hopefully upon an article in the *Spectator* which declared
that perhaps in a few months we might have India to recon-
quer."

As dim as was the prospect of an authentically bloody war,
Churchill had a pleasant and well-behaved time at Sandhurst.
People who remember him there say he did little to attract the

limelight that brightened his path through Harrow. Only infrequently did the tempestuous spirit break out, and then calm was quickly restored. For some reason, these outbursts, as at public school, seemed to come on him near water. At the college swimming pool he made the mistake of heckling the rugby forward, E. M. Panter-Downes, whose daughter, Mollie, born some years later, is now the British correspondent for *The New Yorker* magazine. Panter-Downes, not only a fine athlete but a leading student, saw the problem as military in tone. He rapidly outflanked Churchill, established a line of communication between his foot and the enemy's seat, supplied him with a prolonged ducking, and nearly reduced Sandhurst's personnel by one. Churchill was, in fact, half drowned and left Panter-Downes strictly alone thenceforward.

In classrooms he was undistinguished, competent, and quiet, in astonishing contrast to his classroom manner at Harrow, which was thrustful, ignorant, and raspy. He often had the answers to questions and showed, on the whole, if not excellence, a sincere desire to learn. With various roommates, he spent his evenings at work on the next day's lessons, though it is reported that he often launched one of the windy political roundups for which he had earlier become noted. Partly through devotion to his father, he considered himself an expert in matters of state. His quarters in the main building at Sandhurst, a columned, two-story piece of Doric architecture having a 900-foot façade, were cold and comfortless, unadorned by personal elegancies. He had two or three small family photographs on his plain oak desk and little else to remind others of his lofty descent. And besides, good blood was a commonplace at the military college; nearly all the cadets were the sons of army officers of high family.

These, together with the gaudy foreigners previously mentioned, were housed in strict accordance with the enduring philosophy of English school life. A cadet such as the Egyptian prince, for example, could have transported a spare palace to Camberley, equipped it with a staff of fifty servants, and lived

in regal ease without denting the family budget, but like his
fellows he was stabled in the approximate style of one of his
father's horses. Though born to the purple, the cadets lived a
gray life at Sandhurst. The college's heating facilities consisted
of a small fireplace in each room. On a windy, subfreezing day,
with the gusts howling through the halls and tearing at the
loose-fitting doors of the studies, a fireplace picked things up
much as a lighted cigarette might relieve the situation in an
igloo. It has been established that English cold has character;
it is superior to any other kind known. Rather than creeping
into the human frame from the outside, it seems to work from
the inside out. It bears little relation to temperature; with the
thermometer at 40, one can easily drift into a gelid stupor that
will persist until late spring. Few Englishmen ever get entirely
thawed out; their best hope of survival is to wrap up and keep
moving. The island's meteorological peculiarity has been laid
to the conflict that doubtless arises from the unnatural temper-
ing of a far-northern, nearly arctic land by a warm and errant
Gulf Stream. Subtle, icy vibrations are set up that can't be
measured in inches of mercury. In view of these conditions,
and of Sandhurst's especially slender arrangements, Churchill
and his mates studied within arm's reach of the fireplace. They
followed the general English procedure of frying one side,
while the other freezes, and then switching when both become
intolerable. Bad as it sounds, the Sandhurst (and British) approach to weather is filled with merit. Over the years a race has
been developed that can stand nearly anything. Moreover the
Army intended that cadets emerging from Sandhurst should
match in ruggedness the most poverty-hardened soldier of the
line.

To this end they were put through the stiffest possible paces
on horseback—chased up hill and down dale, over fences and
rock walls, through pebbly streams, and in and out of all the
military drills then known to cavalry. Churchill began to find
his niche; he attained the rank of fourth among the cavalry candidates. "I enjoyed the riding school thoroughly, and got on—

and off—as well as most," he wrote, and later he said, "Horses were the greatest of my pleasures at Sandhurst." Noting the boy's growing zest, Lord Randolph arranged a vacation course for him at the Knightsbridge Barracks, in London, with the Royal Horse Guards. Back at school, he and his companions took to spending all their pocket money hiring horses at the village livery stables. They organized point-to-points and even steeplechases on the estate of a nobleman Churchill knew in the neighborhood. So proficient did he become that Lord Randolph relaxed the hostility accumulated at the time of the examinations and took him on several outings, to a fluffy entertainment at the Empire Theatre and to political parties at Lord Rothschild's. Also, at Churchill's behest, they went to several race meetings, functions at which Lord Randolph was extremely well known, both as horse owner and as miscellaneous horse backer. Altogether, the outings represented some splendid educational opportunities for young Churchill, and he made the most of them. But even now there was no intimacy or warmth in Lord Randolph's manner. "If ever I began to show the slightest idea of comradeship, he was immediately offended," Churchill was to write, in the sad vein of a boy who had and yet never actually knew a father.

Besides the formal instruction at Sandhurst, he learned refinements in the behavior code of British officer-gentlemen. One of his fellow cadets recalls a lesson taught Churchill by his company commander, a martinet major named Ball. Wishing to visit a friend in a militia battalion training at nearby Aldershot, the boy hired a rig and drove over from Sandhurst rather early in the morning. On the road coming back, getting the utmost out of his horse, he dusted by a tandem in which, sitting bolt upright, was Ball, who nodded stiffly and continued at his reasonable gait. Churchill suddenly remembered that he'd either neglected or forgotten to sign the leave-book, a bitter offense. As he pondered his probable punishments, it occurred to him that by beating the major home he could still sign up and nobody would be the wiser. He laid into his indignant horse, which had been accustomed to clack along at a half-dead trot while dreaming of the grassy retirement for which he was years past due, and shot to Sandhurst like a cinema stagecoach. Springing out, he dashed in to where the leave-book was kept and riffled it open, then straightened up in astonishment. Midway down the page was his name written in Major Ball's hand and initialed "O.B." in the margin. This courteous yet reproachful gesture made such an impression on Churchill that he never failed to sign the book again during his remaining time at the college.

The college rules in general were strict but not harsh. The old yearbooks, in discussing the relative systems of Sandhurst, West Point, and St. Cyr, admitted that the former's working day could not compare with that at the American or French schools; it was felt, though, that "the Sandhurst cadet at the end of his course is probably equal if not superior in physique to the American or French cadet." Dancing, it was noted, was a prime exercise at West Point, while not enjoying much popularity at Sandhurst. "St. Cyr likes dancing, too, but no out-of-door games, for they have little attraction for the Frenchman, but in the matter of *esprit de corps* the St. Cyrians are far ahead of the Sandhurst cadets or the West Pointers."

Some of the rules posted in the halls of Sandhurst were:

Shouting in college buildings strictly forbidden.

When cadets go to mess they are to turn down the gas in their bedrooms.

Cadets when in uniform are not permitted to smoke in Camberley, Yorktown or Blackwater.

All gambling is strictly forbidden.

Only gentlemen will be permitted to visit cadets in their rooms at any time.

Afternoon teas may be given in a cadet's room with the sanction of the officer commanding the company, but all other meals are prohibited.

Cadets are cautioned against crossing any land under culti-vation.

When a parent (or guardian) wishes his son to keep a horse during the hunting season, or to be permitted to ride with the drag or hunt, he must send notice to that effect to the assistant commandant.

Greatcoats, buttoned up, are to be worn only in wet or in-clement weather.

No cadet is allowed to exceed the sum of one shilling a day for wine or beer at mess.

Accidental breakages at mess will be charged against the cadet.

Even though its character was at all times military, Sand-hurst offered a stylish sort of program for its gentlemen cadets, in keeping with the British upper-class precept of masking duty and labor with a ritual yawn. Life proceeded in a well-mannered, orderly fashion, only infrequently bumped out of its rut by extracurricular excitements.

It was in his Sandhurst period that Churchill had the first of his unending set-tos with women. Excepting his wife, his mother, his daughters, and one or two others, his experiences with the opposite sex have been more than ordinarily grisly. There can be no doubt that he has been horsewhipped by feminists as often and as passionately as any man living. Part of the fault may be attributed to women, who are occasionally troublesome, but Churchill is by no means free of blame. He has always been regarded as an impatient man living in a man's world, and has never been much inclined to discourse with women on any but a polite basis. Even today at dinners he is not at his best until the ladies leave the room and the men can descend to male topics, brandy, and cigars. At one such function a few years after he left the college, he crushed a bumptious dinner partner with evidence of his maturing repartee. He had political aspirations at the time and was growing a faint, scraggly mustache. The woman on his left said, with true British candor, "Young man, I care for neither your mustache nor your political opinions." "Madam," replied Churchill, "you are as unlikely to come into contact with the one as with the other."

While at Sandhurst, he took violent exception to one Mrs. Ormiston Chant, an elderly fool, who was causing an absurd ruckus around the London music halls. She was rightly considered to be the paramount British nuisance of the year, and she had some claim to a world title, although America was developing a few likely pests: Carrie Nation with her busy hatchet; Frances Willard, who endeavored to put the world on a sarsaparilla basis; Amelia Jenks Bloomer, an advocate of universal pants; and Susan B. Anthony, who ran a publication against men. As in the case of most reformers, various of these ladies suffered from one or another of the popular frustrations—an unelectric sex life, involuntary housework rejection, sour stomach, age, fright, etc.—and in the aggregate they represented a strong argument for the Chinese domestic plan. Mrs. Chant's principal complaint had to do with sipping spirituous beverages at theater bars, and in particular at the Empire, where she felt that people were having an unusually good time. She enlisted the support of a number of sympathetically anti-fun citizens and served notice on the Empire to close its bar. Characteristically with agitators, a countermovement sprang up, headed in London by the *Daily Telegraph,* which described Mrs. Chant and her group as "Prudes on the Prowl," and at Sandhurst by Churchill, who described them in some very picturesque language in private discussions. The meddling ways of Mrs. Chant got to be an obsession with him; in quick order he inflamed Sandhurst to the boiling point. Beardless children who had never seen a theater, and who didn't care if they never drank a drop, walked about the campus cursing her and vowing to tear her down from her false pedestal.

But it fell to Churchill to take positive action. Reading the *Telegraph,* he spied a letter written by a man who was forming "The Entertainments Protection League," an organization to undermine Mrs. Chant and secure freedom of drink for all. A meeting of the Executive Committee was announced for six o'clock of the following Wednesday at a London hotel. Churchill moved quickly. He obtained a two-day leave, by promising to brush up his lessons, and got to work on a long, impassioned speech, in which he touched on the Constitution, the Rights of Man, the nature and denature of alcohol, the sly corrosion of malice, Guy Fawkes Day, Ethelred the Unready, sidelights on the Druids, and additional staples of English history, several of them relevant. Then he committed the effort to memory and boarded a train for London. His monthly allowance of ten pounds was not due for two weeks, and he had only five shillings to his name, but he taxied to the hotel mentioned, and was dismayed by its drab façade and soiled surroundings. He consoled himself with the thought that such a setting was proper to the establishment of a democratic constitution for carousing, and he marched up to a seedy-looking porter.

"I have come to attend the meeting of the Entertainments Protection League," he said.

The porter's verbatim reply has been lost to history, but it was an English equivalent of the American "Pardon?" or "Say which?"

"It states here in the newspaper," Churchill went on, "that the Executive Committee is meeting today in your hotel."

"There's a man setting in the lobby," said the porter.

Churchill walked inside to face an embarrassed, well-dressed youth who rose and said, "Oh, yes, quite—I'm the Committee all right. It's rather hard to get anything worth while started— what?"

"You mean this is all you have so far?"

"They'll flock in once they see we mean business. Now let's get at it—do you suggest a few motions or any of that rot?"

Churchill beat a retreat, and found himself adrift in London at the dinner hour and with nothing in his pocket but cab fare, his speech, and a return ticket. He had counted on an oratorical triumph, an admiring round of congratulations, perhaps an interview or two, and a festive evening on the Committee, the members of which he assumed were wealthy. After this he hoped to gather up the late papers and read the wild announcements of a new political genius as he rode back to Sandhurst.

A disappointing alternative was to hock his watch, which he did, for five pounds. Then he ate a whopping dinner and went to one of the degenerate music halls.

His return to Sandhurst was inglorious. He sat huddled in a wretched train—the shadowy early morning carrier that conveyed the daily toll of London dead to the outlying cemeteries—and rehearsed excuses. Upon arriving, he told his inquiring fellows that the meeting had gone off brilliantly— the Executive Committee had been joined and a bibulous platform was in the works.

"How about the speech? Did it go down well?" they kept asking. He replied with such evasions as, "Couldn't have been a happier occasion in *any* respect—a perfect meeting of minds."

"They like the speech?"

"Naturally, we must proceed with caution; it would be unwise to press public opinion prematurely."

The cadets finally gave up on the speech and concentrated their interest on the developing news in the case. By a tremendous effort, Mrs. Chant forced the Empire management, if not actually to close its bar, to put up canvas partitions with which to screen the drinkers from the merely strolling members of the audience. This capitulation raised a fearful hubbub at Sandhurst. "For shame!" the cadets cried out in lively distress. "These poor devils are being boxed up like donkeys." After some goading from Churchill, it was felt that a large delegation should go in on the Saturday night the canvases were hung. And by chance, a great many young bloods of London had the same idea.

It made a pretty scene. Mrs. Chant and her spastic crew, carrying signboards lettered with messages like "Whiskey is a Curse," "Drop that Bottle!" and "Watch out before it's too Late," patrolled outside the doors, lamenting and moaning piteously. Inside, the atmosphere was rather different. Churchill and upwards of two hundred exponents of *laissez-faire* were draped over the bar, making the canvases bulge and shouting defiance at the teetotaling Mrs. Chant. On stage, a variety show had come to a halt. The noise of the clashing factions was deafening, and anyway nobody was watching. At length, the whiskey group, leaving its grotto, took to the aisles in a snake dance which was stopped when Churchill, or somebody, cried in a ringing voice, "Follow me and charge the barricades!"

Churchill's later account of the riot in the Empire Theatre does not jibe with others presumed to be equally authoritative. He took a modest view of his participation, while it was said by many that he was the sole instigator. In any case, it is fairly definite that he sounded the charge. There was a happy scrambling for the rear, and the canvases came ripping away. And now, typically, Churchill seized the opportunity to deliver his speech. He darted up to the stage, asked a couple of half-dressed chorus girls and a sword-swallower to step aside, and sailed into his remarks about the Constitution, alcohol, and the Druids. Then he departed from his set pattern and concluded with, "You have seen us tear down these barricades tonight; see that you pull down those who are responsible for them at the coming election!" It was his first public address, and while he did not have the undivided attention of his audience (many of the members had repaired to the rear to break sticks and rip up cloth), he bore himself well.

The management ordered drinks for the house, and the victorious party marched to Piccadilly Circus, where they topped off the evening by making a ceremonial bonfire of the debris. Mrs. Chant and her following withdrew to regroup. She was by no means finished; later on, with that hyperthyroid drive that distinguishes morality workers of the front rank, she actually succeeded in screening off all the theater bars in town.

One aspect of his speech troubled Churchill when he returned to Sandhurst. From birth he had suffered from a slight lisp, a not unmelodic impediment in his speech. It made him whistle the letter *s*. The fact that he was not assaulted at the Empire convinced him that he had a future in oratory, and he wanted to shine to best advantage. On his next trip to London he consulted a specialist, Dr. Felix Semon. The burden of the man's report was that little mechanically could be done to correct the flaw; determination, a thick hide, and practice were what was wanted. These Churchill could muster in abundance. He embarked on a program of declaiming in wooded nooks and other secluded spots, enunciating slowly and carefully. But he never quite mastered his lisp; he has the accentuated sibilants yet today. In choosing his words, he avoids terminal *s*'s as far as is practicable.

It is difficult for a biographer to leave Churchill's Sandhurst career without remarking a curious void. Notwithstanding his campaign against Mrs. Chant, and despite his adept horsemanship, few men who attended the college then have a clear recollection of him. As previously mentioned, his manner underwent startling changes. He graduated near the bottom at Harrow, but everybody knew him well, and many even painfully well. His efforts at Sandhurst were satisfactory in every way, but he made no great impression on either the students or the faculty. The *Annals of Sandhurst,* published in 1900 and assembled by Major A. F. Mockler-Ferryman from the available records, contains no mention of Churchill at all. While his old antagonist, E. M. Panter-Downes, who gave him the brisk watering down, turns up as a fighting member of rugby and other teams, Churchill is conspicuously absent from any cadet list. A historian who recently studied an assembled bibliography of Churchill, including both books and newspaper and magazine pieces, was unable to find a single Sandhurst anecdote that had not first appeared in his own writings. Neither can the faculty at the college successfully trace their famous former cadet. As a rule, stories of a rich personality linger on for generations; Churchill left no legend at Sandhurst. Lieutenant Colonel G. A. Shepperd, the genial present librarian of the college, has made it his business to search out evidences of Churchill's stay there, much as Churchill used to search for mementos of the Celts. It has been unrewarding work. Of the two inhabitants, the Celts left the stronger mark. The young man of destiny walked away, was caught up by great events, shot into celebrity, and has never returned. The truth is that, by Sandhurst, Churchill had heard the faint but unsettling bugle call of that dubious product of civilization, the career world. He preferred to step out from the last citadel of his boyhood with his chances unimpaired by mischief. In a class of one hundred and fifty he ranked eighth. The figures have no meaning. Ulysses Grant was twenty-first of thirty-nine in his class at West Point; Robert E. Lee was second in his. Douglas MacArthur was first; Dwight Eisenhower sixty-first and Omar Bradley forty-fourth in a class of about one hundred and sixty.

Certainly Churchill meant to be a professional soldier, and follow in the footsteps of the gory and well-heeled Marlborough. His confidence was never firmer; his voice at graduation soared above the others as he sang "I Am a Gentleman Cadet":

> "Oh! we're the boys to make the noise,
> we won't be taken down.

> And we cut such a dash when we're out on the mash
> in Camberley or Yorktown.

> Our manners at mess are perfect,
> our morals oh so high!

> And you always hear us coming
> with our well known cheery cry."

Over the years Churchill has tried to keep faith with the
old college song. His cry has not always been cheery, but he
has signalized his approach with all the noise possible. And
it has become vividly apparent, and devoutly to be wished,
that he will never be taken down.

# Chapter 8

WITH Sandhurst successfully completed, Churchill stepped out into the exhausting whirl of London society, and of Army protocol. His first duty was to get lodged with a suitably famous regiment. It made a great deal of difference which military unit a highborn Englishman first joined; it affected his whole career. Lord Randolph, despite the contretemps involving the cavalry, still had illusions that he could secure an infantry commission for his son. The Duke of Cambridge had hinted that certain wires might be pulled in inner circles. The Queen was not averse to seeing cadets of promise comfortably placed, no matter what their skill with examinations.

By misfortune, though, this was the deepest winter of Lord Randolph's discontent. He had just returned from an arduous trip around the world, and his health was failing fast. The end was not far away. His last conversations with Winston had to do with the latter's horses; he wished to know if the boy were adequately mounted. His death, on January 24, 1895, cut off a rich source of influence and power for his family; in some measure Churchill was now on his own, although his mother began to pay him increased attention. He was twenty years old, a poised, well-set-up, rusty-haired young man with a bold, humorous, calculating, and rather questioning gaze. The impressions of people who remember his first season in the crazy, rigid, social confusion are of interest. One of his comrades, now Lord ———, was particularly struck by his offhand acceptance of the most coveted invitations. These were secured first of all by virtue of his father's name, by his mother's exceptional beauty and wit, and by his own reputation for being a youth out of the usual aristocratic English mold. "Winston was never self-effacing even amongst the most gorgeous company," says the comrade of those days. "He was polite but condescending. He never *interrupted* the conversations of his notable elders, but he had always the air of waiting patiently until they were finished—then he would give the opinion that seemed to put that topic on the shelf for good."

It was a mellow time of romance and opulence in British history. The Empire was intact, a favorable balance of trade poured wealth into the small island country, the benevolent rule of Queen Victoria imparted to all her subjects that freest of all freedoms—a minimum of government—and the various orders of society were not yet lashed into class furies by neurotics, failures, and professional revolutionaries. There were many abuses of privilege, as there may ever be in an organization lifted above that of the apes, whose communal habits, it has been observed, have put them little forwarder or given them scant protection against the free-enterprise lion. In England of the 1890s it was merely the difference between privileged birth and the equally malodorous but less intelligent privilege of an ideologically experimental proletariat. The latter would come later, and England would not prosper. It must be said that Churchill's world flaunted its favors stupidly. When the Duke of Portland was summoned for driving a pioneer motorcar four miles an hour, and without dispatching two men on foot ahead with red flags, he contemptuously sent his steward into court with the message, "I must warn you that His Grace will be much displeased." The case was dropped. The distinctions were inflexibly drawn. When Lady Ashburton invited the celebrated writer, Thomas Carlyle, and his ill wife to go to Scotland, she put them into a second-class carriage with her maid and a second-class doctor.

But life in the main was easy and genial. Rents were low and food was cheap, good, plentiful, unrationed, and unsubsidized. It is true that the new income tax amounted to nearly two cents in a pound, or something like one-hundredth of its present rate, and there was a certain amount of grumbling, but the secure and lazy state of affairs was such that nobody's mind could dwell on trouble very long. Politics was a game rather than a distemper; inept officeholders were promptly kicked out, and went back to digging coal, or selling garters, or running errands for thugs, or teaching law, or whatever they were doing before the urge to rule hit them. It was before the heyday of that small, venomous blessing, the behind-the-government-scenes intellectual, usually sick and always hate-ridden, who was to be so lofty and sonorous in hauling down a world in which he lacked the courage to compete on normal terms. Writers were enjoyed for what they were: entertaining fellows, a little freakish, who were far less fit for large, unliterary problems than career statesmen were fit for writing. People read Dickens and Thackeray, deplored the social inequities pointed out, and allowed progress to roll on in its ancient, inevitable course.

It was not the best of all possible worlds, but it was Churchill's world, a good world, with some faults and more virtues, and it was to remain substantially the one he believed in for succeeding decades of his bright and useful career. Thanks to the fashionable circles in which he moved, the graduate at last joined a cavalry regiment which for splendor and good connections matched any in the Army. It was the 4th Hussars, commanded by a Colonel Brabazon, a friend of his father and a sidekick of the Prince of Wales. The colonel's qualifications struck a nice balance between the social and the military. Not the least of these on both counts was the fact that he had what was universally viewed as the gaudiest mustache in the English or any Continental army. It was his identifying mark, a carefully tended growth not unlike a pair of ram's horns. Brabazon's mustache got him entree to all the gilded salons and was believed capable of afflicting the boldest enemy with paralysis. He was an Irishman by birth and upbringing, a man who had killed his share of foxes and gone into the Army to make a living, his estates being impoverished. From the outset, what with his natural charm, his bearing, and the mustache, he had flashed through London society like a new Brummell. Churchill speaks amusingly of his old commander's accent, feigned or involuntary, which led him to convert *r*'s into *w*'s. Brabazon, who had changed regiments about as often as he changed his underwear, was once asked, "What do you belong to now, Brab?" He replied, "I never can wemember, but they have gween facings and you get at 'em from Waterloo." There is no detailed record of conversations between him and Churchill, but they must have been interesting, when it is considered that the latter also had a speech peculiarity. The colonel was a man of offhand imperiousness, perhaps a typical product of his class. At Aldershot he once inquired of the stationmaster, "Where is the London twain?" Informed that it was gone, he said, "Gone! Bwing another."

Into Brabazon's regiment, after a six-month recruit period of toughening, Churchill fitted snugly. There was unusual *esprit de corps,* based on social conquests above and beyond the call of duty. Brabazon never let rival commanders forget that his unit had infiltrated everywhere. His manner, though civil, was often deflating. At one mess, after listening to several bragging accounts, he asked the officer in charge, "And at what chemist's do you get your champagne?" In fairness, Brabazon's quality was by no means entirely convivial. His military record was unimpeachable. Notably, he had distinguished himself in the Ashanti campaign, a bloody war of revenge and subjugation fought in 1874 against tribesmen of a small West African country. Like others of his comrades, he was incensed that, in a previous row, the tribesmen had decapitated the governor, Sir Charles M'Carthy, and were using his skull as a drinking cup. This went against both

Brabazon's military and social instincts, and he tore into the natives as though the late governor's skull were the Holy Grail.

In the Afghan War of 1878 and in the Egyptian Sudan he had performed valorously, with the same nonchalant ease he displayed in the London clubs. He had been several times decorated. Brabazon may accurately be held up as the prototype of the English career officer of his day—wellborn, socially versed, good-humored, suicidally brave, sometimes stupid and mulish, but more often competent and tireless in the field. He was of a type now rarely seen. Away from action, it was a point of honor for a man to appear as foppish as possible; under fire, he must walk into the cannon's mouth, if need be, but never under any circumstances accompany the act with dramatics. The whole must always be understated, as only the British can achieve this laudable technique of living. Brabazon's men were as proud of his stylish clothes and sissy airs as of his inevitable gallantry in the face of certain death. During his association with Churchill, a disaster befell both him and the regiment. Sir Evelyn Wood, a martinet general of no doubt envious disposition, ordered the colonel to whack off the mustache. It was a crippling blow. Wood, the story went, had previously essayed a mustache of his own, but the effort had drawn a virtual blank. In a towering rage, Brabazon went to the regiment barber, who with tears running down his cheeks truncated the gorgeous shrub. Brabazon, maintaining a stiff but denuded upper lip, continued to do his duty in the time following, but a shadow had fallen over his spirit. The fire had gone out of him. And the 4th Hussars, also managing a surface equipoise, were far from the same happy group. The mustache was grievously missed.

II

In the days of Churchill's subalternship, the military year was reasonably divided. There were seven months of training in the spring, summer, and fall, and an agreeable five-month leave in the winter, during which the officers could participate in the "London season," as it was called—the continuous round of formal amusements. In the late summer of 1895, Churchill felt himself pursued by that old, nagging frustration, the flimsy prospect of war. He was not alone. All his young companions were champing at the bit. As they often remarked at mess, there was scarcely any further reason for medals, and they knew only a bare handful of lucky senior officers who had been hit by bullets. It was a happy world, but it was not a soldier's world—that of the fading nineteenth century. Except for a slight but undeniable edge at the parties, there was scant motive for wearing a uniform.

Unlike his fellows, Churchill saw a bad situation as something to be corrected, not merely to be deplored. He got out some newspapers and a big map and spent a profitless morning looking for wars. The only thing he could turn up, barring a few bush-league scuffles that could have been matched any evening in Limehouse, was the comic-opera revolution in Cuba. The island people, as yet unofficially aided by their powerful neighbor to the north, were bucking under the Spanish yoke. There was little evidence of mass slaughter, but it was a war, and Churchill determined to see it. At any time in history, small wars attract the adventurous and the ill at ease. In its course, the Cuban revolt was to siphon off nearly all the bored eligibles of North America. Rich and poor alike went down for the military season, for a variety of reasons. A leading statesman, Theodore Roosevelt, attended in order to see if he could ride a horse uphill while wearing bifocals, and others were spurred to arms by similar doubts. It was a strange and fashionable struggle and Churchill was among the first to recognize it as a competitive entertainment, a sort of World's Fair with funerals.

Drawing on the family name, he had no trouble arranging a sight-seeing tour of the Antilles. And, as at Harrow, he roped in a compliant comrade, one Reginald Barnes. "I say, Barnes,"

Churchill brought up the subject the afternoon after he'd studied the maps, "would you care to go to Cuba and get shot at?"

"Oh, rather!" cried Barnes, according to another subaltern in the 4th Hussars. "It *would* be a lark, what? Just hold on till I get my kit and whangee."

With the connivance of his mother, who had become as ambitious for her elder son as she had formerly been for Lord Randolph and for herself, Churchill wrote to Sir Henry Drummond Wolff, once a political aide of his father and now Ambassador to Spain. Then he dropped into the office of the *Daily Graphic,* to which Lord Randolph had once mailed letters from an African journey of several years ago.

"I'm off to Cuba to join the war," Churchill told the editor, "and I'd be willing to be appointed a special correspondent, for a fee, of course."

The editor looked interested and said something in a muffled tone that sounded like "three quid."

"My offer would involve five pounds per letter," said Churchill, with true journalistic fervor. Both editors and publishers have noted that native business genius reaches its zenith in writers. The heads of corporations and international bankers strive for years to attain their financial acumen; nearly all writers are born with an acquisitive and automatic grasp of everything pertaining to money. Alfred Knopf, the American book publisher, once said, "When a writer tells me he doesn't know anything about business, I take a firmer grip on my back teeth." The editor of the *Graphic* knuckled under, and Churchill left with a lucrative commission, his first of many. At home he found an affectionate and understanding reply from Drummond Wolff, saying that he and Barnes must go to Cuba by all means, only thing to do, enclosing permissions from the authorities, and adding a tacit hint that the Spanish commandant would knock off fighting and meet them in Havana with all ceremony.

Things had gone so swimmingly up to now that Churchill

and Barnes decided to throw a big dinner. It was held in a London restaurant and was a success, though it thinned down the spending money of both hosts for about three months. Churchill in his book *My Early Life* makes no mention of this function, but one or two others recall it with pleasure. Everything was done to a nicety, including the serving of first-rate wines with all the courses and two whopping slugs of brandy afterward. Churchill made a fervent but somewhat long-winded speech, just after the brandy, in which he paid tribute to his guests "who are yet under twenty-one years of age, but who in twenty years will control the destinies of the British Empire." The prediction was certainly accurate for himself; it fell short for the others, more than three quarters of whom would be killed in the soon-to-come wars which they all desired so earnestly.

It was not difficult for the two subalterns to obtain leave. They boarded a steamer on November 3, 1895, and had an uneventful trip. The Spanish commandant failed to turn up at the dock, but they were vastly enraptured by the Cuban capital. They registered at the best hotel in town and bought a box of cigars. For two days they did little but smoke cigars and eat oranges, both of which commodities were cheap and superior to anything in those lines seen in England. Then, suffering from a painful surfeit of citrus and nicotine, they presented their credentials to the authorities. Because of the language difference, the Spanish presumably got the notion that their arrival presaged the entrance of England into the war as an ally, and Churchill and Barnes were treated royally. They were presented with several boxes of cigars and a large crate of oranges, which they threw into the harbor. The next day they were assigned to a mission headed by train for the interior.

"Is there anything we ought to know?" asked Barnes.

"*Sí*—if firing commences lie down on the floor," replied the Spanish representative in Havana.

Both subalterns felt that this struck an unnecessarily chill--

ing note in what was intended to be a lighthearted outing. It was the first of a series of very realistic impressions they were to get about war.

The mission proceeded without incident from Havana to Santa Clara, all the passengers riding in the seats from start to finish. At the interior post, Marshal Martinez de Campos received the visiting warriors with great respect. There can be little doubt that he saw their presence as having some profound diplomatic significance. He assigned his best man, a charming young lieutenant with the curious name of Juan O'Donnell, to show the subalterns around. Further confusing his nomenclature, O'Donnell was the son of the Duke of Tetuán, the latter word being, irrelevantly, a Polynesian noun meaning "pigsty."

"Well, what can we do for you?" inquired the duke's son affably.

"Where's the war?" said Churchill.

O'Donnell's reply was that they must find a mobile column, since the fighting around them consisted of invisible guerrilla sniping, vexing but unglamorous. He escorted the Englishmen 150 miles through exceedingly uncomfortable jungle to the town of Sancti-Spíritus, considered by many to be the world capital of mosquitoes and smallpox, and they repaired to a tavern. By this time both Churchill and Barnes were beginning to find the romance of Caribbean revolution slightly dimmed. It was impossible not to recall the good times and military stalemate around the Carlton Club.

One General Valdez, on loan from an O. Henry short story, soon turned up with his mobile column, consisting of 3000 infantry, some cavalry squadrons, and a mule train. An audience was arranged immediately, O'Donnell acting as interpreter. Batting energetically at the mosquitoes, Valdez declared that it was heartening to have the moral support of Great Britain, and he hoped that the main body of her troops was not far behind. Churchill, severely bitten about the face and neck, muttered that it was nothing, and Valdez then paid

tribute to Sancti-Spíritus, saying that the men would march at
daybreak, since if they stayed in town as long as twenty-four
hours they would probably be too sick to leave at all.

The succeeding events proved to Churchill and Barnes that
the Spanish system of conducting a war was eccentric. To begin with, when Valdez said daybreak he apparently meant midnight, for they were on the move in the pitch-dark and they
groped over some very bushy terrain for about eight miles.
Then they pulled up for breakfast, which consisted in the main
of something which the subalterns heard as "runcotelle." It was
bland but powerful. They made an excellent breakfast on stew
and runcotelle, feeling progressively more sympathetic to the
cause, and it was not until several years later that Churchill
identified the mysterious word as "rum cocktail." After breakfast, notwithstanding the frenzied early morning rush to march
eight miles, it was the custom of the Army to lie down on the
ground and sleep until 2 P.M.

Churchill's letters to the *Daily Graphic* began to appear on
December 6. The first one proved such a remarkable dispatch
from a military man that the editor found it necessary to ap-
pend a descriptive paragraph centering on the word "breezy."
The letter was well written and discursive, much of it being
given over to explaining how difficult the writing of such letters
always turns out to be. It was fortunate that General Valdez
had no organized censorship. In that breezy vein which had
caught the editor's eye, Churchill stated that "While the Spanish authorities are masters of the art of suppressing the truth,
the Cubans are adepts at inventing falsehoods." The *pièce de
résistance* of his communiqué had to do with a favorite form
of attack by the rebels, and has been ascribed, no doubt falsely,
to an overdose of runcotelle. Churchill said that the rebels fired
the sugar cane by affixing wax-coated phosphorus to the tails
of grass snakes. The idea was that the snakes would wriggle out
into the sun, the wax would melt, the phosphorus would ignite,
and the countryside would then be hotted up for the enemy. It
was a very fanciful and advanced branch of armament, and it

seems a pity that Churchill did not clarify it with more detail. For instance, it was asked in the London clubs, did the snakes head for the enemy by instruction? What kept them from firing the sugar cane near the *rebels?* It was assumed in the end that the grass snakes were organized into a special unit, on the order of commandos, and were directed by officers from among their own general species, probably rattlesnakes.

Churchill's next letter, equally interesting, announced that he had lost the Army. He was wandering around in an area riddled by patrols from both sides. This was dangerous, he pointed out, because one had to answer a hail with the proper password. That is, if a rebel called out *"Quién va?"* it was imperative to reply "Cuba"; if a federal gave the challenge the answer was, or should be, "Spain." An error committed either way resulted in a volley of gunfire. Churchill's letter indicated, *per se,* that to date he had made some brilliant guesses. It was also assumed that, in his wandering, he had run across a post office.

A third letter the following week put him back among friends. It also contained a very striking remark. "I sympathize with the rebellion—not with the rebels," Churchill said. On the physical side, he related that he had just been under fire, in a running skirmish with the enemy. After several days, or nights, of marching through painfully tangled jungle, General Valdez and his troops, including the British mission, pulled up for the habitual gorge and siesta. It was a pleasant spot—on a grassy knoll, with a fringe of woods around, and in the background tall reeds and rushes, presumed to be free of hostile grass snakes. Suddenly a shot cracked harshly on this quiet, tropical scene. Churchill happened to be sitting down at the time, chewing on a half-roasted chicken. Within ten feet of his head a horse screamed, shook violently, and slumped forward. The young subaltern was amazed. It had not occurred to him that bullets could produce this cruel and disagreeable effect. He was about to cry out, "Watch where you're aiming," when a whole round of rifle fire destroyed all hopes of a normal break-

fast. Two men were grazed and a third, having some connection with the mule train, was reported to have spilled nearly a
pint of runcotelle. Churchill indignantly tossed his chicken
aside. He was still open-minded about war, but this wanton
disruption of meals was going too far. "I began to take a more
thoughtful view of our enterprise than I had hitherto done," he
later wrote in his memoirs.

Intermittent firing from the bush marked their progress of
the next few days. Casualties were light, and there was no sign
of the crawling arsonists. Exhibiting a flair for stratagem of
which Marlborough might well have been proud, Churchill
made a new friend. He stuck close to the side of an enormously
fat Spaniard, whose screening bulk was more reassuring than
the stoutest coat of English mail. When the man, during halts,
strapped up his hammock, there was Churchill, comradely and
voluble, strapping up a hammock right beside him. Obscured
by the shrubs, the rebels retreated before them, expending end-
less rounds of ammunition. General Valdez' men, shouting
carrambas, sapristis, and other federal oaths, shot back in-
dustriously, and the palm trees, both rebel and government,
took a terrible beating. All along the course, both Churchill
and Barnes were nonplussed to note that scarcely anybody on
either side got hit. Nobody was ever killed. But the trees were
badly plastered.

The expedition ended in a brisk set-to within both sight and
sound of the enemy. Valdez brought up his best troops, and the
rebels, "to my relief," as Churchill was to write, quit firing and
vanished for good into the jungle. It had been an expensive and
dubious campaign. So far as could be ascertained, the rebels
had no casualties; the pursuers lost a horse. Nevertheless,
Valdez and his staff celebrated victory with a noisy and un-
interrupted dinner, toasted nearly everything in Cuba, including the snakes, and then pointed the column toward the coast.
Churchill was much gratified; he had seen enough of bush warfare for the moment. Both he and Barnes were anxious to get
back to the Carlton and re-form their lines. Before they left,

for some reason never made entirely clear, the Spaniards presented them with the Order of Military Merit (first class). One of the London bloods, hearing the news, uncharitably commented that the Spanish must have slapped on the decorations on the run, so lively was the British mission in getting clear of the island.

As a parting gesture, Churchill solemnly presented his sword, which he had bought secondhand before leaving London, "to Spain," in the person of a bewildered colonel. His last letter to the *Daily Graphic* was written from Florida. There had been some question of delay in getting a ship to England direct, so the subalterns had grabbed the first thing out. Churchill had intended to compose his valedictory report on the expedition "when under the influence of the sentiment aroused by seeing the shores of Cuba grow dim on the horizon," but he had unluckily come under the influence of seasickness instead and had thrown up all the way across. From Florida they caught a ship home, and turned up back in London early in 1896.

Just after his twenty-first birthday, Churchill inscribed in his birthday book a quotation from Milton:

> To reign is worth ambition, though in Hell;
> Better to reign in Hell than serve in Heaven.

It was apparently his questionable tribute to Cuba.

# Chapter 9

CHURCHILL was barely recovered from Cuba when he was ordered to the military staging center of Hounslow in preparation for duty in India. As it imposed privations upon the cadets at Sandhurst, so did the British Army of that day rise to stern heights in assigning foreign service. When the recently decorated subaltern asked how long he was likely to be in India, he was told, "Around and about fourteen years." In consequence, he and his comrades of the 4th Hussars were given full latitude for the next six months in arranging their affairs. To Churchill this meant traveling back and forth to his mother's home in London and tripping the light fantastic at the season's balls.

Lady Randolph had sensibly decided not to go into permanent mourning after her husband's death. She was a beautiful and vital woman, still young, with a need for self-expression and male companionship. In the course of the years she was to marry again twice, the first time to a man named George Cornwallis-West, a career army man, and, later, to a Montagu Phippen Porch, a civil servant in Nigeria. What with her exotic childhood, Lord Randolph's expeditions, and her succeeding husbands' occupations, she had a wide knowledge of the world, and her counsels became invaluable to Churchill as time went on.

The Lady Randolph was currently not the only American member of the Marlborough clan. The exalted English family seemed to have a predilection for entangling foreign alliances.

The eighth duke had married an American, the wealthy daughter of a commodore in the American Navy. Widowed like the Lady Randolph, she too had embarked upon further matrimonial ventures, and was, at the time of Churchill's subalternship, wedded to Lord William Beresford, with whom the young officer struck up an admiring friendship. Beresford was indeed a man who might appeal to the romantic-minded younger generation. His accomplishments were outstanding even in the rarefied circles in which he moved. For example, he was regarded as the fastest man on a badger draw in all of England. The legend of one feat performed years before when he was attached to the 12th Lancers lived on, and would have been reputation enough for a lesser athlete. On a large bet, he had arisen from the convivial dinner table of his mess at Knightsbridge, walked the ten miles to Hounslow, stolen a badger belonging to the 10th Hussars, and carried it in a bag slung over his shoulder all the way back to Knightsbridge. He made the trip in champion time, too—his record stands to this day.

As if this were not enough, Beresford was an able pigsticker, pony-racer, big-game shot, and polo player. In him were combined all the qualities that young Churchill thought desirable, and many were the reminiscences involving obstinate badgers and elusive pigs that the boy drew forth in quiet tête-à-têtes. Churchill remembers his six-month preparatory leave as "the only idle spell I have ever had." He danced, he lounged in the clubs, he visited the badger king at his handsome estate of Deepdene, and altogether he made splendid gains in the social skills that were to be so helpful to him later. In his works Churchill has given a priceless description of his life and locale in the crowded months before India:

"In those days English Society still existed in its old form [he wrote]. It was a brilliant and powerful body, with standards of conduct and methods of enforcing them now altogether forgotten. In a very large degree everyone knew everyone else and who they were. The few hundred great families who had governed England for so many generations and had seen her rise to the pinnacle of her glory were inter-related to an enormous extent by marriage. Everywhere one met friends and kinsfolk. . . . The leading figures of Society were in many cases the leading statesmen in Parliament, and also the leading sportsmen on the Turf. Lord Salisbury was accustomed scrupulously to avoid calling a Cabinet when there was racing at Newmarket, and the House of Commons made a practice of adjourning for the Derby. In those days the glittering parties at Lansdowne House, Devonshire House or Stafford House comprised all the elements which made a gay and splendid social circle in close relation to the business of Parliament, the hierarchies of the Army and Navy, and the policy of the State. Now Lansdowne House and Devonshire House have been turned into hotels, flats and restaurants; and Stafford House has become the ugliest and stupidest museum in the world, in whose faded saloons Socialist Governments drearily dispense the public hospitality."

Churchill naturally found these high-echelon delights hard to leave, but orders were orders, as he would often point out half a century later when he was in charge of running a great war. Before sailing, he had the good fortune to make one of those useful acquaintances which British society provided for ambitious youngsters. At Beresford's house, he met a high Army officer with the unlikely but fitting name of Sir Bindon Blood, a leader of famous Indian campaigns. During a memorable week end, Blood had shed light on several of his exploits, and Churchill extracted a promise to be allowed to serve under him should any further natives require punishment.

The voyage of the 4th Hussars, a body of 1200 men, was made in a big troopship and took twenty-three days, coming to an end in Bombay Harbor. And there a minor disaster overtook Churchill, an accident destined to plague him steadily until the present day. In stepping from a small boat to grasp the ladders at Sassoon Dock, he wrenched his right shoulder out of place. He wrote afterward that he scrambled up all right but "made a few remarks of a general character, mostly beginning with the earlier letters of the alphabet." The shoulder popped back in, but thenceforward it had the annoying habit of popping out again at unpropitious times—when its owner was swinging a polo mallet, or lifting a champagne glass, or waving derision while making political speeches. It popped out a few years ago during a debate in the House of Commons, and he was compelled to ask a nearby Member, fortunately a party colleague, to yank it back into place. Churchill still uses the shoulder cautiously, performing whatever tasks he can with his left arm.

Soon after the landing it developed that the 4th Hussars were urgently needed in India. The local polo situation had deteriorated; the natives were walking, or galloping, off with nearly every honor. Churchill's regiment settled down at Bangalore to an intensive practice grind. As Army life went, his beginning Indian stint was not onerous. In company with two other second lieutenants, he rented a comfortable cottage and hired twelve servants, in accordance with regional usage. The Indian labor situation was then, and is now, confused. Because of the dark, diverse religions, the limits to what any one person could do were pretty sharply marked out. For example, while a man of one caste or sect might dust a bureau with impunity, he could stir up the gods terribly by dusting the dining-room table. A cook could on no account shine his employer's shoes; the whole theological structure might come tumbling down. When Churchill first arrived, he was told that he must have separate servants for his right and left shoes, but this proved to be only a barracks-room jest.

His wholesale employment of religious Indians often left Churchill in straitened financial condition. His second lieutenant's pay was nominal, barely sufficient to provide food, drink, and tobacco, and his outside income amounted to only five hundred pounds, an allowance from his mother. It was Churchill's practice, upon receiving his salary (a sackful of silver rupees), to go directly home and toss the whole to his butler, who then made out as best he could, shopping in the local equivalent of supermarkets and cooking leftovers. To hike their living standard to what they considered a decent level, Churchill and his fellow officers relied on moneylenders. These mysterious and cosmopolitan brethren were as thick as fleas in the streets, all fairly rich, having as they did the only trade in those parts that offered real security, barring pocket-picking and the clergy. They never made a bad loan; if one of the subalterns neglected to fish up on reckoning day, it was the work of a moment to step around to his commandant and tattle. Churchill and his bungalow mates—Hugo Baring and the former Cuban observer, Barnes—were deep in the toils of the moneylenders nearly all the time they were in India. The immediate cause of their involvement was polo. Every week or so they felt a compulsion to buy a new pony. Next thing was to hop out and find a lender, as a rule easily located on the door-step. The conversation would then go about as follows:

"Good morning, Rajputo. What's the rate today?"

"Very low, Sahib—two per cent a month."

"Outrageous. I need a new pony."

"Service, Bwana. To be procured within the hour."

"A live one."

"I count the teeth personally."

"What's the total rap?"

"A mere nothing, Tuan—three hundred rupees, plus a slight carrying charge."

When the horse was bought, a man would be engaged to untie it, another to give it a shove, a third to curse it, another to lead it down the street, and so on until the gods were ap-peased and the chain of command rather expensively set up to deliver the animal to its terminal owner.

It became plain that Churchill had natural genius as a polo player. Much of his success was attributed to his frenzied style of attack, which was later described by an officer as looking "like a man thrashing at a cobra with a riding crop." Churchill and the other members of the regimental squad made a long trip to Hyderabad to join in a tournament for the Golconda Cup, a sporting event of national interest comparable to that of the Kentucky Derby here. It was considered by all that two native teams, the Golcondas and the Vicar Al Umra, were far and away the best ones entered. By thrashing cobras in especially vicious style, Churchill led his mates to a thundering triumph over the Golcondas, and they went on to take the tournament itself, the first time it had ever been won by a newly arrived regiment; neither was it to happen again. Photographs which exist of Churchill in this summertime of his polo career are those of a youth with a serious purpose. Wearing a sun helmet, he is seen mounted on a milk-white stallion; again, he stands slouched but ready beside a satiny black mare, with four dark-skinned functionaries in the background holding additional testimonials to the moneylenders' skill. None of the early photographs shows him smiling. He is clearly a young man with a mission; perhaps a young man in a hurry, as some journalists were soon to say, with uncomplimentary intent.

In India he got his first real dose of culture, taken voluntarily, without being force-fed. The genesis of this departure was not altogether a lust for learning, or even curiosity. The three hours around noon in southern India are so ominously hot and humid that scarcely any living thing, in the village or in the bush, walks or crawls abroad. Everywhere there is quiet, even in the deepest jungle. Despite a saying of the tropics that only mad dogs and Englishmen go out in the midday sun, Churchill and his colleagues turned in for a snooze. Repose of this sort was appetizing to most subalterns, but it chafed Churchill sorely. He was too highly charged. There was nothing else to do except read. To his surprise, once he had got the first few volumes down, he found the exercise non-toxic. His taste expanded rapidly. In the past he had cheerfully swallowed such confections as *Treasure Island* and *King Solomon's Mines,* but these were wholly for pleasure; there was no notion of self-improvement. As he got into his Indian reading it occurred to him that there were vast fields of knowledge with which he was not even on speaking terms. To anyone with Churchill's sense of personal destiny this was a rude shock, and a challenge. By his account he quickly absorbed, and stored away in perpetuity, Gibbon's *Decline and Fall of the Roman Empire* (an old standby of his father's), Macaulay's various histories and essays, Plato's *Republic,* the *Politics* of Aristotle (edited by Dr. Welldon of Harrow), Southey's *Colloquies on Society,* Darwin's *Origin of Species,* Schopenhauer on *Pessimism,* and the poems of Robert Montgomery (not to be confused with the movie actor).

These down, he decided to take a hitch at religion, with which he had been inoculated repeatedly at Harrow, though it never properly took hold. He read Winwood Reade's *The Martyrdom of Man,* of which, in a Conan Doyle story, Sherlock Holmes was to remark to Watson, "Let me recommend this book—one of the most remarkable ever penned." Broadly speaking, Reade's work is theological, but it does very little for organized religion, since (after a brilliant summary of the main events since Adam) it decides that humankind has nothing to look forward to after death. Not religious to start with, Churchill was by no means evangelically seized by *Martyrdom;* neither was he to get the call from Lecky's *Rise and Influence of Rationalism* and *History of European Morals,* which gave him, he said, "a predominantly secular view." Churchill's religion, or lack of it, has been the source of wide speculation over the years. It has been flippantly suggested that he has a well-organized religion of his own, requiring no outside gods. A few anecdotes, perhaps apocryphal, support this view. During the last war, he was asked by a well-meaning clergyman, "Mr. Churchill, are you prepared to meet your God?" "I'm perfectly prepared," said Churchill. "The question is, is God prepared to meet me?"

Among the most valuable books he found in this period was Bartlett's *Familiar Quotations,* which he read several times from cover to cover, practically committing it to memory. Then he tackled Shakespeare, finding the sacred plays and poems as eloquent as advertised but somewhat verbose and involuted for everyday use. Nevertheless, he plowed through the lot. His style was affected by his reading course. A number of his fellow officers recall that his speech became more richly upholstered with every volume he mastered. Indeed, he developed into such a nuisance around headquarters that he was finally sat on, in the literal sense of the word. At one point, when he had monopolized the conversation for nearly an hour, his mates grabbed him up, pinioned him on the floor, and then shoved him under a sofa, where they kept him captive all evening while they played cards.

The unfailing monotony of barracks, or bungalow, life in Bangalore eventually got on Churchill's nerves. Early in 1897 he wangled a three-month leave to go to London, where he and his mother applied pressures to get him more profitably situated. By a miracle, a nasty tribe of Indians called the Pathans, brigands and torturers, had just erupted on a northern frontier and Sir Bindon Blood was called upon to quell them. Churchill was at the racecourse at Goodwood, a little better than three pounds ahead, when he heard the encouraging news. He promptly telegraphed Sir Bindon to remind him of the promise made at Deepdene. Then he caught the next boat train for India. He was on fire to get at the Pathans, for whom, all in a twinkling, he had developed a raging hatred.

In Bombay he found a somewhat equivocal answer from Sir Bindon Blood, saying, "Very difficult; no vacancies; come up as a correspondent; will try to fit you in. B.B." This was a poser, as Churchill admitted freely. His series on Cuba for the *Graphic* had been gleefully received but had got him no further offers. Journalistically speaking, he was between engagements. But he hopped confidently around to the office of the Allahabad *Pioneer*, a local journal, and had no trouble browbeating the editor into putting him on the staff. And then he had some good news from his mother, who, keeping abreast of developments by wire, had stormed Fleet Street in his behalf. The *Daily Telegraph* had agreed to make him a war correspondent, for the slightly depressing sum of five pounds per column. Churchill was temporarily set back by this niggardly arrangement. "It was not much, considering that I had to pay my own expenses," he complained.

In Bangalore, he wheedled his commanding officer into extending his leave. Then he took his dresser, a confused child named Mohammed Bey, and an armload of books and boarded a train for the front, the whereabouts of which was hazy in his mind. At the station he said, "Give me a couple of tickets to Nowshera. How far is it?" The clerk looked at a map covering a whole wall, made a few calculations, and replied, "Two thousand and twenty-eight miles. Sahib wish a round trip?" Churchill was obliged to sprint back to his house for an additional sack of rupees. The trip took five days and passed comfortably, with Churchill propped up on some cushions reading the books and Mohammed Bey twirling a water-soaked punkah, to keep off the heat and the flies.

Facing the Pathans near Nowshera, the railhead, was a segment of the British Indian Army known as the Malakand Field Force. Churchill and Bey joined it without incident, making the last leg up to the mountains by pony cart. Sir Bindon Blood was temporarily absent, having chased over to a neighboring valley to quell the Bunerwals, a tribe not quite, but almost, as nasty as the Pathans. Hearing that the latter were celebrating, the Bunerwals had understandably voted to kick over the traces, too. Accordingly they had oiled up their handful of antique muskets and opened fire on a British-owned jackass. Blood at this time was a man past middle age, a worn and harried but devoted officer. For years his life had consisted in quelling upstarts. He was interrupted at every turn. If he sat down in his Bombay club, he was likely to be handed a note on a salver, saying, "Rush up to Poontang and quell the Durkees." He even took night calls, like a country physician. His family's whole history was adventurous; its most distinguished member, a Colonel Blood, had given the line something to shoot at by trying to steal the crown jewels, in the time of Charles II. A guard had caught him on the Tower stairs and had him arrested, but the attempt was much praised in court circles, even by the King himself. In waiting for Blood to quell the Bunerwals, Churchill, by his own story, "acquired an entirely new faculty," one that he was to refine to famous heights of artistry. He learned to drink whiskey. Heretofore, he had downed wine, and even brandy, in recommended British style, but had avoided encounters with whiskey. In a flash of vision now with the field force he saw whiskey as man's best friend, giving it priority over the traditional dog. Of all the accounts of this distilled epiphany on the hilltop, his is incomparably the best.

After commenting adversely on the heat and favorably on his discovery, he wrote, "Wishing to fit myself for active service conditions I overcame the ordinary weakness of the flesh. By the end of five days I had completely overcome my repugnance to the taste of whiskey. Nor was this a momentary acquirement. On the contrary the ground I gained in those days I have firmly entrenched, and held throughout my whole life. Once one got the knack of it, the very repulsion from the flavour developed an attraction of its own; and to this day, although I have always practised true temperance, I have never shrunk when occasion warranted it from the main basic standing refreshment of the white officer in the East."

Churchill's candor in connection with his quick and lasting toehold on the bottle is refreshing in a world filled with inveterate apologists. Perhaps because of the proscribed delicatessen at Eden, the majority of mankind spends a great deal of time feeling guilty about something or other. Only infrequently do people come along who can pick a course, stick to it, and remain perfectly satisfied through thick and thin. Churchill is pre-eminently one of these; his early liberation from doubt shows today in his face, which has real character. It is the strong, well-nourished face of a man who long ago decided to drink what he pleased, gorge at will, suit himself in any way it seemed convenient, and in general to follow lines of self-centered behavior popularly supposed to stamp the countenance with a look of weakness. It is a free-enterprise face, somewhat gothic in feeling. The heroic visage stands out in healthy contrast among cautious, remorseful drinkers.

His brother officers warmed to him in the Indian mountains as he demonstrated an easy ascendancy over veterans who had been drinking whiskey since long before his birth. By the day of Sir Bindon's return from the Bunerwals, Churchill was established on the road to a continuous and sober whiskey-drinking career that has had few parallels in his time. And now, said Blood, the hour had struck for quelling the Pathans. The Malakand Field Force became mobile. To accompany it in style, Churchill had to buy two horses and hire a groom; he also bought some military haberdashery formerly owned by soldiers who had fallen during the campaign. The fighting in these mountains differed from that in the Cuban jungle, being dangerous. Properly speaking, Churchill had never been ex-posed to fatal warfare before. The three brigades of the force moved carefully from one hostile area to another and at length, in the Mamund Valley, had the intense satisfaction of being fired upon. A few minutes later, the battle was joined in earnest. Churchill asked and got permission to penetrate into the most forward sector, where a couple of officers and a few Sikhs were arranged on the outskirts of a suspiciously empty village.

The village and the countryside suddenly sprang to life. Voicing a number of unsettling animal yelps, a group of Pathans dashed out of the houses; and from all the mountain ledges others dropped in clusters. Their first fire wounded a Sikh in the calf of the leg and felled one of the officers. When two Sikhs attempted to drag him back, a second burst drove them off, and the leading Pathan, a hideous and apelike giant, fell upon his body with flashing sword. It was at this point that the descendant of Marlborough showed his colors. The drums and trumpets of Malplaquet and Blenheim were sounding hotly in his ears. With that aroused spirit which was to cause Adolf Hitler such acute suffering, he drew his own sword, uttered a frightful rallying cry of Harrow (where he had won the Public

School Fencing Championship) and advanced singlehanded to the attack. The Pathan pulled up, frozen by what appeared to be a series of novel but highly expert flourishes. Then he dropped his blade, picked up a handy rock, and let fly. Here again Churchill displayed traces of the cunning and resourceful first duke. He tossed his own sword aside and drew his revolver. His first shot sent the Pathan howling and limping toward the mountains; the second and third accelerated his pace wonderfully. As Churchill looked around, however, he saw himself to be at this moment the one-man apex of the Malakand Field Force's thrust into the Pathan hills. Supporting the wounded officer, he beat a quick retreat, with a covering fire from the more judicious troops to the rear.

These latter cheered his progress down the slope. Several of them said afterward that the rescue was among the finest examples of individual valor they had ever seen. But Churchill was far from finished; like J. P. Jones, he had not yet begun to fight. Flushed by the prehistoric male fever of combat, he laid down his human burden and snatched a Martini-Henry rifle from the hands of a dead trooper. He straightened up, making a splendid target, and fired about forty rounds at the rapidly advancing arc of Pathans, who began to drop on all sides while others leaped forward in great numbers. The British lieutenant colonel in charge crawled up and yelled, "Dash to the rear and try to bring up the Buffs!" "Sorry, but you'll have to put that in writing," replied Churchill, as he drew a bead on the closest tribesman. The lieutenant colonel gave up and crawled back to his Sikhs, who were demoralized, somebody said, as much by the superhuman conduct of Churchill as by the imminence of an untidy death.

Despite the reckless defense put up by the correspondent of the London *Daily Telegraph* and the Allahabad *Pioneer,* the situation was about as dark as it could be. The unit was nearly surrounded and out of ammunition; its members awaited the climax of what promised to turn into a very messy tribal fiesta. As they watched, little clouds of Pathans burst from behind

rocks everywhere and started on in a last, furious rush. And
then, in the best American movie style, the shrill and garbled
notes of bugles at the charge sounded at the foot of the hill.
"Get down, Churchill, for God's sake!" cried the lieutenant
colonel. "It's the Buffs and the 11th Bengal Lancers!" The
relief party swept on up past the commander, and past Churchill, who had thrown down his rifle and retrieved his sword, and
into the enemy, who fled in wild disorder. The battle was over.
It was said to have been the first time the Pathans had ever
been balked by a cub reporter working at space rates.

For his part in the Malakand campaign, which continued for
some weeks further, Churchill won rewards both military and
journalistic. He was mentioned in dispatches, an extraordinary
honor for one so young. Sir Bindon stated that the officer commanding the forward force "has praised the courage and
resolution of Lieutenant W. L. S. Churchill, 4th Hussars, the
correspondent of the *Pioneer* newspaper, who made himself
useful at a critical moment." Journalistically, the restless subaltern climbed even higher. His pieces were an instantaneous
success. Indeed, they were the talk of London. Since Cuba, his
style had matured and his knowledge had widened. Perhaps
equally important, he had a good deal more to write about.
While the Pathans were without incendiary grass-snakes, they
were well organized and venomously disposed, and Sir Bindon
Blood's army was obliged to take every tactical advantage to
bring them under control.

*The Story of the Malakand Field Force,* an expanded collection of war articles by Winston Spencer Churchill, was published in book form in March 1898. Among the rich harvest
of comments it reaped was a letter to the author from the
Prince of Wales, afterward King Edward VII. It went as follows:

My dear Winston:
    I cannot resist writing a few lines to congratulate you on the
success of your book! I have read it with the greatest possible interest and I think the descriptions and the language generally excel-

lent. Everybody is reading it, and I only hear it spoken of with praise. Having now seen active service you will wish to see more, and have as great a chance I am sure of winning the V.C. as Fincastle had; and I hope you will not follow the example of the latter, who I regret to say intends leaving the Army in order to go into Parliament.

You have plenty of time before you, and you should certainly stick to the Army before adding M.P. to your name.

Hoping that you are flourishing, I am, Yours very sincerely,

A.E.

It was a kindly and generous encouragement from a royal prince to the promising son of an old drinking companion. Churchill never forgot it. Many years later, he in turn would stand staunchly by Edward's grandson, who was renouncing the throne to marry an American divorcee. On that controversial occasion, bidding the young King good-by, his peculiar hat in one hand and his favorite walking stick in the other, Churchill recited the lines by Andrew Marvell on the beheading of Charles I, tapping out the meter on the floor:

> "He nothing common did, or mean,
> Upon that memorable scene."

Churchill of course prized this stick even more highly after it had rendered its historic service. Toward the close of the Second World War, he was making a tour of Roehampton Hospital and met a veteran who was having an artificial leg fitted.

"With your special limb you will be able to walk without extra support," Churchill commented.

The soldier said, "I think so, sir, but I have a favor to ask. I'd like that old stick of yours."

Churchill hesitated a moment, then replied, "Here are my heart, my hand, and my stick. Now you must take good care of this bit of wood—it's been all over the world with me."

# Chapter 10

NOT ALL the talk about *The Malakand Field Force* was rhapsodic. With a sublime disregard for consequences that endures to the moment, Churchill stepped on a lot of expensively shod toes. The whole book, though brilliant, was written with an Olympian finality that would have been more digestible from the pen of, say, Napoleon, or Wellington. The second lieutenant resolved problems of military procedure that had plagued the British General Staff for years. In connection with one sweeping censure, he said, "I am aware that those who criticise an existing state of things ought to be prepared with some constructive legislation, which should remedy the evils they denounce. Though it is unlikely that the Government of India will take my advice, either wholly or in part, I hereby exhort them to quit the folly of a penny-wise policy, and to adhere consistently to the principles of employing British and native troops in India in a regular proportion."

Churchill advised the government to retitle many ranks in the Army. "Deputy-Assistant-Adjutant-General" should be "Brigade Adjutant," he said, and "Deputy-Assistant-Quartermaster-General" should be "Brigade Quartermaster."

The question was raised in London, even by some of the friendliest critics, What the deuce did this have to do with the Pathans? One fellow, as keen about changed titles as Churchill himself, suggested that the title of the book be changed to *A Subaltern's Hints to Generals.*

Nevertheless, the notices were sufficiently excited to warm the heart of any beginning writer. "A wisdom and comprehension far beyond his years" was attributed to the author in one leading paper, and in others there were like hosannas. An editorial defect irritated nearly everybody. Being awkwardly placed in India, Churchill had entrusted the proofreading to the only literary member of his family, an uncle who had once composed a sprightly monograph on Devonshire subsoil. The uncle was a leisurely chap, and his correction of Churchill's proofs had apparently taken place during a light nap. The finished product was filled with typographical miswhackers of the most embarrassing kind. He had scored with particular violence on punctuation, seemingly having gone at it much as one dances the conga—"one, two, three—comma; one, two, three—dash," and so on. The *Athenaeum* was moved to describe the volume as "Pages of Napier, punctuated by a mad printer's reader."

A critic who especially fancied the book noted that, offsetting his chastising of the British, Churchill had unloaded some pretty personal remarks about the Pathans.

It was true, as charged, that he had conceived a vast dislike for the tribesmen and their ungallant ways. He related sourly how they were forever trying to swap their wives for rifles, a practice that would have got a man black-listed in any club in London. "Their system of ethics, which regards treachery and violence as virtues rather than vices, has produced a code of honour so strange and inconsistent, that it is incomprehensible to a logical mind," said Churchill. He had been unappeased to learn that they fought among themselves entirely without malice, two rival sides frequently sitting down on the bodies of their slain comrades to discuss the fine points of the fracas. Their real estate procedures he considered to be ineffectual. When a piece of land was in dispute, each claimant by tribal law was compelled to take a Koran in hand and walk the boundary as he saw it, meanwhile swearing that he trod an accurate path. The results overlapped terribly. By good for-

tune, said Churchill, "the dismal farce of swearing is usually
soon abandoned in favor of an appeal to force."

One aspect of *Malakand* that went unremarked but would
stand out grotesquely in a modern report of war was the in-
vigorating lack of attention to the author's own activities.
Though Churchill was in the thick of several battles, and could
be expected to see the fighting subjectively, he wrote about
the others. His account was about as opinionated as it could
be, but the doings of the correspondent were subordinated to
those of the main army. It was a sensible and largely un-
political appraisal of the terrain, the people involved, their
aims and tactics, and, as already stated, containing a fair
sprinkling of impersonal clues to world, or military, betterment.

Many of his descriptions were said to rank with the best war
writing by the masters in this field: Stendhal, the haughty
plagiarist; Joshua the Stylite, the best-known correspondent
assigned to cover the war between the Greeks and the Persians,
in 430 B.C.; and Stephen Crane, who had never been within
ten miles of an activated battlefield in his life but who contrived, in *The Red Badge of Courage,* probably the vividest
detail about fighting in existence. As a capper, a man who
claimed to have read *War and Peace* clear through compared
Churchill's scene-setting touches with the sharpest in Tolstoy.
"The bullets passed in the air with a curious sucking noise, like
that produced by drawing the air between the lips," wrote the
subaltern at one place, and at another, "The company whose
operations I watched—Lieutenant Lockhart's—killed one of
these [tribesmen] with a volley and we found him sitting by a
little pool, propped against a stone. He had been an ugly man
originally, but now that the bones of his jaw and face were
broken in pieces he was hideous to look upon. His only garment was a ragged blue linen cloak fastened at the waist. There
he sat—a typical tribesman, ignorant, degraded and squalid,
yet brave and warlike, his only property his weapon and that
his countrymen had carried off."

The sale of his book netted Churchill the equivalent of two

years' pay as a second lieutenant. Even at this young age—
twenty-three—he had begun to see the many useful facets of
money. In essence, it provided the vital link between the life
of a gentleman-soldier and that of a man of affairs. Journalism
and fighting formed a kind of cycle: with money he could buy
railroad tickets to far places, kill a few natives, describe the
battle, sell the story, and then be in a position to buy additional
railroad tickets. Keeping this in mind, he noted with delight that
the Afridis, up near the Khyber Pass, had gotten completely
out of hand. His course was clear. He must join the expedition,
in the name of Queen Victoria, the London *Daily Telegraph,*
and the Allahabad *Pioneer.*

Now, for the first time, Churchill ran into opposition. His
exploits and notoriety began to backfire. The *Daily Chronicle*
had been so unkind as to dub him "Pushful, the Younger," and
another paper had described him as being one of that band of
"disconsolate young gentlemen endeavouring to fight their
country's battles disguised as journalists." Moreover, his phenomenally long-suffering colonel of the 4th Hussars was at last
growing restive. The colonel saw his precocious subaltern very
infrequently. Now and then Churchill would drop by for some
copy paper, or to pick up his laundry, or to arrange an ex-
tension to his already attenuated leave. At these times he
presented such a gleaming appearance, what with his Cuban
medal, the ribbon from Sir Bindon's campaign, and his general
air of Fleet Street prosperity, that the colonel had fallen into
the habit of initiating salutes and escorting him around as one
might receive a visiting dignitary. The colonel's manner now
frosted up. Even Churchill's brother officers seemed out of
patience. They were "extremely civil," he later wrote, "but I
found a very general opinion that I had had enough leave and
should now do a steady spell of routine duty."

With his reserves thus weakened, Churchill fell back to a
previously prepared position. He settled down to regimental
life in Bangalore, but he did it ungraciously, and continued to
send out feelers for advancement at each opportunity. The

truth is that his reverence for a career of soldiering in India had faded. Among other things, he had encountered certain difficulties with the language. As a rule, when subalterns arrived in the romantic colony, they immediately set to work learning the native tongues. Churchill at Harrow had been marked as a linguistic cripple. He either wouldn't, or couldn't, tackle anything but English. He was a dead loss at Latin, and his French is still a subject for international flippancy. In the midst of the last war, he was showing a French minister some London military units and was asked to identify a marching company of the Women's Voluntary Service. *"Elles sont des femmes gratuités,"* replied Churchill in his confident style. The Frenchman afterward repeated the curious explanation at the embassy, and added, *"Mon Dieu, quelle situation!"* He had apparently never before seen what he took to be female camp followers dressed in pretty uniforms and drilling on the streets.

During his months in India, Churchill had picked up three Indian words, or, more properly, two and a half: *Maro,* meaning "kill," *chalo,* "get on," and "tally-ho," the English fox-hunting term which had been adopted as an Indian word meaning practically everything, like the Hawaiian *aloha.* With *maro, chalo* and "tally-ho," Churchill felt that he could rise in India, but not very far. In consequence, and because of the rich vistas opened out by his writing, he decided against a cautious succession to eminence through the normal channels of promotion.

Sir William Lockhart was in charge of the expedition to Tirah, where the Afridis were howling under the Khyber Pass. Churchill wrote him a letter expressing a willingness to join the outing, if the arrangements were sufficiently attractive. From a staff officer he got back a succinctly phrased telegram well within the ten-word economy limit and revolving around the word "No." Churchill's mother then wrote to influential government acquaintances, to Lord Roberts, to Lord Wolseley, and to Sir George White, the Army commander-in-chief in India. Their replies, no doubt tinted by the offhand advice in

*The Story of the Malakand Field Force,* were similar in spirit to the telegram. Churchill interpreted the attitude of these functionaries as one of restrained entreaty. So he packed up, browbeat another leave out of his colonel, and shoved off for Calcutta, the seat of government, where he meant to pick up his orders. What was his amazement when the Adjutant General declined categorically to interview him. However, by applying continuous pressures, Churchill actually got himself appointed Sir William's orderly. When the campaign proved disappointing, he saw that his only recourse was to go back to Bangalore and write a novel.

Churchill began work on *Savrola, a Tale of the Revolution in Laurania,* within the fortnight. The writing went at a gallop. His comrades gave him every assistance in outlining the character of Lucile, his heroine. Their remarks were of such a crude and unvirginal nature that he was compelled to sequester himself in his bedroom and stuff cotton in his ears. His manuscript was completed in only a few weeks. He sent it to Longmans, his London publisher, and the serial rights were sold to *Macmillan's* magazine. *Macmillan's* readers in general regarded the effort with interest. When the book appeared, Churchill had introduced a brief preface which said in part, "Since its first reception was not unfriendly, I resolved to publish it as a book, and I now submit it with considerable trepidation to the judgment or clemency of the public."

*Savrola* is an eventful narrative, bumpy in spots, and certainly must be rated a singular creation for a twenty-three-yearold. The scene was laid in Laurania, one of those indeterminate fictional states with which Europe was overstocked by authors around the turn of the century. The boundaries were often casually drawn, giving rise to geographic perplexities that landed more than one reader on the verge of lunacy. Sending her footman into Prague for snails, a heroine might step down the path for a dip in the Mediterranean, picking edelweiss en route and singing a beer-garden aria in Flemish. Laurania looked out on the Mediterranean in front and in the back to some mountains that could have been anything from the Apennines to the Urals. It was a pleasant spot, said Churchill, whose climate "had made the Lauranian capital the home of the artist, the invalid, and the sybarite."

As the story opened, the capital was predominantly the home of an articulate rogue named Antonio Molara, the "President," who had raised himself up to be dictator and was making things tough for the workers. Tension prevailed throughout the nation. Brisk rifle fire broke out on page 13, and an unidentified man in a straw hat was killed. The President himself was beaned by an accurately thrown rock as he descended from the official carriage. In response to hopeful inquiries from his staff, he said, "It is nothing. They threw stones; we used bullets; they are better arguments." Then, ignoring his streaming temple, he stepped on into the palace, presumably to raise everybody's taxes another 12 per cent.

While Molara was nothing special to look at, his wife Lucile was an angel in very thin disguise. She was as saintly as her husband was rapacious. Churchill's low barracks-room friends had made no headway in shaping either her looks or her character. She had "perfect features," her "tall figure was instinct with grace," and her nature was mellowed by a yet unmatured passion for the workers. Within the limits of her unconsciously democratic persuasion, Lucile was a good wife to Molara. "Her salon was crowded with the most famous men from every country." This wanton depletion of other countries of their personages made for very gay doings in Laurania. Reactionary balls were the order of the day, and there were other entertainments nearly as pleasant. Lucile had a pretty wit, and she kept things moving, but she recognized faintly, even if her husband did not, that something was missing. Her life was courtly, polysyllabic, and hollow. All unawares, she awaited the onset of Love.

It was at this point that Churchill's readers were introduced to Savrola, the leader of the opposition, who has been mentioned as being perhaps the most relentlessly political hero in

literature. He was thirty-two and "looked magnificent," with
a "high and ample forehead" and a promising air of election
triumphs just around the corner. From some unstated source,
possibly kickbacks, he was a man of means, and his apartment
was "tasteful and luxurious," built around a library coinci-
dentally featuring the very authors that Churchill himself had
been reading at Bangalore: Darwin, Macaulay, Gibbon, etc.
Though an idealist, Savrola fitted in perfectly with the Lauranian scene. The country itself was an administrative nightmare. Ballot-stuffing, oratory, graft, and assassination were the
main occupations, and the nation's foreign policy was a model
of universal bad will.

Like most politicians, Savrola hoped to repair the confusion
while retaining the politics. President Molara had other ideas.
He preferred to keep the confusion while jettisoning Savrola.
And here, as the dictator pondered a more permanent method
of subduing his rival than outstuffing him at the ballot boxes,
he had what proved to be a uniquely frail idea. Why not sick
the ravishing Lucile onto Savrola, learn his secrets, undermine
his strength, and then, eventually, snip off his locks, even as
Delilah had barbered the muscle-bound Samson? Molara's
wife was naturally reluctant. She argued that she had her principles, same as anybody else. When Molara insisted, in the
iron-jawed style that had accounted for his rise to power,
Lucile made plans for a gigantic state ball and sent an invitation to Savrola.

Churchill's description of this resplendent social function
was confident and sound. His childhood had been spent in
close proximity to the pomp and glitter of Blenheim and other
big houses, and he knew what he was talking about. His
familiar mention of trumpets, powdered footmen, stringed
bands, and potted plants provided a believable backdrop for
the dirty work that Molara had mapped out for Lucile. Savrola
almost didn't go. His advisers, an extremely shifty collection,
felt that his presence might be an affront to the trade unions.

The evening got off to a radiant start. The Russian am-

bassador arrived, kissed Lucile's hand and entered into one of
the cerebral exchanges that distinguished the amenities of that
period.

R: The scene is an appropriate setting to a peerless diamond.

L: Would it sparkle as brightly in the Winter Palace?

R: Assuredly the frosty nights of Russia would intensify its
brilliance.

L: Among so many others it would be lost.

R: Among all others it would be unrivalled and alone.

L: Ah, I hate publicity, and as for solitude, the thought of it
alone makes me shiver.

The British ambassador, Sir Richard Shalgrove, turned up
wearing the Order of the Garter and got off some merry jests,
which had a decidedly unfestive overtone, centering on a fleet
of English battleships that he hinted were lying a little distance
offshore. This was presumably routine British diplomacy, since
nobody paid any attention to him but just laughed at his jokes
and let him maunder on. Savrola, arriving, commanded instant
attention, for he was in plain evening dress, with "no decorations and no stars," and was also strikingly "calm, confident
and composed." About three waltzes later he and Lucile found
themselves tête-à-tête, and the reader sensed the unmistakable
imminence of a romance. This was a skillful touch of Churchill's; an atmosphere of jungle expectancy, of mate calling to
mate, settled down over the story.

Things now moved swiftly. With a firm but tender grasp,
Savrola led Lucile out onto a moonlit balcony, edged her into
a shadowed recess, and drew her into an impassioned political
argument that went on for eleven pages.

The evening was not altogether a success. The King of
Ethiopia, the principal guest, a man with a "black but vivacious
face," left in a huff because of the low-cut dresses of the
women, and no amount of coquetry or low-cut dresses could
stop Savrola from babbling politics. As Molara reflected when
he and his wife were undressing for bed, they had spent a lot

of money and hadn't got to first base. He turned in with plans
for another hike in taxes.

After this the situation went from bad to worse. If Laurania
thought it had been political before, it changed its mind once
Savrola hit his full stride. He made a corker of a speech in the
public square and caused a full-scale riot. Lucile, who had
slipped into the throng to study his style, was trivially injured
in a crush of excited workers. Savrola assisted her to his home
and, with his housekeeper, tried to get her into bed but she
slipped away, laughing, and scampered up to the roof, where
she looked at his telescope.

"I ought to hate you," she said when he joined her, "and yet
I don't feel that we are enemies."

"We are on opposite sides," Savralo replied. "Only politics
can come between us."

Still hacking at the same old line.

As he was about to make some advance of a perhaps more
genially political nature, the dogged Molara burst in and denounced Lucile as a "Strumpet!" This was certainly a loose
choice of words, for her guilt, if any, was ideological rather
than erotic. Nevertheless, Molara cursed her horribly ("The
common, ugly material of his character showed through the
veneer and polish") and took a shot at Savrola, which was
high.

Savrola knocked him flat, and the revolution began. A re-
viewer has complained that it was next to impossible to follow
the twists and turns the fighting took in the capital in the next
few days. At one point a fleet of ships figured prominently in
the talk. They could have been those mentioned by Sir Richard
Shalgrove at the ball, since Churchill earlier had caused one
Lauranian to remark, "Ah these English—how grasping, how
domineering!" It is known for sure that the government suffered
1400 casualties, that the Senate was seized, and that looting
broke out everywhere.

In the manner of most European revolutions, the movement
got out of hand. A German corporal among Savrola's follow-

ing, a foaming maniac named Kreutze who bore a clairvoyant
resemblance to another ambitious Teuton, then still a baby,
screamed himself into command as the new Socialist messiah.
Molara and his gang were liquidated, and Savrola and Lucile
were compelled to flee into exile.

On their way out, standing on a hill overlooking the home
of the artist, the invalid, and the sybarite, Savrola expressed
his determination to return and clean up the mess. If the book
had a flaw, it might be that no reader in his right mind could
be persuaded to believe that any one man this side of heaven
was up to the job.

The evasion and temporary cessation of politics did one
thing for Savrola and Lucile: it enabled them at last to enjoy
an authentic love scene. In the midst of a tropical embrace,
they exchanged endearments.

"Goddess!" whispered Savrola.

"Philosopher!" returned Lucile.

They went on up the alien path, headed for Graustark, or
Hentzau, or another friendly, fictional haven. Politics had
missed fire, but love seemed strong enough to carry them
through to the next general election.

In a sort of epilogue, Churchill quoted his old favorite,
Gibbon, as saying that history is "little more than the register
of the crimes, follies and misfortunes of mankind." It is interesting to speculate whether he would have presented these
dubious nouns had he foreseen how much history he himself
was to help manufacture in the coming fifty years.

Some time after *Savrola* appeared, Churchill epitomized his
novel as a story in which he "traced the fortunes of a liberal
leader who overthrew an arbitrary government only to be
swallowed up by a socialist revolution."

His summary has since been characterized as one of the most
dazzling pieces of unconscious personal prophecy on record.

# Chapter 11

CHURCHILL collected a total of $3500 for *Savrola* and was content, though he finally took a dislike to his book and wrote that "I have consistently urged my friends to abstain from reading it." He felt that there was more money, and more fun, in war correspondence. Barring writer's cramp, there was little chance of incurring serious personal damage while composing a novel, and fictional criticism had an oblique, softened air that he found unsatisfying. With Antonio Molara tumbled down from his high place, he saw that it was time for a second version of *A Subaltern's Hints to Generals*.

At every step in Churchill's career a convenient war has opened up when he was ready for it. In fact, the cry of "warmonger" has been hurled at him repeatedly, in increasing volume since the Socialists took England into protective custody. Today's fevered orators in Hyde Park harp with gleeful malevolence on his long and intimate connection with fighting. As a rule, they refrain from pointing out that he has been uniquely influential in bringing wars to a triumphant close and making England safe for orators in Hyde Park to climb up on stepladders and complain about warmongers.

His unsuccessful attempt to punish and serialize the Afridis had given Churchill a heightened urge to score in some other direction. A golden opportunity awaited him now in 1898. The war offering itself for exploitation was of a romantic nature far exceeding that in the Indian mountains. In the African Sudan, a dark, dusty, superstitious region lying south of Egypt and the Sahara, one Mohammed Ahmed had proclaimed himself the long-lost Mahdi, or guide, of Islam and was goading the people to terrible wrath. The Sudan had been governed by Egypt, which in turn was governed by England. The Mahdi was an early communist; he advocated "universal equality," a catchall phrase that continues to trap disgruntled minorities, and community property. He had dubbed his followers "Dervishes," which, loosely translated, means "holy beggars," and counseled them to keep moving, as a stimulus to the better life. Consequently, they developed a sort of convulsive wriggle that eventually won them the name "Whirling Dervishes," enriching the language of the demon whites. The Mahdi hated all foreigners, whom he referred to, for reasons he never made clear, as "Turks."

Like most communist states, the Mahdi's Sudan soon shook itself down into an inferior species of capitalism, wherein he and his assistant bureaucrats ran the community's property and the Dervishes had little left but their whirl. And in a pattern familiar to strong, utopian leaders, he kept his flock apathetic about its hungry lack of property by putting the members out to war. Of late they had slaughtered several thousand Egyptians as well as the English commander in those parts, General C. G. Gordon. At last, moving with characteristic deliberation, the British military were grouping to retaliate. A relief unit had previously been mentioned for Gordon, but by the time it was organized, with protocol settled, the campaign ribbon decided upon, the quadruplicate files made of all the equipment issued, the unfortunate general was long dead and buried and the Mahdi was looking for some new Turks.

The man whose resistance Churchill had to overcome to join this second punitive thrust was Sir Herbert Kitchener, the Sirdar, or commandant, of the English-Egyptian Army. By mischance, Kitchener was unimpressed by pushy second lieutenants, in general by young men of destiny with exalted antecedents and in particular by Churchill. All the latter's entreaties to the War Office met with rebuffs that implicitly originated in the highest quarter. The reaction to his quick advancements had gathered wide momentum. Writing of this dismaying period, Churchill later said, "Others proceeded to be actually abusive. 'Medal-hunter' and 'Self-advertiser' were used from time to time in some high and some low military circles in a manner which would, I am sure, surprise and pain the reader of these notes." Even the well-groomed enterprise of Lady Randolph was all unavailing. She had dinner upon dinner, at which the best-situated men of military and government were approached without restraint. Their response was an embarrassed mutter that the Egyptian Sirdar was all-powerful in the matter of appointments.

Throughout his life, Churchill's luck has been a point of confusion to his rivals and his enemies. It now appeared that even Kitchener could not stand against it. Lord Salisbury, the Prime Minister, picked up a copy of *The Story of the Malakand Field Force* in his club, retreated to a secluded corner, and read it through in a single sitting. His approval was so uncontained that he sent immediately for the author, who was again in London on leave. Churchill for once was mildly apprehensive about an interview, going to the length of having his clothes pressed, his shoes shined, and combing his hair. Moreover, without precedent in his social history, he presented himself at 10 Downing Street on time, after calculating that he would make the gesture to leave in exactly twenty minutes. The Prime Minister kept him for nearly an hour and said, at his dismissal, "If there is anything I can do to help you, please let me know."

He had scarcely got the words out when the accommodating youth replied, "Indeed there is, sir—I'd like to join Sir Herbert's expedition into the Egyptian Sudan."

A few days later he received a notice from the War Office that he had been attached as "a supernumerary Lieutenant to the 21st Lancers for the Sudan campaign." The information included the rather cheerless corollary that he would pay his own expenses and see to it that he was buried or patched up without cost to the government if he were killed or wounded.

Very rightly, Churchill considered that such items should be taken care of by some newspaper or other. Once again he made the rounds of Fleet Street, and this time he nailed down a good assignment, as correspondent for the *Morning Post,* at the improved rate of fifteen pounds a column. The employment was very welcome, but another macabre note was struck when a funereal-looking stringbean came up to him after a dinner and begged an interview, which went about as follows, according to one of Churchill's clubmates.

"Ah, I'm the president of the Psychical Research Society," said the diner.

"To be sure," replied Churchill, in excellent spirits as a result of his appointment. "Any news?"

"Tolerably slow at this season. We've had one or two little triumphs, but nothing of public interest. To be candid, a spectacular abridgment would not be at all amiss."

When Churchill seemed puzzled, he went on: "You are, I believe, preparing to go into the Egyptian Sudan on a mission of some danger?"

"Why, no more than a routine———"

"In plainer terms, there is an excellent chance you will be shot?"

"Why, I wouldn't say———"

"Precisely. Now I wonder if you would do me a favor," said the man, producing a card. "In case you should Depart, or Muster Out, as it were, would you be so good as to get in touch with me at my flat? I'm generally in in the evenings. Just rap on anything handy, though I'd be obliged if you would avoid the piece of crockery on the mantel. It's been patched."

"Three raps do?" inquired Churchill, falling into a bantering vein.

"The number is immaterial."

With assignments both mundane and spiritual, Churchill felt that he was richly equipped for his outing. He boarded a train for Marseilles. Six days later he was in Cairo, and he pushed on to the Abassiyeh Barracks. There he found a certain amount of resentment at what was interpreted by some as a bumptious intrusion. The 21st Lancers were a proud regiment, known as the "Saucy Devils," and its officers felt that it was not necessarily reinforced by a warrior who would probably appear on the battlefield with a sword in one hand and a pen in the other.

In the beginning, then, instead of getting a troop command as he had expected, Churchill was put in charge of the mess store. His own subsequent report of this snarl indicated that his tardy arrival accounted for his lowly command; one or two others remember the facts differently. All the versions agree that Marlborough's descendant was in no way humbled by the slights and setbacks.

One day a junior officer met him coming up a path leading a rickety mule and two donkeys. The recollection of the officer, now long in distinguished retirement, is that Churchill said, "Look at that. There's a trust for a British officer! It's not even a job for a non-commissioned officer. They've said, 'We'll break young Churchill's heart if he comes to us.' Poor little men! They think I'm as small as they are. But it's my object to write a big book on this campaign, and as long as I get there I don't mind how they employ me. Even if they give me a sweeper's job I shan't demur."

Many of Churchill's present associates think that part of his greatness has always been his refusal to waste time in petty angers, personal bickering, and dreams of vengeance. Neither his equanimity nor his effectiveness is ever impaired by attempts to frustrate him. Another junior officer having to do with the mess store, Robert Smyth, who later rose to be a brigadier general, wrote to his sister in England, saying, "Winston Churchill is only 23 and frightfully keen. Started by telling me he was more interested in men than horses, so I asked him to look after rations etc. and said I would do the horses. He asked to see the men and spoke to them (very well, too) and had a great success; in fact, they liked him."

Robert Grenfell, the subaltern assigned to the command that Churchill had hoped to get, wrote back to his family:

"Fancy how lucky I am. Here I have got the troop that would have been Winston's, and we are to be the first to start."

History is violently altered by very small decisions, as somebody has already noted. A few days later, in the terrible charge at Omdurman, Grenfell was pulled off his horse and cut to pieces by a howling Dervish mob. It is engrossing but idle to ponder the probable course of England had Churchill ridden out in the van instead of Grenfell. It is not fantastic to suggest, however, that today's government in London would be in the hands of either a German or a Russian gauleiter, and that mankind would be much farther advanced on its determined return to all-fours.

When Kitchener's army started its hot, hazardous trip up the Nile, Churchill's duties became less onerous and the tension about his presence slackened. The expedition made its way 350 miles southward by train to Asyut; from there by sternwheel steamers to Wadi Halfa; thence 400 miles via the new military railroad to the Egyptian Army base at the confluence of the Nile and the Atbara. Omdurman and Khartoum, where the Mahdi and his Khalifa, or chief lieutenant and successor, had killed General Gordon, lay less than 200 miles farther down through the desert.

Churchill spent much of this trip reading background literature on the Sudan and its troubles and in ingratiating himself with his fellow officers, an occupation for which he had immense talent. People who knew him then say that he was irresistibly entertaining when he chose; few ill-wishers could hold out against his charm. He could talk on a great variety of subjects with an odd quality of infectious excitement. In those days, too, he was an able listener, a skill that he has not seen fit to sharpen with the passage of time. The fact is that Churchill at present is a captive audience of the itchiest sort. He is slightly deaf, and he leans heavily on this useful infirmity. At dinners especially, when he is apt to be flanked by garrulous women, his hearing is nearly invulnerable to the human voice. In the midst of anecdotes about petunias and woman's suffrage, he will cup one hand over an ear, frequently the far ear, and call out "Hah?" Meetings of defense officers during the last war were a painful trial to him. On one occasion, a minor functionary arose, cleared his throat, and began what promised to be a two-hour report on "buffer stocks." Churchill endured it for about ten minutes, then whispered hoarsely to a neighbor, "Who is that man?" The expert droned on, and a few minutes later, Churchill's whisper again interrupted with, "What's he talking about?"

"Buffer stocks," replied the embarrassed neighbor.

"Butterscotch!" cried Churchill. "Let's wind this up and get back to the war. He can investigate butterscotch on his own time."

The expert threw in the sponge and sat down. Everybody had a pretty good idea that Churchill could hear all right. He simply preferred to talk.

As the British force pushed into the desert toward Omdurman, reports of a mirage-like enemy filtered in from patrols. It was a parched, uneasy Mohammedan world, alien to the British soldier and his dreams of a green and ordered England. The usual techniques of warfare might be futile against these receding but watchful bands of horsemen. Kitchener's Egyptian infantry and mounted English lancers moved slowly over the hot dunes, while naval units—gunboats, stern-wheelers, and sailboats carrying supplies—proceeded up the Nile not far away. Churchill was with a forward patrol that caught occasional glimpses of fast-riding scouts but no concentrations of Dervishes. Early on September 1, as he rested his horse near some thornbushes, a sergeant major came galloping back with the welcome shout, "Enemy in sight!"

"How many are there?" asked Churchill.

"A good army. Quite a good army," replied the sergeant major, beaming with pleasure.

Churchill's patrol moved forward to a shallow ravine, where he found his commander, Colonel Martin, also in exuberant spirits. Martin's first greeting was "Good morning!" Then, hav-

ing disposed of the amenities, he hastened on to say to Churchill, "The enemy has just begun to advance. They are coming
on pretty fast. I want you to see the situation for yourself, and
then go back as quickly as you can without knocking up your
horse, and report personally to the Sirdar. You will find him
marching with the infantry."

Churchill reconnoitered and put his horse, a gray Arab polo
pony, to a gallop toward the rear, with feelings of trepidation.
His anxiety was aroused by Kitchener rather than by the
Dervishes. The question was, how would the commander-in-
chief react when the subaltern to whom he had given an emphatic "No!" came riding up here in the desert with a first
report on the enemy? Churchill could not help but wonder if
Kitchener's ire would be so fearsome that he would defer his
campaign against the Dervishes and concentrate his resources,
both mounted and afoot, on Churchill.

Everything went off without a hitch. It is believed that
Churchill to this day is piqued by the impersonal abstraction
with which the Sirdar took his message. Kitchener was riding
alone, an impressive figure, with purple jowls, long, waving
mustaches, and a mien of portentous solemnity. He listened
without interrupting while the author of *Malakand* gave an
eloquent military précis of the situation (well rehearsed as he
had sped back over the sand), and then asked, "How long do
you think I have got?"

"You have got at least an hour—probably an hour and a
half, sir, even if they come on at their present rate," replied
Churchill. This was a brash and chancy estimate, involving
heavy responsibility, but Churchill had no doubts whatever, as
usual. Kitchener dismissed him with a slight bow, and the
subaltern joined the junior officers for a prebattle luncheon of
bully beef, mixed pickles, and stout wines. He gave an excellent
account of himself during these preliminaries. Seated at an upturned cracker box, Kitchener dined apart from everybody, on
a few dry biscuits. The duties of a commanding general are
somewhat more serious than those of lieutenants, as Churchill

perhaps began to realize for the first time. The gage of battle, the conduct of the troops, the final outcome with its historic consequences, would be summed up in headlines approximating either "Kitchener Wins" or "Kitchener Loses."

When the front was still quiet at sundown, it was rumored that the Dervishes would attack by night. Orders for strict silence were given out up and down the lines. Thorn fences, or *bomas,* as they are called farther west in the Congo, were thrown up by the infantry. Churchill's sleep was fitful, and he had arisen, with the others, long before dawn. As the sun came up, the scene was one of preparation and hopeful excitement. The Nile with its crowded flotilla was within view on the left flank, and the cavalry units were disposed at points beside and in front of the infantry, ready for charge and countercharge. Churchill's squadron leader, a Major Finn, a big, leisurely Australian with the rough-and-tumble sense of humor characteristic of those southern people, had for days carried on a harangue about how he meant to put the untried subaltern-correspondent through his paces. Now he summoned him and sent him forward on reconnaissance, with a half-joking admonition not to try to win the war by himself. Churchill took a patrol and rode ahead into the glassy fields of sand. Far away on both sides he could see other patrols setting out. And behind them Kitchener's mounted units—the 21st Lancers, the Camel Corps, and the Horse Artillery—started up slowly. Members of patrols on that day recall that from hillocks one could see through binoculars the spectral white buildings and mud huts of Omdurman, and opposite it across the Nile the arsenal and ruins of Khartoum, the ancient former capital.

But the "good army" reported the day before was no longer in evidence; only black and brown smears of thorn relieved the tumbled white, and now and then a scattered, hurrying group of riders. One of these came within range of the new British Lee-Metford carbines. A volley of shots spilled two Dervishes from their saddles. Their companions reined up, puzzled, and then waved their rifles in an obvious signal. All

across the desert, for as far as anybody could see through his
glasses, the black and brown smears of what had appeared to
be thorn materialized into human life, the well-trained rows of
60,000 fanatics who comprised the Khalifa's army. They came
on in waves, pouring out of gulleys and springing up from behind every sand ridge that offered concealment. Prisoners
quizzed afterward gave the composition of the Khalifa's forces
and the names of his leaders. The center of the army, formed
in squares and commanded by Osman Sheikh-ed-din and Osman Azrak, included 12,000 black riflemen and 13,000 black
and Arab spearmen. The Ali-Wad-Helu rode in front with
5000 horsemen of the Degheim and Kenana tribes. The
Khalifa's bodyguard of 2000 followed the center force, and
behind him marched Yakub Emir with 13,000 swordsmen and
spearmen. The right wing was the brigade of the Khalifa Sherif,
with 2000 Danagla tribesmen; the left flank was formed by
1700 Hadendoa commanded by Osman Digna, a villain of
such horrifying reputation that whole villages in his path had
been known to fold up and vanish. These first-named leaders
flew identifying green, red, or black flags from many spear-
heads, but the troop of Osman Digna flew no flags at all, feeling that its fame was sufficient without further advertisement.
As the infantry drew closer, the British could see the ritual
dancing of the Dervishes, intending to establish their fury and
discourage the bravest enemy. All in all, as one of Churchill's
patrol nervously remarked, it looked as though there was apt
to be "quite a brush."

### THE FIGHT

Churchill at his advance post ripped a page from his note-
book and rushed back a message to Kitchener: "The Dervish
army is still in position a mile and a half south-west of Jebel
Surgham." He marked it XXX, meaning Urgent, or With
All Dispatch, according to the drill book. With his patrol he

rode to the top of a sand ridge and pulled up to watch. In a bright, quivering crescent, the Khalifa's army was coming on, the sun glinting from thousands of spears, swords, and rifles. Preceding it was a shocking tumult of sound, the roar of 60,000 Mohammedans screaming to Allah for victory over the invader infidel.

"They're at less than four hundred yards!" Churchill yelled to his troopers. "Open fire!" The several rapid-fire shots they directed into the wildly surging lines went unnoticed, and Churchill gave a more sensible order: "Let's get out of here." Even in his haste, he was unable to avoid adding a footnote, as identifying in his case as the black flag of the Sheikh-ed-din: "This is no place for a Christian." They scrambled off the ridge and spurred their way back toward the regiment, only to meet a corporal coming up who drew in his horse so savagely that it stood upright. Churchill was handed a note from Kitchener's Chief of Staff: "Remain as long as possible, and report how the masses of attack are moving."

Both the gunboats and the artillery opened fire a moment later, the shells slamming through the air overhead with a steely bucketing reminiscent of rolling boxcars. Holes appeared momentarily in the Khalifa's lines, and dozens of banners dropped into the sand. However, the general pace of the army was undiminished, and Churchill was not dismayed to get a note from Major Finn, saying, "Come back at once into the *zereba* [thorn fence] as the infantry are about to open fire." In the smoky confusion of the next few minutes the recklessly advancing Dervishes suffered several thousand casualties, while no more than two or three hundred of the crouching and protected British infantrymen went down. The left flank of the enemy overshot the mark entirely, and the center, crumbling, broke into flight. But Kitchener's Camel Corps had run into trouble. The ungainly beasts shuffled through the sand at only about seven miles an hour, and it was easy for Dervish infantrymen to overtake them and pull down their riders, who were cut to pieces instantly. The Camel Corps appeared to be headed in a rout toward the river. Simultaneously, the main body of the enemy were rallying for an entrenched stand before and inside of Omdurman. It was at this moment that the bugles of the 21st Lancers sounded the charge and Churchill found himself in the midst of his first cavalry attack.

The horses started up slowly, at a trot, the outriding patrols with sabers drawn. Young Lieutenant Grenfell, on the right, was somewhat ahead of the others. He would not survive; all of his younger brothers would eventually fall in England's wars, one after winning the Victoria Cross at Château-Thierry. As the tempo of the mounted lines quickened into a gallop, with all horsemen still in a perfect, jingling line, the swelling cry of 400 Englishmen, with accents ranging from Limehouse to the halls of Eton and Harrow, mingled with the *"Ul, ul, ul Akbar!"* of the enemy. The fight was to be on even terms; in the main, the British would use mostly lances and swords, against the spears, scimitars, and rifles of the Dervishes. Churchill was one of the few exceptions. Because of his defective shoulder, he sheathed his sword and drew from its wooden holster his Mauser pistol, which held a clip of ten cartridges. Over the brow of a hill, as the ground fell away from his horse's feet, he saw a long row of dark figures, cowled like monks, ride up suddenly out of a *khor,* or dry watercourse. It was the Hadendoa brigade of the unsavory Osman Digna.

The two lines came together with a terrible collision, the familiar clash of steel against steel, on this occasion to be virtually the last of its kind in history. Churchill leaped his horse over two blue-robed infantrymen who lay in his path. Both raised themselves up and fired, and the trooper behind him gave a cry and fell. In the smoke and flying sand a dozen or more of the enemy pressed close, seeking a decapitating cut at Churchill or a hamstringing blow at his horse. He and the subaltern on his right, Wormald, formerly of the 7th Hussars, spurred their way out to higher ground. Churchill fired at one man so closely that the pistol struck him in the face, and he rode off another with polo tactics—a gaunt

Arab wearing a steel helmet and chain mail. Many of Churchill's comrades on his far left were being pulled from their
horses and hacked apart. "In one respect a cavalry charge is
very like ordinary life," he was to record years later. "So long
as you are all right, firmly in your saddle, your horse in hand,
and well armed, lots of enemies will give you a wide berth. But
as soon as you have lost a stirrup, have a rein cut, have
dropped your weapon, are wounded, or your horse is wounded,
then is the moment when from all quarters enemies rush upon
you."

A young officer writing to his family about the fight at
Omdurman said that the screams of the torn and bleeding
horses formed his worst impressions of the field. "Their
great rolling eyes flashing panic and the foaming saliva
squeezed up by tortured nerves were printed on my memory
even in the hottest din of battle. After all, they were not there
by choice, poor beasts. I was there, I suppose, because I
thought it would mean good sport. It was not sport. I am afraid
that I have killed several men." Churchill killed a Dervish
who lunged up from the ground with a savage spear thrust.
In the midst of the polyglot bedlam of curses and prayers, he
emptied his Mauser and tried to draw his troop aside. Several men were missing, he noticed, but he felt that the Lancers
had inflicted overwhelming casualties on the enemy without
themselves sustaining very heavy losses. "But now," he was to
write, "from the direction of the enemy there came a succession of grisly apparitions; horses spouting blood, struggling
on three legs, men staggering on foot, men bleeding from
terrible wounds, fish-hook spears stuck right through them,
arms and faces cut to pieces, bowels protruding, men gasping,
crying, collapsing, expiring."

When trumpets over the field sounded the call for a dismounted and enfilading fire, the Dervishes picked up their
injured and fled toward their doomed city. Both sides had won
the traditional victory of proving their valor and losing many
men. Half an hour later, breakfasting in the watercourse where

he had first shot at the enemy, Churchill asked his sergeant, "Did you enjoy yourself?"

"Well, I don't exactly say I enjoyed it, sir, but I think I'll get more used to it next time," the man replied, and all the troop laughed.

Churchill modestly left certain personal details out of his account of the charge. Others there recall that he and a fellow subaltern, after riding out of the melee, sprang off their horses and dashed back to rescue from certain death two non-commissioned officers who had been dragged down into Dervish hands. Both men were pulled away and both afterward recovered from their wounds.

The right arm of Dick Molyneux, a subaltern friend of Churchill's, had been all but severed by a sword cut. The muscles had been sliced through, and his weapon had dropped from his useless hand. Only the gallantry of one of his troopers, who dismounted, beat off three spearmen in a frenzied attack, and carried him to safety, saved his life. Before being returned to England, Molyneux was patched up by a doctor who desired that part of the wound be "skinned over" as soon as possible. A nurse volunteered some skin but fainted when an incision was started in her arm. Churchill then entered the tent, offered the services of any epidermal area that the doctor thought suitable, and stood in a corner smoking a cigar and chatting while a chunk the size of a fifty-cent piece was cut from the inside of his forearm. He still wears the scar, the only one he got from the battle of Omdurman.

The Khalifa cagily disappeared up the river, into the dim, unmarked reaches of the Nubian Desert, where pursuit by a large, adequately supplied force was impossible. But his army was broken, his capital taken, and his reign of terror in southern Egypt ended.

In the afternoon, when the regiment entered Omdurman, Churchill became a father, or a kind of foster father. He had been trotting along leisurely and noticed at the roadside a small bundle wrapped in soiled cloth. Something about it, some extrasensory identification that always betrays humanity, impelled him to get down and investigate. It was a baby girl three or four hours old, abandoned by a refugee mother. The situation was entirely new to Churchill. First he laid the infant out of reach of the horses; then, when it started to cry, he sat down on a bank to consider. The child was quite obviously hungry. From his kit Churchill took his only fodder, a piece of very sustaining sausage of about the same consistency as a rhino's hide. It was inexplicably rejected. By good fortune, an Arab now came along to whom Churchill had offered clemency on the battlefield. The man had some biscuits, and these, crumbled up, were seized on eagerly. "Allah be with you—you've fought well and acquired a family," said Churchill, and he pushed the pair along on the road to Omdurman.

In search of information, he visited Kitchener's headquarters in town and met Charles Neufeld, an Englishman who was having irons struck off his legs. Neufeld had been a prisoner of the Dervishes for thirteen years, during which he had lain chained to a stone floor. "Have I forgotten how to walk?" he kept saying. Later on, Churchill and a friend, the soon-to-be Duke of Atholl, rode back out to the battlefield. There they found two horribly wounded Dervishes crawling on their bellies toward the river. Churchill gave them water from his bottle, but they died soon afterward. The sight and stench everywhere around were so affecting that Churchill and his comrade rode away. They were sick and depressed, in the hollow, confused, too quiet lull that the most seasoned veterans usually find after a battle. The campaign was over. An important victory had been won. Nothing remained but to bury the dead.

# Chapter 12

WHEN Churchill returned to England his head was spinning with dreams of grandeur. The ideas came tumbling through so fast that he was incapable of isolating them for exact appraisal. Underlying all was a resolve to quit the Army, for financial reasons. The golden vistas of journalism had knocked the Queen's pittance into a cocked hat. Next in line was a sneaking desire to go to Oxford and become a famous scholar. This proved to be one of the worst notions he ever had. Taking the matter up, he was handed a sort of prospectus, or assay of examinations that it was necessary to pass before proceeding to his higher studies. The sheet was filled with the deadliest kind of allusions to both Latin and Greek, in about equal proportions. Churchill dropped it as though it had been a live hand grenade and turned his mind to more worthy problems.

At a dinner one evening he remarked to a friend of his father's, an august member of the Cabinet, that he was "considering politics." He said it somewhat in the manner of an impoverished stage actor bearding a Hollywood producer.

"How long have you been bent on a political career?" asked the minister courteously.

"Ever since I was so high," replied Churchill, who had been visited by the inspiration shortly after the fish course.

"Ah, then, my advice is to drop around to party headquarters and announce yourself as available," the minister went on, convinced that he had heard the end of it. Together with his colleagues he was amazed to learn that, the very next afternoon, Churchill had strolled jauntily into the Conservative offices in St. Stephen's Chambers and made himself comfortable. He was stunningly got up, according to a man then employed there as a clerk. His uniform was brilliantly cut, and he was festooned with polychromatic reminders of his global excursions with pen and sword. One of his wealthy kinsmen, a Mr. Fitzroy-Stewart, held an honorary position in the establishment, and he showed the youngster around. It was mentioned conversationally that a speech or two might be in order.

"A speech?" inquired Churchill. "Where?"

"One of a dozen places," said Fitzroy-Stewart. "Take your pick."

"What shall I choose as my subject?"

"Anything that comes handy."

Churchill in his memoirs mentions Bath as the scene of his "official maiden effort." One of his friends was more forcibly struck by an unofficial warm-up canter he ran through in the outlying Rotherhithe Town Hall. Had it been well covered by the press, the chances are it would have got England into an immediate war with France. Relations between the two countries were already mildly tense; Churchill's address would likely have snapped the cord. Certainly it was one of the most jingoistic first speeches ever heard, and it set the pace for some classic ones to follow. France, he told the ordinarily somnolent but now alarmed folk at Rotherhithe, "has deliberately crossed our path and brought upon us what cannot be regarded as less than a personal affront." He continued in this vein as though he were still chasing Dervishes.

"My impression is," says the friend who heard the speech, "that quite a number of the audience slipped outside to buy newspapers and find out precisely what was the nature of the schism referred to."

"It is fortunate that our Government is strong," shouted the speaker; "it is fortunate that those who compose it are possessed of the confidence of the country, for in the course of a few days, perhaps even a few hours, we may be called upon to make a great effort to hold what really belongs to us. War clouds are hovering over us."

By this stage of the address, says the witness, several men quietly got up and went out to put their affairs in order, since it was plain that the recruiting officer could scarcely be more than half an hour behind Churchill. The audience was relieved to hear the latter say, a moment afterward, "I think probable—we all hope that it is probable—that these clouds may pass away."

However, Churchill was by no means done with France. Only a few days later he attended a dinner at Dover and sailed into the unfortunate nation again. It was, by chance, an excellent, well-rounded meal, and the orator was admirably fueled for his onslaught. At one important climax he held up his right arm, shook it, and challenged an anonymous but "well-known" foreign power "to come on." Nothing happened; France was busy.

By contrast, his official opener at Bath was tepid. France got off surprisingly well, which was probably a good thing, since the *Morning Post,* perhaps stimulated by the high jinks at Rotherhithe, sent a correspondent down to report the occasion in full. Churchill was somewhat moved to find the man seated in a first-class carriage and attired in a gray frock coat. They became acquainted by intuition. With his easy charm, the veteran of Omdurman sat down and made himself agreeable. By the time they reached Bath, the correspondent was a devoted fan, and when the speech was delivered in a tent before a sprinkling of townsfolk, he stood glassy-eyed in front of Churchill and took down the remarks word for word. In its essence the talk was political. It was pro-Government in tone, or, rather, pro a Government that he took to be a developing "Tory democracy," his father's old phrase, and it contained a pretty sharp dig at "the dried-up drain pipe of Radicalism." The audience received everything genially, with more calm than that attending the crowd at Rotherhithe. In London, the *Post's* readers were informed editorially that "a new figure has arrived on the political scene," and other papers included thumbnail portraits of the young genius. Among the comments made, a writer noted that Churchill "was born a demagogue and happens to know it," and added that "at dinner he talks and talks, and you can hardly tell when he leaves off quoting his one idol, Macaulay, and begins his other, Winston Churchill."

Before resigning from the Army, Churchill patriotically rejoined his regiment in India for a short tour of duty. Trouble was brewing at Meerut. One of the toughest polo tournaments of the year was in the offing, and he was needed. But soon after his arrival he slipped on a stairway, going in to dinner, and threw his shoulder out of joint again, this time very painfully. After the shoulder was strapped tightly into place, Churchill's comrades persuaded him to take the field for a trial gallop. He performed creditably in the first two games, and in the finals, against the 4th Dragoon Guards (whose Captain Hardress Lloyd would afterward score brilliantly in international matches against the United States) he played with such incautious fervor that he accounted for three goals and the tournament. Churchill still considers the finals at Meerut to have been the athletic high point of his life.

At dinner of the day he mustered out, his regiment drank him a toast and wished him well. In the two years since he joined them, Churchill had seen remarkably little of the 4th Hussars. While the regiment was going about its humdrum business, he had fought three separate wars and was an object of considerable glamor. Bronzed, widely read, hardened to gunfire and oratory, he represented what many of the Hussars hoped to turn into when they grew up and took advantage of their opportunities. Quite a few of the officers, replacements, knew him only by reputation; some of these were introduced to him before they went in to dinner and toasted him. Churchill made a brief but telling acknowledg-

ment, in which he said that he would never forget his old
regiment, and he implied that, even in absentia, it had been
uniquely satisfying. As he looked about at the flushed, unfa-
miliar faces, he became quite visibly emotional. He essayed
to single out for special mention one or two officers here and
there, but he was apparently unable to recall their names
and was heard to mumble things that sounded like "you there
in the corner" and "the chap with the beige goatee." It was a
memorable leave-taking; several of the regiment treasure it
to this day.

Churchill went to Cairo to put together the manuscript
of his book on the campaign in the Sudan, to be named *The
River War*. In the Egyptian capital he called on several British
officials for help; among them was Sir Percy Girouard, one
of Kitchener's young assistants, in charge of the desert railway. Girouard was dismayed to learn that Churchill's only
reason for returning to India had been to play polo.

"Really now, you know, you can't be serious," he said
several times.

Churchill, unmoved as always, equably continued to smoke
a cigar, a habit he had fallen into, and asked numerous questions about the high-level policies of the war against the
Dervishes. Girouard at length unbent and gave him valuable
advice, of which Churchill took note in his writings and for
which he rewarded Girouard more substantially some years
later by appointing him governor of Northern Nigeria.

When he finished his chapters on General Gordon's death,
the author took them to Lord Cromer, then head of the
British-Egyptian Agency, to be checked for accuracy. Cromer
interpreted his duties as somewhat broader and indeed marked
up the manuscript as though it were a public school quiz. At
one point, dealing with the General's post as private secretary
to Lord Ripon, Churchill had said, in his evolving style, "the
brilliant sun had become the satellite of a farthing dip." Lord
Cromer conscientiously penciled this out and observed in
the margin, " 'brilliant sun' appears to be extravagant eulogy

and 'farthing dip' does less than justice to Lord Ripon's position as Viceroy." Oddly enough, Churchill submitted meekly to criticism and made many alterations, losing some of his trickiest phrases. The final version was far from humble, however. Published in 1899, it provoked both lavish praise and widespread indignation, the latter because of Churchill's breezy censure of his old antagonist, Kitchener.

The tenor of his comments about Kitchener was, as a critic noted, "patronizing." Two passages aroused special umbrage. "Before the attack on Mahmud's zereba the Sirdar issued orders that the wounded were to be spared," Churchill wrote, adding, "It is scarcely possible to believe that he wished otherwise at Omdurman. It is nevertheless a pity that his former order was not republished to the troops for I must personally record that there was a very general impression that the fewer the prisoners, the greater would be the satisfaction to the commander."

Again, Churchill referred to the destruction of the Mahdi's tomb: "By Sir H. Kitchener's order the tomb has been profaned and razed to the ground. The corpse of the Mahdi was dug up. The head was separated from the body and . . . passed from hand to hand till it reached Cairo. . . . The limbs and trunk were flung into the Nile. Such was the chivalry of the conquerors!" If things were to continue thus in the Sudan, the author went on, "it would be better if Gordon had never given his life nor Kitchener won his victories."

If *The Malakand Field Force* should rightly have been titled *A Subaltern's Hints to Generals,* then *The River War* could have been called *A Subaltern's Hints to Kitchener.* Nevertheless, the new book won many admirers. *The Outlook* said that "in 'The River War' Mr. Winston Churchill comes, we think, very near doing for the Sudan what Kinglake did for the Crimea." Two expensive editions were printed in quick succession and sold rapidly; Churchill felt more than ever that his decision to leave the Army had been well conceived. Besides his remuneration from the book, he had skill-

fully arranged for another source of income. Before he left
India he had worked up a kind of reverse arrangement with
the Allahabad *Pioneer*. Instead of keeping its readers informed
about Indian turbulence, he would mail back weekly letters
from the battle fronts in London, at the rate of three pounds
per dispatch. The break was now complete; Churchill had
become a full-fledged peace correspondent, and he took off his
uniform, bought some civilian clothes, including a black,
barrel-shaped hat, and tried to settle down.

The year 1899 will remain a bright one in the long, unhappy annals of politics. Winston Churchill, after nearly five
weeks of relaxation from the wars, decided to toss his singular
hat into his first election ring. The scene of this milestone
grapple was Oldham, a northern industrial center, described
by the rising young lawyer, H. H. Asquith, as "one of the
most dismal places in the country, peopled by wan-faced,
grimy, tired artisans who have never known life in its real
sense and never will know it till their dying day."

Asquith, whose fiery spirit and liberal tenets were to make
him one of the most important men in England, was destined
to work in political partnership with Churchill for years, but
in 1899 their views were divergent. More accurately, Churchill's views were formless and shifting, pulled along as a sort
of kite tail to his central motive force of ambition. He had
Liberal stirrings, but he was still a technical Tory.

His opportunity arose when one of the two Conservative
members from Oldham fell ill. The other, a Mr. Robert Ascroft, inexplicably chose Churchill to fill the gap. Churchill
accepted the honor without astonishment, and at the party's
"adoption meeting" he caused the utmost consternation by
arising to confront a veteran strategist with the precocious
words, "I disagree with you." At Tory headquarters in London it was wondered if the party had another intractable
Lord Randolph on its hands. Everybody sat back to watch
with interest, and apprehension, the outcome of this fledgling

effort. In the matter of independent thought, Churchill disappointed nobody. It was an unusual contest in nearly every way. To start off, Robert Ascroft died in mid-campaign and was succeeded by a Tory workingman, James Mawdsley, whose cockney accent contrasted sharply with the educated drawl of his running mate from Blenheim. The fact is, the two men presented an incongruous unit on the platform. Mawdsley was attired in the stout but ungorgeous threads of the laborer, while Churchill was a sartorial blossom, in a swallow-tail coat and carrying a gold-headed cane. Neither could the two ever get together on their remarks; no matter what line Mawdsley took, Churchill was pretty apt to be yawing away on a different tack. On one occasion, Mawdsley rose to passionate heights in outlining a utopian program for labor, to be followed by Churchill in an hour and a half's blanket denunciation of the Church of England. His complaint was based on ritualism: too much mumbling, far too many tassels, too much shaking of censers, too many cabalistic signs marked out in the air. "I introduce the subject," he said at one point, to the relief of many, "because I am sure that it is uppermost in the minds of the voters of Oldham." It did not appear to be uppermost in the mind of anybody at the meeting, since his explanation caused a general guffaw and not a few gibes of a basically unreligious nature.

The people of Oldham, strapped for amusement, as Asquith had indicated, took the campaign as a kind of street carnival. The press also treated it flippantly. The Conservative candidates were commonly referred to as "The Scion and the Socialist." It was noted by one paper that Churchill, though the grandson of a duke, was not himself titled, while Mawdsley was the bona fide secretary of the Amalgamated Society of Operative Spinners. The opposition was strong but not distinguished. The Liberal candidates were Alfred Emmott, who ran a factory, and Walter Runciman, the son of a shipping-line owner, who had the temerity in one speech to suggest that Churchill had been "a swashbuckler around the world."

This injudicious barb provoked the Scion to depart from the lofty generalities to which he had cleaved and introduce a personal tirade, demanding of the electors whether "this is the sort of welcome you will give the Lancashire Fusiliers when they come home from Omdurman. Mr. Runciman has not had the experience of the Lancashire Fusiliers; his contests have been more pacific. The difference between Mr. Runciman and the Lancashire Fusiliers is that, while they were fighting at Omdurman for their country, he was fighting at Gravesend for himself. And another difference between them is that, while the Fusiliers were gaining a victory, Mr. Runciman at Gravesend was being defeated."

There was agreement that the last part of this was vague, because the family ship business was afloat and bustling and young Runciman himself looked perfectly successful; nevertheless, the remark was digested and enjoyed.

A note of unfairness crept into the election when Churchill and Mawdsley were branded as representing the vested interests. Emmott and Runciman were held up as the champions of the underprivileged. Since both Runciman and Emmott were extremely rich and, as Churchill tried futilely to point out, he and Mawdsley would have had "great difficulty in finding five hundred pounds between us," this stigma was a bitter pill. At the conclusion of a meeting, Churchill and his vested harness mate would retire to an inexpensive pub to dine on pig's knuckles and beer, while the champions of the underprivileged held a gaudy wassail in the leading hotel.

As the campaign matured, a feeling of confusion pervaded Tory headquarters in London. Churchill appeared to be fighting a contest along very bizarre lines, not entirely connected with the party. Mawdsley, too, was going it alone, having come out openly for something he described as "Tory Socialism," to which only Mawdsley had the key. There was anxiety as to how Churchill would handle the pet Clerical Tithes Bill; it was felt that a few more allusions to the Church of England and to the disturbance at Omdurman might muddle the issue. Arthur Balfour, the leader of the House of Commons, was reputed to have remarked, in the interest of cheering his fellows up, "We need have no worry. The boy's young and he's flighty, but he's not Randolph's son for nothing—he'll bat his heart out in a pinch." The way things went, all this was worry wasted. Churchill came through in dazzling style. At the climactic meeting of the campaign, he batted the bill overboard altogether. "A tragic mistake," he described it airily, and passed on to some additional foolishness of the Church. When news of the ditching reached Balfour, he changed his opinion slightly. "I thought he was a young man of promise," he said, "but it appears he is a young man of promises."

What with Mawdsley bawling about Socialism at one of their platforms and Churchill conducting a revival from the other, the Tories put up a very poor show. When the results were all in, Emmott led the quartet with 12,976 votes, Runciman came in second with 12,773, Churchill was next with 11,477, and Mawdsley with his plans for a workers' paradise brought up the rear with 11,449. The Conservatives had lost both of their Oldham seats, and the party heads were in a state of advanced peeve. Writing of this, Churchill observed, "Everybody threw the blame on me. I have noticed that they nearly always do." The consensus was that his abortive reform of the Church of England had done the trick.

Perhaps the most mystifying aspect of the whole election was Churchill's attitude when he lost. His manner was indistinguishable from that of the victors. At the "declaration of the poll," when each candidate makes a species of post-election statement, he far outshone his colleagues. All the Tories present concurred that he scored his best impression of the campaign; even Emmott was moved to declare publicly that Churchill's words had been "noble and gallant."

One of the local newspapers reported that "Lady Randolph Churchill, who had listened to the result with a tinge of regret, bore herself proudly as she retired from the room with her talented son."

When they reached the door, Churchill turned sportingly to Runciman and observed, "I don't think the world has heard the last of either of us." In view of the fact that Runciman had won a seat and was in an excellent position to be heard, the remark was baffling in the extreme. Runciman was said to have stepped down to a nearby newspaper office and checked the returns again. The first tabulation was correct: Oldham had returned Churchill to journalism.

## Chapter 13

THE AUTUMN of 1899 brought a welcome diversion to Churchill, whose premature retirement from politics was growing tiresome. For the first time since the Crimea, Britain was about to open fire on white soldiers. The trouble zone was South Africa, where President Paul Kruger of the fanatically religious republic of Transvaal was finding the English settlers on all sides growing in uncomfortable numbers. Kruger and his faithful were of Dutch and French extraction, a weird and headstrong band, called Boers, after the Anglo-Saxon word meaning "farmer."

Kruger himself was nearly enough to cause a war on sight. He was an angular man who wore a hat shaped like a coal scuttle and had eyes that flashed piety as the prehistoric dragon was said to have exhaled flame from its nose. Kruger was a Dopper and claimed to know God. Periodically he disappeared into the veldt for several days of communion, subsisting on bark and insects. His regime was conducted with an iron hand; he had decreed that the world was flat, and any statements to the contrary in his presence brought on an immediate fuss. When the New Englander, Captain Joshua Slocum, called on him while sailing a 36-foot boat around the world, Kruger declined to say more than a few gruff words, on the ground that Slocum was trying to peddle a dangerous physical theory and go against nature.

Kruger himself had gone against the English in every way, petty and large, that he could contrive, from supplying free

liquor to the natives (whom he detested), thus preventing them
from working in the English industries, to cutting off trade between the Transvaal and the British Cape Colony. For their
part, the British were keenly anxious to cultivate a friendship
with Kruger and give him a hand with his rich diamond mines.

In consequence of Kruger's hostility, and the extreme amity
of the British, which had lately taken the form of transport-
ing troops to the Transvaal border, in the hope of forcing
the issue and paving the way for the diamond-studded camaraderie to follow, the situation in South Africa had deteriorated. Kruger now sent London an ultimatum to withdraw the
troops, and the war was on.

The collective force of these events stirred Churchill patriotically. Muttering imprecations against Kruger, whose eccentricities he did not find intimidating, he went round to the
*Morning Post* and made a pretty bargain. He would report
this struggle, even as he had covered the one farther north in
the Sudan. By now he was a veteran warrior-correspondent;
only recently a newspaper had noted that, except for Napoleon,
he alone was known to have waged campaigns on three continents. Publicity of this sort seemed to Churchill to weigh
heavily in favor of an increase in rate. The *Morning Post,* after
some backing and filling, agreed to pay him £250 a month and
all expenses. This certainly represented progress, since his
other English papers had allowed him practically no expense
money and the Allahabad *Pioneer* refused to cough up as much
as the price of a cigar.

Once again, Churchill packed up and bade his friends
good-by in a series of exhausting dinners, which reached a
climax with a rousing celebration for him and one of his
father's closest friends, Sir William Gerard, who was also joining the African campaign. The Prince of Wales was among the
guests. Gerard, an elderly man, was presented with several
cases of choice champagne and brandy and told to share them
freely with young Churchill. After the dinner, in happy but
muddled spirits, Gerard and Churchill thought it expedient to

label the cases "Castor Oil" for shipping purposes. Two months later in Natal, Gerard tried to check up on his supplies by telegram. He received a reply that the drugs consigned to him had already been delivered to the hospital by mistake but that the base had a full store of castor oil and was rushing him a crate marked "Emergency." Later on, a friend of Gerard checked further at the hospital and learned that the morale there had brightened out of all bounds.

Churchill sailed on October 11 aboard the *Dunottar Castle* for Capetown. Also on the ship was Sir Redvers Buller, who had been appointed to command the South African Field Force. Churchill saw very little of Buller either on the journey or in Africa, but he was to write about him with informality, as he had about so many other generals. His shipboard impression of the commander was that "He said little, and what he said was obscure." Churchill's military impression of him, given some years afterward, was that "he was a man of considerable scale. He plodded on from blunder to blunder and from one disaster to another, without losing either the regard of his country or the trust of his troops, to whose feeding as well as his own he paid serious attention."

Arrived in Capetown, the passengers learned that the Boers had invaded Natal and were putting up a surprising fight. This came as agreeable news, since it had been feared on the *Dunottar Castle* that the dispute would be settled before the ship landed. It remained now for Churchill to make his way north to the front. In company with J. B. Atkins, the correspondent for the *Manchester Guardian,* he went by train to Stormberg and then sailed from nearby East London for Durban in a small coastal steamer. Up to this point his South African adventure had unfolded genially; three hours out on the coaster the roof caved in. Churchill took to his bunk with a case of seasickness that made his Caribbean trouble seem like a momentary giddiness. For several days, as the wind blew, he remained prostrate, arising only to perform the ancient rites of the ailment. He clung tenaciously to life, he said, by re-

minding himself "that Titus Oates lived in good health for
many years after his prodigious floggings."

The sea subsided, the ship landed, and Churchill, several
pounds lighter, continued with Atkins toward the fighting
region, at last reaching Estcourt, which was held by a small
detachment of British and was in danger of being cut off by a
large force of Boers. Here Churchill ran into an old acquaintance of Harrow days, Leo Amery, the boy who had so patiently
censored his dispatches to the *Harrovian*. He was in Africa
representing the *Times*. The relationship between them had
changed; Amery's old contributor was now fairly well known
and in a furious hurry to move onward and upward. And by
good luck, a Captain Haldane he found at Estcourt, a friend
from the Indian wars, was the means of providing him with
an opportunity that, as it developed, made him the most famous
young man of the decade.

The great Armored Train episode started as a piece of military stupidity and ended in a personal triumph for Churchill.
His name was quite literally sung throughout England, even as
the heroes of medieval legend became staples in the musical
diet of the land. Churchill's song went as follows:

> You've heard of Winston Churchill;
> This is all I need to say—
> He's the latest and the greatest
> Correspondent of the day.

Forty miles to the north of Estcourt, Sir George White was
encircled at Ladysmith by strong units of hard-riding Boers. It
was judged by the British commander at Estcourt that the
thing to do was send down a reconnoitering party via the railway, on which service had been suspended. The vehicle
selected for this foolhardy venture was a locomotive and six
armored trucks, with a 6-pound naval gun and crew together
with a company of the Dublin Fusiliers and a company of the
Durban Light Infantry. Now an armored train is only as strong
as its railroad's weakest culvert, and to remove a culvert re-

quires the use of but a single stick of dynamite, or less. Churchill was brash enough to point this out at headquarters, but the commander (by proxy) said, "Nonsense! Why, a handful of ignorant, ill-equipped rustics would never dare ride against Her Majesty's artillery!"

Unfortunately for England, the high-level thinking of the whole Boer War was pitched in just about that key. At the start, it was opined at No. 10 Downing Street that the skirmish would be over in three months and that the total cost to the government would be around ten million pounds. Churchill's contract with the *Morning Post* had a clause that gave him a minimum four months of employment. As it turned out, the war lasted three years and cost England something over two hundred million pounds, or twenty times the original estimate. Complacency was never higher. In reply to an offer of help from Australia, the War Office had cabled, "Unmounted men preferred." The several units of cavalry on hand were regarded as quite adequate to quell this mounted enemy. Before Buller left England, Intelligence had sent him several volumes on the theater of operations, but he had returned them with a note saying that he knew "everything about South Africa."

It would be difficult to underestimate a foe more dangerously than Britain did the Boers. Because they were generally bucolic, canting, and untutored, they were thought to be a military joke. After all, it was argued, what could these bushmen know of cavalry maneuvers? It was doubted if they could even ride a straight line. What they could do, though, was ride for days on end with little food or rest, cover with dazzling speed a country they knew thoroughly, and think for themselves, according to the rules of common sense rather than those of antiquated army textbooks. The Boers had been toughened by a code of religious spartanism incomprehensible to the average Britisher. They were a suspicious people, with an implacable God, and were disinclined to frivolity or friendship. If immigrants settled within a day's ride of a man's farm, that neighborhood was viewed as congested, and he picked up and

moved. A Boer usually carried a Bible with him and read it as
he did his chores, accepting the Old Testament as the Law and
discarding the New as untested and disreputable. In the main,
a man's chores consisted in caring for huge herds and in hunting, at which he was expert. Most Boers were exceptional shots
and could drop an antelope or a wildebeest, in which the
country abounded, at distances up to several hundred yards.
Agriculture was in bad repute with the Boers; for some reason
they thought it sissified. Also, herds were movable while crops
were uncomfortably fixative. Household recreation in the
Transvaal depended upon the daily singing of a collection of
pretty frightening hymns that left no doubt where a person was
likely to lodge if he strayed from the paths of righteousness.
Further spicing up life, each family annually made a giddy expedition a hundred or so miles to the nearest church for Holy
Communion. And now and then a number of Boers got together to war on the nearby natives—the Zulus, the Hottentots,
the Tembus, and the Swazis.

Captain Haldane was chosen to lead the Armored Train into
the little-known land of these strange and hostile folk. It was
an assignment to which he had not aspired and he talked it
over gloomily with Churchill. "Never mind," said the latter,
"I'll go along with you. I consider it my duty to the *Morning
Post*." Haldane was said to have brightened up perceptibly,
it having become gospel that including Churchill in the roster
of any company was tantamount to dividing the management. Preparations got under way forthwith. The train creaked
out from a siding, the engine in the middle of a string of six
cars. It was loaded with the naval gun and crew, the infantry
climbed aboard, Churchill and Haldane took up a stand beside
the engineer, and they all rolled off into the bush, to the accompaniment of some halfhearted cheers.

All went serenely for about fourteen miles, or to a spot some
little distance beyond the tiny station of Chieveley. Haldane
had called a halt at Chieveley to telegraph their progress to the
commander at Estcourt. Rolling along now, they suddenly

noticed several groups of riders who seemed to be hurrying to a
hill between the Armored Train and home. "Back, men!" cried
Haldane, and he ordered the engineer to throw the train into
reverse. Before this was accomplished, Churchill jumped down
and sprinted to the (now) rear truck, which he mounted, and
then crouched down with his eyes just above the steel plates.
From the hill, three or four lazy puffs of white smoke arose,
and shrapnel zinged off the armored sides. British Intelligence
had neglected to determine that the Boers had for months been
obtaining a new kind of Maxim gun and other artillery from
Germany. Starting back, Churchill heard an unpleasant whistling over his head and threw himself on the floor, as a series
of sharp explosions shook the front of the train. It had just
occurred to him that the Boers might also be apt to tamper
with the track when there came a paralyzing shock and the
train skewed off the rails to a grinding, bumpy stop.

The situation was decidedly awkward. The rustic hymn-
singers had bushwhacked the reconnoitering party almost directly between two hills, from which poured a steady and
accurate rifle fire. For a group of unprofessional illiterates it was
a competent maneuver. Churchill scrambled out of his car and
was able to see that the two front trucks had overturned, badly
injuring several occupants. As he ran up toward the engine, a
shrapnel burst struck near by and grazed the engineer, who was
in the act of leaping from his cab. The man was outraged; he
was a civilian, he pointed out, and entitled to all the civil benefits of a democratic state, which included freedom from shrapnel. "Be calm!" cried Churchill, and then gave him a singular
bit of comfort: "Nobody is ever wounded twice on the same
day." The engineer wrapped some cotton waste around his cuts
and seemed much keener. "Furthermore," Churchill went on,
expansive and happy in the emergency, "devotion to duty will
win you fine honors." Even as the shrapnel struck around them,
his memory was in its usual working order. Eleven years later,
he arose in the House of Commons and recommended the engineer and his fireman for the Albert Medal.

The Armored Train as a whole was in a condition of wild confusion, but Churchill appeared to take on a new personality as things got worse. He trotted back and forth, in full view of the enemy gunners, advised Captain Haldane, joked with the Irishmen, gave crisp, sensible directions, and altogether had a splendid time. In his opinion, he told Haldane (who was directing the return fire), by uncoupling the overturned trucks, a train crew could clear the debris and enable them all to break out for home. Haldane assigned him nine workers, whom Churchill spurred to courageous effort by standing carelessly on an eminence and smoking a cigarette. From all accounts, the fact that he did not get hit was a marvel of good chance, since the bullets and shells were whistling and crashing about with increased fury.

When the trucks were freed, Churchill had the engineer push the wreckage from the tracks and try to re-engage the other cars. This proved useless. The engine itself got clear; the rest of the train was trapped. Haldane and Churchill loaded the forty-odd wounded into the engine and tender, and, with the Dublins and Durban soldiers creeping along close beside, the bruised party started back. Some of the wounded men were clinging to the cowcatcher and sitting on top of the cab. Slow as the engine went, the pace was too much for the exhausted soldiers, who fell two hundred yards to the rear. Churchill jumped down and ran back to join them. His act was simultaneous with a charge from the hills by Boer horsemen. "Go ahead! Get the wounded out," he yelled to the engine crew, waving his arms, and to the infantry he said, "Take cover, men. It's everybody for himself."

Churchill dashed for a ravine and threw himself down, then crawled along rapidly, but a rider pulled up on the far bank and threatened him with a rifle. Churchill felt for his revolver, remembered that he had left it in the engine, and threw up his hands. The rider motioned him toward the Boer lines. Churchill has since said that this was a bitter moment in his life; he had been on the scene for one day and for him the war seemed to be over. Besides, he was unaccustomed to defeat. He walked along, occasionally scowling up into the not particularly hostile face of his captor. Indeed, he was obliged to admit to himself that it was a moderately attractive face, rather English in feeling, a far cry from the barbarous expressions of the Indians and Dervishes he had been fighting. He was to remember the face of this victorious Dutch farmer with a real shock six years later when, as Under-Secretary for the Colonies, he welcomed a delegation of leaders from South Africa in London. "And this is General Botha [soon to be the first Prime Minister of the Union of South Africa]," said a functionary performing the introductions. "The Right Honorable Winston Churchill."

They shook hands and studied each other carefully.

"Don't you recognize me?" asked Botha.

"Aha!" cried Churchill. "The day of the Armored Train!"

"It was I who took you prisoner. I myself."

Several persons present have verified that Churchill, while wholly gracious, was unable to resist commenting that, had he had his Mauser, it would probably have been a different story. General Botha looked unconvinced, but they went into lunch and enjoyed a friendly reminiscence. Their acquaintance, begun under adverse conditions, developed into a friendship that was much valued by both of them. Botha visited Churchill frequently and worked in close co-operation with him during the First World War.

But the Botha of the day of the Armored Train, a subordinate officer in the Boer cavalry, delivered his unusual prize and turned to other duties. The sky had been overcast, and now it began to pour rain; the weather was a bedraggled match for Churchill's spirits as he stood in a leaky tent and awaited his fate. He was not reassured to consider that, as a civilian who had engaged in active fighting, he could legally expect a quick court-martial and a trip before an official firing squad. The Boers looked him over with interest. At length, a field cornet came up and, with a delightful British accent, said, "We are

not going to let you go, old chappie, although you *are* a correspondent. We don't catch the son of a lord every day."

It had been decided to send him south to the Boer capital
of Pretoria as a formal prisoner of war.

## II

On the evening of Churchill's capture, the following letter
was sent to the general manager of the Natal Railways:

Sir:—The railwaymen who accompanied the armoured train this
morning ask me to convey to you their admiration of the coolness
and pluck displayed by Mr. Winston Churchill, the war correspondent who accompanied the train, and to whose efforts, backed
up by those of the driver, Wagner, is due the fact that the armoured
engine and tender were brought successfully out after being
hampered by the derailed trucks in front, and that it became possible to bring the wounded in here. The whole of our men are loud
in their praise of Mr. Churchill, who, I regret to say, is a prisoner.
I respectfully ask you to convey their admiration to a brave man.
I am, dear Sir, yours truly,

J. Campbell
Inspector, Natal Government Railways

A member of the wounded party wrote back to his mother
in London: "If it hadn't been for Churchill, not one of us
would have escaped."

According to the English historian, Ephesian, several men
high in the government said that, beyond a doubt, if Churchill
had been a regular officer he would have been awarded the
Victoria Cross.

## III

The subject of these panegyrics recovered his good spirits
when he learned that the firing squad had been cheated. He
began to talk with his old gusto. He was marched to the head-

quarters of General Joubert, to whom he gave important advice. In his later writings Churchill omitted these events preliminary to his departure for Pretoria, probably because his efforts were unavailing. First of all, he assured Joubert that the entire Boer campaign was futile, and, in effect, urged him to turn over his sword. Waiting to be removed to the lockup, he painted a black picture of the enemy cause. General Joubert listened courteously, then, after a whispered conversation with his aides, decided to go on with the war. At this point, Churchill became slightly abusive and demanded to be released, on the ground that he was a civilian. A lieutenant in the room afterward said he had the distinct impression that the prisoner was threatening to sue. In any case, his attitude in brief was: "You'll be sorry. And don't come whining to me later. I won't have the least sympathy for you." Presumably, Churchill had forgotten that a few hours ago he was grateful not to be shot.

The Boers heard him out, informed him that "had it not been for you, we should have captured the engine," and sent him on his way, to Churchill's offended astonishment. He was compelled to walk across fields for six hours in a driving rain, without food or drink. He noted uneasily that his captors finished this trip in perfectly fresh condition, and he began to wonder about the probable length of the war. Near the small town of Colenso, they slaughtered an ox and roasted it over an open, sputtering fire. That night, sleeping on a pile of straw in a shed, Churchill reflected on escape. But each time he sat up, he stared into the impassive, leathery face of an armed Boer guard.

The trip by train to Pretoria began the next day at Elandslaagte station. Churchill once more became voluble. He argued all the way down, having hit on some paradoxical technicalities that struck him as first-rate. For instance, if he were *not* a civilian, why shouldn't he be treated as a captive officer? An official replied with some skill that there was no reason not to consider him a private. The force of this quelled Churchill for nearly fifteen minutes; then he got up and went to the lavatory and tried to escape, but the window was stuck, in the historic style of all windows on all railway cars everywhere. Thanks to his eloquence he was herded with the combatant soldiers of the line when they reached Pretoria; however, a Boer colonel rescinded this order and Churchill was marched with a group of officer-prisoners to the State Model School, where they found sixty additional Englishmen. Among them was his old friend, Captain Haldane, who had been taken with most of his Dublin and Durban infantry.

We have the word of several witnesses that Churchill wasted no time in idle vapors. He got promptly to work. Before the afternoon was gone he had composed a long, rhetorical, acidulous, and thoroughly unconvincing beef. This he sent to the authorities by a janitor to whom he gave a half crown. Stripped of its verbiage, the burden of his message was that the prisoner wanted out. The authorities countered with "No." Churchill then sent a shorter dispatch restating his conviction that he was a civilian. The authorities replied that so far as the Boers were concerned, he was a combatant officer. In submission to this, Churchill cashed a check for twenty pounds, went to the commissary, and bought a civilian suit, which he put on, complete except for a hat. He looked around for a hat and ran into a bit of luck. In one of the rooms was a Dutch clergyman whose views had not coincided precisely with those of President Kruger; that is, the man had been so foolish as to suggest that the world, if not round, was slightly bent at the edges. He was being allowed to meditate in confinement while the world smoothed itself out in his mind. Hanging from a hook in his room the parson had a sort of low-comedy black hat, with rolled-up edges and no crown. Churchill dropped in for a courtesy visit and on his way out abstracted the hat. Then he borrowed a copy of John Stuart Mill's inappropriate essay *On Liberty,* and went to bed, fully clothed. In a mood of unexampled self-confidence, he had decided to read awhile, get a good night's sleep, and climb out over the fence early the next morning.

Churchill has written entertainingly about his escapade amidst the Boers, and other sources add abundant material. All agree that he proved to be the most dedicated jailbreaker since Edmond Dantès entered the Château d'If. When he arose from his first night's slumber, he saw that an evasion was impractical in the daylight hours; the place was swarming with sentries. During the morning, according to a fellow prisoner, he proposed and abandoned four separate plans for escape, one of them involving a wholesale mutiny of the seventy officers in the school, the two thousand men in a nearby enclosure, and the disaffected cleric. The ramifications of this plan, which he sketched out in detail, transcended the prison: his notion was to go ahead and seize the capital. Churchill has never been easy to convince, but he dropped this scheme without argument when the other sixty-nine officers voted it "a trifle ornate."

Much of his first day was spent compliantly parading himself before curiosity-seekers who had come to see "the lord's son." Before nightfall the guards were addressing him as "Lord Churchill," and one of the local newspapers labeled him thus throughout his adventure. "They all talked at once, especially Churchill," one of the prisoners has said. For about a week Churchill enjoyed his role of side-show freak, then the prison routine grew irksome. The other officers were given to playing chess, checkers, and cards, conversation-stifling amusements that he has detested most of his life, and besides, his audience showed general signs of becoming stagnate. He stepped up his escape plans and hit at length on one that impressed him as foolproof. Taking along several bars of chocolate and a can of meatballs, he would climb the fence around midnight, stroll leisurely through town, and walk the three hundred miles to Portuguese East Africa, navigating by the stars. He was to come surprisingly close to doing just that.

"I've found a spot in the fence that the searchlight misses, and the guard passes every five minutes," Churchill told Haldane, who wearily acquiesced, having no further strength to find flaws in the Plans which were now materializing every hour or so. Together they talked it over. The fence where Churchill meant to climb it looked on to a garden that offered easy access to a main thoroughfare. "And what do we do then?" inquired Haldane.

"We proceed down the street," said Churchill.

"And what if we're hailed?"

"We reply in conversational tones."

"Any particular language?" Haldane wanted to know.

Since he had hit on an obvious weakness, Churchill enlisted a third man, a sergeant who spoke both Dutch and Kaffir, the local native tongue. That night, carrying the chocolate, the meatballs, a compass, and several maps, they crouched in the bushes by the fateful spot. But a lazy sentry perversely took up a stand there and refused to budge.

"We'll have to put it off until tomorrow," Churchill told his colleagues.

The next night, they hid in a lavatory near the fence, with the intention of sprinting out one at a time and clambering over. The area was free of sentries and the moon was obscured by flying clouds—the road to freedom beckoned. As might have been expected, Churchill was the first man out. He scrambled up the six-foot enclosure, looked around briefly, dropped down, and disappeared into a flowering shrub. As the minutes ticked by slowly, nobody came to join him. A man appeared from the house that the garden adjoined and lit a cigar. He walked back and forth for a while, stopping once to stare directly at the bush which Churchill had gathered round him like a Turkish towel. Presumably he saw nothing, for eventually he strolled on and re-entered the house. At the end of an hour, there was heard an anguished hiss from across the fence and the strained voice of Haldane explained that they were stuck. The sentries had become grouped in the escape zone like a pack of beagles. For some reason that Churchill never understood, then or later, the sergeant repeated the situation in both Dutch and Kaffir.

"You'd better come back," added Haldane.

It was an unkind blow. Having made a daring advance, Churchill was now unable to bring up his reinforcements. Tactically, he was in an unenviable spot; to go on minus Haldane and the polyglot sergeant was risky, to retreat raised the chance of getting shot, and to take up an indefinite residence in the shrub was unthinkable. To make his plight more odious, a cat closely followed by a pair of hungry bulldogs now cut across the yard, doubled back, and ran right under him, creating a frightful snarl. This last indignity was too much. Churchill emerged from his covert and stepped down the street. He had only four bars of chocolate. Mapless, minus meatballs, without a compass, absurdly hatted, and lacking even a rudimentary knowledge of any tongue save English, he was footloose in Africa at last.

# Chapter 14

THE Boers were outraged by the loss of their gaudy exhibit. His absence went unnoticed until nearly noon the next day. Playing it as low-down as he could, Churchill had left a dummy in his bed, arranged in a sprawling position and clutching the copy of Mill's *Liberty*. Even the Boers, saintly and unamused in a flat world, recognized the sarcastic touch of this grouping. They appropriated the book and classified it as "dangerous," a piece of literary criticism that ranks among the most arbitrary in history. Their feelings were not eased by an exceedingly pompous letter that Churchill left behind. Addressed to the Minister of War, it expressed the hope and belief that they would soon "meet again" in Pretoria under different circumstances. Had it not been Churchill's morning for a shave, his flight would likely have been undiscovered for days. The prison barber called out his name, ready for the periodic outpouring of rhetoric, and the search was begun.

Haldane first told the barber that his garrulous client was in the bathroom, but when a suitable time had elapsed this was felt to be exaggerated. Churchill's room was entered, the dummy unmasked, and the incendiary volume carted off to headquarters. For their pains in helping him, his comrades were relieved of their small prerogatives. Chess, checkers, and cards were rationed, and room-to-room visiting was held up for a while. The sole person undismayed by these stringencies was the preacher with the missing hat. In a rather worldly vein, he observed testily that the hat was the only one he had

The boy Winston with
his lovely mother and
his brother John

The young man about
school, age twelve

future First Sea Lord at age
seven

*Left,* an early formal pose; *right,* as correspondent to the *Morning Post,* South
Africa, in 1900

Wanted, Dead or Alive: the poster issued by the Boers after Churchill's famous
escape

and God knew where he would get another. As far as he was concerned, he said, they could cut out the visiting altogether.

The Boer newspapers broke out in a rash of rumors. The prisoner, the Duke of Churchill, had fled from the State Model School disguised as a woman, a paper in Pretoria said. The article implied that it would be well for everybody to watch strange females carefully on the streets, see how they walked, look for drooping petticoats, and so on. Two editions later, this same paper ran a bulletin killing the woman. The duke had made his escape while dressed as a policeman. He was reputed to be violent. The policeman lasted nearly twenty-four hours and then expired in favor of a waiter. This latest suggestion entertained Haldane and his friends, who could hardly imagine a man less fitted for the job. Simultaneously, a reward was flashed over the countryside. Handbills were struck off by the military; they went as follows:

# £25

TWENTY-FIVE POUNDS REWARD IS OFFERED BY THE SUB-COMMISSION OF THE FIFTH DIVISION, ON BEHALF OF THE SPECIAL CONSTABLE OF THIS DIVISION, TO WHOEVER BRINGS TO THIS OFFICE, DEAD OR ALIVE, THE ESCAPED PRISONER OF WAR CHURCHILL.

*For the Sub-Commission of the Fifth Division,*
*LODK. DE HAAS, Secretary.*

Churchill has always been piqued by the uninspired description of himself that was appended to the reward:

ENGLISHMAN, 25 YEARS OLD, ABOUT FIVE FEET EIGHT INCHES TALL, INDIFFERENT BUILD, WALKS WITH A FORWARD STOOP, PALE APPEARANCE, RED-BROWNISH HAIR, SMALL AND HARDLY NOTICEABLE MOUSTACHE, TALKS THROUGH HIS NOSE AND CANNOT PRONOUNCE THE LETTER "S" PROPERLY.

Every means was seized by the Boers to take him into custody again. Their enterprise was so clamorous that they ap-

peared to view his attempt as the war in microcosm. Warrants
were issued by the wholesale, most of them granting permission
to ransack the houses of known British sympathizers, and those
of some suspected ones, bringing about the usual number of
senseless and unjust incidents. Several of his former jailers
were sent to patrol the railways leading from the town. And a
perfectly innocent nurse was drummed out of the country on
the suspicion she had harbored the captive and contrived his
escape. The wildest insinuations were made about this apocryphal connection; Churchill was presented as a lover more
potent than the late Benvenuto Cellini. It was said that the
girl, hysterical and abandoned, had managed to nurse him
right out of prison and onto the road to safety in a manner not
made public. This account had all the documented authority of
President Kruger's unspherical world; nevertheless, the nurse
lost her position and was deported. Beyond doubt, the most
reprehensible act committed by the Boers during Churchill's
escape was General Joubert's announcement that the prisoner
had been officially declared a civilian and was going to be released. When this ruse failed to flush him, the Boers stepped
up their hunt. "For some days the whole state machinery came
to a standstill," Captain Haldane said later.

Not all of the Boers viewed the escape as critical. The truth
is that many of them were ripe for a spiritual backslide.
Kruger's godly manifestoes were beginning to bind and chafe.
In recent years, some of the farmers—renegades whose reading
had ventured beyond the Old Testament and the sulphurous
hymnals—would have liked to relax and take a few trips out
past Kruger's Flats. De Haas, for example, the officer who had
composed the laconic reward bill, saw the hue and cry as pretty
much of a joke. He was an upper-class native of the Nether-
lands who had gone out to help the Boer cause in response to
the promptings of both sympathy and boredom. Transferred
from the volunteer cavalry to police duties, he was playing
cards in his hut with a Boer plumber and two Kaffir boys when
the phone rang on December 13 to announce the glittering

jailbreak. In 1946 he wrote an article for the *Strand,* a British magazine now defunct, in which he explained, somewhat jocularly, his part in the attempted recapture.

Upon receiving the first news, De Haas inquired what all the commotion was about. "Headquarters seemed to consider us responsible," he said later.

"What is so sacred about this Churchill chap?" he wanted to know.

He was severely rebuked. Pretoria replied that Churchill, the son of the Duke of Marlborough, was "a very dangerous individual," a correspondent who had taken part in the fighting and "sabotaged" an armored train. He was known to be a "leading Jingo."

"I conferred with my colleagues," said De Haas. The plumber raised the relevant question whether the sons of dukes were dukes themselves. One of the Kaffirs settled this by assuring him that this was so, except if illegitimate, when they were known as "marquesses." De Haas broke out a bottle of wine he'd been saving and there was some discussion about calling Pretoria and ascertaining if the fugitive was legitimate.

"We had just decided that he wasn't worth bothering with," says De Haas, "when the phone rang again, to say, 'What are you doing about the escaped prisoner?' "

De Haas advised headquarters to relax; he would see to everything. Then he got a piece of paper and scribbled off what struck him as a well-conceived reward notice. "Having to provide the cash myself, I decided that twenty-five pounds was ample," he said in his article. "So I took pen and ink and then and there wrote the proclamation. When it was dry we pinned it up outside and confidently awaited."

Sure enough, a minor constable turned up a few hours later with a prisoner in tow. "Haul him in," cried De Haas, delighted that the nuisance was finished. "Put him in the chair."

"Now, sir," he went on, according to witnesses, "what have you got to say for yourself?"

"Ay ban vish to go home," replied the captive.

"Why, confound it, this fellow's a Swede!" cried De Haas.

"Will that affect the reward?" asked the constable. "I'd like to get the money right away. I want to buy some things."

After more urgent goading from headquarters, De Haas organized a house-to-house search. He himself led one party, in a desultory fashion. His first call was upon the Bishop of Pretoria, who looked at the guns in their belts and said, "I hope there will be no occasion to use those." De Haas murmured something propitiatory and asked what was inside a huge wooden bin that stood in a hallway. "I was wondering if Churchill might be in there?" he inquired pleasantly.

When the bishop refused to open the bin, De Haas had a soldier force it, to reveal some garments in use before their host had succeeded to his bishophood. In the nearby home of a rich English woman, De Haas insisted on entering a briskly defended wardrobe and found a cache of whiskey and gin that would easily have carried her for several years.

In some ways, however, the search netted a skimpy haul, and De Haas went back to his hut to resume his card game. Before he could think up any further devices, the news of Churchill had taken another turn, and he was relieved of all responsibility.

In later years De Haas himself became a correspondent, for the English news agency Reuters. In conversation with friends in the House of Lords he was often pressed as to how he fixed on the niggardly twenty-five pounds as the price of the reward. And Churchill, too, queried the sum. In 1908, when the former fugitive, now the president of the Board of Trade, was being married, De Haas wrote him a little note of felicitation. Churchill replied:

Sir—

I am very much obliged to you for your courtesy and good wishes. I look back with feelings of thankfulness to my share in that long South Africa story. I earnestly hope that all will now be peace.

I think you might have gone as high as 50 pounds without an overestimate of the value of the prize—if living! Yours faithfully,

Winston Churchill

II

The central figure in all this commotion had assumed an air of proprietary ease after vacating his shrub. It had not required any unnatural effort. He strolled past the lighted windows of the house, out into the street, and toward the center of town. He was, he says, humming a tune, and he is known to have tipped his unlovely hat to various of the burghers. In response, seeing the disheveled but consecrated young cleric, they executed little bows and spoke the Boer and Kaffir equivalents of "Good evening, Father," and "Your Worship." Past the illuminated business area, Churchill accelerated his gait and made toward the railroad, any railroad. There remained in his mind a plan to strike for the nearest neutral territory, in this case Delagoa Bay, in Portuguese East Africa, three hundred miles distant. From his inconclusive schooling he had unwillingly absorbed a knowledge of astronomy that centered on the constellation Orion. Once before, while looking for Dervishes, he had wandered off into the desert and found his way back by studying his old favorite. He now looked to Orion for guidance, as Shadrach and his associates had followed Cassiopeia.

Good luck soon led him to a railroad, and Orion led him eastward along the tracks, walking out of town. Almost immediately he came perilously close to being retaken. The bridges were all picketed—he saw the pickets just in time. Very carefully, he crept around them, gave a suburban station a wide berth, and hid in a ditch on the far side, waiting to snag a freight, as the saying goes. This represented an important comedown for Churchill. Since the time of the first duke, the Marlboroughs had all ridden first class, and he was now reduced to seeking accommodations amongst the crates and livestock. It was a bitter thought, but the time was not ripe for titled distinctions. Churchill was as joyous as if he had been in the brasserie of Waterloo Station when he heard the sickly hoot of a Boer mixed freight and saw it laboring past the station and up the gradient in his direction. To scramble from his ditch and hurl himself toward the nearest rungs was the work of a few seconds. And again, his adventure all but ended in disaster, as he missed one handhold and went banging between the cars and against the couplings. But instead of falling, he grabbed a projecting piece of iron, hung on, and exhaustedly hauled himself up. From the couplings, he climbed into an open truck filled with empty coal sacks. Then he made himself blackly comfortable and slept like a baby until the first gray streaks of morning.

Not long after he awakened, it came over Churchill that he was starving. He ate the chocolate and decided to leave the train, though it was rolling briskly and visibility was next to zero. Unhappily, as a public school man he had not enjoyed the advantages of the professional bindle stiff, or hobo, and was unacquainted with the orthodox methods of descending from a fast freight. It is a skill not to be despised, particularly in an era of quick economic change. Standing on the low-hung ladder, one pushes backward with a violent heave from the *right* foot, lands on the left, and takes three or four short, running steps. The secret lies in the rearward shove, to counteract the forward motion of the train, and in starting from the right rather than the left foot, which to an amateur would seem to be the logical choice. Churchill leaped forward from his left foot, hit the roadbed, executed a series of admirable gymnastic loops in the air, then came to rest, somewhat loosely, in a ravine. He pulled himself together and took inventory. Everything accounted for.

In the growing dawn, he saw that he was near a Kaffir kraal, or native village (from whose term is derived the Western "corral"), and at the fringe of a wood. The great thing now was to find some water, since the chocolate had given him a raging thirst. A pool lay in tantalizing sight between the kraal and the wood, but he was afraid to creep forward and drink lest he be noticed and seized, enriching some native herdsman to the tune of twenty-five pounds. He spent an exceedingly miserable day hidden in the trees, with an African sun blazing overhead. His only companion was a gigantic vulture that sat patiently on a nearby limb, plainly confident that luncheon was soon to materialize. Because of his weeks in captivity, Churchill was in inferior physical condition at this time, and the rigors of the trip now began to tell. Famished, thirsty, and with fading hope, he spent much of the afternoon on his knees, praying. There are few instances of overt prayer in Churchill's early history; this genuflection in the South African glade must be classed as extraordinary to unique. While not anti- or unreligious, he has never been (as previously stated) notable for those humbling devotions that mark the God-fearing man. His treatment of the Lord's servants, for example, has been distinguished by amiable jocularity, often tinged with respect. The business of taking the Boer's hat should not be taken as typical. Churchill is keenly aware that the leading churchmen of England are, like the royal family, valuable symbols of stability and cohesion.

At the start of the recent London bombings, he sent a note to the Archbishop of Canterbury, saying, "Can you spare me a few minutes?" The Archbishop rushed up to London to see him, and Churchill said, "Hitler is threatening us with destruction from the air. What steps have you taken to protect your person?"

A little startled, the Archbishop replied, "We have a perfectly fine cellar and have moved some beds into it."

"That won't do at all," said the Prime Minister. "You must go down to the farthest recesses of the cathedral and get a crypt. Put sandbags in it, place girders along the top, and then put on more sandbags and more sandbags. I want it so strong that it will survive anything but a direct hit. If it takes a direct hit, Your Grace may regard it as a Summons."

When darkness fell over the kraal, Churchill scuttled like a land crab across the veldt to the pool, where he drank long

and noisily. Then, his hunger sharpened, he began hiking eastward along the railroad again. The moon rose and shed its pale
radiance on the bridges and trestles, around which he trudged
through swamps and razorlike weeds soaked with dew. He
was, he estimated later, less than halfway to the frontier. His
clothing was now in tatters and he had despaired of finding
another friendly freight train; all traffic seemed to have
stopped. As he rounded a curve in the track, he observed the
tipples of a mining village off to the right, and he resolved to
essay a bluffing account of being a lost English-Boer recruit,
tumbled from a train. Ironically enough, in making for the village he became authentically lost. He found himself at length
on the steps of a cottage a good distance from town. Half
fainting, he knocked, saw the intelligent-looking proprietor
stare out of the window, hesitate, and then come to the door.

Even in his frazzled condition Churchill was able instantly
to discard his first account and come up with an alternative,
an easy product of his richly inventive brain. "Ah, good evening," he gasped, jiggling the funny hat, "I'm the Reverend
Hjalmar T. Buglemeister, currently a poor war worker
who——"

"Come in, come in," said the man abruptly. "You needn't
lie to me; you're Winston Churchill, and this is the only house
for twenty miles where you wouldn't be given up."

His host was John Howard, manager of the Transvaal Col-
lieries, a mine now staffed by a skeleton crew, because of the
military drafts upon labor. Howard himself was an Englishman
who had become a naturalized burgher of the Transvaal Republic; his three key employees were also British. One of these,
a Mr. Dewsnap, turned out to be from Oldham, the scene of
the fugitive's political fiasco. "Don't worry," Dewsnap told
Churchill, crushing his hand in a miner's grip, "they'll vote for
you next time."

Churchill meditated upon this cheering news as he was low-
ered two hundred feet into the earth. Howard had related that
the surface regions were swarming with spies; he had two

sleep-in maids who were Dutch and intensely inquisitive. "You will be better off in the mine," he insisted to Churchill, who had asked for food, a pistol, a guide, and a pony, so that he could flee, in nocturnal stages, to the sea. Before being dropped in the cable car, he had been invited to make himself free with a bottle of whiskey and a siphon. By the time of the actual descent, he was a shade better than fully recovered in mind and body.

The developing plot grew more elaborate. As indicated, Kruger and his Republic were righteous but dull; Howard had lived for years in a state of uneventful torpor. Now he was privy to an adventure of resounding quality, and he went to work on it in the manner of Tom Sawyer freeing a runaway slave. During a council of war, held in the bowels of the earth, he advised the underground party that Churchill would be known, in the colliery, as Dr. Bentock. He did not vouchsafe the origin of this singular name. In the opinion of Bentock, the plot grew almost *too* elaborate. For the first few nights, the doctor was lodged in a stable room with the pit ponies, which seemed friendly but not as friendly as the several dozen rats that made use of the place. From Howard's library, Churchill had selected a book to read—Stevenson's appropriate *Kidnapped*—and prone on his subterranean pallet he tried to review the problems of David Balfour and Alan Breck. Stuck in the mine, the rats had little or no access to literature, and they kept creeping up to look over his shoulder. In an hour or so he called it quits, blew out his candles, and settled himself to sleep. The rats—uncommonly large ones, pink and with phosphorescent eyes—then dug under his pillow to get at the candles. It was hard to tell whether they were starved for tallow or crazy about Stevenson.

In four days Dr. Bentock was brought up to an office adjoining Howard's and several Englishmen of the neighborhood called in that evening to see him. The night following, they transferred him to the barn of a sympathetic Dutchman, a man who had once gone round the world in a windjammer and held

important geographic differences with Kruger. The Dutchman
was preparing to ship some bales of wool to Delagoa Bay. Into
a railroad car with these Dr. Bentock was carefully secreted.
He shook hands with his benefactors, feelingly told Howard
that he hoped to meet him again, preferably in London, and
soon afterward the train started rolling. Churchill did meet
Howard again, and in London, as he had suggested. The un-
selfish colliery manager eventually wearied of South Africa
and moved back home. He met Churchill several times to
reminisce happily about the touchy days in the coal mine.
Howard died in England in 1941, not long after his former
ragged protégé had become Prime Minister, and the most important man in the world.

For two and a half days the freight train bumped its way
toward the frontier; then it sat on a siding for eighteen hours
so that Boer officials could examine it. Dr. Bentock, a man
of more than ordinary impatience, had improved the journey
by sticking his head out every ten minutes or so in an effort to
catch the names of towns. On Howard's advice, he had memorized a whole string of station stops: Dalmanutha, Machado-
dorp, Waterval Boven, Waterval Onder, Elands, Nooidge-
dacht, and so on, and he kept a fair track of his progress. But
it was a long ride, and for the most part he squirmed restlessly
amid the bales—woolgathering, as it were. At a dinner thirty
years later, in a remarkable demonstration of his memory,
Churchill rattled off a series of eighteen of the Boer railroad
towns without making a single error. During the inspection he
had burrowed down deep, and although he heard somebody
pull off the covering tarpaulin, and sensed the inquisitive stare,
he was not discovered.

When the train rolled slowly on and past the frontier,
Churchill crawled out for a celebration. Perched on top of his
sleeper, he drew a revolver that Howard had given him and
emptied its six chambers into the quiet, African air. Then he
added something fairly special in the way of howls and yelps.
But noting that the train, not too surprisingly, was beginning

to slow down, he reflected that the less known about the details of his flight the better for Howard and his associates. Accordingly he plopped back into his grotto and subsided. The train crew could find no accounting for the unholy racket and are undoubtedly, if still living, wondering what hit them that day near the Transvaal border.

Covered with grime, the onetime prisoner disembarked at the town of Lourenço Marques and hurried to the office of the British consul, where he had a dampening experience. A subordinate, haughty and officious in the subconsular tradition, took him for a fireman from one of the vessels in the harbor and was unaccommodating. He had picked the wrong man. Churchill has ever been competent to deal with the petty snobberies of small officials. With a manner painfully ducal, soot or no soot, he sent the flunky hiking for his superior. Immediately all was changed. The refugee was welcomed with shouts of congratulations. The English colony in the town turned out in a body, offering refreshment, clean clothes, and other benefits.

"Name it, just name it," one patriot cried, and Churchill, after practically no reflection, ordered a telegraph blank. He wrote out a long and stinging announcement of his safe arrival and dispatched it to the Boer Minister of War.

An inspiriting celebration proceeded until he boarded the steamer *Induna* for Durban. He was escorted onto the ship by a large group of armed Englishmen, who had taken the notion that, at this late date, he might still be kidnapped and returned to durance vile. Their precautions were unwarranted. Except for a pair of elderly ladies in deck chairs, who seemed annoyed at the boisterous arrival, everybody within sight was amiable and sympathetic.

At Durban, the lid of British enthusiasm was blown off more emphatically. All the ships in the harbor were flying a colorful laundry of bunting, numberless small craft swarmed about, bells, bosun's pipes, whistles, sirens, and foghorns set up a joyous chorus, and a monster gathering with three bands was

on the quay as the *Induna* was warped alongside. After succes-
sions of bitter defeats—at Stormberg, Magersfontein, and
Colenso—the British had a victorious hero at last. Bareheaded,
Churchill stood in the bow and, in the idiom of the ring, mitted
the crowd. His hour had come at last. For several years he had
repined under the odium of a limited notoriety. From this day
on he would be all but impossible to hold.

It might have been difficult to find a young man more brilliantly suited to the mantle of public benefactor. In the midst
of the color and the noise, Churchill shone like a gem. With
that indefinable air compounded of nonchalance, an awareness
of great things, and suppressed excitement (for which the over-
worked "glamour" is the best available label), he fulfilled exactly the hopes of a people in carnival mood. To deafening
sounds, he descended the gangplank with stately warmth and
shook hands with the mayor, the local admiral, and the local
general, who were dignitaries of the highest accessible voltage.
The bands, consecutively and, by accident, concurrently,
played everything in their repertory, and then Churchill made
a speech.

There exists a photograph of Churchill on this halcyon date.
Mounted on a makeshift platform before the City Hall, hatless,
wearing an ill-fitting black suit with a vest, his hands on his
hips, his thinning red hair tumbled over his forehead, he is addressing the crowd with an expression of patriotic intensity.
Beside him stands an unidentified young man wearing a straw
hat and holding aloft a huge British flag. The crowd includes
both blacks and whites, and there is a sway-backed horse with
a buggy in the foreground. The men are wearing straw hats, or
bowlers, or caps, ducking a little from the sun. It looks like a
hot day. And in some vague, nostalgic way, it looks like 1900,
as 1900 must have looked—lazy, unhurried, comfortable, and
relaxed despite the war. The faces are peaceful, lacking that
ashen strangulation that an eminent neurologist has recently
classified as Uranium Cramp, the nerve cancer of technocracy.

When the hubbub had died down slightly, Churchill resumed

his work with the telegraph blanks. Having thoughtfully reported his safety to the Boer Minister of War, he could scarcely do less for the London *Morning Post,* upon whose expense account he was theoretically traveling. In wiring his paper, Churchill became carried away and launched a critique of the entire conduct of the war. In the British phrase, it did not "go down very well." Certain passages, such as his query, "Are the gentlemen of England all fox-hunting?" were construed as impertinent. His tributes to the fighting qualities of the Boer also were regarded as overdrawn. "The individual Boer," said Churchill, "mounted in suitable country, is worth from three to five regular soldiers," and he added that the only way to treat the problem was "either to get men equal in character and intelligence as riflemen, or, failing the individual, huge masses of troops."

Replies to his broadside were quickly forthcoming. While Churchill had reviewed the government's whole prosecution of the war, several papers reviewed Churchill's. The periodical *Truth* led off with a few remarks about the Armored Train. ". . . Mr. Churchill is described as having rallied the force by calling out 'Be men! Be men!' But what can the officers have been doing who were in command of the detachment? Again, were the men showing signs of behaving otherwise than as men? Would officers in command on the battlefield permit a journalist to 'rally' those who were under their orders?"

The *Phoenix* commented, "That Mr. Winston Churchill saved the life of a wounded man in an armoured train is very likely. Possibly he also seized a rifle and fired at a Boer. But the question occurs what was he doing in the armoured train? He had no right there whatever. He is not now a soldier, although he once held a commission in the Fourth Hussars, and I hear that he no longer represents the *Morning Post*."

The *Daily Nation* got in a similar plug: "Mr. Churchill's escape is not regarded in military circles as either a brilliant or honorable exploit. He was captured as a combatant, and of course placed under the same parole as the officers taken prisoners. He has however chosen to disregard an honorable undertaking, and it would not be surprising if the Pretoria authorities adopted more strenuous measures to prevent such conduct."

There were many other notices in a similar vein. The *Morning Leader* struck a fresh note, a departure from its accustomed sobriety, by saying that, "We have received no confirmation of the statement that Lord Lansdowne has, pending the arrival of Lord Roberts, appointed Mr. Winston Churchill to command the troops in South Africa, with General Sir Redvers Buller, V.C., as his Chief of Staff."

Perhaps the pithiest observation was composed by the generals and colonels of London's most exclusive military club, who, no doubt feeling that Randolph's son needed counsel in these trying times, sent him the following telegram: "Best friends here hope you will not continue making further ass of yourself."

The attacks on Churchill grew so reckless that later, as he said, "I have been forced to extort damages and public apologies by prosecution for libel on at least four separate occasions." These were mostly in connection with the untrue statement that he had broken a parole, but the fact is that Churchill, in general, is a zealous protector of his legal rights, as his chief secretary once warned an unauthorized biographer. He customarily reads magazine and newspaper pieces about himself while making frequent asides to members of his staff. "Aha, we'll sue on that sentence!" he will say, or, again, "An outrageous misstatement—institute proceedings immediately."

The *Phoenix* was wrong about Churchill's job on the *Morning Post*. His plan of procedure after his arrival in Durban was to re-enter the military. But he did not wish to relinquish his well-paying job, so he got General Buller to appoint him, as an unpaid lieutenant, to an irregular regiment, the South African Light Horse, or Cockyolibirds, as the members were informally known (from the plumes in their hats). In this way the hero was able to continue with his writing, and among the first things he turned out were some pretty sharp criticisms of Buller.

Laden with telegrams from all parts of the world, Churchill made his way from Durban to rejoin the Army. The meeting took place within a hundred yards of the spot where he had been captured. He recognized a platelayer's hut that he had used as a landmark on that hurried and disappointing day. Only six weeks had elapsed since he had jumped down from the train and scurried into the grasp of Louis Botha, but in that time he had become internationally famous. The pangs of ambition were appeased for the moment. He gathered together all the fine foods and wines he could buy and gave a dinner to his friends. It went on through the evening, past midnight, and into Christmas morning. The slow century of Victorian England was drawing to a close. Churchill had begun the merry season, as he would so many others, "on the flinty and steel couch of war," a gift of the tyrant custom.

*Part*

# III

# Chapter 15

A FEW details of Churchill's later career in the Boer War should be mentioned briefly before the bizarre events of his political life are considered. The war itself was not concluded until May 31, 1902, but he detached himself from the Army in 1900, when the back of Boer resistance was unmistakably broken. As usual in Churchill's life, his span of service had not been barren of incident. Despite the newly won honors, he distinguished himself further. At the relief of Ladysmith, he was the first horseman to enter the city, and there is some basis for the story that the English prisoners there thought for a while that he had delivered them singlehanded. At Dewetsdorp, his saddle girth was shot through and he tumbled to the ground to watch his unharmed mount gallop away. For an awful moment it looked as though he might repeat the dark experience of Pretoria. Precisely what the Boers would have done with Churchill had they retaken him is not known, but it may be assumed that the Minister of War, clutching his jolly telegram, could scarcely have been genial. In any case, the crisis passed; Churchill thumbed a ride from a mounted British trooper, who said later that his passenger "didn't mind a bit. That man could stand anything. He didn't show the least sign of fear, and wanted to talk when he got up behind me. But I thought it was no time for talking and I told him so."

For his pains in halting, scooping up Churchill, and carting him to safety, the trooper, whose name was Roberts, was awarded the D.C.M.

It was reported that Churchill himself was considered for decoration after he had stormed an occupied town in search of bottled beer. He had understood that the place had been evacuated; however, minus the beer, or perhaps incensed by failing to get it, he conducted a bristling withdrawal that was much admired.

There were indications that, as the war went on, Churchill took the notion that he was fighting it alone. His movements bore little relation to those of his unit. Not unnaturally, the Queen was less severe about individualism on the part of unpaid soldiers; it was considered that no matter how far afield such a man might wander, it could cost nobody but himself to get him back. In Churchill's case, the expense was defrayed by the *Morning Post,* which received its money's worth. There was no end to the lively anecdotes he sent in. At one point, he told of a soldier who was found skulking in the wake of the Army. A general asked him why. "Because I'm only a third-class shot," said the man (according to Churchill of the *Morning Post*). "That's a great pity," remarked the general, "because we'll have to put you three times as close to the enemy to make you effective. *Forward!"*

At Lindley, Churchill made a reconnaissance based on information that the Boer President, Two-dimension Kruger, was hiding in an old house. Churchill cased the dwelling, as the gangsters say, then broke in to make the capture. The President was absent, but he captured two bottles of enemy champagne, which he executed on the spot.

A good many of Churchill's activities in the Boer War centered on fodder. He took some outrageous chances to dine luxuriously. He got a name for being a scrounger above and beyond the call of duty. There was the matter of the purloined goose. Traveling through a country sparse in produce, he scouted an unexpected flock of fat geese. He chose a spot downwind and crouched in the underbrush, waiting his chance. It was a fretful operation, since other units were coming up and there was a danger of losing the flock to attrition. At length Churchill spied a straggler, then pranced out and delivered a heroic kick, aimed to hoist the bird over a fence. Owing to a miscalculation, and a cross wind, it sailed into the highway and the lap of a martinet colonel, who hauled Churchill up for a public rebuke. It is a matter of pride to Churchill's political allies that he has taken some of the fieriest tongue-lashings in history without turning a hair. His knowledge of his qualities has always been too secure to permit wilting from censure by mediocrities. He listened attentively to the colonel, returned a brisk salute, wheeled, snatched up the goose, which was lying in the road, and fled. Later, squatting in the bush, he cooked the bird himself, after which he shared it with some like-minded unregenerates.

While accompanying the campaign of his old friend Ian Hamilton, who was marching on Johannesburg, Churchill concocted a typical escapade. With Hamilton's troops, he found himself on one side of the city, and Lord Roberts, at the only telegraph outlet, was cut off on the opposite side. It seemed vital to send a dispatch to the *Morning Post,* which had been scooping London on things like loitering soldiers, geese, and miscellaneous flaws in the high-level planning. Churchill was sitting at a roadside, wondering what to do, when two civilians came riding along on bicycles. They were conversing in French. He jumped up promptly and hailed them in his Harrovian approximation of the subtle Gallic language. Did they think it possible, he asked, for him to cycle through the city dressed as a civilian? Whatever their answer, Churchill cried "Splendid!" and fastened onto one of the wheels, giving the owner a fistful of bank notes as rental. As if the fellow's plight were not sad enough, he soon saw himself talked out of a first-rate seersucker suit and garbed in the faded drab of the Cockyolibirds. The exchange took only a few moments. Without rightly knowing what had hit him, the peasant came to seated in Churchill's old spot and, for all general purposes, on the reverse side of the struggle. He waved in halfhearted fashion as his comrade and the cyclone from the north rode off toward Johannesburg.

Churchill's tactic en route through the city was to shout what he considered to be French to his bewildered partner. In order to gesticulate in the accepted fashion, he frequently rode with no hands, and why he was not apprehended has never been cleared up by the Johannesburg authorities, for he was not only suspicious-looking, he was a municipal nuisance. However, he got through town all right and dragged the unwilling cyclist with him. At Roberts' headquarters he paid off his helper, shook his hand, and sent him reeling back. He himself recounted his adventures with such bumptious good cheer that Roberts stood him a bottle of wine and put him up for the night.

At one time, Churchill's path crossed that of his brother Jack, who happened to be spending his first day under fire. The veteran of three continents had the uncomfortable experience of seeing his young brother shot in the leg; he assisted him back to the rear and by dint of addressing a stripling surgeon as "Major" got him the best of care. It also occurred that, simultaneously, his mother, ever busy, had put in to Durban with a hospital ship she had casually outfitted. The Lady Randolph continued to be a handsome and persuasive woman. She had just talked a pliable American millionaire into making a staggering anti-Boer donation. Using the money to equip a vessel of mercy, she found, in Durban, that the first patient admitted for treatment was her son Jack. Her son Winston, to whose ears had come a rumor that the ship was rich in provisions, arrived soon afterward. He stayed some days, dining in style and recounting his vivid adventures. Altogether, it was a warm, if uncommon, reunion.

Before quitting the war, Churchill arranged a transfer from the Light Horse to resume his duties as general correspondent, in order to have a wider range. The old trouble of confinement to a single unit had been plaguing him again. But in transferring he had run into unexpected and severe resistance, provided by his former campmate, Kitchener, who had taken over one of the highest commands in the South African Army. The ex-Egyptian Sirdar was piqued on two counts; one had to do with the many generous hints Churchill had given him in the Sudan, via the *Morning Post,* and the other was of more recent origin, resting on a dispatch that Churchill had written about chaplains. In the course of his young career it was difficult for Churchill to keep out of religious squabbles. For a man not especially devout, he expended a lot of time on theology.

The immediate friction involved a blend of religious and military theory. Listening one Sunday to an earnest army chaplain preach, Churchill took umbrage at the reported tactics of the Israelites in felling the Walls of Jericho. He saw the account as a garbled piece of journalism, and said so, in the *Post.* Possibly fearing a libel action by a descendant, he did not come out openly and charge the man at the scene with distortion; instead, he laid the heaviest burden of error on the chaplain. "These strictures," he afterward wrote, "had, it appeared, caused commotion in the Established Church." Kitchener took the line that the chaplain was doing his best and did not deserve to be called down on a point that was basically military. He implied that he, unlike Churchill, was satisfied with the siege of Jericho, and indicated that anyhow it was too late to change it: the walls were gone.

After much talk and wirepulling, Churchill finally got himself detached, and went on to riper glories. He was the first man in at the capture of Pretoria, from which he had been the first man out. The joyous deliverance has been described by him in *My Early Life:*

"The prisoners rushed out of the house into the yard, some in uniform, some in flannels, hatless, coatless, but all violently excited. The sentries threw down their rifles, the gates were flung open, and while the last of the guard (they numbered 52 in all) stood uncertain what to do, the long penned up officers surrounded them and seized their weapons. Someone produced a Union Jack, the Transvaal emblem was torn down, and amidst wild cheers from our captive friends, the first British flag was hoisted over Praetoria. Time: 8.47, June 5. Tableau!"

There followed a fitting carouse at the State Model School. An old boy had come back for Class Day, and the long term was over.

It was the emotional climax of Churchill's deeds of derring-do. Ahead lay the safe but vexing problems of a life in public service.

# *Chapter 16*

CHURCHILL's trip from Capetown to Southampton, made in July of 1900, is worthy of passing note. He was an object of immense curiosity to his fellow passengers, whose interest was not lessened by his conduct during the voyage. His plans had crystallized: he would return to Oldham and take it by storm. To this end he had written several speeches with which to sow the wind. Cramped as he was, and with time short (for an election impended), he had little opportunity for proper rehearsal, so he stationed himself in the prow of the ship and, in the words of a fellow passenger, borrowing from Demosthenes, "harangued the waves and winds."

Characteristically, he was wholly oblivious of the eccentric spectacle he presented, nor was he regardful of the excited buzzing from the onlookers. Gesticulating wildly, with red hair flying, tossed up and down with the motion of the ship, he shouted out his emphatic platform, which went about as follows: "My Liberal opponents will tell you [glaring into the frightened face of some unoffending planter or missionary] that this war is unjust and unnecessary. Now I say to you that their opposition, their unreasonable hampering of its prosecution from start to finish, have jeopardized the very roots of empire. *It must be fought to an indisputable conclusion.* Do you agree?"

At this point, a number of the less hardy among the passengers would retire to their cabins, preferring to hide rather than make a public statement of policy.

By the time they reached England, Churchill was elocuting
smoothly; the rest of the ship's company was exhausted but
sold on his candidacy. He stepped ashore to a unique and
unremitting ovation. Indeed, it went on so long that several
of the Conservative leaders were fearful that he might try to
buck for Prime Minister.

In London he attended the wedding of his mother to the
career soldier, George Cornwallis-West, and then went on
to Oldham, where he plunged immediately into the campaign. The line-up this time was only slightly different. Representing the Liberals were still Emmott and Runciman, but
Churchill's running mate was now Charles B. Crisp, a broker
who was later to found the British Bank of Foreign Trade
and achieve world-wide fame as a financier. James Mawdsley,
the secretary of the Amalgamated Society of Operative Spinners, had met with a regrettable accident. He was an enormous
man and had been gaining a little more weight each year. A
large china tub in which he was accustomed to bathing had
at last collapsed under the growing avoirdupois and Mawdsley
was destroyed in the wreckage. Replacing him, Crisp had no
utopian program for labor, but he was an able speaker, could
foot his own bills, and was respectful toward Churchill, the
lion of the hour. It was a strong ticket.

Eleven other constituencies had invited Churchill to stand,
but he gave out an interview in which he said that he preferred to avenge the "smack in the eye" of the year before.
All the bands in town were assembled when he arrived, and
the prevailing melody was "See the Conquering Hero Comes."
Through streets lined with cheering thousands, he rode in an
open carriage to the Town Hall, where he made his first address. It was observed that, when somebody opened a door
to hand him down, Churchill vaulted to the street over the
other side. He related the story of his escape from the Boers
and laid the credit almost entirely to Mr. Dewsnap, the
former resident of Oldham. This was remarked as odd in view
of the fact that the mine manager, Howard, had engineered

the whole business. Dewsnap had, in fact, contributed little more than a handshake. However, the revelation brought down the house, and a number of small girls in the front row, wearing sashes that said, "God bless Churchill, England's Noblest Hero," arose and sang a song in which he was described as the savior of the downtrodden. This was a far cry from the sentiment of the previous election, in which he and the ill-fated Mawdsley were branded as creatures of the vested interests.

In the two months that followed, Churchill addressed 150 meetings, winding up one of the last in a half swoon, which was seized upon by the opposition as false, to his raging indignation. Indeed, the campaign was marked by surprising personal vilification. The other side went so far as to accuse him of both cowardice and the abandonment of his fellow prisoners at Pretoria. These charges set in motion the long, crowded train of Churchill's libel actions. It is still merrily rolling.

To refute the slanderous indictments, he produced statements of prisoners and additional testimonials. A Captain Haserick wrote to the *Daily Mail* as follows:

Sir: I have been shown a letter which appeared in the *Daily Mail* a short time ago, and the subject of which is Mr. Winston Churchill. I regret that, owing to travel, I did not see it at an earlier date.

The writer says, *inter alia;* "Before his (Mr. Churchill's) brief excursion to South Africa, when he escaped by prematurely leaving his fellow prisoners, with whom he had agreed to make the attempt co-jointly, we find him, etc."

As one of these fellow prisoners—five of us intended to make the attempt, in two parties—I desire to state emphatically that there is no truth in this accusation.

We were at the time in the Model School, Praetoria, and the escape was to be made at night over the playground wall, at a very dark and badly guarded part of it. Mr. Churchill was the first to make the attempt, and succeeded in getting over safely. An officer who followed bungled, and the noise attracted the attention of a guard who ordered him off the wall, but fortunately made no further investigation. Mr. Churchill, I know for a fact, waited a considerable time in the garden into which he had dropped before making off.

I may add that one of the officers who was to have accompanied him, a Colonial, spoke the Taal fluently, and Mr. Churchill, who spoke not a word of Dutch, had naturally relied very much upon his officer for an escape from the Transvaal. Under the circumstances only a miracle could save him, and this took place, for, compelled by exhaustion to seek help, he approached a house the tenant of which happened to be the only Englishman in the district. I know that I can rely upon your sense of fairness to publish this letter.

A. E. Haserick, Captain

The Oldham voters apparently preferred this version of Churchill's adventure to that of the Liberals, for Runciman was rudely unhorsed in the election. Emmott led the quartet with 12,947 votes; Churchill was a very close second, with 12,931; Runciman and Crisp, not elected, were third and fourth.

And now, on the first of October 1900, at the advanced age of twenty-five, and having already provided a rich legend for the minnesingers, Churchill was ready for his life of service. There was little faltering in his manner. Notwithstanding his youth, he was a master planner, and his next step was loudly applauded in a limited circle: he decided to go to America and make some money. The word had reached him that there was a gold mine in lectures. His informant pointed out somewhat impertinently that, since Churchill was in process of lecturing almost continuously, he might as well corral a formal audience and store up some cash before settling down in Parliament.

It was not a difficult choice. Despite his haughty lineage, Churchill was far from wealthy. Outside of a moderate allowance from his mother, and about twenty thousand dollars he had made from his books, he had no source of support. Furthermore, the Members of Parliament were then unpaid. As the congratulations poured in on his campaign triumph, Churchill went ahead with his scheme. Lord Salisbury, the Prime Minister, telegraphed him; Arthur Balfour, the Leader of the House, asked him to share a speaking platform; and Joseph Chamberlain, the Colonial Secretary, introduced him everywhere. Churchill concluded that an English lecture tour might be in order before he began his American journey. It was enthusiastically arranged. Lord Wolseley presided at his successful debut in St. James's Hall in London.

In this period, according to his contemporaries, Churchill's lecture technique was the envy of his enemies and his imitators. He had adopted a style that, while sufficiently confident to prevent nervousness in his listeners, was yet tinged with a certain appealing timidity. This latter quirk might have been the result of his working with a magic lantern, which was apt to blow up in critical passages. He also had a careless habit of shoving the slides in upside down, and it is well known that neither Boers nor the African landscapes are at their best exhibited in this way. A journalist of the day was unkind enough to suggest that the shyness was "very largely humbug," assumed for its effect on ladies. The old lisp was still in evidence, and here, too, a defect seemed to militate for the general good. In writing his speeches, Churchill continued to avoid beginning and terminal *s*'s and struck a rueful, boyish expression whenever one accidentally reared its hissing head. But it was probably in his sincerity, or vehemence (the quality lay somewhere between the two nouns), that his real strength was rooted. It has been suggested that had Churchill been selling medicine or razor blades he could have retired with a fortune. His evident belief in his words has perhaps never been surpassed by anybody before or since. In fact he is admired yet today for the way he can hold a hostile audience that is silently rejecting his offering in toto.

Even those Englishmen who opposed the Boer War, and there were many, enjoyed Churchill's passionate remarks in favor of it. The audiences were gorgeous. Both society and the proletariat bought tickets with abandon. Sir Arthur Conan

Doyle served as chairman at his second address; Lord Rosebery introduced him at Edinburgh, Lord Dufferin at Belfast,
and his cousin, the incumbent Duke of Marlborough, at Oxford. As the acclaim and the money piled up, the Marlborough
motto of "Faithful but Unfortunate" began to appear as though
it had been chosen in sport. Churchill was hailed everywhere
as the most fortunate man in all of Britain. His average take
was the equivalent of $500 a night, a rare sum in those days
of the honest pound and dollar. At St. George's Hall in Liver-
pool, he hauled in $1500, and in the month of November he
banked a cool $22,500, with only half of his English swing
completed.

These golden successes continued until he left for America,
where the climate unexpectedly frosted up. The former colony
was not altogether imperialistic in its views, and a great many
people, Churchill found, were hoping that the Boers would
win. Taking the lead in this unfriendly contingent were the
Irish, who had no use for the English then and have found
little reason to thaw in the years that have passed. The opening lecture was in New York; the atmosphere was one of restrained cordiality. A fair crowd attended, perhaps partly out
of a desire to see Mark Twain, who presided with good-
humored finesse. In Baltimore no more than a comparative
handful showed up, and in Chicago, a citadel of Hibernianism,
there were indications that Churchill might be ridden out of
town on a rail, a custom of the raw, new country. In this
crisis, the visitor proved again that he was a man of more than
ordinary mettle. Imperturbable on the platform, he placated
the galleries with the laudatory observations on the Irish
Fusiliers that were described in Chapter 2, and then, as he
wrote later, "made a few jokes against myself, and paid a
sincere tribute to the courage and humanity of the Boers."
From then on, the tour went smoothly, climaxed by a tremendous turnout, together with an organized pro-British demonstration, in Boston. "On the whole," he has said, summing
up, "I found it easy to make friends with American audiences.

They were cool and critical, but also urbane and good-natured."

The American tour had been organized by a Major Pond, an impresario of the period, who offered Churchill a guarantee of ten thousand dollars with clauses about percentages, etc. Pond was a man with dynamic qualities and ideas even larger than his client's, as evidenced by some advance publicity he got out. It advertised the forthcoming lecturer as "the hero of five wars, the author of six books, and the future Prime Minister of Great Britain." Officially horrified, Churchill ordered him to withdraw it. Pond did so, but under protest. Before returning, Churchill extended the foreign tour to Canada, where all was joyous welcome. He concluded his engagement in January and sailed for home. Altogether, he had managed admirably. For more than five months he had spoken every day except Sunday, had seldom slept twice in the same bed, and had saved his money prudently. The tour had been rigorous, but he had been fed and housed much better than during his preceding outing in South Africa. Besides, he now had nearly fifty thousand dollars put aside. Conditions were propitious for his fling at politics. Churchill journeyed to London and prepared for a kind of postscript lecture to the series—his maiden speech in the House of Commons.

II

The serene and widely mourned death of Queen Victoria had occurred on the twenty-second of January 1901 without causing a political ripple. She had "received a crown that had been tarnished by ineptitude and vice" and had made it "the symbol of private virtue and public honor." Her eldest son and successor, Edward VII, a chemistry expert, was a man of such wise and judicial qualities that even the Radical and Socialist parties voted to extend the royal prerogatives, and the country entered upon another governmental phase that exemplified the best of the monarchical system. In the main it was a period of calm, refinement, and poise, suitable to the development of skilled parliamentarians. Onto this tranquil scene strode the young Churchill, fired with change and reform. He was a Conservative but he had inherited an errant Liberalism. In the matter of his opening address, he got down to business with uncommon speed. As a rule, fledgling Members were expected to sit by with deference while their elders showed them the ropes. It was not considered seemly for a youngster to disclose too early that he had the gift of speech. Often as much as a year went by before a new Member came forward with opinions. Even Lord Randolph, a stormy petrel of exceptional intransigence, waited two months before entering his first demurrer, and he took almost no part in the debates for three years thereafter.

Within two days after his son had entered the chamber, it became painfully clear to everybody that a major oration was imminent. Bristling with activity, Churchill sat at a desk making notes on slips of paper and tossing them ostentatiously into an upturned hat. A certain nervousness ran through the House. His offhand remarks about the Church of England were recalled by some, and others remembered his unsuccessful attempt to start a war with France, at the Rotherhithe Town Hall. When he first came in, there had been a momentary confusion about where he should sit. The confusion was in the minds of the other Members only. Churchill stepped up to the seat formerly occupied by his father, made himself comfortable, and laid out quite a substantial array of equipment: scratch pads, loose-leaf notebooks, a variety of memoranda, and works of reference. He seemed as much at home, said one writer, "as if he were the oldest, not the youngest, man present."

"Men who watch 'the Boy' detect many resemblances between him and his father," wrote the English biographer C. E. B. Roberts in 1927. "He has the same large eyes and square forehead; the same habit of throwing up his head and laughing loudly at anything that amuses him; the same manner-

With Lloyd George, Chancellor of
the Exchequer, on Budget Day,
1910

At Portsmouth, 1914, after a flight
from Upavon, Wiltshire

Captain Winston Churchill during World War I, in France

The ardent orator ad-
dressing munition
workers at Enfield,
Middlesex, 1915

*Picture Post Library*

The confident Chancellor
of the Exchequer leaving
11 Downing Street on
Budget Day, 1925

*Picture Post Library*

With Paddy hat and shil-
lelagh to Ulster Hall in
Belfast

*Picture Post Library*

isms—rubbing his hand over his coat as if his heart pained him, twisting order-papers endlessly into spills, bending forward to listen to conversations with strained attention and his hands folded, and walking at great speed through the lobby with a pronounced stoop and his hat swinging in his hand like a cane. Even his voice, resonant and with a touch of asperity, is curiously similar to Lord Randolph's."

On the third day after his seating, Churchill arose and teed off, in the golfing term. All did not go exactly as he had planned. There was in the House of Commons at this time another rising young man, a dissatisfied and bitterly eloquent Welshman named David Lloyd George, a Liberal, who popped up before Churchill and sailed into a full-dress impromptu speech. As Churchill wrote afterward, "he soon became animated and even violent. I constructed in succession sentence after sentence to hook on with after he should sit down. Each of these poor couplings became in turn obsolete. A sense of alarm and even despair crept over me."

For a few minutes it seemed as though the veteran of the Chicago hecklings had met his match. The angry and unexpected grumblings (Lloyd George had planned only to move an amendment) had pulled the carpet from under Churchill's pithiest phrases. He was groping for a well-turned *mot* when the Member on his left, Thomas Gibson Bowles, a Conservative of long experience in manufacturing spot witticisms, leaned over and suggested, "You might say 'Instead of making his violent speech without moving his moderate amendment, he had better have moved his moderate amendment without making his violent speech.'" Churchill gratefully jumped up and broke in, and to his surprise heard Lloyd George say, "I will curtail my remarks as I am sure the House wishes to hear a new Member."

Bowles' offering had saved the day; everybody agreed that it was a very passable barb, and they gave Churchill all the credit. In the British Parliament considerable weight has always been attached to graceful rhetoric. Previous to the Socialist revolution, its Members were largely men of taste and classical education, and their utterances were important contributions to the world's store of beautiful letters. This is in unfortunate contrast to the American Congress, in which most Members seek only to clothe their remarks in syntax palatable to constituencies nurtured by soap opera and vulgarisms exalting the improbable therapeutics of tobacco. It must be said that all too often the speakers fail to come up even to that dismal level. Besides the borrowed wisecrack, the body of Churchill's first speech was regarded as commensurate to the House of Commons standard. The topic under discussion was the Boer War, and he got off many positive statements that he assured them were made from firsthand knowledge: "I have traveled a good deal about South Africa during the last ten months, and I should like to lay before the House some of the considerations which have been very forcibly borne in upon me during that period." At the beginning of his remarks, he was heard to stutter rather badly, and he looked nervous. "Here and there he paused in his sentences as if searching for a word," says one witness. "But the more he stumbled and halted, the more determined his expression grew, and there was no doubt in any listener's mind that he would be heard through and often."

As in Chicago, he drew his warmest responses from the Irish Nationalists, sometimes in favor, sometimes against. "The Boers," he said, "may prefer to stand by their old cry, 'Death or Independence.' " (Loud cheers from the Irish Members.) "I do not see anything to rejoice at in that prospect," he added, "because, if it be so, the war will enter upon a very sad and gloomy phase." (Fairly loud boos from the Irish Members.) "Besides, the Nationalists ought not to regard the war as they do, both because of the great achievements of the Irish commanders in South Africa and because there can be no hope of reforms in Ireland until the end of the conflict in South Africa leaves men free to deal with other questions." (Quite loud but exceedingly puzzled boos and cheers, in about equal measure.)

It has been said of the speech that it was often difficult to tell which side Churchill was on. Some of the Conservatives finally concluded that he formed a kind of side of his own. Reaching one climactic part, he shouted, in connection with the high qualities of the enemy, "The Boers who are fighting in the field—*and if I were a Boer, I hope I should be fighting in the field*——" and Joseph Chamberlain, the Colonial Secretary, took advantage of a lull to remark to a neighbor, "That's the way to throw away seats!" Nevertheless, he and the others applauded courteously when the young firebrand had finished, and they shook his hand warmly afterward in the lounge. According to Churchill's own account, he was done up, in need of medication. "The usual restoratives were applied," he wrote, "and I sat in a comfortable coma till I was strong enough to go home."

The speech had interesting repercussions. Immediately after Churchill finished, Sir Robert Reid arose and said, "I am sure the House is glad to recognize that the honorable Member who has just sat down possesses the same courage which so distinguished Lord Randolph Churchill during his short and brilliant career in the House. I have listened with great pleasure to the honorable gentleman." Joseph Chamberlain, despite his complaint about the possible loss of seats, described the address as "very admirable," and Herbert Asquith, the Liberal leader, called it "interesting and eloquent." The Secretary for War, Sir William Brodrick, a vague and myopic man, contributed a bizarre touch when he apparently got the notion that Winston Churchill *was* Lord Randolph. Brodrick enjoyed the speech, he said, just as he had always enjoyed Randolph's speeches—more power to the "right honorable" Member. Unquestionably the most curious reaction of all was registered by an Irish Member, who, plainly overstimulated, sprang to his feet and attempted to make an address in Erse, the Irish form of Gaelic. He was quelled, and the startled House adjourned. It had been a gala day.

Not long afterward, in a series in the *Daily News* called

"Parliamentary Sketches," the journalist H. W. Massingham said of Churchill's effort: "Address, accent, appearance do not help him. But he has one quality—intellect. He has an eye —and he can judge and think for himself. Parts of the speech were faulty enough—there was clap-trap with the wisdom and insight. But such remarks as the impossibility of the country returning to prosperity under military government—the picture of the old Boers—more squires than peasants—ordered about by boy subalterns, the appeal for easy and honorable terms of surrender, showed that this young man has kept his critical faculty through the glamour of association with our arms. The tone was, on the whole, quiet, and through the speech ran, as I have said, the subdued but obvious plea for sympathy towards the foe."

Churchill settled into his new position quickly. The truth is that he settled into it so fast as to cause a certain amount of embarrassment. Only a week after his first speech, he advised his colleagues not to embark on a full-dress inquiry into the conduct of the war; however, he sympathized with their anxiety, realizing as he did that satisfactory information was scarce. "I have in many cases myself supplied the only report given to the country on some of the most important matters. I feel keenly the responsibility which has thus been placed upon me, and I think it is time for the Government and the War Office to relieve me of some of it." Asquith, a man of wry spirit, was unable to resist a comment on this self-conscious pronouncement. He hoped that "every possible step" would be taken to lighten "that burden of responsibility which at present weighs so heavily on the honorable Member's shoulders."

III

While Churchill started his parliamentary career with a solemn sense of his importance, he soon allowed his native humor a loose reign. Before very long he had acquired a reputation for wit that persists to the present hour. He also became noted for unorthodox and even impudent departures from the House of Commons ritual. In general, his witticisms have always been somewhat personal.

Once, when he was making an acidulous speech, a heckler jumped up and tried to expostulate but could produce only a few choked bubbles, like a defective drain. Churchill departed from his set remarks to observe to the House and to the gallery, "My right honorable friend should not develop more indignation than he can contain."

Churchill himself is a heckler of unparalleled talent. His disagreements take a rich variety of forms. Sir William Joynson-Hicks, once defeated by Churchill, was making a speech before Commons and noticed him, on the front bench of the Opposition, shaking his head in such vigorous style that attention was distracted from the address. "I see my right honorable friend shaking his head," cried Joynson-Hicks in exasperation. "I wish to remind him that I am only expressing my own opinion."

"And I wish to remind the speaker that I am only shaking my own head," replied Churchill.

Not long after he had been criticized for making literary capital out of his public life, he advised the House sternly: "Leave the Past to History, particularly since I intend to write the History myself."

Addressing himself to the War Office, which had issued angry appeals for manpower but which had been guilty of husbanding all its own clerks, he shouted, "Physician, comb thyself."

Churchill seldom misses a chance at a slapstick gesture. During one of his speeches, to a crowded House, a junior Socialist member wished to retrieve a paper from the broad desk that separates the front benches of the Government and the Opposition. To be inconspicuous, he dropped to all fours and crawled silently around the corner of the desk. On the other side, Churchill stopped talking, leaned over the desk, and, after an embarrassing silence, said, "Well, where did *you* come from?" The man sprang up, red as a beet, and retired from the Chamber.

Periodically Churchill has attacked the House of Lords, which he once described as "onesided, hereditary, unpurged, unrepresented, irresponsible and absentee." But he has been just as vitriolic about the other side. He called the Socialist regime a "government of the duds, by the duds, and for the duds," and predicted that it would vanish "unwept, unhonoured, unsung and unhung."

Churchill has always been more than ordinarily discourteous toward Oswald Mosley, the leader of Britain's tiny Fascist group. He listens to the counterfeit Hitler's speeches with obvious impatience. On one occasion he arose, when Mosley had finished an address that was both empty and awkward, to say, "I can well understand the honorable Member's wishing to speak for practice. He needs it badly."

Once in a while Churchill will introduce a personal touch of a homely nature. When the elderly and well-known Glasgow Socialist, David Kirkwood, was bouncing and sputtering at one of his speeches, Churchill stopped and said, "Now, David, behave yourself." To everybody's surprise, Kirkwood subsided and made no further racket.

At every step in his development, Churchill has shown a brilliant and generous flair for eulogizing his contemporaries. Of Lord Charles Beresford, he said that "he can best be described as one of those orators who, before they get up, do not know what they are going to say; when they are speaking, do not know what they are saying; and, when they have sat down, do not know what they have said."

Of Trotsky he remarked to his colleagues that "He sits disconsolate—a skin of malice stranded for a time on the shores of the Black Sea and now washed up in the Gulf of Mexico."

Nearly everybody has some pet aversion, and Sir Stafford Cripps has long been Churchill's. Several times he confusedly mentioned Cripps as Sir Stifford Crapps, and in the House, on

December 12, 1946, he said that "None of his colleagues can compare with him in that acuteness and energy of mind with which he devotes himself to so many topics injurious to the strength and welfare of the State."

Having once branded Ramsay MacDonald as a "boneless wonder," Churchill could not resist amplifying the theme. "I remember, when I was a child," he said, "being taken to the celebrated Barnum's Circus, which contained an exhibition of freaks and monstrosities, but the exhibit on the programme which I most desired to see was the one described as 'The Boneless Wonder.' My parents judged that the spectacle would be too revolting and demoralizing for my youthful eyes, and I have waited fifty years to see the Boneless Wonder sitting on the Treasury Bench."

Regarding MacDonald's mistakes and airy explanations, Churchill observed that he was "the greatest living master of falling without hurting himself."

Churchill's briefer descriptions have always been regarded as excellent. Aneurin Bevan, he said, had been a "squalid nuisance" all through the last war. It was seldom that he referred to Prince Paul of Yugoslavia as anything but "Prince Palsy," and nobody has yet come up with a better thumbnail biography of Hitler than Churchill's "bloodthirsty guttersnipe." Mussolini took second rhetorical billing in his fascist catalogue as a "whipped jackal." The pious followers of Gandhi were outraged to hear the Indian Mahatma depicted as "a seditious Middle Temple lawyer." On one occasion, having painted lurid pictures of several rogues, Churchill arrived at Pierre Laval, groped for a suitable phrase, and then said, "I am afraid I have rather exhausted the possibilities of the English language."

Churchill's friends and foes alike suffer from his barbs. After one of the members of his Nationalist Government had gone over to the Labour Party, he commented that it was the first time he had ever heard of a rat swimming *toward* a sinking ship.

When the new Conservative M.P., Alfred Bossom, was mak-

ing a speech in the House, Churchill turned around to stare at
him, and then asked in his hoarse, winged whisper, "Who is
that man?" Upon hearing his name, he said, "Bossom? Bossom?
Why, it's neither the one thing nor the other."

For many years the House of Commons has been richly
entertained by Churchill's easy treatment of foreign affairs.

"We shall continue to operate on the Italian donkey at both
ends," he once said—"with a carrot and with a stick."

"I have no hostility for the Arabs," he told the Members in
1936. "The Emir Abdullah is in Transjordania, where I put
him one Sunday afternoon in Jerusalem."

Quite a long time ago he summed up the Far Eastern situation by saying that "China, as the years pass, is being eaten
by Japan like an artichoke, leaf by leaf." Later, feeling that
this needed clarification, he told the Members that Japan's
policy was "to make hell while the sun shines."

"France," he said, "though armed to the teeth, is pacifist
to the core."

Of his mother's native land, he noted sarcastically in 1918
that America was making great strides in helping to settle
international problems and had "proposed to send a detachment of the Young Men's Christian Association to offer moral
guidance to the Russian people."

One of the qualities most admired about Churchill in Commons is his unique gift of impenitence. He has great resistance
to embarrassment. Finding himself on the wrong side of a
question, he can switch with the speedy grace of a ballet
dancer, and explain it entertainingly. Of one prodigious leap
to safety, he said, "I acted with great promptitude. In the nick
of time, just as Mr. Snowden was rising with overwhelming
fury, I got up and withdrew [the tax on kerosene]. Was I
humiliated? Was I accused of running away? No! Everyone
said: 'How clever! How quick! How right!' Pardon me referring
to it. It was one of my best days."

The subjective strain in Churchill's remarks makes them
the more lovable. It is often difficult for him to censure a

miscreant without presenting himself in contrast. This was especially true concerning Hitler, who was driven to a belated grave by Churchill's sharp tongue. "Then Hitler made his second great blunder," said the latter in discussing the German Army's round trip to Moscow. "He forgot about the winter. There is a winter, you know, in Russia. For a good many months the temperature is apt to fall very low. There is snow, there is frost, and all that. Hitler forgot about this Russian winter. He must have been very loosely educated. We all heard about it at school, but he forgot it. I have never made such a bad mistake as that."

From the start, it has been understood that Churchill gets as much enjoyment out of his parliamentary antics as his colleagues do. When it was decided to hold secret sessions in wartime, he showed up for the first one in high humor. Arising and looking around at the austere, spectatorless chamber, he led off by saying, "Isn't this fun?"

Oddly enough, while being pretty generally busy breaching the rules, he is by far the most furious Member when somebody else departs from them. On one occasion, badgering an Opposition orator by jumping up every few seconds to interpolate "supplementaries," he was astounded to hear the presiding officer, known as the Speaker, call out, "Really, you know, we simply can't have this gate-crashing by the right honorable gentleman." Churchill stopped and swung around slowly, frozen by the unaccustomed slang from a dignitary of normally impeccable diction. Moreover, the Speaker, Clifton Brown, was a Conservative and had rebuked his own party boss. Churchill executed a stiff but savage bow, made a few formally apologetic remarks that sounded peculiarly like curses, and sat down. But he was cool to Brown for weeks.

There has always been some dispute about the aside that Churchill tacked onto his famous speech in which he promised that "We shall fight on the beaches," and in other local spots. After crying out the now familiar repetitions, accenting the "We shall fights" like hammer blows, he finished, then added a half-whispered comment as he sat down. The best authorities say that his words were: "But God knows what we'll fight with." The version of the speech that he broadcast carried a positive amplification of this aside. One of England's highest clergymen, who was present in the studio, reports that Churchill ended his speech, placed his hand over the microphone, and added, "And we will hit them over the heads with beer bottles, which is about all we have got to work with."

# Chapter 17

CHURCHILL's reputation as a wit in Commons began in connection with one of his departures from Tory principles. He had not been seated a month before it was evident that his tastes were frequently to run counter to those of his party leaders. Not only did he advocate a soft peace for the Boers, who were doggedly holding out against the best military brains Britain could muster, but he created an uproar by savagely attacking a proposed high military budget. It was no wonder that Brodrick, the War Minister, confused Churchill with his father, for this last measure was the very one against which Lord Randolph had shattered his best lances. But it was the question of Free Trade that separated Churchill with real emphasis from his fellow Conservatives. When Joseph Chamberlain abandoned the historic laissez-faire policy for tariff protection, with particular reference to Birmingham industries, Churchill arose in the House and said, "Mr. Chamberlain loves the workingman, he loves to see him work."

As his father had done, the hero of Pretoria steered a small group of dissidents away from the official party course. They included Ian (later Sir Ian) Malcolm, Lord Hugh Cecil, and Ivor Guest (later Lord Wimborne), Churchill's cousin, and were much relished by the press, which referred to them by various nicknames worked out from the names of the participants—"Malcolmtents," "Hughligans," etc. Churchill became so exercised about Free Trade and the workingman that he was scarcely distinguishable from his old running mate, the late Mawdsley. He took his best friend, Hugh Cecil, and spent the summer of 1903 barnstorming directly on the heels of Joseph Chamberlain, who was speaking from town to town in favor of "Free Trade Within the Empire." The fact that the Hughligans were coming up astern was said to have nettled Chamberlain to the point where he forsook his message and spent most of his time preaching about the immature absurdities of Churchill, whom he took to be the instigator of practically everything troublesome in that era. The net result of this was very beneficial to the mop-up pair; Chamberlain's blasts acted as a kind of preliminary billing; he was cast in the role of advance man, like Frank Braden with the Ringling Brothers Circus.

By the time Churchill and Cecil reached a town, everybody was stimulated to receive them, sometimes with cheers and encouragement and occasionally with ropes. They were almost lynched in Birmingham, Chamberlain's native city. Birmingham was a traditionally impulsive spot, from which Lloyd George, after a pacifist rally, had recently withdrawn in safety only by donning a policeman's uniform. Warned that a genuinely hostile crowd was planning a necktie party, in the Western term, Churchill drove his carriage into the midst of the people, lit a cigar, got down leisurely, and made a path to the speaking platform, puffing away as serenely as if he had been in the Carlton Club. At first stunned, the crowd finally relaxed and then cheered him in admiration.

Churchill had some club trouble on this trip. In one town, he and Cecil repaired to the Conservative Club only to find themselves locked out. From the front windows a number of indignant, elderly faces stared down, and several bony fists were brandished. Churchill shrugged and led his comrade to a pub, where they found refreshment just as satisfying.

The incident was one of a series that ended in a sensational move by Churchill. Continuing, he wrote to one Liberal candidate wishing him success against his protectionist Conservative opponent; then, at a meeting in Halifax, he ended a speech

by crying, "Thank God we have a Liberal Party"; and in the
House he arose during a Liberal address to say, "Mr. Speaker,
I rise to a point of order. I am quite unable to hear what my
honorable friend is saying owing to the vulgar clamor maintained by the Conservative Party." At his constituency of Oldham, the Conservative Association passed a resolution saying
that he had "forfeited its confidence" and officially disowned
him. Then occurred a spontaneous group discourtesy that has
no parallel before or since in the House of Commons. When
Churchill essayed another speech, Arthur Balfour, who had
succeeded Lord Salisbury as Prime Minister, and the rest of
the Conservatives got up and filed out noisily. To reduce the
scene to bedrock comedy, each one except Balfour paused in
the doorway and jeered at Churchill like a schoolboy. In its
way, the episode brought him as much notoriety as his escape
from the Boers.

The fact is that Churchill touched off one of the racketiest
sessions the House has ever known. In the succeeding debates,
the antagonists descended to a name-calling remarkably
sprightly for Englishmen. A Colonel Kenyon-Slaney had the
effrontery to call Churchill a traitor; the accused replied, "I
have noticed that when political controversy becomes excited,
persons of choleric dispositions and limited intelligence are
apt to become rude. If I was a traitor, at any rate I was fighting the Boers in South Africa when Colonel Kenyon-Slaney
was slandering them at home. I had the honor of serving in the
field for our country while this gallant, fire-eating colonel was
content to kill Kruger with his mouth in the comfortable security of England."

A young Conservative, Claude Lowther, tensely informed
the House that beriberi was known to have broken out in
South Africa and suggested that Churchill had contracted the
disease. He documented this diagnosis by saying that "I made
that remark because I have heard that the most marked
characteristic symptom of the disease is a terrific swelling of
the head."

Churchill got up and changed seats, moving over to the Liberal side, from which he conducted a heckling campaign of Joseph Chamberlain that is still fondly remembered. In rebuttal, the Conservatives raised such a howl every time he opened his mouth that the usually decorous Parliament came to a complete standstill. Raising his voice over the din, Churchill shouted that the chaos was a calculated "conspiracy" in which Chamberlain was an "accomplice." There were shocked cries of "Oh, oh!" and Chamberlain came bouncing out of his seat like a man stung by a wasp. This slur from a stripling on one of England's most venerated servants was regarded as beyond the pale, and Churchill made a sort of apology. In general, however, he continued his agitations.

Psychiatrists have observed that a few people appear destined to envelop themselves in trouble, as Jove wrapped thunderclouds around his head. Something about the atmospheric conditions when they are born, perhaps an uncommon presence of static electricity, produces a low equanimity quotient. They are the destroyers of serenity, and the builders of the world. Churchill is pre-eminently one of these. He fixed his course very early in his career: he chose to row upstream and drag trouble along in his wake. His appearance in the House on any day was sufficient to ruffle Members of established torpor. His facial expression—bellicose, tardy, unconvinced, and half pouting—drew rejoinders automatically. Often there was no need for him to speak; somebody, after a glance at him, would spring up and shout, in effect, "You're another." He put Arthur Balfour to flight so consistently that he thoughtfully cautioned, as one session got under way, "The right honorable gentleman need not run away. I am not attacking him today."

To add to his stress, Churchill was trying to change his methods of oratory at this time. Heretofore he had memorized his speeches and rehearsed them carefully. Now (for a brief while) he was trying to improvise from notes. It was tough going. He found that he had a genius for digression; his mind wandered off on side issues, all of them entertaining. On one occasion he marshaled his thoughts successfully for nearly an hour, arrived at the last paragraph of his remarks, stammered, floundered, and then collapsed in his seat. The press was instantly alerted to the similarity of this breakdown to one Lord Randolph had suffered in the House shortly before the end. Several theories were advanced, including the suggestion that his recreational habits were sapping. It was true that Churchill, in this period of his closing twenties, went at his amusements as though he were attacking Tories. He had been making the rounds of the ducal houses of his acquaintance, enjoying convivial dinners, dances, and hunts. He was still especially fond of both hunting and polo and had suffered a painful accident while engaged in the former. At one meeting, during which the fox had shown an annoying reluctance to give up its brush, Churchill had ricocheted off a horse and broken his shoulder. The injury had healed but in doing so had not improved his general health.

His close friends in these days included Lord Hugh Cecil (later to calm down amazingly, become Lord Quickswood and Provost of Eton College); Max Aitken, a young Canadian-born promoter who had come to England for the candid purpose of making money (and would succeed admirably as Lord Beaverbrook, the publisher); and one of the genuinely gifted roisterers of all time, F. E. ("Galloper") Smith, who is still considered in many clubs the greatest drinker England has produced. Smith (who in the inevitable upper-class progression finally got to be Lord Birkenhead, as well as a famous trial lawyer) once remarked of his friend, "Mr. Churchill is easily satisfied with the best." The latter's companions were forever saying memorable things about him. Max Aitken told a reporter, "I would pay five pounds an hour just to listen to him talk." While one and another of this group was noted for special talents—Aitken for spotting cash, Smith for his ability to haul genies out of bottles, etc.—Churchill was hailed as the most talkative young man in England and her Colonies (including India). His monologues at dinners were renowned for the brilliant variety of their topics and for the expediency of their classical allusions, a gift from Bartlett's *Familiar Quotations*. Unquestionably the rising politician was, and is, one of the most eloquent conversationalists ever known, inferior to the clacking Johnson only in the technical sense that he had no long-suffering Boswell.

His political associates formed a scintillating collection. Besides some of the men just named, there were John Morley, who had written a biography of Gladstone; Ivor Guest; Sir Gilbert Parker, the novelist; Major Jack Seely; Sir John Gorst, his father's old political ally; Gibson Bowles; Reginald McKenna; and, incongruously enough, Walter Runciman, who had just got back into Parliament as Liberal Member for Dewsbury. Churchill was not in the least embarrassed to find himself shoulder to shoulder with Runciman after all the mean things they had said about each other. Merely reminding the shipping heir of his prediction that "the world has not heard the last of either of us," Churchill went ahead denouncing the Tories and their tariffs. Leader of the Liberals was Sir Henry Campbell-Bannerman, and it was understood that young Herbert Asquith would succeed him, but the flaming Welsh orator, David Lloyd George, was still the undisputed party prodigy.

This was a peevish situation for Churchill, who preferred to be the party prodigy himself. He found in general that going over to the Liberals had its drawbacks. High on his list of complaints was the fact that the Marlborough family dropped him for a space, cutting off a bountiful source of influence near the Crown. The Marlboroughs and many others of his Tory connections balked at some of the things he had begun to advocate. The list now looks unbelievable, in view of the successful propaganda the Socialists have spread about Churchill, describing him as the arch-enemy of labor and a professional warmonger. "When one considers how vast the Labour interest is," he said in a speech at this time, "how vital, how human; when one considers the gigantic powers which by the consent of both Parties have been given to the working classes; when, on the other hand, one considers the influence on this House of company directors, the learned professions, the service members, the railway, landed and liquor interests; it will surely be admitted that the influence of Labour on the course of legislation is even ludicrously small." He campaigned so forcibly in favor of stopping the war that he became known as "Peace-at-any-Price Churchill." His argument was that the struggle should be "ended with a handshake."

Despite the corrosive malice of Socialist and Communist publicity, it is difficult to construe these as the attitudes of a warmongering labor-hater.

## II

In the Churchill household, the general election of 1880 had ushered in a time of mourning, with the Liberal Gladstone throwing the Tories, including Winston's grandfather, out of office. Now a strange cycle was being completed: the general election of 1906 again removed the Tories from power, but in doing so it established Winston Churchill, the Liberal, as a Cabinet minister. (His appointment had actually taken place some weeks previously, when the Conservatives had failed to form a government.) Lord Randolph had attained Cabinet rank at the precocious age of thirty-six; his son clipped five years from this record. Churchill's post—Under-Secretary for the Colonies—was relatively unimposing, but in securing it he continued the legend of Boy Wonder, adding another to his string of infant stupendities. The outcome of the election also perpetuated his history of stunning good luck. Oldham having given Churchill a disapproving eye, he accepted a constituency in Manchester, from which a popular Conservative Member had just retired, to be replaced by candidate William Joynson-Hicks, a temperance lecturer and church devotee.

Churchill's meetings got off to a mediocre start. After one speech at the Coal Exchange, a number of people rushed the stairs to watch him leave, but they overshot their mark and all tumbled down, injuring several. A few days later he was declaiming in well-oiled style at a large public building when the crowd cheered, there was a noisy crash, and about half of the group disappeared, the stands having fallen into the bed of a swimming pool. Seeing that the damage was slight, Churchill cried out strongly, "Let justice be done, even though the floor falls in!"

It seemed that his fights for public office could never be ordinary. He and his opponent were again in odd contrast on the platform. While Joynson-Hicks was for the Church and against whiskey, Churchill was in favor of whiskey and critical of the Church. And although the issues of the day transcended these two points, religion did play an eccentric part in the contest. During one speech, Churchill declared against the Government's Aliens Bill and made a few affectionate remarks about Zionism. The Manchester Jews promptly fell in line behind him as though he were a kind of latter-day Moses. One of their leaders got up at an all-Jewish meeting and announced that "any Jew who votes against Winston Churchill is a traitor to the common cause." Another suggested the slogan, "Vote for Winston the Winsome." The candidate modestly amended this by saying that "On Saturday, after the poll, you may call me Winston the winner."

The unfortunate Joynson-Hicks, cleaving stoutly to his principles, jarred the Jewish contingent by declining to address an audience of them on Sunday. "Never," he cried, with a pious and sober gesture toward the heavens, "never so long as I am your candidate or your member, will I go electioneering on a Sunday!" That settled it. The Jews all went down and voted for Churchill, who enjoyed electioneering on Sunday, there being little else to do except go to church. Joynson-Hicks remained their candidate a great deal longer than he was their member. When the results were in, Manchester had embraced

the unreconstructed Churchill; his opponent went back to good
works and resumed his vilification of the demon rum.

### III

Churchill's cause in the election was considered by many
to have been helped by a brilliant biography of his father that
he had just published. In two volumes, it had the unqualified
praise of practically every critic and literary person in the
kingdom, including those of contrary political beliefs. Lord
Rosebery, who also had written about Lord Randolph, called
it "little less than marvelous" and "one to be marked among
the first dozen, perhaps the first half-dozen, biographies in our
language."

During this election there had flown into Churchill's life the
screeching magpie of Woman's Suffrage. From a distance of
fifty years it is hard to determine why the movement selected
him as its personal devil. Something about his face, something
emphatically male in his attitude, acted on the ladies like
catnip. The mention of his name once started a free-for-all in
the dining saloon of a train, painfully injuring an elderly man
reading a sporting journal, and a group of suffragettes were
removed from the street of one northern city while pelting an
enlarged picture of Churchill with dried apricots. The tocsin
had been sounded by Miss Sylvia Pankhurst, a member of an
old and distinguished family, who announced abruptly that
"in Winston Churchill the Liberal Government will receive
the weight of the women's opposition." Her campaign tactics,
presented candidly, were to appear at his meetings and break
them up, tearing down the stands if necessary. Accordingly, as
Churchill, Sir Edward Grey, and Lord Durham mounted one
platform in Manchester, a paralyzing uproar broke out in the
rear of the crowd and a flying wedge of aroused females, wearing the bonnets and badges of their guild, came charging to the
fore, where they wrought ingenious havoc. Sir Edward Grey

was, as he afterward said, "jostled," and Lord Durham was
clapped over the head with an umbrella. Churchill got off
scot-free, if some fairly bisexual epithets may be discounted.

The meeting might easily have had melancholy results had
it not been for the opportune arrival of the police, who had
come with strong reinforcements, it being widely known that
a suffragette in full cry can fight like a tiger. Miss Pankhurst
and her chief of staff, a Miss Kenney, were lodged in the nearest lockup, whence they issued a formal statement, their first
communiqué of the war. It affirmed their refusal to be bailed
out by "anything in pants." The next day, in communiqué No.
2, same sector, they declared that Churchill had visited the jail
and offered money; they had hustled him on his way. The commanders were then fined but on principle they elected to sit it
out rather than pay up. This was held by the press to be obtuse,
in view of the fact that the Pankhurst family was extremely
wealthy and could have bailed out all the women in Manchester, had the occasion arisen.

After their release, Miss Pankhurst and Miss Kenney organized their battalions in a drive to plaster all the posters of
Churchill with pictures of Miss Pankhurst and Miss Kenney,
together with paragraphs on their credo. Churchill then issued
a communiqué of his own, declaring that he was being "henpecked." He was so miserably harassed that Joynson-Hicks, a
man of ironclad character, made a public appeal for fair play.
For his pains he was advised that the suffragettes' actions "will
be determined without reference to the words of yourself *or*
of your opponent." Soon afterward, at a meeting in a hall, Miss
Pankhurst was invited to the platform to ask questions—it was
the only way Churchill could contrive to prevent her from having hysterics in the audience. Once seated on the platform,
however, Miss Pankhurst took him so literally that she jumped
up with a question every time he opened his mouth. Also, she
had a trick, possibly just a nervous habit, of going "yah, yah,
yah" between questions. Churchill has never been the most
patient man in the world, and he finally exploded. "You are

bringing disgrace upon an honored name," he told her, and then he shouted (nailing down his perfidy forever in the eyes of the suffragettes), "Nothing would induce me to vote for giving women the franchise. I am not going to be henpecked into a question of such importance."

What transpired has been described by Miss Pankhurst in her book, *The Suffragette Movement,* which compares favorably in spirit with *Mein Kampf.* "I would have gone then," her account went, "but in a scuffle, during which all the men on the platform stood up to hide what was happening from the audience, I was pushed into a side room. I was left there, the door being locked on the outside, but not before I had opened the window and called to the people in the side street to witness the conduct of an enthusiastic Liberal who was jumping about like a madman and threatening to scratch my face. It appeared that I was a prisoner, for the windows were barred, but the people who had gathered outside called to me that a window at the other end of the room had a couple of bars missing. They helped me out and called for a speech. When the night's talking was done, I gave my story to the press. It appeared with big headlines next day, producing innumerable jokes at the candidate's expense. There was no more kidnapping."

The merry spat continued. Indeed it went on without any interruption except for the First World War until as late as 1928, when unlimited suffrage was belatedly passed by Parliament. The situation was not eased by the abrupt participation of Rudyard Kipling, who wrote a rather violent anti-women poem for the *Evening Standard* entitled, *The Female of the Species.* During this fretful period Churchill remained the leading scapegoat, harried and derided, but Asquith, who succeeded Campbell-Bannerman as Prime Minister in 1908, was the bitterest foe of the movement. Eventually Churchill came to profess a sort of unaggressive regard for the women's vote, but the tragic fact is that nobody believed him. Wherever he went, the ladies followed. The gruff bark of his Pied Piper's voice sent a queue of angry reformers dancing through the streets.

They snapped and bayed at his public speeches. In Bristol he stepped off a train and was horsewhipped by one Theresa Garnett, a sublieutenant of the Order, whose demoniac cries indicated her belief that he had once said, "These ladies ought to be horsewhipped." This was incorrect; it was another member of the Liberal Party who had made the remark. So Churchill took the trouncing for nothing. Struck once across the face, he warded off further blows by throwing up an arm, and jumped back into his car. The gentle Garnett was led off to the jail (already crowded with her sisters) and charged with being a public nuisance. When Churchill made inquiries about her health, she issued the usual statement saying she had no personal antagonism against him but had hit him in the face as a means of showing her general aptitude for politics. Churchill's reply was, it is said, that he would never dream of taking the horsewhipping personally.

He was not much hurt—only a rosy welt remained—and he proceeded to Colston Hall, where he dined on a terrace, while a friend of Miss Garnett's threw stones at him from the roof of an adjoining building. The shots were wide. One waiter carrying a dish of soup was struck on the foot; otherwise the meal was normal. At a meeting in Bradford a male suffragette (a good many had joined the cause, most of them youths of goldfish-swallowing intellect from universities like Oxford and Cambridge) was so forcibly ejected from the hall that his leg was broken. There followed a noisy hue and cry. His female supporters claimed that his conduct had not been sufficiently eccentric for such punishment—he had only been shouting, "Honk! Honk!" and breaking eggs on his head. But the sting persisted until one of his fellows, an acne-ridden child suckled by Mid-Victorian poets, assaulted Churchill in a train corridor. "Take this, you dirty cur," cried the suffragette, and lashed at the Minister with a dog whip. By this time Churchill was traveling with a corps of "detectives," or bodyguards, and they caught the impassioned collegian in time. Later on, in police court, the defendant based his demand for release on an allega-

tion that he had been misquoted. "I did *not* say 'You dirty
cur,' " he told the magistrate, stamping his foot, "I only said,
'You cur.' " The ruling was that, adjective or no adjective, attention must be centered on the dog whip.

At one political dinner party, attendants rushed in to
Churchill with the news that suffragettes were chaining themselves to railings in the public square and would stay there
until they received the vote. Churchill answered loudly, "A
man might as well chain himself to the railings of St. Thomas
Hospital and say he wouldn't move until he has had a baby."
(His moderate conversion to suffrage came sometime after
this.) Despite his witticism, the movement continued apace. In
1907 there occurred the well-known "Mud March" through
London. The ladies had thought to conduct a large public
demonstration in order to arouse sympathy over their voteless
plight. They printed a great many placards, laid in a supply of
chalk with which to scribble messages on sidewalks and buildings, and got spruced up in suffrage finery, a kind of festive
black with belligerently shaped bonnets. By misfortune, a
whopper of a downpour started up two hours before the event,
and the ladies ran into as much trouble as the Children of Israel
had getting out of Egypt. Their path lay through many dirt
lanes, paving being spotty in those days, and before long the
demonstration had all the earmarks of a hog wallow. To their
credit, it must be said that the suffragettes were not dismayed
by the experience. In a sort of religious frenzy they took to
the gumbo, whooping, splashing, and stumbling. A report that
a number of them had been hitting things up in a pub was never
proved, but several did make so free with the mud that three
shopowners were compelled to summon the law. If the purpose
of the march was to provoke interest, the event was successful,
for people came forth to look who hadn't been out in the rain
for years. Their convulsed laughter rocked through the city.

The ladies took these attentions as complimentary and organized several more demonstrations, which went off unremarked, the weather having refused to co-operate, turning fine.

A gaudier scheme was then devised. It was announced from one headquarters, a corset works, that any suffragettes arrested would knock off eating. No more food until they were released. At first, the authorities were bored, and then worried. The ladies lounged about the prisons, very gaunt, declining nourishment with such martyred sighs that the turnkeys quit eating in sympathy. Parliament thereupon stepped into the crisis with the Prisoners Temporary Discharge for Ill Health Act, popularly known as the "Cat and Mouse Act." It provided that women released for hunger-striking could be rearrested when they had got their strength back. It was a curious law. Under it, the irrepressible Miss Pankhurst was collared and tossed into jail eight times. Her weight went up and down like a barometer. She would be arrested, say for throwing a brick through a plate-glass window, setting fire to a mailbox, and hitting a policeman with a wagon tongue, and would sit down and go foodless for five days, and then would be turned loose. A detective assigned to follow her would decide, perhaps on the following Tuesday, that she was back up to par and restore her to the lockup, where she would cut off the calories again. And so it went everywhere.

The suffragettes actually defeated Churchill in 1908. Upon the death of Campbell-Bannerman, Asquith, who succeeded him, reappointed Churchill to the Cabinet but in a superior post, that of President of the Board of Trade. He followed Lloyd George, who was advanced to be Chancellor of the Exchequer. By an old ruling, it was necessary for such an appointee to go to his constituency again. Churchill found himself facing his former opponent, the pious Joynson-Hicks, in a by-election at Northwest Manchester. The suffragettes turned out by the hundreds, making his meetings a nightmare of confusion. Joynson-Hicks, on the other hand, was able to bawl on without interruption in favor of ecclesiastics and pink lemonade. When the returns were in, Churchill was out, by a score of 5517 to 4988. As he was leaving the Town Hall, a wildly celebrating suffragette seized his arm and yelled, "It's the women who have done this—now you will understand that we must have our vote." Churchill angrily wrenched his arm free and said, "Get away, woman."

His defeat had a silver lining: he received a telegram inviting him to stand from a constituency in Dundee, Scotland, where a vacancy had been caused by the raising of Edmund Robertson to the peerage. This was certainly a blow to the suffragettes after their exhausting crusade in Manchester, but they rallied with spirit. In fact, they assigned one of their ablest field workers, a specialist, to the zone. It should be explained that, in the movement, particular skills were encouraged. A few women were deadly accurate with rocks and empty bottles, others could outrun the speediest police. One worker, no more than a child, could "heehaw" like a jackass, and a representative from Bath was a virtuoso on the ticktack, or window-rattler. The emissary assigned to Dundee was a Miss Malony, with a very high rating. Her line was carrying a large brass bell around and clanging it during speeches. It was a neat contrivance and had earned her the sobriquet, amongst her fellows and the press, of "La Bell Malony." At Dundee Miss Malony laid into her instrument with the selfless zeal that had seen Miss Pankhurst jailed eight times for irregular eating habits. However, according to newspaper advices of the region, the Dundeeites did not take kindly to the obbligato, but admonished her, in the local idiom, to "gang awa' and mak' your perritch."

La Bell Malony rang on, and Churchill, at one point deafened by the clamor, stopped his speech and sat down to smoke a cigarette. "I won't attempt to compete with a young and pretty lady in a high state of excitement," he told the crowd. "It's no use your being cross," returned Miss Malony sternly. Her severity was not unique in the campaign. Churchill's opponent this time, destroying all the laws of probability, was a Mr. Scrymgeour, whose sole claim on the public was a wild compulsion to spread teetotalism. As if Joynson-Hicks and his temperance were not enough, along came Scrymgeour to babble about chopping down the distilleries and pouring all the alcohol into the sea. It was almost too much for Churchill, who rarely ascended a platform without having a few warming nips beforehand. Luckily for him, Dundee was about the least likely place in the world for Scrymgeour to get his desiccated start. The pleasant constituency had earned the name, through municipal pride and devoted effort, of being "the drunkenest city in Scotland." The louder Scrymgeour brayed for abstinence, the more people flocked to gaze on the convivial countenance of Churchill. And as Malony futilely dingdonged, he carried the election, leaving Scrymgeour to ponder a more arid locality. Unquenched, in true suffrage style, La Bell accompanied the victor to the railroad station, clanging away beside his carriage. But she didn't look happy. Churchill had evened his score with the ladies.

# Chapter 18

AT THE HEIGHT of his bedevilment by suffragettes, Churchill got married. The event was the fashionable climax of an especially gay year in London. Several other Cabinet ministers, spurred on by the success of the Liberal Party, also took wives. Churchill's was a distinguished beauty, Miss Clementine Hozier, whose father, Colonel Sir H. M. Hozier, had been an officer of the 3rd Dragoons and was for many years before his death secretary of Lloyd's. The bride's mother was Lady Blanche Ogilvy, daughter of the Countess of Airlie, of the principal family in Dundee. Churchill and Miss Hozier had first met at a house party and it was through her people's influence that he was provided with his new constituency.

The wedding took place in September of 1908 in the hyperexclusive St. Margaret's Church, the little church that sits in the yard of Westminster Abbey. For a pageant of such precise ritual, everything went off splendidly, with the exception that Churchill was reported to be wearing brown shoes. There was universal agreement on the handsome appearance of the bride; Churchill's was described by one guest as being "powerful if ugly." When the couple marched down the aisle, Lord Rosebery remarked. "There go two lively chips—the marriage won't last six months." The groom had gathered his intimates and drinking companions around him (Hugh Cecil was his best man), and in the words of one of his biographers, he seemed to have been in a "less solemn mood than anyone else." Besides his close friends, one of the largest crowds that ever to this day has thronged the churchyard turned out to wish the couple well. Then as now the country was about equally divided between those who favored Churchill and those who opposed him, but everybody has always been proud to have him around.

The wedding presents were piled high, including handsome ones from the King and Queen and from all the members of the Cabinet. A fractional breakdown showed 25 pairs of candlesticks, 21 inkstands, 15 vases, 20 bowls, 10 cigarette cases, 14 trays, and 8 salt and pepper sets. Churchill in this period had made a speech in which he spoke bitterly of the "vulgar and joyless luxuries" of the Tory rich, but he took his bride on a brief honeymoon to his ancestral home of Blenheim Palace, where they enjoyed many of its vulgar luxuries, and then they journeyed to Lake Maggiore, in Italy. Their first domicile was a small house in Queen Anne's Gate, an establishment organized inexpensively, since neither the bride nor the groom had an independent income, although Churchill had added thirty thousand dollars to his savings as proceeds from the biography of Lord Randolph. They shortly moved to a slightly more pretentious home in Eccleston Square. From those first happy days of their marriage until recently, the Churchills have been hard-pressed to find sufficient funds with which to meet their standard of living.

The groom's departure from solemnity at his wedding was indeed unusual at this time. His habits had undergone changes of late. The carousing with his spirited comrades had given way to a solemn, if refreshment-fortified, perusal of his career. Before his marriage he had occupied a flat in Bruton Street with his brother, Major John Churchill, a bond salesman who had no particular ambition and was as festive as anybody around town, a prime figure at the dances and other entertainments. Brother Winston had given these up; he went mainly to functions that combined business with pleasure—club luncheons attended by politicians and quiet soirées of the policy-makers.

On the rare occasions when he did attend a social event, he was the instant center of the group, almost certain to say something biting and memorable. A contemporary wrote, "When he emerges, however, he imposes his personality on the company. His is not the studied effectiveness of Mr. Bernard Shaw in earlier days, when the young dramatist-novelist-Fabian would visit a party to deliver a prepared epigram and then hasten elsewhere to repeat it. Churchill's *bon mots* are spontaneous."

The years from 1907 to the First World War were ones of violent change for Churchill in several ways. As Under-Secretary for the Colonies he had embraced many liberal, and even socialistic, measures; as President of the Board of Trade he entered upon a course that then constituted dangerous radicalism. He became what one of his affectionate biographers has ruefully described as "the most hated politician in the country." The phase represented, perhaps, a variation of his love for the adventurous and the new. After his years of literary barnstorming, Churchill was finding the life of a serious legislator a little stifling. And before his term as Under-Secretary had ended, he had been able to concoct a sort of good-will tour, during which he could survey a few of the lands of his charge, and have some fun. Ever alert for business opportunities, he also took the precaution of obtaining a commission from *Strand* magazine to do several articles on his travels, at fancy rates.

His route lay past Malta and Cyprus through the Red Sea to Mombasa, thence by way of British East Africa, Uganda, and the Sudan to Cairo, and then back home. He had a lot of interesting experiences. Members of his African safaris said afterward that he was the most undisciplined man on a hunt it had ever been their misfortune to attend. He often refused to obey even the ordinary rules of safety. On one occasion, advised to give a movement of army ants a wide berth, he investigated, was surrounded, fell down, and, in escaping in the nick of time, abandoned a prized walking stick, which was devoured. Behaving with caution, Churchill shot a white rhino, but in the hottest lion country of Uganda he insisted on ventur-

ing out alone with a makeshift butterfly net (looking for butterflies). He took innumerable pictures with which to imple-
ment his articles, but was dissuaded from trying to photograph
crocodiles while floating down the Nile on a log. It was noted
that he argued politics with everybody, including native chiefs
whose English was pretty well limited to "Me thirty-two wives"
and "Gottum baccy?" In Kampala he tried to moderate the
time-honored noise of the rickshaw coolies, who egg themselves on with strange and impetuous cries. He relented when
it was pointed out that silence was taking all the spring out of
their legs. A strange coincidence was that, approaching Khartoum, before which he had seen so much bloodshed and sorrow, his valet fell ill and died, and was buried the next day.
Churchill stood in melancholy silence by the grave, not far
from the spot where, a few years ago, he had saved the life of
a newborn baby.

The tour aroused some criticism, but it was trifling compared to the over-all criticism that Churchill had begun to
reap. The Liberal Party as a whole, after a bland voyage of
two years, was running into the first signs of heavy weather.
An English political student wrote that the Liberal landslide
of 1906 "went too far." Nothing could hide the fact, he added,
that the ranks of the Government were "honey-combed with
cranks, faddists, pacifists, and other strange political wild
fowl." Churchill was doing his part in championing unpopular
measures. He fought hard for the Miners' Eight Hours Bill,
the Scottish Small-landholders' Act, the Labour Exchanges Act
(a means of combating unemployment), and the Old Age Pensions Bill. As President of the Board of Trade, he introduced
a Port of London Bill, which established government control
over all the docks and wharves in the port. In arguing for this
legislation, he told the House that, if the bill was not passed,
"the docks, which have already been called obsolescent, will
have to be allowed to obsolesce into obsoleteness."

Without doubt he was the hardest-working minister ever to
fill his position, given to stints far into the night at his White-

hall office and in Commons, and to incessant trips of inspection. He visited the famous shipyards at Newcastle, where the local suffragettes were so grateful that they deployed behind stacks of cargo and pelted him with coke. Their inverse allegiance to Churchill was unshaken; they never let him down. When he took his bride along on a speaking journey to Southport, three women ascended to the roof of the hall and bellowed at him through ventilators. The new Mrs. Churchill waved to them sweetly. Friends of the Churchills say that the bride was worried about her husband's travail in this period; she was especially so when it was erroneously reported that he had entered a night session in Commons clad in a pair of pink pajamas. Churchill was disregardful of his dress then, as he is now. There had been a tremendous hubbub over his appearance at Windsor Castle when King Edward elevated him to the status of Privy Councilor. For a hundred years, ritual had prescribed that the new Privy Councilors be uniformly dressed in tail coats. On the occasion of Churchill's visit everybody was rigged out impeccably except him. He had on a kind of old cutaway that looked as though it might have been handed down by his great-grandfather. The audience was shocked; however, the King chose not to see it. He even kept Churchill for a chat after the others had gone.

When the opposition to the Liberal Party became serious in 1910, a general election was held in which Churchill was again returned from Dundee, defeating the parched Scrymgeour. In the new Liberal Cabinet, the former President of the Board of Trade was advanced to the post of Home Secretary, and he promptly redoubled his work on the House of Lords, where his ancestors had sat in comfortable torpor, all unaware of the black sheep who was to come along and attack their sanctuary. Churchill's comrade, F. E. Smith, a Conservative, finally took umbrage at his reckless language about the Upper House and exploded in Commons with a very uncomradely speech. "The Home Secretary is beginning to play Lady Macbeth to the Prime Minister's Thane of Cawdor," he said. "No more shameful speech has ever been made by a member of the Commons than that in which the Home Secretary said, 'The time has come for the Crown and the Commons acting together, to override the Lords.' Everyone knows that the Home Secretary does not mean that the Crown and the House of Commons are to act together. What he means is that the time has come for the Crown and the Liberal Party and the Labour Party and the Irish Party to act together and go against the House of Lords. This is an insolent appropriation of the name of the Sovereign to purely Party purposes. It is analagous, physically, to the act of striking a woman."

In many parts of the United States these frank words would have ended a happy friendship, probably with gunfire, but Churchill and Smith shortly went off together on a yachting trip, during which they had many a chuckle over their political rages. They were particularly amused, it is said, because a report had recently been current that the two foregathered before sessions and set up their bombastic tangles, providing one another with leads upon which to base the waspish epithets that aroused such widespread dismay. Their trip was aboard the Baron de Forest's yacht, *Honor,* whose party included Churchill and his bride, Mr. and Mrs. Smith, Churchill's brother, and several others. In most ways it was a typical outing of Churchill's. At Vesuvius the group, save for him, made the usual spiral ascent to the top. Churchill chose to climb in a beeline from the base. Inevitably getting stuck on an impossible slope, he had to be taken off by a rescue unit. Somewhat later, he had the good sense to turn back when Smith, after a number of champagne cocktails, elected to swim the harbor at Syracuse and write an original poem on the Messina earthquake. Smith contributed several skillful touches to the holiday. At Crete the officials had planned a gigantic welcome for the Home Secretary, but Smith, having arisen earlier than the others, went ashore and allowed himself to be feted by error. He professed an extraordinary interest in the production of Cretan wines and was persuaded, as Home Secretary, to sample most of them. Churchill finally turned up, rather hastily dressed, and explained the situation to everybody's great embarrassment except Smith's, who kept smiling at the baffled officials and giving them to understand, in a sort of patois, that he was not on a very solid footing in either Greek *or* English.

Not long after the yachting trip, Churchill was entangled in the separate incidents involving "Peter the Painter" and the "Dartmoor Shepherd," which netted him about the usual amount of abuse. In the first case, a gang of Russian desperados under the leadership of one Peter the Painter, whose real name was Jacob Peters, broke into a Houndsditch jeweler's and, in escaping, shot and killed three policemen. The public, always on the prowl for an easy culprit, decided that Churchill, as Home Secretary, was somehow negligent. He was therefore relieved when, soon afterward, the gang was bottled up in a house in nearby Sidney Street, a poor and run-down section. The news got around fast. Before very long the scene resembled New York around the Gotham Hotel when a man stood on a seventeenth-story ledge the whole day through before leaping to his death. As more and more London police rushed to Sidney Street, the Painter and his associates poured a steady fire from the windows of their squalid citadel. Under their barrage, a policeman went down and was hauled back for treatment. Besides the crowds in the street, every window in the neighborhood was bursting with the morbid curious.

Churchill arrived just before noon, wearing a silk hat and a black opera cape. He looked a little as though a professional dresser had made him up to play Auguste Dupin in a suburban presentation of *The Murders in the Rue Morgue*. He was full of enterprise, shouting, waving, and pacing back and forth within easy range of the criminals. He had not come alone; the Scots Guards from the Tower of London marched in a few moments later, and then came an artillery piece from the St. John's Wood Barracks. It was the first time the Scots Guards had been called out since 1820. In a twinkling, what with the field gun booming, the Guards kneeling and firing, and the policemen and the others trying to get out of the way, the spectacle bore a positive resemblance to the Storming of the Bastille. The result was a foregone conclusion; the house burst into flames and collapsed on its inmates, two of whose bodies were recovered. Peter the Painter had apparently escaped. He would later be identified with Bolshevist agitations.

Churchill was the goat, as always. The press and the public, which had found him negligent before, now declared that he had no business taking charge and raising such a ruckus. What did he mean coming down there with the Scots Guards and a cannon? He had turned a picturesque residence into a battlefield shambles. At the inquest, Churchill denied most of the allegations and went on his way, no more disturbed than ever at this fickle turn of mass sentiment.

The Dartmoor Shepherd provided the richest buffoonery of that year of 1911. The aged Welshman in question had a remarkable record: except for a few years in his infancy, when he was gathering strength, he had spent his entire life in jail, for a succession of mean and uninspired larcenies. David Lloyd George, a man of hasty Welsh Liberalism, chose to stir up a general belief that the unfortunate was a typical victim of "the landlord system." This was about as farfetched as excusing a triple murderer on the ground that he was reared in a tenement, but it hit the public right in the eye. "Oh, the poor old man! All those wasted years!" was the widespread feeling, and the blinking unregenerate was led out of prison, where he burst into tears and agreed wholeheartedly that he had been framed. Churchill and Lloyd George both made speeches pillorying the landlords, and Churchill found the derelict a situation at Wrexham, as caretaker. For several days the public wallowed in bathos, with many an "I told you so!" and then the Shepherd, terribly sick of his job, took two sprinkling cans and a lawnmower and went over the wall. With the proceeds from these as a new start in life, he bought some grade-A burglar's tools and took care of a nearby mansion to the tune of $112.50. Reapprehended and returned to his prison abode—one of the many fruits of the landlord system—he expressed himself as being without bitterness. The kind gentlemen, Mr. Churchill and Mr. Lloyd George, had done their best by him, and if it had not been for a neighbor's dog, the reformation would have gone through on schedule. By-passing Lloyd George, a discriminating public selected Churchill as the target for its ridicule.

Politically, he continued his near-socialistic pressures. Urging a confiscatory income tax, he made a speech saying that in the future the tax collector would not ask, "What have you got?" but "How did you get it?" In retrospect, these sound like odd words indeed from the latter-day opposition leader who would rage at British Socialism. He fought through the anti-military budget and won his feud with the House of Lords, when that hoary and paternal chamber was reduced to impotency by the Parliament Bill of 1911. One of Churchill's pet legislations, when he was Home Secretary, bounced back in his face. Despite the sad incident of the Dartmoor Shepherd, he became anxiety-ridden about the conditions in British prisons and instituted a bill carrying certain reforms, centering on lectures and concerts for the inmates. Surely, he must have thought, this will appeal to everybody, outside and in. But no, the ever faithful suffragettes raised a lamentable howl, for the singular reason that such alleviations of prison misery might tend to lessen their martyrdom. This was seen by nearly everybody as selfishness of a very high order, and the Cause, which all along had been right and just, though regrettably managed, took a sharp setback.

Like so many politicians before and after him, Churchill now found that, in the midst of his efforts for labor, the workers of the country showed their gratitude by marching out in a succession of paralyzing strikes. First came the dock strikes in South Wales, always a trouble center, where troops had to be called out to see that the strikers obeyed the laws, as ordinary citizens were compelled to do. Then came a railway strike, also attended by soldiers, and after that a complete breakdown in the weaving industry. Churchill worked hard to restore harmony everywhere. The method he favored most was to gather the disputing leaders together and ply them with liquor. As a rule the tension was eased and friendly talks followed.

II

Internationally at this time friendly talks were at a premium. The brawling state of Germany had been at peace for several years and was growing very restive. Kaiser Wilhelm II, its Emperor, a man whose main attributes of leadership were a gift for practical joking and a fondness for street carnivals, was never very interested in war, or anything adult, but his ministers and advisers, drawn from the Prussian military class, were keenly anxious to put some nation or other in its place. As usual with Germany, the principal contender was France. An opportunity for a squabble arose in 1911, when France decided to broaden the scope of its protectorate over Morocco. This was entirely within its legal right, but a pair of German industrialists, the Mannesmann brothers, complained bitterly that their commerce was being jeopardized. The Kaiser was busy when the emergency arose—he was said to be occupied in contriving a sort of hotfoot to be tried out on one of the servants (believed to be among the earliest recorded examples of this hilarious trick) and his Secretary of State, Herr von Kiderlen-Waechter, happily sent a gunboat into the Moroccan port of Agadir.

The gesture touched off a deal more anger than even Kiderlen-Waechter had bargained for. It aroused France to prompt resistance, it called the world's attention to the failing relations between the two countries, and, far more important, it kindled a great fire under Winston Churchill. The English Home Secretary now sailed off on yet another tack. During his years as war correspondent, he had been fiercely jingoistic; as a young politician he had turned pacifistic; and now, as a moderately young politician, he was yawing about again. It takes a wise and plucky man to change his mind, and in the light of history, there can be no question that Churchill almost alone saved England's skin in the First World War.

Although the Germans withdrew their gunboat, he pitched himself headlong into the cause of preparedness. He did it with habitual thoroughness. He was at a garden party when it was remarked by another minister that the nation's supply of cordite, used by the Navy, was loosely guarded.

"Under whose jurisdiction is it?" inquired the Home Secretary.

"Why, yours, I believe," replied the minister.

Churchill tossed aside a teacup and a remnant of biscuit, cried, "Good-by!" and rushed from the scene, with a lot of curious eyes staring after him. He telephoned the acting First Lord of the Admiralty and demanded that a guard be turned out.

"I say, what is all this?" the man kept asking, and when it was borne in upon him that the Home Secretary wished the cordite guarded, he said, "Why, I haven't got a guard, don't you know—they've all gone off to the races."

In a furious temper, Churchill persuaded Richard Haldane, the War Minister, to dispatch troops to the cordite cache; then he got to work on a bill enabling him to open "the correspondence to and from spies." While this amounted practically to carte blanche to intercept all the correspondence in the land, the bill went through, and, by the outbreak of the war, it had been utilized with such skill that nearly every dangerous spy was easily rounded up.

Heretofore, even in his own government, Churchill had not been admitted to the inner circle to which Asquith confided the secrets of foreign policy. Both Churchill and Lloyd George were regarded as too pacifistic to be entrusted with information touching on war. Now the doors were thrown open to both men, Lloyd George, too, having turned around and made a speech in which he said that "peace at that price [surrender of

her great and beneficent position] would be a humiliation intolerable for a great country like ours to endure."

Privy to all the facts, Churchill drew up a historic document, a timetable of probable developments in the case of war.
It is still viewed, even by his enemies, as one of the world's
classics of prophecy, laying the groundwork for the many
uncanny predictions of his that have followed.

The document started off, "It is assumed that an alliance
exists between Great Britain, France and Russia, and that these
Powers are attacked by Germany and Austria," and went on
with details. The highest military leaders in England had declared, in closed meeting, that the French Army was sufficiently
strong to counterattack sometime between the ninth and thir-
teenth days after the start, and then roll the Teuton back.
Churchill presented a scintillating argument why the French
strength was easily exaggerated, and countered with an analysis
of his own. The French, he said, would still be in full retreat
from the Meuse on the twentieth day and would not be in a
position to attack until at least the fortieth day, when the
Germans had extended their lines, been engaged at sea, and
begun to worry about the Russian pachyderm to their rear.

*Three years later, the French would be in retreat on the
twenty-first day, and the Battle of the Marne, generally con-
ceded to mark the turning point of the war, would begin on the
thirty-sixth day.*

The English Army, with General Henry Wilson as spokes-
man, rejected Churchill's document as "that silly memoran-
dum" and called it publicly an "utterly amateur legend." The
Army's jealous indifference to this opinion from a civilian
brain of the first order was only typical of the professional military attitude before any war. Despite the fact that generals and
admirals are trained at the public expense and presumed to
be competent, most wars begin with a series of blunders, disasters, setbacks, and stupidities, such as Dunkirk, Pearl Harbor, and the rest.

Embarrassingly enough for the British generals and admirals, including Harry Wilson, Churchill was soon elevated right over their heads, after which he began to issue documents marked "Orders." The astute Asquith invited the Home Secretary on a trip to Scotland, where they played some extremely questionable golf. While Churchill was carrying out a program of excavation in a sand trap, Asquith, up above, inquired, "Did you ever hear the word, *Weltpolitik?*" He had touched a raw wound. Churchill had heard of, and nearly assimilated, *"Agricola in horto est,"* but he had got little further in a linguistic way. At a recent party he had jokingly said that he intended to learn German when the Kaiser's legions hit the beach at Dover. As he stalled for time, Asquith went on to explain the bristling German dream—the *Weltpolitik* of the Kaiser and *Lebensraum* of that latter Brahman, Adolf Hitler: the dream of "living space," of a world-spanning chain of colonies wherein the flaxen-haired clods of Bavaria and the swarthy street gamins of Hamburg could stretch and grow, spreading the national neurosis.

Churchill expressed himself as being alive to this problem, and Asquith changed the subject. "Would you be interested in taking over the Admiralty?" he inquired. Churchill's answer, which came with great rapidity, was, "Indeed I would."

"We have only the Navy," said Asquith. "It is our only hope."

In an unheard-of move, Churchill and Reginald McKenna, then head of the Admiralty, exchanged ministries. This was doubly peculiar in that, two years before, the two had quarreled bitterly in Commons, McKenna advocating larger Naval Estimates and Churchill, the pacifist, opposing them.

Now the fighting pacifist had disappeared. Churchill embarked on a pugnacious reshuffling of the Admiralty that had the majority of high naval brass sulking in their tents. After the start of hostilities, he cajoled out of retirement a brilliant and balky sailor, Lord Fisher, who was regarded by about half the Navy as being a ripe candidate for observation. It was well known that he favored all manner of new ideas, including

absurd notions about faster ships and bigger guns, and he had
never shown the least respect for seniority. This had given him
a standing in the British Navy, as it would in any navy, roughly
equivalent to that of a leper at a 4-H conference.

Fisher was just the man for Churchill, whose ideas also had
never conformed to the popular pattern. The two arranged a
meeting at Fisher's home in Reigate, where they mapped out
strategy. The retired admiral finally agreed to become First
Sea Lord, which means second in command in the British
Admiralty. (The minister himself is known as the "First
Lord.") Then Churchill made some unpopular promotions,
lifting Admiral Sir John Jellicoe up to command the Home
Fleet, by-passing many senior officers, and naming as Naval
Secretary to the First Lord, David Beatty, a young rear ad-
miral whose talents Churchill had appreciated ever since the
Battle of Omdurman, when Beatty, aboard one of the gun-
boats, had tossed him a bottle of spare champagne.

With Fisher's tacit approval, Churchill flew in the face of
public opinion and ordered 15-inch guns, instead of the usual
13.5-inch ones, for all his new battleships. It was a decision
of grave responsibility, since, if they failed, the fleet would
be impotent. A heart-rending cry arose from many naval people. But Churchill bulled right ahead, and when the war began, his ships could outfire anything the Germans had to offer,
and often did.

Even amidst these martial omens, he took brief time out
for other considerations. His espousal of the Home Rule for
Ireland Bill (whereby the destiny of the northern Protestant
counties of Ulster would be decided by Ireland rather than by
Britain) was so vigorous that Ronald McNeill, an Ulsterman,
arose in Commons, wound up, took careful aim, and scored a
direct hit on Churchill's nose with a copy of the Parliamentary
Rules and Etiquette. Criticism of McNeill was outspoken; it
was felt that he could have selected a more fitting volume. However, his apology was so handsome that, later, Churchill made
him his chief financial assistant at the Treasury. Leo Amery,

the former Harrovian, jumped on Churchill in the House for deploying the fleet near Ireland at a time of high feeling. He wished to know if this "would lead to bloodshed and fighting." Momentarily forgetting Amery's onetime role as editor of the *Harrovian,* Churchill leapt up and denounced "this hellish suggestion." In the words of the historian Ephesian, the minister "is at once called to order by the Speaker, and, for the second time only on the fourteen years in Parliament, has to withdraw an offensive epithet."

Churchill's name was mentioned peripherally in connection with a financial scandal of the time. It brought charges that Lloyd George and the Attorney General Rufus Isaacs, had used secret government information to speculate in shares of the Marconi Company. Asked to give evidence, Churchill impatiently arrived in what has been described as "his most characteristically Napoleonic manner" and complained that he had been wrenched away from vital work at the Admiralty to testify in connection with "the merest unsupported tittle-tattle." He denied any knowledge of the transactions and sought to establish Lloyd George's reputation by saying that "hardly a day passes in Parliament when we do not converse on current topics for at least half an hour."

One of the questioners, a Mr. Birrell, commented only that "Neither of you can be very easily bored."

As the events of Europe marched in inevitable succession toward conflict, Churchill continued his efforts to build a supreme Navy. He created the first "Fast Division" of battle-ships, a variation of which was still widely used in the Second World War, and he brought about a greatly disputed change-over from coal to oil fuel in the fleet. This led to Britain's purchase of a controlling interest in the Anglo-Persian Oil Company, which Churchill has lately seen frittered away by a fully socialized England. In 1913 and 1914 he introduced the largest Naval Estimates ever given to Parliament, saying in an accompanying speech, "Unless our Naval strength were solidly, amply, and unswervingly maintained, the Government could

not feel that they were doing their duty to the country." In
the early summer of 1914, he called off the usual maneuvers
and announced instead a "practice mobilization." His decision
again displayed prescience of an almost mystical quality. The
fleet concentrated at Spithead on July 17. On June 28 the
Austrian Archduke Franz Ferdinand had been assassinated by
students of his vassal state of Serbia. A month later, on July 29,
Austria-Hungary marched on Serbia, Russia backed up the tiny
Slavic country, Germany mobilized, and Europe was at war.

# Chapter 19

T HE HISTORY of Winston Churchill in the First World War is divided into about equal parts of tragedy and comedy. On the whole, it makes remarkable reading. Perhaps never before had such a whirlwind of human energy been loosed upon a wartime government. The Admiralty was groggy within a week, and it did not shake its head entirely clear until ten months later, when he was rather summarily removed. In that time, he had effected changes, embraced new conceptions, and followed lines of enterprise that revolutionized the British Navy and nearly brought the war to a close in 1915.

But at the crucial moment, as often happens, things hung delicately in the balance and then went wrong altogether. To use Churchill's old refrain—one of his happiest inspirations— "Everyone threw the blame on me." This blame—for the entrapment at Antwerp and, more importantly, for the fiasco of the Dardanelles—pursued and harried him for years, crippling his career, establishing him as a national butt, and depriving his country of his uniquely valuable services. A lesser man would doubtless have wilted beneath the hot blasts of slander and accusation. Churchill, untroubled, did his best within the limits so harshly imposed upon him.

In the beginning, he and the recalled Lord Fisher were in warm agreement, exchanging letters, notes, and memos at a brisk clip. Fisher's, for reasons best known to himself, were ended with picturesque inventions that included, "Yours till charcoal sprouts," "Yours till Hell freezes," and "Yours till

battleships fly." Ice had scarcely started to form on the fringes
of hell before the two men were to part in anger, but the temperature remained steady in the opening weeks. Anti-Conserva-
tive historians are apt to dismiss Churchill's contributions to
this period. In a quick round of inspections, he traveled aboard
the Admiralty yacht *Enchantress,* flew in the several rickety and
frowned-upon aircraft owned by the Navy, and made land trips
to the European front. His first unpopular (and then loudly
applauded) decision had been completed on August 1, three
days before Britain's formal declaration of war. In the face
of a Cabinet veto, without the King's signature, wholly il-
legally, he ordered full mobilization of the Navy, calling out
the total naval reserve strength of the nation. Because of this
audacious act, the fleet was ready to fight when the war began,
one of the few times on record when a defending Navy has
been even halfway prepared.

Churchill took a fancy to his aircraft and set in motion the
development of an air arm. He and Fisher hammered it
through, between them laying the foundations for the present
Royal Air Force, and Churchill continued his agitations for
Air in succeeding posts. His new "hobby," as Prime Minister
Asquith acidly termed it, was a heavy bane to his associates,
who were kept busy declining invitations to ride with him. It
was Churchill's pleasure to take to the skies with some junior
officer and then pre-empt the controls. He persuaded one young
friend to go up in a three-seater. The passenger arrived a little
late, with apologies. "Where have you been?" growled Churchill. "Making my will," said the man cheerfully. Some time
afterward, when he had won the Victoria Cross, he explained
that he had not actually been afraid of Churchill but had
thought it only tidy to put his affairs in order.

The War Office, too, was becoming interested in airplanes,
but Churchill's relentless drive overshadowed everything. In
the memoirs of Sir Sefton Brancker, who was then Deputy
Director of Military Aeronautics and later became Air Vice-
Marshal (and died in 1930 in the crash of the dirigible R 101)

is found a description of the situation: "Immediately after mobilization," he wrote, "I went over to the Admiralty and had a talk with my opposite number, Murray Sueter, about the allocation of available contractors, aircraft and engines. He was prepared to draw up as clear a line of delimitation as possible between the trade activities of the two departments. . . .

"I endeavored to cooperate thoroughly with him and I think that he was anxious to meet the wishes of the War Office in every way possible: but he was not his own master, for the vigorous and enthusiastic personality of Mr. Winston Churchill had come into play. He believed in aviation. Even at that time he had realized the enormous possibilities of the attack on hostile territory by an independent air force, and had grasped the necessity of some central control over all aeronautical matters. But the Admiralty conceived that this control should be vested in the Admiralty, with the independent force part and parcel of the Navy, his particular responsibility at the moment; and to this end he worked assiduously during the last months of 1914.

"The first sign of this policy was his sudden announcement that the Naval Wing of the Royal Flying Corps had become the Royal Naval Air Service—this without any reason or warning being given to the War Office."

Churchill's hungry bites at the air potential became so voracious that Lord Kitchener, his old nemesis, lately made a field marshal and called to head the War Office, reluctantly asked him to undertake the Aerial Home Defense. On the theory that the best defense is a good offense, Churchill directed his aircraft to proceed to Europe and win the war. There began a series of rash and unlikely operations that are still mentioned with awe in the British military.

The planes flew first to Cologne and Friedrichshafen, where, to the stunned astonishment of the Kaiser and his generals, they beat to a pulp the German airship sheds. Then the pilots turned their attention to Zeebrugge and the submarine bases. Even the War Office monitors, not necessarily inclined to be friendly, reported that the attacks were "sound and justified." From this start, Churchill branched out fast. Kitchener had only to mutter something about a "diversionary gesture" at Dunkirk before Churchill was in full stride with his notorious marine "Circus." Unluckily for Kitchener, the word was of his own selection; Churchill interpreted it literally. On August 27, three weeks after the start of the war, Commander Samson landed in France with some naval troop units—marines and yeomen—several double-decker buses that Churchill had ordered covered with iron plating, and a few of the growing squadron of airplanes. The activities of this joyous band undoubtedly represented the most bizarre excursion of the war. To begin with, they traveled so fast that the Germans could never get anywhere near them. According to one observer, they were "here, there and everywhere terrorizing marauding Uhlans and inspiring French Territorials." The force looked much like a group of wildly celebrating fans returning from a successful football match. In Churchill's view, a circus was aimed to make noise; his units rode while singing, shouting at the top of their lungs, and heaving beer bottles into the streets. Their impudence had such scope that they once dispatched a telegram to one of the Allied armies in the neighborhood, asking details of its movements, as they wished to "co-operate." A British Army officer of the period wistfully commented in a meeting that the Navy, heretofore, had always been known as "the Silent Service."

Churchill often went over and joined his repertory company, and had a grand time. And as he did so, Prime Minister Asquith, who had to run the Admiralty in the interim, grew increasingly peevish. He finally ordered the Circus disbanded, and the wandering minister returned to take up other matters.

Churchill may unequivocally be described as the father of the tank. It was due solely to his farsightedness that the tank came into being as a weapon of modern warfare. One night he had sat long at his desk, thinking about the armor that the crafty Hannibal had used on elephants. A few others had since made tentative suggestions for a protected vehicle of attack. Churchill went somewhat further, blandly earmarking $350,-000 for the production of eighteen "landships." When the news got about, it was transposed into a huge joke, known as "Winston's folly." And when the foolish Churchill gave up the Admiralty to Arthur Balfour, the latter quickly canceled the tank order though not in time to prevent one machine from going through. On September 15, 1916, it and (by courtesy of a belatedly convinced War Office) forty-eight of its brothers took the field in the Battle of Thiepval. The Germans threw down their guns and fled, and warfare underwent another lasting alteration, comparable to the effect of the *Merrimac* and the *Monitor* in the American Civil War. About the only person to give Churchill the proper credit was General Ludendorff, who said in his memoirs that he had sought an armistice because of "enemy tanks in unexpectedly large numbers."

Very little resulted from Churchill's Steam Troop Crusher or from his personal shield. He had suggested, as an alternative to humans going over the top and suffering casualties, a gigantic iron roller which would grind its way into enemy trenches and chew up all the personnel they contained. He had bright visions of riding to Berlin and victory over roads of flattened-out troops, and of a war ended mechanically. The effect of his improvisation on the War Office was something less than genial. "Stark, staring mad" was the general feeling, and the device was noisily pigeonholed. "I remained impenitent and unconvinced," Churchill wrote afterward. There was a similar reaction to his urging of individual shields for the soldiers. Despite his dual lack of success, a good many reputable officers now think the ideas sound; eventually they may come to pass.

The word "tank" was about the only new military term of these years that Churchill did not coin. From his fertile pen there sprang such staples of our present vocabulary as "seaplane," "flight" (of airplanes), and "fog of war." All his direc-

tives were models of painstaking composition, as if the writer
meant to put them to use later, but he would tolerate nothing
but brevity from his associates. "Winston made us all write
what we had to say on one side only of one piece of paper,"
one of them said lately. "He would call up and ask for information, but he wanted just the skeleton facts. He filled out the
rest from his extraordinary understanding." A number of people who know Churchill feel quite frankly that, with his usual
farsightedness, he took special care in keeping his documents
because he knew he would compose a history of the war and
sell it. And sure enough, when the smoke rolled away, there
appeared his monumental *The World Crisis,* a very controversial work, in four volumes. They hasten to point out that
there is nothing shabby about this procedure; military leaders
from Caesar on have presented accounts of their stewardship,
and the public, discounting school children, has always bene-
fited.

There began to be some doubt, even in the minds of the
principals, as to whether Churchill or Asquith was Prime
Minister. In his passion for management, Churchill often
reached across ministerial lines, and his repeated trips, such as
the ones to the Circus, left Asquith in frequent charge of
the Admiralty. A cooling-off process was noted in their relations. It was not retarded by an outing that Churchill had
arranged for their families, aboard the *Enchantress.* He was
thunderstruck to find that none of the Asquiths, with particular reference to the head of the Government, planned to spend
several days listening to a monologue by Churchill. If anything,
the shoe was on the other foot. The First Lord was rendered
extremely disgruntled by Asquith's recital of exhaustive data
about every part of the world. Up till then, Churchill had been
regarded as the Empire's premier talker; Asquith put him in
the shade aboard the *Enchantress.* To make matters worse,
the Prime Minister steered the group into parlor games that required harkbacks to a college education. There were mentions
of Greek, and even Latin, a language that the Churchill family

had tacitly agreed was dead beyond any hope of resurrection. When Asquith took to improvising Greek verses, Churchill took to refreshment. He suffered terribly while his learned guest paraded his erudition. "No one could write down in a five-minute period more generals beginning with L or poets beginning with T," said biographer René Kraus of the loquacious Asquith. Altogether, the ordeal on the *Enchantress* proved so strenuous that Churchill was a little suspicious of his boss from that point onward.

The Antwerp affair widened the breach. It was in the month of October, after a time of rout, bad losses, and fading hopes. The Battle of the Marne had started, but the French were still in retreat all across the littered and smoking front. Protecting the Allied left flank, the Belgian Army already had capitulated at Liége and Namur but was holding out at Antwerp, which the Germans had been ordered to take at any cost. To prevent this, 8000 men of the Royal Naval Division had been rushed to bolster up the sagging lines. These and other problems vexed Churchill as he rode on a train between London and Dover, heading for Dunkirk and his exuberant Circus. In mid-flight a very emphatic telegram from Kitchener put an abrupt end to his visit. As if taking no chances, the telegram ordered train, First Lord and all back to London. Then, at a meeting in his home, Kitchener explained that Churchill was urgently needed in Belgium, to lend "moral support in a vital and deteriorating situation." "Nobody but you can provide the necessary spark to stem the tide," the field marshal said in effect. Churchill agreed instantly and left before morning. A number of reports exist that touch on both his departure and his arrival at the scene.

From Mr. Asquith's memoirs comes the following notation: "I was away but Grey [the Foreign Secretary], Kitchener and Winston held a late meeting and, I fancy with Grey's rather reluctant consent, the intrepid Winston set off at midnight and ought to have reached Antwerp at about nine o'clock this

morning. He will go straightaway and see the Belgian Ministers; Sir John French is making preparation to send assistance
by way of Lille. I have had a talk with K. this morning and we
are both rather anxiously awaiting Winston's report. I do not
know how fluent he is in French, but if he was able to do himself justice in a foreign tongue the Belges will have listened to
a discourse the like of which they have never heard before. I
cannot but think that he will stiffen them up."

Churchill's arrival was one of the high lights of the war. It
was ably described by the American correspondent, E. Alexander Powell. "At one o'clock that afternoon," he wrote, "a
big drab-coloured touring-car, filled with British naval officers,
drove down the *Place de Mer,* its horn sounding a hoarse
warning, took the turn into the *Marché-aux-Souliers* on two
wheels, and drew up in front of the hotel. Before the car had
fairly come to a stop, the door of the tonneau was thrown
violently open and out jumped a smooth-faced, sandy-haired,
stoop-shouldered, youthful-looking man in undress Trinity
House [a sailors' fraternity] uniform. . . .

"As he charged into the packed lobby he flung his arms out,
in a nervous characteristic gesture, as though pushing his way
through a crowd. It was a most spectacular entrance, and re-
minded me for all the world of a scene in a melodrama where
the hero dashes up bare-headed on a foam-flecked horse, and
saves the heroine, or the old homestead, or the family fortune,
as the case may be."

Asquith's speculation about Churchill's linguistic skill was
not entirely idle. When the First Lord rushed in to confront
the Belgian ministers, one of them, pointing to his peculiar
uniform, asked what he was. In attempting to explain that he
had been made an elder brother of Trinity House, he said, *"Je
suis le frère aîné de la Trinité."* Confused as they were, the
Belgians got the impression that Churchill was announcing his
divinity, and they spoke more softly. When the French group
arrived, it was suggested that perhaps he had better converse in
English. But he insisted on sticking to his French and sailed

into a stirring and garbled summation of the crisis. When it was over, the Frenchmen quietly conferred for a moment, obviously moved, and then sent one of their subordinates across the room for a translation.

The language problem was finally ironed out, and Churchill, in his excitement, decided to withdraw from the Admiralty and plunge personally into the land fighting. He therefore got off a telegram to the Prime Minister, saying: "If it is thought by H. M. Government that I can be of service here, I am willing to resign my office and undertake command of all relieving and defensive forces assigned to Antwerp in conjunction with Belgian Army, provided that I am given necessary military rank and authority, and full powers of a commander of a detached force in the field. . . ."

Asquith turned down this impulsive offer, wearily noting in his memoirs that "Winston is an ex-lieutenant of Hussars and would, if his proposal had been accepted, have been in command of two distinguished major-generals not to mention brigadiers, colonels, etc., while the Navy were only contributing their little brigades."

The refusal did not prevent Churchill from taking full command. One of his old Harrovian contemporaries, Lord Mottistone, who had been sent to the scene as an observer by Sir John French, the British commander-in-chief, afterward wrote, "From the moment I arrived, it was apparent that the whole business was in Winston's hands. He dominated the whole place—the King, Ministers, soldiers, sailors. So great was his influence that I am convinced that with 20,000 British troops he could have held Antwerp against almost any onslaught."

And speaking of the naval brigade, Sir Ian Hamilton, also on the spot, added, "Churchill handled them as if he were Napoleon and they were the Old Guard, [flinging] them right into the enemy's opening jaws."

The outcome of the Antwerp incident, and Churchill's part in it, have been a matter of controversy for more than thirty years. He was accused of a reckless, even a wanton, expendi-

ture of lives to no purpose. The fact that he had recently been
studying Napoleon was pointed out as significant by his critics.
Had the city's defense successfully held off the Germans, he
would doubtless have been feted as a savior, and welcomed
in triumph back to London. But the oncoming hordes were too
powerful, and at last, after five days of titanic effort, the Allies
gave way. As they did so, part of one naval brigade was
trapped and interned in Holland for the rest of the war. What
is largely overlooked is that the Belgians, together with their
main British support, were able to fight backward along the
coast, opening sluices and flooding the country so thoroughly
that the Germans were sealed off from the Channel ports. Also,
a sizable English army had time to rush up and engage the
enemy at Ypres, where a major battle was fought, in which
cooks, batmen, and other supernumeraries helped hold the
lines fast. Students of the war now agree that, without the five
days' delaying action at Antwerp, the Hun would quickly have
swept on and been in a position to strike at England.

Notwithstanding, Churchill came in for the usual stinging
censure. It is a curious truth that, all his life, something about
him, his mood of truculence, an excess of vigor, his defiant
scowl, have aroused antagonism in people almost automatically. They rally around happily to bait him, as the townsfolk
of Pamplona appear annually in the streets to bait the season's
bulls. This has been deplored by the less thoughtful among his
friends. Actually, the public's unseemly attentions to Churchill
are a compliment of very rare quality: weaklings are tormented
but never baited; only championship class attracts the best opposition.

The results of his next ruckus gave Churchill a chance to
exercise all of his champion's powers. Over the vociferous protests of his side-kick, Lord Fisher, he invented an intricate
scheme to force the Dardanelles, detach Turkey from the Central Powers, win over the Balkan States, and pave the way for
a sweeping Russian victory in the east. It was his blueprint for
smothering the war early, a "back-door" attack on the enemy.

Fisher had at first been in favor of the plan; then he veered around to oppose it. He was a testy and unpredictable but effective man. All of these traits were manifest in the Battle of the Falkland Islands, when two of Germany's best ships, the *Gneisenau* and *Scharnhorst,* were destroyed along with several smaller cruisers. It was due to Fisher that the English cruisers *Inflexible* and *Invincible* were refitted and at sea in time to tackle the enemy. He had directed the dock people, at Devonport, to have the ships out in three days. "It will take the laborers a week to finish the brickwork on the boilers," they telegraphed him. The First Sea Lord's unemotional reply was that, if the workmen were not finished in three days, they could put the bricks aboard the cruisers and sail with them. Without benefit of entertainment units or further begging from the government, they finished in two days and a half.

Fisher's and Churchill's hours did not precisely coincide. In these years the First Lord was working a comparatively normal day; Fisher preferred to start at 3 A.M. and continue without interruption until 3 P.M. To preserve the peace, Churchill accommodated his hours to the Sea Lord's eccentric ones, and he has never since shaken off his acquired habit of working at night.

Fisher's pique over the Dardanelles can be ascribed in part to the fact that he had a similar plan of his own. In a contest of wills, the results were inevitable: Fisher found that he was, in fact and in spirit, second in command. In the beginning, Kitchener, too, was in accord with Churchill's stratagem, but he was against using troops to support the naval action. After lengthy talks by the Cabinet, it was agreed to proceed, using the oldest ships in the Fleet, supported by the long-range guns of the new superdreadnought, *Queen Elizabeth.* Churchill rode over all further objections and the catastrophe got under way, on March 18, 1915.

It was not long in taking form. While entering the straits, Admiral de Robeck, commanding the assault group, ran into trouble in the form of a mine field and lost three battleships.

This was a heavy blow, but there were more to follow. To the amazement of the Turks and Germans, he broke off the action. In the light of postwar reports, he chose an extraordinarily bad time to do it, for the enemy were all but out of ammunition. "The Turkish gun crews were demoralized and even the German officers present had, apparently, little hope of successful resistance if the Fleet attacked next day," says the official British history of the war, prepared by men not necessarily friendly to Churchill. In London, the First Lord assembled his "Admiralty War Group" and showed them a telegram instructing De Robeck to renew the action. It was never sent; Fisher and the other admirals refused to overrule the man on the spot. This can now be seen only as a very great pity. After the war, the able German general at the Dardanelles, Liman von Sanders, wrote, "If the orders given at that moment had been carried out, the course of the world war would have changed after the spring of 1915, and Germany and Austria would have been constrained to continue the fight alone."

Now followed a disastrous lull in the campaign, during which it was decided to bolster the naval thrust with a troop attack on nearby Gallipoli. By the time the soldiers arrived, the Turks had dug trenches, thrown up barbed wire, and made other preparations. And at the critical moment, Fisher ordered the *Queen Elizabeth* home. This drew a frenzied protest from Kitchener, who charged that the Navy was "deserting" the Army. The whole effort became tangled up in a many-sided quarrel, which was not helped by a secret note that Fisher disloyally sent to Asquith, saying, "I desire to convey to you that I honestly feel that I cannot remain where I am much longer, as there is an inevitable drain *daily* (almost hourly) on the resources in the decisive theatre of the war.

"But that is not the worst. Instead of the whole time of the whole of the Admiralty being concentrated on the daily increasing submarine menace in home waters, we are all diverted to the Dardanelles, and the unceasing activities of the First Lord, both day and night, are engaged in ceaseless *prodding*

of everyone in every department afloat and ashore in the interest of the Dardanelles Fleet, with the result of the huge Armada
now there, whose size is sufficiently indicated by their having
as many battleships out there as in the German High Seas
Fleet! Therefore this purely private and personal letter, intended for your eye alone and not to be quoted, as there is no
use threatening without acting, is to mention to the one person
who I feel *ought* to know *that I feel that my time is short.*"

Whatever his grievances, Fisher's methods were those of a
schoolboy tattling on a companion. In any case, his companion
went ahead with the eastern campaign. After being bullied
and badgered, Kitchener dispatched the 29th Division to reinforce the Gallipolian army, but the paper work was so faulty
that the unit was obliged to go first to Egypt in order to sort
out its stores. On June 7, Churchill had made a speech in Dundee that was injudicious from a security standpoint; he said of
the Dardanelles campaign, "There never was a great subsidiary
operation of war which a more complete harmony of strategic,
political and economic advantages has combined, or which
stood in truer relation to the main decision which is in the central theatre. Through the narrows of the Dardanelles, and
across the ridges of the Gallipoli Peninsula, lie some of the
shortest paths to triumphant peace."

Before this address, which was widely printed, the Turks
had not judged that the British Army in their area would be
reinforced and the fight continued. General Liman von Sanders
said afterward that the speech helped him "to realize that the
British attacks would surely be resumed with increasing violence." He and the Turks accordingly hastened to increase their
defenses, and the ensuing actions provide one of the goriest
chapters in the ugly and unending history of war. The total
British casualties reached 205,000; those of the French were
47,000. The British dead, English, Australian, and New Zealand officers and men, amounted to 43,000. One of these
young unfortunates, a splendid veteran of Churchill's naval
force at Antwerp, the poet Rupert Brooke, spent the last few

weeks of his life in the alien land to which the Admiralty had
dispatched him recording his metric impressions for posterity:

> If I should die, think only this of me:
> That there's some corner of a foreign field
> That is for ever England. There shall be
> In that rich earth a richer dust concealed;
> A dust whom England bore, shaped, made aware,
> Gave, once, her flowers to love, her ways to roam,
> A body of England's, breathing English air,
> Washed by the rivers, blest by suns of home.
>
> And think, this heart, all evil shed away,
> A pulse in the eternal mind, no less
> Gives somewhere back the thoughts by England given;
> Her sights and sounds; dreams happy as her day;
> And laughter, learnt of friends; and gentleness,
> In hearts at peace, under an English heaven.

Churchill countered with a well-composed obituary: "He
expected to die for the dear England whose beauty and majesty
he knew; and he advanced towards the brink in perfect serenity,
with absolute conviction of the rightness of his country's cause
and a heart devoid of hate for fellow-men."

The sad and straggling remnants of the Army and the Navy
were evacuated from Gallipoli and the Dardanelles; Fisher resigned his post with angry words; and the public's wrath rose
up in a terrible storm, whose epicenter was Churchill. New
Zealand and Australia, with a frightful loss of their best youths,
were especially bitter. In the official Australian history of the
war, an account of the campaign ends, "So through a Churchill's excess of imagination, a layman's ignorance of artillery
and the fatal power of a young enthusiasm to convince older
and slower brains, the tragedy of Gallipoli was born."

Politically, the aftermath was swift and destructive. The
Tories, thirsting for Churchill's blood, were able to force a
Coalition Government, and the tempestuous First Lord was
removed from his post. A visitor calling at the Admiralty has

said that he found Churchill slumped over at his desk, broken-hearted. "This," the fallen idol was quoted as saying, "is what I live for," waving toward the charts on the walls. "Yes, I am finished in respect of all I care for—the waging of the war, the defeat of the Germans."

In company with Rupert Brooke, Churchill himself was among the early casualties.

# Chapter 20

ONE MORNING in December 1915 I fell in with the Transport Officer in the unsavory courtyard of the farm which housed the Battalion H.Q. of the 6th Royal Scots Fusiliers, and in exchanging rumors he told me as a fact that almost immediately Winston Churchill was coming to take over the Battalion."

The writer of those words—a "Captain X"—went on to say that, hearing the rumor, he agreed and then added that Lord Curzon would probably be made transport officer. He was about to offer a few more predictions of a similar nature— Arthur Balfour, Lloyd George, and the Duke of Norfolk had been named mess attendants, and so on—when he began to suspect from his informant's "unquenchable solemnity that he might after all be making an essay in the truth."

It was the truth all right. Churchill was at last taking the field as the logical successor to, the lineal descendant of, the mighty Marlborough. Stepping from the debris of his shattered career, he had asked for a command at the front. After being deposed at the Admiralty, he had been given a token ministry, as Chancellor of the Duchy of Lancaster, but he was excluded from the War Council, the influential group of policy-makers. So he declared in favor of active service.

A friend of Churchill's has described his leave-taking, as reported by British biographer Lewis Broad: "The household was upside down as he completed his preparations. Downstairs his faithful secretary, Eddie (later Sir Edward) Marsh, was in tears, upstairs Lady Randolph was in despair at the thought of her brilliant son leaving for the trenches, their discomforts and their danger. Mrs. Churchill alone remained calm."

Of the ménage, she had the least reason to be composed. The Churchills by now had two daughters and a son: Diana, born in July, 1909, Randolph, born in 1911, and Sarah, who had come along soon after the war started. With two small children and an infant, a tiny income, and a husband whose rash acts were England's principal gossip, the former Miss Clementine Hozier could scarcely have been reconciled to his colorful decision. By a kind fortune, for her and for the nation, his holiday amidst the bursting shells would be wholly unsanguinary, and would indeed provide an episode of high comedy in a generally bleak drama.

The warrior first went to France and visited Sir John French (in his last weeks as commander-in-chief), who was talked into offering Churchill a brigade. When news of this reached Asquith, his frenzied reply was, paraphrased, "For God's sake, don't give him a brigade—don't give him anything more than a battalion!" One of the minister's associates said later that Asquith was afraid that Churchill, perhaps under cover of darkness, might march the brigade directly on Berlin.

The command eventually simmered down to colonel in charge of the 6th Royal Scots Fusiliers. Several extant sources, including "Captain X," who wrote his small, anonymous memoirs, contribute valuable data on the union.

Churchill arrived early on an afternoon and held a compulsory levee in his headquarters, described by Captain X as a "more than usually dirty farm." The new C.O. took an elevated seat in a corner of the orderly room and asked that the company commanders be brought in one by one and formally introduced. This was accomplished in a hushed and constrained atmosphere; the rest of the officers were then presented. During the absurd ritual, the figure in the chair, says one bystander, "looked uncommonly like Napoleon, with the same forward thrust in his pose, the same brooding scowl, the hand in the tunic, and even the same baldish head with its vagrant forelock."

After the presentation, several awkward minutes ticked by as Churchill regarded everybody stonily. "It was not easy to parry this unconventional attack on one's composure," wrote Captain X. "It was necessary to stand at attention, of course, so that no relief could be sought in the diversion of a mere social and friendly observation. I found myself forced to stare hard back at him and trust to time to bring this, like all other trials, to an end." When fully five minutes had elapsed without so much as a whisper breaking the tension of the room, the extraordinary new commander got up and lumbered out. There was no possible way to tell whether he liked or disliked what he saw.

His first order, issued via the adjutant, read, "Clear the cats from the orderly room." This was done. Next day he held a second levee, of a vastly different character. It was as verbose as the other session had been mute. Also, Churchill had presumably found fault with the way the sergeant major was dressed for the opening. For the repeat performance, the unfortunate stood by the doorway outfitted with every device known to the soldier of that period, with a full pack, including pup tent, a rifle with bayonet attached, various things like hatchets, spades, frying pans, and hand grenades attached to his belt, and on his face a look of terrible misery. He had anticipated correctly: there were titters as the company passed him going in.

The eccentric chieftain was seated in his old place. When his visitors were settled into uncomfortable attention, he opened his mouth and said, hoarsely, "War is declared, gentlemen, on the lice." "With these words," declared Captain X, "did the great scion of the house of Marlborough first address his Scottish Captains assembled in council. And with these words was inaugurated such a discourse on *Pulex Europaeus*, its origin, growth, and nature, its habitat and its importance as a factor in wars ancient and modern, as left one agape with

wonder at the erudition and force of its author. I became forthwith a prey to the most lively apprehensions lest I should fall
a victim to its foul attentions, in which event I saw but little
likelihood of ever being clean again."

Fate at last had thrown in Churchill's path a captive audience of the first rank. He rumbled on with facts, statistics,
philosophic generalities on lice, and some capital anecdotes
about individual lice who had made their mark. It was an entertaining if unusual wartime speech. When it was concluded, he
ordered the entire battalion to turn-to and get after the enemy
on the double. Soldiers and officers assembled at various spots
on the grounds, and, taking a few precautions to avoid the
inquisitive gaze of the farm ladies, peeled off their clothes and
began tossing them into pots of boiling water. The operation
took three days; when it was over the lice had thrown in the
towel. They were finished—the only major defeat they had
suffered thus far in the war.

After its first shock, and resentment, the battalion began to
take pride in having a former Cabinet minister at its head. For
two or three weeks only a few persons got his name and rank
correctly; "Viscount Churchill" led the list of mistakes, and
there was frequent usage of "Lord Churchill," "Sir Winston
Churchill," and even the "Duke of Churchill," as in Pretoria.
The Royal Scots were and are a proud unit, with traditions of
accomplishment dating back to 1678, when its Highland forebears were prominent, as one of its members says, "chiefly in
certain hanging dramas not altogether unconnected with the
stealing of cattle." A rank outsider, and an Englishman at that,
coming in to take over was nearly sure to have trouble, and
anybody but Churchill might have wrought a lasting breach between battalion and leader. But he undertook the improvement
of his officers and men with such hilarious verve that they relaxed and watched him with great satisfaction. He invited the
company commanders to dine with him in the headquarters
mess, and they were astounded at the gorgeous style in which
he received them. The setting he had contrived was more

reminiscent of a London club than of a squalid French farm on
the western front. It was noted in the conversation that Churchill, by now, had learned the name, history, tastes, and preferences of every officer present. "No doubt he sought to win us,"
says Captain X, "but for that he is only to be admired, and his
capacity for coaxing and charming the best even out of the
most boorish is a gift which I never ceased to wonder at. He
materially altered the feelings of the officers toward him by this
kindliness and by the first insight we thus gained into the wonderful genius of the man."

The enthusiasm of the troops kept pace with that of the
officers, but for different reasons. Somebody divined, and
passed along down the line, that the Duke of Churchill was
bound to have connections. Whereupon there started a tremendous flow of letters between France and Scotland, seeking
favors and services of the most bizarre kind. A woman living
near Glasgow wondered if the duke could help locate her
errant husband, who had stolen her father's pig and was reported to have joined the Fusiliers, presumably using the pig
as an entrance fee. One member of the battalion, a Mr. Mac-
Gregor, slightly rheumatic, submitted a request for a month's
vacation in the South of France, and a corporal named Muck-
leroy set in motion a claim to the peerage. There were any
number of petitions for raises in pay, and one or two for shorter
hours. A wife in Edinburgh, who had cousins in Düsseldorf,
wondered if it would be possible to switch enemies; she hadn't
kept up with the war very well and thought it wouldn't matter
to anybody *who* they were fighting so long as they fought somebody. "If it wouldn't be inconvenient," she added courteously.
"The Adjutant grew more rapidly bald in the conduct of his
administrative duties in this period," says Captain X, "as the
Colonel insisted on the most scrupulous justice being done to
every inquiry, however trifling."

Once the lice were cleaned up and the cats cleared out,
Churchill undertook several changes of procedure. The first of
these, and the hardest to swallow, was a prohibition on the use

of "Yes, sir" and "No, sir" in response to orders. From now on all orders would be answered with the simple "Sir." The officers of the 6th Royal Scots have told how they struggled to capture the shades of inflection necessary to make the tiny word cover its many meanings. (One fellow went so far as to declare it "a silly little monosyllable.") For instance, should the commander ask the balding adjutant, "Do the men seem to be taking to the new music program?" the resulting "Sir!" might easily be construed to indicate that they were having a bad time. The fact is that they were. Although he himself was practically a monotone, Churchill was a staunch believer in the therapeutics of song. He had decreed that the men, henceforward, would sing, individually or in groups, every time they found themselves in motion, even if they were only going to the privy.

In theory, as some of the Royal Scots have since admitted, this melodic support was worth while—singing on the march lessens fatigue, or at least disguises it. But Churchill's regimen was thought to be extreme. By bad luck, the 6th Fusiliers were about as unmusical an outfit as could be found outside a Chinese monastery, and for most of the men to lower or elevate their pitch half a tone was a severe trial. Despite their other fine qualities, the Scotch are not a melodic race. In all of recorded history, they have produced but a handful of composers worthy of any notice at all. And to make matters worse, the Fusiliers knew only one song, a one-verse job not suitable for use outside the barracks. Using the generic word "paint," it went as follows:

> "I'll paint, and you'll paint,
>  We'll both paint together—oh
>  Won't we have a hell of a time,
>  Painting one another, oh!"

It was the custom to switch "paint" for one or another of the lively Anglo-Saxon verbs, producing a quatrain that any soldier might be proud to try. Churchill had noticed, and

balked at, this "inexhaustible fountain of impurity" during the
very first march on which he accompanied the unit. Passing
through the village of Merris, with its pretty girls waving and
blowing kisses, the men had written new chapters in Scotland's
meager musical annals. The commander was badly shocked as
his charges leaned into the faces of the innocent *jeunes filles*
and screamed:

> "Won't we have a hell of a time,
> ——ing one another, oh!"

That evening, the adjutant, who now had practically no hair
left at all, posted orders for a gigantic sing in a neighborhood
barn—a "rehearsal." It was to be a regular thing. A number of
new and antiseptic tunes were tried out, many of them of a
religious nature. They went down badly. On the occasion of the
next march, out came the paint again. Incredibly enough, in
Churchill's eyes, the women seemed to like it, and appeared to
be gesticulating wildly toward handy copses and haymows. It
was later decided that they had caught sight of various field
rations that were furtively being brandished to augment the
paint.

The following rehearsal was held in a bog, where the men
seemed to catch on to the new songs a lot faster. Progress from
then on out was slow but steady.

Churchill soon announced a battalion parade, with the company commanders mounted. This was a bitter pill, since the
6th Fusiliers were an infantry unit and nobody knew anything
about horses. Furthermore, the function was to be performed
in step to the company piper, who had asthma and besides
could play only snatches of "The Campbells of Redcastle." The
parade turned out to be a perfect nightmare of confusion. The
commanders got on their unaccustomed mounts all right, but
the horse carrying Captain Foulkes wandered off to a sink-hole
to drink, while his company continued to march across the
field. Churchill sat on a white mare and watched. The men ar-

rived at a fence and seemed indecisive. Some of them marked time while others climbed over, attempting to maintain a certain cadence. As the roll was being taken, it was noted that D Company, the entire company, was missing. However, to everybody's relief, before the roll was finished, young Lieutenant Sinclair came lurching up on a wretched-looking animal, reined in before Churchill, saluted, and said, "D Company absent, sir." There was a murmur of appreciation when the colonel returned the salute and nodded as if the report were the most natural thing in the world. It was at this point that the saddle girth of Captain Whelkins broke and spilled him into the mud (the day was damp). To relieve the situation, Churchill called out, "Wheel!" and the majority of the company commanders inexplicably found themselves *behind* their men. It was a tense moment. In Captain X's account, he says, "Sometimes I was beside my company, sometimes in front, sometimes behind." One horse walked *through* a company, nuzzling men out of the way. The parade ended in what has been described as "a *melee* of blasphemous humanity and outraged horseflesh." Churchill studied it impassively throughout.

A few days later the great news arrived. The 6th Fusiliers were moving up to the trenches. As the western front went, this was a quiet sector, but Churchill promised the men that he would strive to his utmost to keep them from getting dull. In a brief but unsettling speech, he said, "We will go easy at first: a little digging and feeling our way, and then perhaps later on we may attempt a Deed." An outsider would have got the notion that, whatever they did, it would be independently of the main Allied effort. In any case, his words did nothing to comfort the unit. On previous visits to the front lines, the Fusiliers, like all other troops past and present who are not ordered to go out and get killed, were content to idle the days away, now and then peering through a telescopic sight, flinging jibes and jokes at the hidden enemy across the turf, doing their laundry, and once in a protested while planting a little wire. It seemed evident that Churchill was deliberately going to try to make somebody mad. Captain X has said that "our attitude to trenches was hostile and more than ever hostile in view of the possibility of a definite rupture with whatever enemy chanced to be opposite to us."

The black pall was temporarily rolled away by a classic dinner the colonel threw in celebration of the impending gore. He went into nearby Hazebrouck and chartered the Station Hotel, in its entirety, for a fete in the Marlborough tradition. He took the precaution of inviting two guests in addition to his own officers—the brigade major and the officer commanding the divisional train—and then blandly drew on them for almost unlimited goodies. A couple of lieutenants who checked later, after the unit and the town had recovered, decided that Churchill, out of his own pocket, had literally bought up all the liquors offered for sale in Hazebrouck. The dinner got off to a whooping start. The piper was drunk within half an hour and spent the whole evening stamping in circles around the table playing a new tune he had learned, not inappropriately entitled "The Drunken Piper." His contribution was characterized as "a most devilish row." Churchill delivered an eloquent, if overlong, address in which he touched on his "three ties with Scotland"— his wife, his constituency, and his regiment. At the suggestion of a subaltern, this was corrected to include scotch whiskey. Toward the end of the speech, the transport officer slid under the table and was laid out with a brandy keg under his head. As soon as Churchill subsided, and it was not soon, the brigade major weaved to his feet and started to address the group but was told to "sit down and mind your manners."

The dinner had started at seven thirty, and at eleven, when the liquor was exhausted, many of the company headed vaguely for home. Only a handful made it. Unluckily, they had nearly all come on horseback, as Churchill had been trying to teach them to ride. Flinging out of the hotel, they leaped on, or at, their mounts (one man actually put a foot in a stirrup, gave a healthy push, and sailed clear over and into a puddle), and clattered away over the village cobbles. A train was coming into the station, and the crossing gate was down, but several of the guests put the gate back up and halted the train. "What's going on down there?" yelled the engineer. "Dinner breaking up," he was told.

The bulk of the guests were finally located in three main towns: Meteren, Rouge Croix, and Strazeele. Churchill publicly commended the adjutant for the exceptional job done on search. The man, now completely bald, made charts of the countryside, dividing it into twelve segments, each to be explored by a sergeant with a small salvage party. While Meteren, Rouge Croix, and Strazeele turned up the bulk of the diners, a number of smaller towns had suffered damage, too. The transport officer was belatedly found in the shattered billiard room of the hotel, but the doctor was overlooked altogether. He reported in two days later: he had been taken ill at a farm where he was trying to buy a flock of sheep and had received excellent medical attention from the French farm family.

Before going up to the front, Churchill acquired a French tin helmet, in a vivid blue, which he wore during the rest of his time with the battalion. It got to be a widely known landmark and starred in many photographs printed across the world. The actual trip to the trenches was accomplished by marching and in omnibuses. His assignment was to relieve the Gordon Highlanders near Ploegsteert, in the Armentières sector. Churchill established his headquarters in a nunnery, where the cooking was said to be superb, and made an official statement to his officers. "Here we are," he said, "torn away from the Senate and the Forum to fight in the battlefields of France." There was little to be contrived in the way of a reply except the usual "Sirs," although one lieutenant said later that he greatly admired Churchill's choice of the literal "torn away."

The good people of Ploegsteert cheered warmly as the battalion marched through, and Captain X observed that "had they only known, [our arrival] meant that most of them would say farewell to their homes within a very few days as a result

of the retaliation of the enemy for the bellicose attitude of our
Division as a whole."

Churchill's personal attitude changed sharply as the unit approached the guns. He began to take on a professionally
martial manner and seemed to be quietly playing a role pitched
somewhere between Marlborough and Napoleon. At 3 A.M. on
the night before they entered the lines, he sent orderlies to
arouse everybody to "make preparations against a possible gas
attack." Since gas had not been reported that far back for upwards of a year, one of the officers, declining to rise, with suitable oaths, cried, "What for? The man's daft!" "Colonel says
the wind has shifted to the right direction, sir," answered the
orderly. Nobody got up, and the gas did not materialize. The
next night at 2 A.M. the battalion crept into the trenches. Word
from the colonel was soon sent along the lines that tomorrow
was the Kaiser's birthday. There was considerable exclaiming
over this, the men not knowing quite what was expected of
them. It was bitterly regretted that they had not remembered to
get him anything, and one or two offered to bake him a cake.
"We may expect a bombardment," said Churchill's next message, clearing the air. Sure enough, not long after daylight, a
couple of enemy guns spoke up and knocked several grooves in
a Fusilier parapet. Two men scornfully grabbed shovels and
began to repair the damage, in the style of children playing at
a beach. Churchill came sprinting up with a look of terrible
agitation. "Throw them down!" he cried. "Stand back—leave
everything as it is—they mustn't know that they've harmed us."

"Why, bless you, sir, they haven't harmed us," said one of
the soldiers. "They've only kicked up a bit of dirt."

"Stand back!" cried Churchill. "Leave the holes!"

The men threw down their shovels and retired, and a few
minutes later a bullet whistled through one of the openings and
struck a corporal named Bisbee in the rump. He was conveyed
to the rear while shouting happily at the fellows, "The colonel
was sure right about that dirt! Leave it lay—no more trenches
for me!"

Of Churchill in these first days at the front, one of his officers says, "Early and late he was in the line. On an average he went round three times a day, which was no mean task in itself, as he had plenty of other work to do. At least one of these visits was after dark, usually about 1 A.M. In wet weather he would appear in a complete outfit of waterproof stuff, including trousers, or overalls, and with his French light-blue helmet he presented a remarkable and unusual figure." It was a fetish of Churchill's to keep his finger on each operation in progress, no matter how trivial, and this enduring nosiness was a heavy burden on his unit. He had, for example, set up as an authority on sandbagging, presumably having stolen aside to do some light reading on the subject. He would appear in the trenches when sandbags were being handled and deliver a formal lecture. "To see Winston giving a dissertation on the laying of sandbags, with practical illustrations," says Captain X, "was to come inevitably to the conclusion that his life-study had been purely in poliorketics and the corresponding counter-measures. You felt sure from his grasp of practice that he must have served apprentice to a bricklayer and a master-mason, while his theoretical knowledge rendered you certain that Wren would have been proud to sit at his feet, or even such a master of the subject as Uncle Toby Shandy."

The only trouble with Churchill's applied omniscience was that it often didn't work. In nearly every case wherein he imposed his sandbag erudition on some ignorant sergeant, the latter turned out to be right. Also, as one of his men has said, he had an unfortunate method of egging on his troops. This consisted of comparing their efforts adversely with those of the Gordon Highlanders. And yet, an officer says, "While at times his demands were a little extravagant, his kindliness and the humor that never failed to flash out made everybody only too keen to get on with the work, whether the ideal he pointed out to them was an unattainable one or not."

One of Churchill's most unattainable ideals was to provide a bodyguard for each of his officers. In a meeting one day he said that, in future, officers in the trenches would keep their batmen at their sides "at all times." It was explained that, officers being valuable, they could be succored with more celerity in this way should catastrophe strike. The plan was given only a cursory tryout. Its great defect was that batmen were scarce, one usually being shared by three officers, and in addition they served as mess attendants. However, since the colonel's orders were plain, a gesture or so was made. During the first day of the project, several groups of four persons— three officers and a batman—were seen moving awkwardly here and there, trying to correlate their business. At mess, the situation worsened. One triumvirate of three officers tried to eat *en bloc*, so as to ease their batman's problem, and another, whose man was assigned to a different shift, stood unobtrusively in a corner until he was finished. But the system as a whole broke down over the matter of sleeping. There was clearly no way for three officers and a batman to get into one bunk, and somebody finally summoned the courage to tell Churchill so. The order was withdrawn.

The battalion slept, of course, but not very much during Churchill's stay. He kept everybody busy, organizing huge working parties and decreeing that the jobs must be finished in some ludicrously inadequate time. One day when he was dining at his convent headquarters, a shell plopped through the roof and, in exploding, broke a soup plate, which wounded the adjutant in the right thumb. "That little farm presented such a scene for the next few days as must have been witnessed at the erection of the Pyramids," says Captain X. "It swarmed with activity—men coming and going and carrying (and cursing) and climbing and hammering and shoveling, while Ramsey [the adjutant] looked on and commanded and implored and directed and misdirected and a thousand times a day wished himself back in B Company."

Besides building, Churchill was very keen on artillery. In fact, the entire village of Ploegsteert moved out in disgust only a few days after he arrived. Helpful and good-neighborly to the end, he lent them battalion transport wagons in which to haul their household goods, and waved them down the road with many a cry of *"C'est la guerre."* If the growls of the Ploegsteerters were any indication, the general feeling was that *"C'est le Churchill,"* since, as the village midwife said, they had never had any trouble of this kind before he came. The nuns were among the very first to leave, and it was remarked that only their religion prevented them from speaking their minds. The 6th Fusiliers owned a battery of 18-pounders, which the colonel liked to keep booming at odd hours. "We'll scramble the Hun's sleep," he told his men. Aside, they pointed out to each other that what he was doing was scrambling *their* sleep, too, but they knuckled under and kept the ammunition handy. The gun crew would be bounced out of bed at 2 A.M. or 3 A.M. and told to "fire ten rounds—wake those fellows up." The firing would commence, and the enemy would shortly start lobbing shells over in retaliation, and maybe knock down another church in Ploegsteert. Churchill soon tired of the 18-pounder and made friends with General Tudor, who commanded the divisional artillery. From then on the nights were a perfect hell. The colonel had his officers telephoning back for bombardments every hour or two, and the Germans apparently moved up several more big guns to keep pace. When it began to dawn on everybody that the sector threatened to become dangerous, the divisional artillery crews took to presenting arguments during the night shifts. At these times, Churchill would get on the telephone personally and explain the largely imaginary situation, drawing on technical gibberish culled from his Sandhurst days to suggest that the Hun was poised to go over the top—something that had not yet started in that area. "And after a while and after much further argument," says Captain X, "they would give in and the night would be rendered hideous by repeated series of shocking explosions, during which the entire Division awoke from its slumbers and asked itself if this was the Great Push or only another of Winston's tunes on a borrowed fiddle."

One of the most heart-warming aspects of Churchill's residence in the trenches was his paternal attitude toward his troops. It grieved him to find young boys trembling in fear on sentry-go; he would quit his other duties to mount the fire step and explain in a kind and patient manner that little likelihood existed of their being hit. He lived in mortal terror, too, of having men reported for sleeping on the job, and was forever making up excuses that might mitigate their crime if they were caught. His feeling was, perhaps, not unlike that of Lincoln, who could never take a stern and unrelenting view of this capital military mistake. When somebody was wounded, Churchill was all bustle and concern. He hopped right down to the spot and carried on a learned dialogue with the doctor, and, if feasible, with the patient. He would pad along beside the stretcher, offering medical reasons, conspicuously inexpert, why the sufferer would be up and around soon. The men were devoted to him and took enormous pride in him, but the doctor finally became exasperated. "The confounded fellow treats me like a surgeon's orderly," he told one lieutenant, now a high officer in the British Army. Churchill's apprehension about the chance of his men getting into trouble, any kind of trouble, was so sharp that he always lined up new recruits at his headquarters for a personal indoctrination. And for some reason not largely understood, this invariably took the form of a lecture on drunkenness. On one occasion, twenty youngsters reported in, filled with fright at the horrendous stories about this region to which the enemy appeared to give priority, and Churchill left his dinner to attend them. He ordered a bottle of champagne to be recorked as he left, and he hurried outside, where he tendered them all a fatherly tongue-lashing on the evils of drink.

There is good reason to believe that the Germans knew Churchill was at the front near Ploegsteert. It was an unending point of speculation with the Fusiliers. Certainly more shelling went on between those lines than in any other area near by. Churchill himself felt that the Hun thought he was in the trenches but did not know exactly where. He told his officers at one mess, "I am just as well known in Germany as Tirpitz is in England and they don't like me there: they hate me. If they knew I was in the line here they wouldn't send over a few shells like this. They would turn on all their guns and blot the place out. They would love to do that."

The colonel could always find extenuating circumstances for soldiers talking back to non-commissioned officers. His leniency in this regard was so notorious that many of his officers resented it mildly. The situation actually descended to a point, say several members of the battalion, where the stock answer from a soldier to a sergeant, upon being given an order, was "Kindly go to hell." Churchill's staff had to work hard to maintain discipline. The colonel himself did not insist on rigor in his relationships with subordinates. He loved argument and was never so happy as when one of the most colorful and unreconstructed products of the war, Canadian Captain H. T. ("Foghorn") MacDonald, was attached to his group as observer. MacDonald took over altogether. Without precedent in Churchill's history, the newcomer monopolized all mess conversations, using the most frightful profanity, and bragged and blew until the whole battalion was all but paralyzed with admiration. "He was the embodiment or incarnation of that rude hustling force both in word and action which by a long tract of experience we have come to associate with persons bred in America," said Captain X.

Churchill loved him. One of the unit later remarked that he had never seen the colonel "take second place in conversation to anyone save Foghorn, who treated with noisy scorn such of Winston's ideas as differed from his own, and who when he found that they were in agreement would suffer no other person than himself to expound their common views." Churchill's laughter at MacDonald's Paul Bunyanesque statements rocked the nunnery; the C.O.'s contribution was to draw the observer out. Under pressure, MacDonald admitted that, once the war was over and he had become a soldier of fortune, he would

probably wind up as King of Mexico. He had been turning the
plan over. Churchill modestly urged him to present his ideas
on the political situation there. As reported by Captain X, "His
opinion of Villa was that he hadn't a — of use for the — son
of a ———. His opinion of Carranza on the other hand was to
the effect that —————————————————."

Churchill had a cavalier manner with distinguished sight-
seers and high military brass. Even his commanding generals
trod softly around him, having the uneasy feeling that a former
Cabinet minister just *might* get to be a minister again, and
maybe even Secretary for War. The colonel's great friend, Lord
Birkenhead (F. E. ["Galloper"] Smith), who had risen to be
one of England's foremost legal minds and had a delicate job
at GHQ, came to inspect Churchill's battalion. One of the
guards looked over his credentials and found them in im-
proper legal shape. Churchill seemed mildly rueful as Smith
was arrested and led away, and reportedly commented that it
was "the fortunes of both war and law."

After one dinner party (an occasion mentioned with awe
and laughter for years by the 6th Fusiliers) Churchill asked
a scintillant collection of guests, including some of the most
famous generals then at the front, if they would like "a little
entertainment." They responded eagerly, with visions of
French dancing girls, and he led them on a relaxing stroll to
the trenches. He did not go by way of the communications
trench, but on top of the ground, as he made all his own inspection trips. In the darkness there were muffled giggles from
the unseen troops as these dignitaries stumbled over sandbags,
tore holes in their gorgeous uniforms at the wire, and wallowed
in mudholes. "What a lovely night," remarked their host. "But
isn't there considerable danger of being hit up here?" asked a
well-known paper-work general who had never been near the
lines before. "This is a very dangerous war," replied the former
Cabinet minister.

The chances are that there will never be another Mess like
Churchill's. He had his couriers scouring the countryside for

tasty viands, and he once sent a man to bespeak Hazebrouck's entire seasonal production of peach and apricot brandy. He also bought all the lobster and tinned fruit in Armentières, paying good prices. Sometimes the money came out of the Mess Treasury, usually presided over by the doctor, and sometimes the officers suspected that the colonel supplied the funds himself. The main reason for the Lucullan flavor to their dining was that Churchill enjoyed good living; moreover, they were obliged to entertain a steady queue of guests, of high and low degree. Churchill was a celebrity, one of the best-known in the world, and it was hard for many people to believe that he actually was in Ploegsteert with a bunch of wild Scotsmen. The skeptics, if they could wangle a pass, came over to see. Churchill treated the bright spirits with punctilio, and with the aid of Foghorn MacDonald pulled the legs of the bores.

His officers were surprised at the candor with which their colonel spoke of the most delicate aspects of his career. He characterized Fisher, Kitchener, and Asquith, calling the first a greathearted fighter (and a "ferocious brute"), the second a "very nice old cup of tea," and the last a number of things not altogether complimentary. However, the epithets were used without bitterness and were the seemingly dispassionate views of an observer of tested ability. Churchill talked freely about his experiences in connection with Antwerp and the Dardanelles, and, says one officer, "I for my part was quite won over and believed, as I believe to this hour, in the justness of the decision he then took."

To a man, the 6th Fusiliers backed Churchill solidly. They were enthusiastic about both his faults and his virtues. If he overrode them about sandbags, they listened with respect, then made things right later. If his methods seemed eccentric, they thought up excuses, generally saying that it was high time the Army provided such-and-such for everybody. This had particular application to his tin bathtub. One morning Churchill hailed an itinerant tinker and put him to work; the upshot was a bathtub of a type never seen before or since. It was shaped like a giant soap dish, and, perhaps as a result of some latent humor in the workman, had a suggestion of fluted sides, in the manner of Venus' shell. It was the colonel's custom to board this outrageous vehicle around ten o'clock each morning, at a spot beneath some trees in the farmyard. And, generously, he lent it to others. Perhaps the only man not sold on the tub was Watt, Churchill's batman, who had to fill it with hot water. Churchill liked to set up a phonograph on a beer barrel alongside, whereupon Watt was instructed to keep the records moving. As the melodies soared up into the smoke-filled air, contending with the divisional artillery, Churchill sat reading a pocket edition of Shakespeare. If the shelling was severe, he bathed with his blue tin hat on.

The commanding officer was probably the solitary member of the battalion who considered the recordings melodious. Thoroughly unmusical, Churchill was autocratic in his choice of numbers. His favorites were "Dear Old Dublin," not especially popular with the Royal Scots, and something called "Chalk Farm to Camberwell Green," a jerky piece of nostalgia about a place the Scots had never seen. "What an excellent composition—that gets to you, does it not?" Churchill would say to his officers, and they would wander off on trumped-up errands. Even so, it was a melancholy day when he left. In May of 1916 orders came for the battalion to be dispersed and amalgamated with other units of the regiment. At the same time, a political crisis had arisen back home. The question of conscription, which Churchill had fiercely supported, was hanging in the balance, and pressures were being applied to have him resume his parliamentary duties. During his stay, his tactical genius had never been tried, but he had left a soldierly mark. The 6th Royal Scots Fusiliers held a final orderly-room session near the town of Béthune. There were refreshments. Churchill looked tired; he had spent days beating paths to all the high rank he knew, seeking good billets for his officers. The adjutant, a noted teetotaler, showed up drunk. He made no apology but said, rather, "I have never made a speech before, but in the last hour I have prepared myself to do so now." He then went on to tell an embarrassed Churchill that the assembly would never again have a commanding officer they liked half so well. He made a good many heartfelt remarks, and the officers all cried, "Hear! Hear!" Churchill then delivered himself of what must be regarded as a singular farewell. "Whatever else they may say of me as a soldier," he told his charges with obvious affection, "at least nobody can say I have ever failed to display a meet and proper appreciation of the virtues of alcohol."

As he walked across the yard to the bus that was to take him away, both officers and men cheered. Then they struck up a tune—one of the dismal substitutes for the lively painting song—and the piper marched out and tootled the best of *his* feeble repertory. Churchill turned abruptly, with a curt, victorious sign similar to one that would become famous in another war a quarter of a century later, and without more ado went on his way, missed by all.

A graceful obituary to his life in the trenches has been written by Captain X, who said, "He came to be looked on really as a possession of our own, and one of which we were intensely proud. And much more, he became our friend. He is a man who apparently is always to have enemies. He made none in his old regiment, but left behind him men who will always be his loyal partizans and admirers, and who are proud of having served in the Great War under the leadership of one who is beyond question a great man."

# Chapter 21

ETURNING home to stir up Parliament, Churchill found himself in a frustrating position—without power, portfolio, or backing. But he was still the Member for Dundee, and he set about destroying complacency wherever he could find it, which was nearly everywhere. First he made a rackety speech urging the creation of a separate Air Ministry, and succeeded in cementing the foundation of the present Royal Air Force. More or less in return, he was informed that a Committee of Inquiry would be held on the Dardanelles campaign; not too surprisingly, Churchill was to be given prominent billing as the star witness.

With the herculean energies that had never flagged, he went to work preparing his case and had plenty of time left over to turn out a great number of magazine articles on the war, receiving for most the praiseworthy sum of twenty-five hundred dollars. Warming up to his writing, he composed a thundering document on the Battle of the Somme, which he circulated among the Cabinet. It provoked a near-riot. Its main contention was that Sir Douglas Haig's estimate that "the enemy's losses in men and material have been very considerably higher than those of the Allies" was significantly wrong. Churchill's estimate, stunning all of England, was that Germany had lost men in the proportion of 1 to 2.3 of the British. Deposed from power or not, he had been right too often in the past to ignore. A careful examination of the facts, completed after the war, showed that the true figures for the Somme were 1 German killed to 2.27 British. His document contained a good many more upsets and predictions, but it did not, for a while, restore him his crown and scepter. Nothwithstanding that it was received with scorn, the Army adopted it in after years as "a model for Staff Officers to show how the deductive process can be used in military calculations."

This was a provoking period for Churchill, a lull in a career bristling with action. As a self-styled "Opposition Member" in a Coalition Government, he was tilting with invisible dragons; it was all but impossible to separate foes from friends. Perhaps out of desperation, and to take up the slack, he turned to painting, at first only a pastime and today a polished facet of his creative life. Churchill made his entrance into the arena of art through the back door, so to speak. The Armored Car Division in France, a unit he had brought into being against the sagest council of the existing military minds, wished to tender him an appreciation and commissioned Sir John Lavery, an accomplished and famous artist, to do his portrait. Sir John did a splendid job, as may now be seen in the Municipal Gallery of Dublin, but he did it under stresses. Churchill became fascinated by the technical end of the project and refused to remain in the pose. He was eternally popping around to check on the artist's progress; after a few days he began to give Lavery helpful little hints. Sir John countered with several priceless lectures on painting, and before long Churchill had swung into full stride. Characteristically, he provided himself with every known accessory of the guild—a gigantic easel, a light blue smock, and a flapping beret the size of a small tent. In the words of one of his friends, "He was a hell of sight, if you know what I mean."

Regardless of his visual impression, Churchill forged ahead rapidly. In almost no time the boulevardiers of war-torn Paris were treated to an exhibition by an unknown and probably struggling artist named Charles Morin, which was the succinct *nom de brush* that the former First Lord of the British Admiralty had ·chosen. It was noted that foremost among the

budding Morin's offerings was a quite recognizable portrait of
Sir John Lavery, the well-known English artist.

Some details of Churchill's artistic bent will be considered
later in this volume; now in 1916 his beginning work with
brush and easel tided him over a bad time and simultaneously
nurtured a strong talent that might have withered had he been
otherwise fully occupied.

Churchill's personal bad time was negligible compared with
the dark days that had descended upon England as a result of
blundering by the war government. Catastrophe followed close
on the heels of calamity. Sir Douglas Haig's campaign of the
Somme had cost 600,000 casualties. Unmoved, with the English phlegm that is so admirable in some connections and has
proved so tragic in others, he announced himself as still in
favor of a "war of attrition," in which British manpower would
be matched against German and emerge triumphant, though
possibly with only a couple of dozen men left. In accordance
with this cynical view, he went ahead with his unholy action at
Passchendaele, where he expended 500,000 soldiers in an unworkable effort to gain possession of a swamp that was without
military significance and of whose terrain, it was later shown,
neither he nor his chief of intelligence had any concrete knowledge whatever. Besides these setbacks, Asquith's Government
had abandoned Rumania and Serbia to be run over, allowed
Bulgaria to join the enemy, watched Russia disintegrate, and
let a British expedition in Mesopotamia expire for lack of
supply and Ireland flare up in the Sinn Fein Rebellion.

To give the holocaust flavor, Arthur Balfour, as Churchill's
successor in the Admiralty, urged a timid hide-and-seek program for his fleet, then saw it decimated at the Battle of Jutland, in which he and the tentative Admiral Jellicoe claimed a
victory on the technical ground that the Germans (though with
smaller losses) fled first from the scene. Balfour was not apprehensive about submarines. In consequence, the Germans were
able to develop an underwater flotilla that, by 1917, had sunk
almost every Allied and neutral vessel in all the sea lanes lead-

ing to Europe. For his part, Kitchener, as War Minister, had been dilatory to the point where he had managed to arrive just short of the nick of time in nearly every instance in which troops or matériel were critically wanted. In Malcolm Thompson's *Life of Churchill,* the author observes that "After the Dardanelles campaign he [Kitchener] seemed to lose his nerve entirely, and the nation's war effort floundered and halted in consequence."

The situation plainly indicated an infusion of new blood with a higher red corpuscle count. In December of 1916, Lloyd George brought about the resignation of Asquith and succeeded him as Prime Minister. And when a good deal of savage Tory opposition was quelled, he appointed his old friend Churchill Minister of Munitions. The appointment was opportune, since the new minister had just come out of the Dardanelles quiz with a surprisingly clean bill of health, considering the popular notion of his culpability. With typical British candor, the Committee of Inquiry, whose members had been appointed by Asquith, issued a report in which Asquith himself was rather severely criticized. It was felt that Churchill's basic plan was sound but that Kitchener's halfhearted troop support had botched things fatally. Asquith was condemned for not exerting the necessary pressures on his reluctant field marshal. The fact that Churchill got off lightly gave him a vast amount of badly needed prestige; and some favorable publicity in the press, which had harried him devotedly of late, provided what he interpreted as a green light for gala operations at the Ministry of Munitions.

These took the form of a mobilization of the kingdom's resources so all-embracing that it wrung piteous howls from several other ministries, which succeeded in hauling him up before a Priorities Committee on the old complaint that he was trying to hog the show. Churchill was advised of his limitations, after which he continued his reforms. He arranged a means of commuting to the front: he arrived at his Whitehall office early in the morning, worked hard for several hours, rushed by motorcar to Hendon Airport, and took a plane to a fancy château the French Government had been persuaded to supply him near Verchocq. Before each day was finished, he had usually managed to hop off in another, smaller plane from his château and fly recklessly over the hottest actions. He dropped in on the French military leaders so frequently with ideas and gigantic plans that, according to excellent sources, they adopted the practice of hiding when they heard he was coming. On one occasion, he took the frail and aged Clemenceau on an exhausting visit to the front-line trenches, where the bombs burst all about them. "Did you enjoy it?" asked Churchill on the way back. "What a delicious moment," replied the French Premier.

A heartening aspect of his ministry was that, upon the first inkling of American intervention in the war, Churchill displayed that practical view of his overseas cousins for which he has always been noted. In a ringing speech, he cried, "Bring on the American millions! And, meanwhile, maintain an active defensive on the Western Front, so as to economize French and British lives and to train, increase, and perfect our armies and our methods for a decisive effort later." When the United States entered the war, Churchill was given the job of equipping the American millions he had spoken of, and he did it so well that, afterward, General Pershing presented him with the Distinguished Service Medal. He was the only Englishman to wear this decoration. His assignment to prepare American soldiers for combat brought him into contact with Bernard Baruch, who was then chairman of the War Industries Board at Washington. They developed a close friendship that has continued without interruption to the present.

In the last year of the war Churchill committed himself to an "anti-liberal" action that gave him his envied start toward becoming the premier target of the left-wingers, or plotters against society. Despite his history of fifty years of humanitarian endeavors, he stands today as a sort of free-enterprise lightning rod, drawing off the furies of ideological conspiracy. His first such unpopularity was gained in the strikes of 1918, which were similar to the Communist-planned stoppages that swept America in the recent war. Like President Truman in the later crisis, Churchill threatened to end the strikers' immunity from military service unless they returned to work. Though the mass lamentations and wails of the radical press were heart-rending, he held fast to his convictions. It was pointed out that men fighting with guns were not permitted to strike for higher pay, or for a four-hour day, and that industrialists were discouraged by law from war profiteering; the question was then raised why workers should be treated with special deference. Faced with the prospect of a low-paid and even dangerous life in the trenches, the men went back to their jobs, and the war was allowed to continue to its successful conclusion.

When peace came, it returned to Churchill much of his lost favor. The ghost of the Dardanelles had been laid, or at least forgotten for the moment, and traces of the victorious youth who had escaped from the Boers were again seen by a forgiving public. On the night of the Armistice, he and his wife entered their automobile in front of their house in Northumberland Avenue and started for the Prime Minister's. People in the street saw them and started a cheering stampede that swarmed upon the car from every direction. The couple were driven slowly through Trafalgar Square and into Whitehall, while what seemed to be half of London waved and applauded and sought to shake the minister's hand. In the Government he soon consolidated his gains with such speed that, as the Tories blinked, he found himself in the unprecedented position of holding two offices—Secretary for War and Secretary for Air. The protests that arose over this artistic coup shook the Cabinet. The old epithet of "medal snatcher" was changed to "portfolio collector." A Captain Wedgwood Benn, a Liberal M.P., arose in Parliament and complained so testily that General Seely, the Under-Secretary for Air, was suddenly convinced of Churchill's villainy and resigned. The Minister for Air and War placidly continued with the business at hand. His

sang-froid had been so firmly re-established that he had not even
bothered to campaign in the "Khaki election" of 1918. At
Dundee the inexhaustible Scrymgeour made enough racket for
both of them. The teetotaler had settled into a career of being
defeated at the polls by Winston Churchill. Before this last setback, he had learned—the news had somehow leaked out in
Scotland through relatives of the 6th Fusiliers—that Churchill
was in the habit of taking an occasional nip. Screaming imprecations on strong drink and all of its acolytes, Scrymgeour implored Dundee to turn the tippler out. Instead, the city stamped
its approval on Churchill's manners by voting him an immense
majority. Biding his time for the next opportunity, Scrymgeour
sought solace in his water jug.

As Minister for Air, Churchill established a reputation for
being the worst pilot yet developed by aviation. He appeared to
have an uncanny instinct for making the wrong move. The fact
is, he crashed with regularity. To carry out the business of
demobilization, he found it convenient to fly often into France,
and the peasants in outlying areas came to know him well. In
the last days of the war he had enjoyed the distinction of crashing twice in the same day, a record still admired in aeronautics
circles. Along with a "co-pilot," he had taken off for London
from the French General Headquarters in a plane that nobody
else would touch (he had a patriotic bias against pre-empting
aircraft that might be put to better work elsewhere). Five
miles out in the Channel, the engine quit and they headed
toward the sea. Churchill was trying to get out of his heavy
clothing when a few strangled pops hauled them back up
briefly. They made it to Gris Nez and flapped down near the
aerodrome. The plane was patched up, serviced, and assisted
into the air again. This time Churchill and his pilot were more
than halfway across when the engine sighed feebly and dimin-
ished to one or two cylinders. With fifty feet of altitude left at
the English shore, they crash-landed safely in a grove of elms.

Churchill's pilot after the war was Captain Jack Scott, an
ace who had been decorated several times and had a crooked

leg from an aviation injury. The procedure was for the two to fly in a dual-control plane with Churchill doing the actual piloting and Scott keeping an eye open for mishaps. They left a small airport in southeast England one morning headed for London. A light drizzle set in and Churchill quickly deduced that they needed altitude. He took the plane up to 15,000 feet, an unusual height in those days, and made his reckoning for the London field. He came down three hours later at an aerodrome in France. Several hours later, the weather clearing, he got them back to London, as originally planned. They could have made the return trip more speedily had not the plane burst into flames over the English Channel, presumably as a result of some maneuvers Churchill was attempting. Scott put the craft into a power dive and the fire went out.

Not long afterward, Churchill was in a hurry to keep an appointment in Paris and he and Scott made a fast take-off in an antiquated biplane, which rose a foot or so into the air, turned over, and collapsed. As usual, Churchill and Scott climbed out of the wreckage unhurt. Churchill seemed to have been born under some benign celestial influence. His rashest acts—errors that caused him immense immediate concern—commonly turned out to have a long-term silver lining. In the summer of 1919 he and Scott flew neatly into a vicious sideslip and hit the turf with vigor. Churchill gathered himself together, intact in his essentials, but Scott had said farewell to aviation for some time to come. He lay senseless and bleeding on the ground. As rapidly as possible, he was carried off to a hospital, from which the news at first was bad: the famous ace was not apt to fly again. A later bulletin rolled away the pall: Scott would recover. A third report carried on Churchill's tradition for winning the war no matter how the battles went. Owing to the peculiarity of his fall, Scott's crippled leg was twisted in such a way that an operation was necessitated which set it absolutely straight again. He walked out of the hospital a whole man, though in a somewhat different direction from where he was likely to find Churchill.

As it developed, Scott could have gone in any direction with an easy mind, for the Secretary for War and Air had decided to give up flying. The truth is that the accident which injured Scott so beneficially had soured Churchill on piloting. The first faint hint that there were flaws in his technique had begun to enter his mind. According to one of his friends, he even was persuaded, with his wife's help, and further aided by the counsel of unbiased experts, that unless he laid off the controls he could not expect to live over a few months more at the outside.

His attention was focused on sterner matters, notably the business of demobilization and with it the connected state of affairs in Russia. The charge had arisen that Churchill was impeding demobilization in order to assist the White Russians, Admiral Kolchak and General Denikin. As Kipling had put it, this was "the time of peril—the time of the Truce of the Bear." The ugly mooncalf of Bolshevism was climbing out of its cradle. The revolution led by Lenin and Trotsky had ended Russia's participation in the war and had provided the sprawling and benighted country with civil strife instead. Now the Bolshevists wished to come to terms with the civilized world, and especially with England, where Red Russian agents were diligently at work propagandizing their cause. Two top agents, Comrades Litvinoff and Rothstein, had found useful employment in London, the former as confidential adviser to the Russian section of the British Foreign Office, and the latter in the Foreign Press section of the War Office. They had been doing a masterly job of distortion, and a certain few among the ignorant, the gullible, and the conniving were favorably affected.

Churchill came into his dual ministerhood with a heritage of commitments to the White Russians. Despite current Communist statements to the contrary, he inclined at first to the Bolshevist upheaval over the rotting regime of czarism. However, being a man of at least normal perception, he was quickly able to see Bolshevism, or Communism, in its true and sickly light of suppression and mass murder. And being Churchill, he did not hesitate to say so. "A man is called reactionary in Russia," he observed in Commons, "if he objects to having his property stolen and his wife and children slaughtered." Touching on his new resolve to assist the Whites with all the power of his offices, he said, "Britain is not unmindful of our obligations to the gallant men in Russia who helped us to fight the Germans when the Bolshevist leaders were betraying the Allies on that Front." Before long he unburdened himself of a sort of definitive statement on Communism that stands up remarkably well today:

"Was there ever a more awful spectacle in the whole history of the world than is unfolded by the agony of Russia? This vast country, this mighty branch of the human family, not only produced enough food for itself but, before the War, was one of the great granaries of the world, from which food was exported to every country. It is now reduced to famine of the most terrible kind—not because there is no food—there is plenty of food—but because the theories of Lenin and Trotsky have fatally and, it may be, finally ruptured the means of intercourse between man and man, between workman and peasant, between town and country; because they have shattered the system of scientific communication by rail and river on which the life of great countries depends; because they have raised class against class and race against race in fratricidal war; because they have given vast regions where a little time ago were smiling villages or prosperous townships back to the wolves and the bears; because they have driven man from the civilization of the twentieth century into a condition of barbarism worse than the Stone Age, and left him the most awful and pitiable spectacle in human experience, devoured by vermin, racked by pestilence, and deprived of hope."

This address was received with calmness by the long-range planners in Moscow. They held an elaborate ceremony in which was conferred on Churchill (in absentia) the Order of the Red Flag, in mock appreciation of his devoted contributions to the Cause.

Notwithstanding the War Secretary's clairvoyant efforts, Lloyd George (who had also been exercised by the plight of the Dartmoor Shepherd) went ahead and recognized the Bolshevists as the government of Russia, and granted them fine trade privileges.

Six years later, Churchill would be vindicated and England would kick the plotters out.

## II

Toward the end of 1920 the Government decided that the Cabinet post most needful of an aggressive spirit was the Colonial Office. A number of vexing predicaments, in the Far East and elsewhere, were costing England enormous sums of money. Through appeals to his patriotism, Churchill was persuaded to lay aside the doublet of Mars and don the toga of conciliation. He became Colonial Secretary, a ministerhood in which he had begun his Cabinet career, in 1906, as Under-Secretary. His immediate problem was Iraq, so explosive that a large army of occupation had to be maintained in the desert country at all times. The cost of this one military commitment alone ran to about $200,000,000 annually.

Churchill first created a Middle East Department to deal with the diverse interests represented in the area and then stunned everybody by announcing that he was calling in Colonel T. E. Lawrence, the mysterious, nomadic "Lawrence of Arabia," to act as adviser to the Government. In the England of the period, this was regarded as beyond the pale. Lawrence had proved himself to be a renegade from his race, a man who had disappeared into the shifting dunes of a dark and inscrutable land to take up life with a heathen people. His appearances in the world of stilted speech and tea sets were both brief and inconclusive. During the peace conference after the war, he had turned up in Paris on behalf of his Arab brothers. His visit did nothing to endear him to his fellow Englishmen. He strode the boulevards of the French capital garbed in an Arabian burnous and hood and with a formidable dagger thrust into a wide red belt. Once offered the order of Commander of the Bath and the Distinguished Service Order (for his unifying work in Arabia in the war), he turned the honors aside casually. At the peace conference he had been snubbed socially by everybody except Churchill, who invited him to lunch and then dressed him down for being so offhand with the King.

In spite of the general snub, or perhaps because of the lunch, Lawrence now presented himself in Cairo at Churchill's request and plunged into the work of ironing out the Iraqi difficulties with easy, unobtrusive co-operation. Churchill was delighted and, at the conclusion of a meeting with him, said, "Now we must secure for you some commensurately high office in His Majesty's service."

"All you will see of me," replied Lawrence, "is a small cloud of dust on the horizon." He was swallowed up forthwith by the blazing sands that he had chosen for his home. Later on, in his monumental memoirs, *The Seven Pillars of Wisdom* (of which the first manuscript was lost, requiring him to spend several years writing another), Lawrence said of his sessions with the new Colonial Secretary, "Churchill in a few weeks made straight all the tangle, finding solutions, fulfilling, I think, our promises in letter and spirit, where humanly possible, without sacrificing any interests of our Empire or of the peoples concerned."

It might be noted of the strange and unpredictable Lawrence that he finally tired of the desert, and, for some reason changing his name to Shaw, enlisted in the Royal Air Force as a lowly mechanic. He was killed in a motorcycle accident, in England, in 1935.

As a result of Churchill's bizarre Middle East Department, he was able to inform Commons that the army of occupation would be withdrawn, to be replaced only by a patrolling air force, at a yearly saving of $165,000,000. There was some discussion whether an air force was competent to keep order, but the Secretary was permitted to continue, and he proved to be right.

It was during his tenure in the Colonial Office, and largely because of his efforts, that the Anglo-Irish Treaty was passed, giving Ireland Dominion status and leaving the Protestant counties of Ulster in an alliance with England. Churchill's soothing ways with the fiery revolutionists prevailed where touchier diplomats had failed. One evening in Churchill's home, Michael Collins, the leader of the Sinn Fein, blew up and began to rant about the fact of Britain's having once placed a price of $50,000 on his head. He abused Churchill with variety and fervor. The Colonial Secretary listened throughout with respectful attention, then, during an unexpected lull, stepped into his study and brought out a framed sample of the Boers' £25 reward after his escape from Pretoria. "If you were offended at the price on your head, imagine how I must feel," he told Collins, who relaxed, started to laugh, and kept it up most of the evening. Speaking of the newly created Irish Free State, or Eire, Collins afterward said, "Tell Winston we could never have done anything without him." Two days later he was struck down and killed by the gunfire of Dublin extremists.

As Colonial Secretary, Churchill did important work to make Palestine a national home for Jews. He was often bitterly opposed by anti-Zionists, who accused him of all manner of perfidy. At one point their ire was centered on his granting of an irrigation concession to a Phineas Rutenberg, described by the press and in Parliament as a "Jewish Bolshevist." The opposition died down when documents were produced in which it was revealed that Rutenberg had spent a considerable portion of 1917 trying to get the Russian authorities to hang both Lenin and Trotsky. Speaking in Commons, Churchill complained, "It is hard enough in all conscience to make a new Zion, but if, over the portals of the new Jerusalem you are going to inscribe the legend, 'No Israelite need apply,' I hope the House will permit me in future to confine my attention exclusively to Irish matters."

Due indirectly to his role in the Zionist movement, Churchill became involved in the Crown's criminal libel action against Lord Alfred Douglas, a retired poet. It was a bang-up trial, the pre-eminent entertainment of that year. Everybody concerned (and the defense in particular) agreed that Churchill made one of the most impudent witnesses on record. Douglas had first emerged on the public scene as the inseparable companion of Oscar Wilde, the noted flower fancier. The two had walked together, both night and day, and while it was felt that Douglas' gait was easily as mincing as Wilde's, his verses were regarded as second-rate. Subordination of this kind might alter the mood of an extrovert, and it proved disastrous to a chum of Oscar Wilde's. Douglas lapsed into brooding and biting his nails. His works declined in proportion. Whereas he had formerly dashed off neat but unaggressive little couplets dealing with petunias and the higher aesthetics, he now took to writing *against* things. To make his plight more desperate professionally, these essays were mostly in prose, a medium in which his technique had a distinctly meat-ax cast. In none of his later pieces was this style more evident than the brochure which he produced and circulated, entitled, *The Murder of Lord Kitchener and the Truth about the Battle of Jutland and the Jews.*

The booklet was mostly about Churchill—charging that he and his father's friend, Sir Ernest Cassel, had got out a false communiqué after Jutland in order to drive down the price of some shares and make a lot of money.

Churchill took the stand to answer questions.

"I suppose you know that the cause of the Serajevo assassination is unknown," said the counsel for His Lordship.

"I can assure you that *I* had nothing to do with it," replied Churchill.

"Then perhaps you know that Sir Ernest Cassel started in the City of London as a clerk at two pounds a week?"

"Is that very much against him?" Churchill inquired.

After a whispered conversation with Douglas, whose face gave away that he had hit on a significant point, the counsel wanted to know if Churchill was aware that the word "I" had occurred thirteen times within thirteen lines of one of his books.

"If that is so it is a great pity," Churchill said. "If you will show me the passage, I will endeavor to cut out a few from the next edition."

He explained that he had not written any of the Admiralty communiqués in the war and then outlined in detail the financial relationship between him and Sir Ernest, who had invested various sums for the Churchill family for years. All in all, Douglas' brochure shaped up as being so feebly rooted that it was plain he must be given time to think it over. The judge thereupon gave him six months, and the case was concluded. There was a story, possibly invented, that Churchill sent him round a copy of his old pal Oscar's well-known prison doggerel, *The Ballad of Reading Gaol*, which he was said to have read in a very ambiguous humor.

III

Churchill's star, having risen so brilliantly after the war, was due to set for a space. All unexpectedly he suffered a series of personal and professional setbacks, a recurring theme in the long and sturdy fabric of his life. As he had done before, and has done since, he endured it all stoically and only awaited his time for a successful *coup d'état*. In late 1921 Lloyd George regrouped his Cabinet in the face of growing Tory opposition to the Coalition. In the minds of the public, there was only one logical choice for the coveted post of Chancellor of the Exchequer, which carries with it leadership of the House and traditionally augurs early succession to the premiership. Churchill's speeches in the recent session had been so powerful and persuasive that he was already considered to be Parliament's *de facto* leader. But the Conservative machine, which he had belabored mercilessly, threatened to end the Coalition in the event of his appointment. Lloyd George passed him over.

So profound was England's astonishment that an anonymous author (later revealed as Harold Begbie) sought to explain Churchill and his mishaps, in a behind-the-scenes political volume called *The Mirrors of Downing Street*.

"With the exception of Lloyd George, Mr. Churchill is the most interesting figure in the House," wrote Begbie. "From the start of his career he was an element of great promise. Sometimes he disappointed his admirers, but he never destroyed their hopes. His intellectual gifts, his unique fighting qualities, also in politics, his boundless personal courage are singular. No man is more difficult to shout down. From his youth he fiercely loved England, war and politics. Politics, to him, are almost as exciting as war and quite as dangerous. In war you can only be killed once, but in politics many times.

"He has many qualities of real greatness—but has he the unifying spirit of character? He has truly brilliant gifts, but you cannot quite depend on them. His love for danger runs away with his discretion. His passion for adventure makes him forget the importance of the goal. Mr. Churchill carries great guns, but his navigation is uncertain. His effect on men is one of interest and curiosity, not of admiration and loyalty. His power is the power of gifts, not of character. Men watch him, but do not follow him. He beguiles their reason, but never warms their emotions. You may see in him the wonderful and lightning movements of the brain, but never the beating of a steadfast heart. His inconsistencies have brought him too often into inferior company. . . .

"All Mr. Churchill needs is the direction in his life of a great idea. He is a Saul on the way to Damascus. Let him swing clean away from that road of destruction, and he might well become Paul on his way to immortality. This is to say that to be saved from himself Mr. Churchill must be carried away by

enthusiasm for some great ideal, an ideal so much greater than
his own place in politics that he is willing to face death for its
triumph, even the many deaths of political life. At present he
is but playing with politics. Even in his most earnest moments
he is 'in politics' as a man is 'in business.' But politics for Mr.
Churchill, if they are to make him, if they are to fulfil his
promise, must be a religion. They must have nothing to do
with Mr. Churchill. They must have everything to do with the
salvation of mankind. It is high time he hitched his waggon to
a star."

This frank estimate is important, if it is important at all,
only in that it represented the view of a good many members
of the Tory Party. They respected Churchill's gifts but distrusted his ambition.

As events shaped up, Lloyd George could have appointed
anybody he chose to head the Exchequer, since the Coalition
came crashing down notwithstanding his omission of Churchill.
As is not uncommon after the pressures of war, the national
psychology was ready for change. The identity of the Administration was of little moment; the voters, having lived under
duress and restriction, were happy to seize any chance to re-
affirm their freedom of thought. Churchill has found himself
caught by this illogical reaction on several occasions. The
Conservative Party disavowed the Coalition and took office
under Bonar Law. There followed a calamitous general election. Churchill's participation was handicapped by an accident
of health. Preparing for a journey to Bristol to make a major
speech, he fell ill and was operated on for acute appendicitis.
The popular account was that, when his doctors informed him
of his danger, he nodded vacantly and said he hoped to look
into the matter the minute he returned from Bristol. Whereupon
one of them, summoning enough courage to beard the lion,
stepped forward and declared himself in exceedingly positive
terms. "I do not imagine that anyone had spoken so sharply to
Winston for twenty years," says one of his friends. The burden
of the physician's message, stripped of references to "mulish-

ness" and "stupidity," was that unless an operation were performed immediately, Churchill would probably come back from Bristol in a hearse.

Nevertheless, the candidate arose from his bed of pain dangerously soon after the surgery and summoned a quartet of stretcher-bearers. "Let us proceed to Dundee," he told them. "I have some electioneering to do." He was transported by stretcher and train to his Scottish constituency and carried in a chair onto a platform at the Town Hall. Never deviating from character, he made no mention of his peculiar appearance but addressed a large gathering from his seated position. His effectiveness was perhaps curtailed. Mr. Scrymgeour, on the other hand, was in a rollicking mood. Having been beaten regularly by Churchill since 1906 on the subject of teetotalism, he had wisely switched his emphasis. Scrymgeour was now in favor of the workingman. But a study of his remarks shows that, if he were elected, it would probably be a workingman without a bottle. Promiscuous and disconnected references were made to Scrymgeour's companion of the years. "And I can certainly tell you," his advice went, "that the deplorable condition in the Aberdeen mines is a subject toward which I intend to devote my considerable energies. Wine is a mocker. Neither can the Coalition escape the inevitable consequences of the present high cost of living. Strong drink is a curse. And in conclusion . . ." and so on.

The twin phantoms of Antwerp and the Dardanelles arose to haunt Churchill again. The people had veered away from a triumphant review of the war and were concerned only with its disasters. When the returns were in, the gibbering Scrymgeour was elected at last to Parliament. The reasons are hard to assess, but it is established that Dundee was powerfully grateful that he'd let up, even slightly, on teetotalism. And to the surprise of practically no one, Scrymgeour arose in the storied and well-nourished House and hurled his opening remarks in a frothing assault on booze. His explosion was so intemperate that another Member showed up the next day

with a glass of beer, which he sipped at intervals while presenting some statistics on hops.

Churchill was out. For the first time since 1900 his warning
voice was absent from the nation's forum. In the words of a
contemporary, it was "a high price to pay for the exaltation of
a whiskey-hating fanatic." The time was 1922; Churchill was
forty-seven years old, a man of resounding successes and failures. Lincoln was a penniless and disappointed lawyer at fifty-
one. At forty-seven, Churchill appeared to have ended a career
in public service. He was quoted as saying to a friend, "Sitting
in armchairs in front of the fire and going to sleep—that's what
I am getting used to. It's an unhealthy life, but what is to be
done? You can't do anything in this world of ours without
power." Acquaintances thought that he aged badly in the weeks
after his rude dismissal. But the fighting heart, the buoyant
constitution, the unexampled self-confidence, were in no way
affected by the outward physical change. In Cannes, where he
took his family for a six-month vacation, he was soon seen
studiously attending the international problems of the Casino.
"He drank ample brandy and soda and smoked his big black
cigars," says a man who was there, "but he appeared unquestionably to be waiting for the political call that would
follow." Despite Churchill's prescience in other matters, he
found no short cut to eminence at roulette. He lost a very
considerable sum of money. During a trip he made a few years
ago to the United States, a reporter asked him, "If you had it
all to do over, would you change anything, Mr. Churchill?"
Before replying, the great man weighed the question with a
nostalgic and hungry expression. "Yes," he said finally, "I wish
I had played the black instead of the red at Cannes and Monte
Carlo."

# Chapter 22

THE FINANCIAL standing of Churchill and his family had undergone some improvement. After years of anxious economizing, they were able to vacation in leisure. Churchill's fees for magazine and newspaper articles had grown to be among the highest paid, and his output was colossal. He had established a reputation for making advantageous contracts. To his eternal credit, he has always insisted on being paid in proportion to the quality and popularity of his work. His attention is judiciously divided between what he is going to say and how much he is apt to get for it. Even in the Great War, during a journey to visit Roosevelt, he summoned a New York editor in an effort to hike up one of his magazine rates. In 1921 he had also come into money by inheritance. The Lady Randolph had recently died, leaving him the equivalent of $150,000. Her passing was mourned not only by her family but by the most glittering personages of Europe. To the end, she remained a luminous attraction in the social maelstrom of her adopted land. Like her favorite son, she had been noted for an excess of constructive energy; her interests were nearly as diverse as his. The pet of her last few years was a publication called the *Anglo-Saxon Review,* of which she was both editor and publisher. To fill the pages of this well-bred journal, she gathered together, as contributors, the majority of the crowned heads of Europe and most of the uncrowned royal offshoots. It might be said that within the framework of its titular preference the *Review* was managed democratically.

The aspect of its writers was often about as Anglo-Saxon as the average Eskimo's. While the Maharajah of Mysore, in the July issue, might have some pretty warm things to say about Central European pheasant shooting, the King of Andorra would come back with a blistering rebuttal in December.

Lady Randolph's bequest to her older son included one item aside from the financial. When her first husband, the tempestuous Lord Randolph, resigned from the Exchequer, he had refused to surrender his robe of office. This had given rise to a federal gasp of dismay. The traditional course was plain; one resigned, bowed, made a few misleading comments, and turned in his suit. The courageous attitude of Lord Randolph, in taking the garment home, had always been admired by his wife, who willed it to Churchill with the hope that he would someday succeed to his father's position. Her ambition would be realized posthumously. In the meantime, her bequest, and an unexpected one from a distant relative, Lord Herbert Vane-Tempest, had eased the burden of upper-class living for the Winston Churchill family. (Vane-Tempest had left him an annuity and a castle in Ireland, together with a number of thatched cottages. The Irish revolutionists soon destroyed the castle, in the course of a property-damaging spree, and Churchill gave away the cottages to the peasants of the area.) In the England of that day, before the Socialists had enforced the policy of universal drabness, it was considered graceful, and even nationally therapeutic, to entertain and live generally in a style commensurate with one's abilities and enterprise. This was, at the time, believed to be a principal reward of democracy. The Churchills maintained a high standard, though often precariously. Their dinners were noted for lavish food and drink and for the stimulating qualities of the guests. As a rule, Churchill liked to combine business with relaxation. He invited men in public office, persons with political opinions, men upon whose wits he could sharpen his own.

Shortly before Lady Randolph's death, the Churchills had sold their large residence in Eccleston Square to the Labor

Party, which was rich, and had moved into a rented house in Sussex Square. Not long afterward, with his earnings from writing, he bought a handsome estate, the present familiar establishment of Chartwell Manor, the family's farm home in Kent. There Churchill settled down to write his history of the First World War, called *The World Crisis,* in four large volumes. For recreation, after the stint at the Casino, he pottered around his farm and took one brief whack at a neighboring golf course. The legend of his performance persists in the locality. With next to no preliminary instruction, he wound up on the first tee and drove his ball savagely into a sand trap on an adjoining fairway. After his ninth or tenth retrieving chop, with the ball moving ever farther into the soil, he climbed out of the bunker, voiced a number of immensely fitting remarks, and gave up the game for good.

There were repeated rumors in these days that Churchill's health was failing. His appearance had declined markedly. It was recalled that Lord Randolph had died young. By now son Winston was practically bald and his posture was the despair of physical culturists; he had a forward stoop and shambled as he walked. His head was thrust out and down, giving his jaw a truculent look. If he worked long hours, as he frequently did, he emerged with a pallor that was alarming to his family and friends and the concern of his physician, Lord Moran. Churchill has never taken kindly to medical advice. On the contrary, he prefers to brief his doctors, quoting memorized lore. In 1943, he was ill in Marrakech and was visited by General Eisenhower, who watched the doctors fussing around the sickbed. It seemed that they had no accurate way of ascertaining the patient's temperature, since Churchill always snatched out the instrument when they approached and read it himself. When he saw Eisenhower laughing, he said, "Oh, I always do that, otherwise these fellows would try to keep me in bed for no reason."

In the early twenties Churchill did nothing for his appearance in the matter of dress. His eccentricities along this line

were becoming a public joke, which had gained its first impetus
by the story, right or wrong, that he was wearing brown shoes
at his wedding. He had also been observed riding in London's
fashionable Rotten Row (whose curious appellation had de-
volved from its original name of *Route du Roi*) in a pair of
patent-leather boots with suede tops. On several occasions
while riding with his mother he had been taken for her groom.
His hats had begun to be caricatured in *Punch* and other lighthearted British journals, and tailors' house organs sniped at
him steadily. The Guild of London Tailors was moved to go on
record with an official and published protest against his "sartorial terrifics." At length his clothing came to have a sort of
museum value, greatly sought after by collectors. A man was
arrested and hauled into police court on the complaint that he
had broken into a secondhand store; but he was no ordinary
thief. His explanation, mollifying everybody, was that he had
spied a fur-lined overcoat which he had recognized as having
belonged to Churchill. The proprietor refused to press the
charge and doubled the price of the coat, which was full of
holes. It had an early sale.

The family was now complete. There were three girls—the
third, Mary, having arrived in September of 1922—and one
son, Randolph. A fourth daughter, Marigold Frances, born in
1918, had died in her third year. It was a happy family; Mrs.
Churchill, an excellent wife, geared the household and all of
its activities, business and social, to her husband's important
work. Very quickly she recognized that the pivotal point of his
day was dinner, at which time he ate a substantial amount, and
she began the practice of serving him an outsized roast beef
each evening. She continues to do so today. Her friends say
that foremost among her instructions in the event her death
precedes his is that "Winston must be given a good dinner—it
is essential to his health and happiness." Even during the war,
when meat and other commodities were scarce, the members
of the Government insisted that the Prime Minister be provided

with the beef that was so important in maintaining his priceless energies at a high pitch.

Extraordinary measures had been taken long before to safeguard Churchill's health. At the time of the Irish rackets it was feared that he might be assassinated by terrorists, and Scotland Yard detailed a good man to watch over him. Churchill had been beaten by suffragettes, threatened by strikers, cursed by Irishmen, and made the target of a thrown volume in the House of Commons. He was obviously a mediocre risk. Sergeant (later Detective Inspector) W. H. Thompson came to Churchill's house and, liking the work, remained on for fifteen years. His job was quietly to keep the impulsive minister in view. Perhaps no other member of the famous police force could have carried out this difficult assignment with such good-humored tact. In the morning, Thompson might be crouched in the shade of a willow while the master sketched a country scene; in the afternoon he would be seated in the anteroom of Churchill's parliamentary office; a week afterward he might be observed just out of the firing line at Cannes. Through some patriotic whim, Churchill insisted on paying not only Thompson's official salary but an extra-duty fee as well. Curiously enough for a man religiously devoted to compensation, Churchill laid out money with the reckless haste of a sailor ashore. His attitude about it was and is unusual. His confidant and adviser, Brendan Bracken, feels that Churchill expends considerable thought on the moneys coming in but has no interest whatever in the sums going out. He could give away thatched cottages with never a thought for their value, while in the office of a publisher he could be as alert as a pawnbroker. Most of his friends believe that he regards himself, as a Marlborough, as entitled to the costly prerogatives of the privileged, and that he would buy them—houses, farms, rich furnishings, the best food and wines, domestics, secretaries, bodyguards—whether he could afford them or not. From the start of their marriage, his indifference to expense was such that Mrs. Churchill, the granddaughter of the Countess of Airlie, was compelled to develop a frugality sufficiently strong to keep the ship from foundering. She studied the bills, struck bargains with the help, and tried, without success, to curb the golden outflow at Cannes and elsewhere.

In the social life of aristocratic London, the Churchills were popular. No better example of this can be found than the election at Westminster. Forgoing politics, Churchill had worked on his history of the war for two years when Stanley Baldwin succeeded Bonar Law as Prime Minister and declared in favor of Protectionism. This was a rallying cry to Churchill, who had made some of his liveliest speeches in favor of Free Trade. In the closing weeks of 1923, he had been offered a candidacy at West Leicester and had consented to put up his name, only to be defeated by F. W. Pethick-Lawrence, a veteran of several incarcerations in the cause of Women's Suffrage. Churchill was caught between two fires, being against the old-line Conservatives and, of late, suspicious of the growing socialism in the Liberal and Labor parties. His latter feeling was shortly confirmed when Asquith combined forces with the Socialists to bring down the Conservative Government, install Ramsay MacDonald as Prime Minister, and institute the beginnings of English regimentation. Churchill promptly announced his severance from the Liberals and his emergence as a new party of one member—the "Constitutionalists." It was at this critical point that his friends persuaded him to stand from the unique constituency of Westminster.

In all of British history, there has never been an election quite like the one that followed. Westminster is a division lying in the heart of London and includes Westminster Abbey, the Houses of Parliament, the buildings and offices of state, and a sprinkling of the slum quarters that are usually found huddled in juxtaposition to the important centers of most cities. The official Conservative endorsement, now in 1924, had gone to a Captain Otho Nicholson, not very extravagantly described by one writer as "an estimable young politician who would certainly be too modest to claim for himself rank among the great men of his day." But he was a nephew of the late General Nicholson, who had been the traditional Conservative Member for the division since 1909. Traditional or not, a good many young Conservatives, social colleagues of the Churchills, were sick of mediocre representation from Westminster, which has been called "the Washington of England," and they gathered in vivid support of their companion of the clubs and casinos.

Churchill ran as the logical nominee of his one-man Constitutionalist Party. In addition to him and Captain Nicholson, there were two other hopefuls—Fenner Brockway, a Socialist, and Scott Duckers, a Radical. To get things started, the millionaire, James Rankin, lent Churchill his mansion in nearby North Street as a headquarters. Then the majority of Burke's Peerage, studded with whatever jewels had escaped the loan shops, began arriving to be assigned duties. Nothing loath, Churchill's backers dealt them out tasks both menial and large. Lady Wodehouse sallied into the slums and began knocking on doors. There are still available excellent witnesses to this memorable campaign, and they treasure the details which gave it such a wide and hearty press. Lady Wodehouse's manner with the tired, suspicious slatterns of her list was friendly but baffling. "My deah!" she would cry, as she stood with one foot in the front room of some crumbling ruin, "you really must drop all this and run over to Jimmie Rankin's for tea. We're getting together to elect jolly old Churchill."

These tactics were duplicated by Lady Blandford, Lady Bessborough, Lady Harmsworth, and others of their company, and now and then some curiosity-ridden member of the depressed orders actually did snatch up a shawl and scuttle around to headquarters. The house was regarded as extraordinary even in an era of magnificence. It was hung with Romneys and Gainsboroughs and similar masters, and its bric-a-brac was priceless. No official computation was ever released on the total abstraction of this latter ware, but it is said to have been substantial. Churchill's candidacy reshuffled the property of Westminster far better than the Socialists could have done.

The scene at Rankin's, aside from the pilfering, was one to warm the heart of a socially ambitious caller. The toffs were assembled in full war rig. The best-known names of London fashion were gathered in little knots beneath the frowning portraits, terribly serious, plotting their tempest in a teapot. Striking a visual note of even deeper interest, the busty chorus of Daly's Theatre appeared, the girls, many of them fully clothed, saying that they had "always liked Churchill's face." Some shortsighted committee member put them to work addressing envelopes. Now and then various parts of the great room would burst into song—one of the committees had devised a tune for popular consumption. It focused on the candidate's celebrity as fighter, orator, and diplomat.

As could be expected in a congress of such lineage, things occasionally got out of hand. At one juncture, Churchill was obliged to clap on his hat and sprint into Victoria Street, where the Countess of Bottsley, with a brush and a bucket of paste, was plastering blown-up photographs of his children onto the public buildings. Over the cherubic faces was printed the appalling legend, "Vote for Daddy!" But it was not only the ladies who were busy. The Duke of Marlborough, who long ago had forgiven his relative for having liberal leanings, called from door to door in the state offices. He was said to have taken along a valet who did the actual knocking with a gold-headed stick. The duke's uncringing address, when he entered, was always, "See here, now!" Most of the frightened office workers arose and either curtsied or touched their forelocks.

The tactics of the Socialists were considered, even by the Radicals (as evidenced by one of Scott Duckers' speeches, in which he advocated both that the Socialists be censured and that every existing social custom be scrapped, with a view to a new start), to be outside the bounds of decent electioneering. They organized small but sinewy roving bands, which waylaid and rushed the gilded gentry at work for Churchill. The dregs of Soho emptied into Westminster, and knives and brass knuckles assumed parliamentary importance. In the first few days, nearly all of Churchill's meetings were routed. He would no sooner set up on a street corner than a flying wedge of share-the-wealth addicts would sweep over the stands like cattle, destroying his props and stampeding the crowd. At length, at the suggestion of General Seely, the M.P. from the Isle of Wight, who was in good physical shape, and Lord Darling, a noted croquet player, a volunteer bodyguard was formed to stand off the rowdies. Hearing the news, many of London's prize fighters and jockeys reported in to Rankin's to offer assistance. In the next brush, Sir Philip Sassoon got a black eye, and the shins of Commander Locker-Lampson were rudely barked, but the Socialists suffered worse casualties, and Churchill was able to unburden himself of his message.

By and large, the city was thrown into a turmoil. A good many of its normal functions ceased, so as to allow their participants to become spectators in Westminster. A rather large number of incidents appeared on the police blotters of the district. The most regrettable of these involved an immigrating Italian family that debarked from a train at Victoria Station in the midst of a brisk fist fight between the Socialists and the Peers. The family, according to its later report to correspondents, thought that a revolution had broken out and actually got on a train and went back to Italy.

Throughout the ebb and flow of these melees, Churchill remained calm. In spite of the blue blood running in the streets, he stuck to his main plea—the liquidation of Socialism and the liberalizing of ultra-Conservatism. At a delicate point in the campaign he was aided by two gestures from influential Tory Members. The Hon. Leo Amery, his old school pal from Harrow, wrote an unobtrusive bit in the *Times* stating his belief that the return of the Protectionist-minded Captain Nicholson would weaken the party. Then Lord Balfour, with the permission of Party Leader Baldwin, made public a letter pledging his support to Churchill. These almost did the trick. All of London was discussing the violent upheaval in the Conservative Party. "Families are split in twain," said one writer. "If the parents support Captain Nicholson, as the official Conservative, the younger voters stand for Churchill." At the start of the campaign, Churchill's candidacy was regarded merely as a defiant token, not apt to have any tangible results. The monumental obstacle of Nicholson tradition in Westminster was thought to be decisive. It now appeared that the Conservative Party was in the throes of a real reformation. A significant part of England seemed to feel that Winston Churchill was the element needed to fuse this badly deteriorating compound. By 43 ballots out of more than 16,000 cast, he lost the election to Nicholson, but he won an immeasurable vote of confidence. It was the quality missing in his life for the past two years. He was triumphantly re-established in the public favor. "At no other time has he been so popular," a correspondent wrote, and another spoke of his "giddy moral victory."

Forever alive to his opportunities, the warrior-statesman emerged from his half retirement and was soon under full sail again. Sitting in armchairs in front of the fire was deferred to another time, one that, to date, has not yet come.

# Chapter 23

THE HULLABALOO over Churchill at Westminster acted as a lively stimulant to the Conservative cause. Everybody sensed that the new Constitutionalist Party would assuredly be absorbed, to a man, by the Conservatives and that the union would be healthful for the nation. Churchill's position, in 1924, was soon made even more influential when the constituency of Epping returned him with an overriding majority as its Constitutional Member for Parliament. Anti-Socialist victories all over the country were so resounding that the government of "the Boneless Wonder," Ramsay MacDonald, fell apart and was succeeded by a Tory administration with Stanley Baldwin again at the helm. To the surprise of practically nobody, he made Churchill his new Chancellor of the Exchequer.

This appointment gave Churchill the all-time British record for holding ministerial jobs. He had been, in succession, Under-Secretary for the Colonies, President of the Board of Trade, Home Secretary, First Lord of the Admiralty, Chancellor of the Duchy of Lancaster, Minister of Munitions, Secretary of State for War and for Air, Secretary for the Colonies, and, now, Chancellor of the Exchequer. Even his staunchest enemies admitted that these added up to quite a list.

For the first time in years, Churchill seemed nervous while making a maiden address in a new post. He had put on his father's robe, and he paused frequently to look up and smile at the gallery, where his wife and four children were sitting. He spoke very slowly, with traces of stammering and a noticeable harkback to his old complaint of the sibilants. In his speech presenting the Budget, a tense time for all Exchequer heads, he appeared to have relaxed his adamantine stand on Free Trade. He was now a Free Trader in theory, he implied, but in practice a Free Trader with empire preferences. For purposes of both illustration and nourishment, he had brought a glass of whiskey out of the House bar, and, sipping along, he referred to it in connection with his new tax on liquors. "It is imperative that I should refresh the revenue," he said at one point. "I do so now," and he took a hearty swig.

Important on the list of those not amused were Philip Snowden, the preceding Chancellor of the Exchequer, and the House's leading pair of teetotalers, Lady Astor and Mr. Scrymgeour, the Conscience of Dundee. These last two had formed a strange partnership. In Scrymgeour, the rich, American-born champion of forlorn causes had found a congenial spirit, one who, like her, saw no middle ground in dealing with intoxicants. They were both ardent "Prohibitionists," having borrowed the new and unlovely term from across the Atlantic. During his five years as Chancellor of the Exchequer, Churchill tilted almost daily with the sober pair. As far as parliamentary business went, they were a thoroughgoing nuisance, given to heckling, interruptions, asides, squirrel-like noises, and booing. On one occasion, Churchill talked for nearly half an hour on his revenues to the accompaniment of a continuous chorus that went about as follows: "Haw—Psssst!—Doubt it —Wawk! Wawk!—Sit down!—Fie, for shame!—Phg!—Oh, what a lie!"—and so on. He finally got so fed up that he stopped and addressed a remark directly to Lady Astor, saying, "I have great regard and respect for the noble lady, but I do not think we are likely to learn much from the liquor legislation of the United States." As the House applauded, her answer, studiously conceived, was, "Why?"

Churchill had emerged now as the full-blown nemesis of the Socialist Party. Snowden took exception to everything he did and said. The campaign of nagging opposition was aimed to make life miserable for Churchill, but it only made life miserable for Snowden. Churchill has always been an impossible man to heckle successfully. He cannot be persuaded to rise to the bait. Neither can he be trapped into confessions of guilt, error, bad judgment, or inconsistency. Snowden once sprang to his feet to denounce bitterly the Chancellor's abandonment of strict Free Trade principles.

"There is nothing wrong in change, if it is in the right direction," replied Churchill, with confusing logic.

Snowden thought the sentence over, then said lamely, "You are an authority on that."

In his most sanctimonious vein, Churchill concluded with, "To improve is to change. To be perfect is to have changed often."

Snowden sat down and cast about for a less difficult theme. In his later years, he wrote the usual autobiography and included an articulate passage on Churchill:

"It would be tiresome if I were to deal at length with the innumerable encounters between Mr. Churchill and myself in the Budget debates of this year and succeeding years. As an Ex-Chancellor it fell to me to lead the Opposition in the Budget debates, and I found Mr. Churchill a foeman worthy of my steel. The debates between us became quite a Parliamentary entertainment. They were regarded as the best show in London. When it was expected that we should both be speaking, the public galleries were invariably crowded. After a time I ceased to take very much interest in these duels, but I was expected to play the Parliamentary game of opposition and to provide entertainment for my supporters.

"Mr. Churchill, during these years, gradually developed as a Parliamentary debater. He learnt to rely less on careful preparation of his speeches and more upon spontaneous effort. However much one may differ from Mr. Churchill, one is compelled to like him for his finer qualities. There is an attractiveness in everything he does. His high spirits are irrepressible. It

was said of a French monarch that no one ever lost a kingdom
with so much gaiety. Mr. Churchill was as happy facing a
Budget deficit as in distributing a surplus. He is an adventurer,
a soldier of fortune. An escapade has an irresistible fascination
for him."

Though alert about publishing payments, Churchill has
never been considered a financial wizard, and his Budgets
made about as many foes as friends. Among others, he managed to alienate an entirely new segment of womanhood. The
suffragettes had been more or less quiescent of late, with only
an occasional thrown bottle or a small, organized fit of hysterics to mark their latent fury, and it is likely that Churchill
was enlivened by the distaff wrangle now springing from his
revenues. In a surprise move, he decided to place a tax on horse
bets. The outcry that went up in all quarters of the kingdom
was piteous, but the remarkable truth is that by far the loudest
voices were those of women. They poured letters into his office
in painful abundance. The tone of these baffled experts for a
suitable reply; in essence, the women all threatened to quit
gambling if Churchill didn't ease up on the horse grab. Their
indignation made a pretty sight when he composed a form
letter advising them by all means to go ahead and quit, that the
revenue would probably gain by their "increased usefulness in
other directions."

The principal feature of his first Budget was a return to the
gold standard, in an effort to jack up the sagging pound. Off
the gold standard during the war, England had seen the pound
dip to the alarmingly low price, in the foreign exchange, of
eighteen shillings (it is now worth about twelve). His action
provoked the economist, J. M. Keynes, to write an angry little
pamphlet entitled *The Economic Consequences of Mr.
Churchill*. Its prediction was reminiscent of the familiar statement by Louis XIV—"After me the deluge." Keynes believed
very strongly that Churchill was kowtowing to the bankers,
and said, "To begin with, there will be a great depression in
the export industries. This, in itself, will be helpful, since it will

produce an atmosphere favorable to the reduction of wages. The cost of living will fall somewhat. This will be helpful, too, because it will give you a good argument in favor of reducing wages." These things promptly came to pass, with particular reference to the coal industry, and Keynes pressed the attack. Churchill made a reply in which he asserted that the gold standard was about as responsible for the conditions in the mines as "the Gulf Stream."

Keynes digested this opinion and rejected it, possibly because he was weak in oceanography. He felt strong in economics, though, and went on to say that "Thus Mr. Churchill's policy of improving the exchange by ten percent was, sooner or later, a policy of reducing everybody's wages by two shillings in the pound. In doing what he did in the actual circumstances of last spring, he was just asking for trouble. For he was committing himself to force down wages and all money values, without any idea of how it was to be done. Why did he do such a silly thing?"

Gold standard or Gulf Stream, wise or silly, Keynes or Churchill, there followed a Miners' Lockout and then a gigantic General Strike. A great many experts, most of them employed by colleges, have tried to assay the exact causes of Britain's financial crisis in the middle twenties. The findings vary. Economics, like beauty, exist largely in the eye of the beholder. One economist's chart is another economist's poison. President Roosevelt and Henry Morgenthau once fixed the price of American gold by flipping a coin, and a meeting of learned professors, in the same era, resolved a tough banking procedure by holding a chess tournament. It has been suggested that if economists could foresee the financial future they would probably predict tomorrow's stock prices and retire with a fortune. Most of Keynes' prophecies, during Churchill's Exchequer career, proved uncomfortably correct, but other experts on the scene missed wildly. As for Churchill himself, he stuck to his Gulf Stream theory and continued with the business of breaking the strike.

In the words of one of his hostile biographers, a Welsh M.P. named Emrys Hughes, "The General Strike gave Churchill another opportunity for playing the Napoleon." This statement was founded partly on the Chancellor's zest for inspecting the strike-breaking milk trucks. Churchill saw the marshaling of the nation's non-union facilities as a gigantic military operation, rushed into being to avert a catastrophe. Whatever the faults or virtues of his basic stand, he took every step necessary to maintain the national commerce and good health, in the manner of President Truman invoking the Taft-Hartley Act. It was not so much his thinking as the fact of his seeming to enjoy himself that appeared to enrage many people. When the emergency horses and milk carts assembled each morning on the streets of London, he appeared, with a small retinue, and went down the line on inspection. The similarity between his procession and the average general's parade was striking. With courtly grace (the essence of successful command) he paused to question a driver here, or pat a horse there, and if in his haste he inadvertently switched the procedure, it must be laid to the confusion of the moment.

All the newspapers of London quit publishing, except for a tiny, four-page version of the *Times,* and Churchill quickly showed his surest leadership of the strike. His friends agreed that, all his life, he had felt possessed of unexploited potentialities as an editor. The collapse of the London papers in the face of union walkouts gave him his chance. He rushed into the office of the *Morning Post,* which had never been known as a champion of labor, and set up a national newspaper called the *British Gazette,* with himself in charge. The precise relevancy this bore to the job of Chancellor of the Exchequer was not revealed. Nevertheless, Churchill established himself in a plushy office, put on a green eyeshade and a pair of sleeve garters, draped himself with wet galleys, and began bawling out directions in the approximate idiom of the Fourth Estate. By mischance, there was practically nobody on hand to take them, barring a few of the city's best-known editors, who dropped in to help, and these displayed notable apathy upon hearing cries of "Copy!" and "Here, boy!" So bizarre was this whole enterprise that a good many distinguished persons came to visit and were taken on conducted tours of the plant. And in one of the most aggravating coincidences on record, Lord Birkenhead, who had been arrested while attempting to call on Churchill at Ploegsteert, was turned away from the door by an officious special constable. Birkenhead left with the observation that, in future, he thought he would let Churchill come to him.

The new editor's selection of material for his paper was rich with bias. All the articles seemed to pick rather heavily on labor. Proceeding along this line, Churchill suddenly took the patriotic notion that the workers were, after all, British, so he lifted a piece from a French journal in which it was suggested that the English General Strike was fomented by the Bolsheviks. Thereafter, the *Gazette* stuck pretty closely to the theory that the strikers were merely unhappy dupes. The Russian accusation naturally stirred up resentment in circles notoriously sympathetic to Communism. Not long after it appeared, the Archbishop of Canterbury blew up a noisy bladder described as a "Peace Manifesto," which was rushed by messenger to Churchill's office. The man was ushered from the premises with detailed instructions about what the Archbishop could do with his Manifesto. For eight days Churchill reigned as the preeminent news dispenser of England. He pointed out with editorial pride that the *Gazette's* circulation had risen, through his management, to 3,000,000, but his critics countered with the opinion that it was because he had no competition. His plans for expansion were maturing rapidly when the strike caved in. Under the direction of Commander Locker-Lampson, his sidekick of the Westminster election, he had organized a subsidiary paper in a defunct printing works in Gough Square and was offering a free course in linotype operation to college students. By all accounts, Churchill returned the *Gazette* to the *Morning Post* with vast reluctance.

The most slavish of Churchill's followers seldom wax eloquent over his course as Chancellor of the Exchequer. The
abrupt return to the gold standard, the economic decline, the
dissatisfaction of labor, and the flamboyant strikes did much
to destroy his rewon popularity. Plainly enough he had veered
away from the all-out compassion for the workers he had exhibited while in political tandem with Asquith and, perhaps
infected by the fear of Socialism or Communism, had turned
more sharply to the right than most of his new Tory colleagues.
The old cry was raised that, as often before, he had gone too
far, had been too impulsive. Even the Tories, with a rekindled
suspicion of the firebrand, were moved to wonder if Lord Oxford was right when he called Churchill "a genius without
judgment." Another admiring but vexed critic remarked that
he was "jaywalking through life." Stanley Baldwin had spoken
nervously of "Winston's hundred horsepower brain." It was
felt that Churchill's career, and his weather-vane convictions,
had whipped about in the wind of political opportunism. In a
word, he was too much for nearly everybody. And once again,
as the Tories crashed before MacDonald's Socialist, or Labor,
upsurge of 1929, "everyone threw the blame on me." While
still a Member of Parliament, Churchill stepped down from his
high Government post. He was entering upon his desert period,
a ten-year span of near-oblivion. In the busy time since Sandhurst, he had fought five wars, held nine Cabinet offices, made
8000 public speeches, and seen himself, in quick order, the
most popular and the most unpopular man in England. It was
a dazzling record, and it was far from finished. Unlike Alexander, he had yet more worlds to conquer.

II

The interval between 1929 and 1939 in Churchill's life has
been variously described as "the lotus years," "the time between," his "out of step" period, and several other circum-

locutions aimed to indicate public disfavor without actually saying so. The fact is that he was retired rather abruptly to Chartwell, following which he occupied himself chiefly in writing and otherwise making a living. This took the form, soon after his banishment, of journeying to the United States to undertake another lecture tour. His first one, at the time of the Boer War, had been lucrative and even pleasant, barring the Irish yammering, and he was anxious to reap a similar harvest now in his distinguished middle age. Ship news reporters in New York were impressed by the sprightly way in which he received them, aboard the *Europa;* the *Times* spoke of "the twinkle in his eye." Because of his recent ambiguous success with the *British Gazette,* Churchill addressed the boys as "colleagues" and threw in a number of professional phrases.

The speaking tour itself was rudely interrupted. Churchill left the Waldorf-Astoria Hotel one afternoon to visit his old friend of the First World War, Bernard Baruch, and got mixed up about the location of Baruch's house, at 1055 Fifth Avenue. He descended from a taxicab at Sixty-seventh Street and wandered around looking at numbers. Crossing from one corner to another, with an automatic British glance for drivers on the left side of the road, he heard a screaming of hard-braked tires and felt a tremendous shock. He came to in the Lenox Hill Hospital. He had been struck by a taxicab in the hands of one Mario Contasino, who was at the moment out in the corridor setting up lamentations of a superior order. Churchill, who had a sprained right shoulder and multiple lacerations of the face and nose, insisted in taking all the blame. He suggested, and the driver verified, that he had managed to say "It's my fault" before lapsing into semiconsciousness. Churchill spoke to an anxious King George V on the telephone, then summoned Contasino and gave him an autographed copy of *The World Crisis.* He had a restful visit in the hospital, not at all unsettled by Sergeant Thompson's extreme measures, which included flinging all the clothes out of incoming laundry baskets, to prevent reporters from disturbing the sickroom. For once,

Churchill was in agreement with his doctors that he should be guarded from upsets. His concern, while identical to theirs, was prompted by a different reason. Propped up in bed, he was busily at work on a rush article for an American magazine, tentatively titled, "My New York Misadventure." He finished it without distraction, sold it for twenty-five hundred dollars, then got up and took a convalescent trip to the Bahamas on the proceeds.

Some weeks later, back home at Chartwell, he resumed the massive writing projects to which he was now dedicated. *The World Crisis* had been a financial and critical triumph. Before publication of this work, his prose, in England, had been viewed with a certain amount of skepticism. Unlike Americans, the English are nurtured on good literature from the cradle to the grave and are not easily wooed by writers who ply the artistic trade as partial employment, or as the offshoot of a more favored vocation. The four volumes of *The World Crisis* had appeared at different times in the twenties; from them Churchill had realized something over a hundred thousand dollars, after earning out his advance of sixteen thousand dollars. His personal interpretation of the war stirred up unprecedented comment all over the world. It was an argumentative work, and, naturally, not slighting of his own part in the great events he was narrating. As the series began appearing, the critics were at first tentative and then increasingly devoted when Sir Arthur Conan Doyle came forward with the bland announcement, "I have long recognized that Winston Churchill has the finest prose style of any contemporary." Most reviewers fell in line behind this clarion call; a few were seriously antagonized by it. The novelist Arnold Bennett felt that "Churchill *will* write for effect, when he has neither the leisure nor the natural ability to do that." The poet John Masefield, on the other hand, thought the volumes "masterly." The *Observer* took up a diplomatic perch astride the fence, beating the drum for the man and cautiously including his writings. "None in the line of English statesmen is more sure of a lasting place in

literature," observed the editor, adding that the author was
"one of the born organists of language. He is all vigor, personality. There is a style because there is a man."

As if this apologia for his prose on account of its human
origin were not peculiar enough, H. G. Wells, in the burbling
fever of his hottest Liberal period, jumped on Churchill for
having an unromantic attitude toward the Russians, and went
on to say that "He believes quite naively that he belongs to a
peculiarly gifted and privileged class of beings to whom the
lives and affairs of common men are given over, the raw material of brilliant careers. His imagination is obsessed by dreams
of exploits and a career. It is an imagination closely akin to the
d'Annunzio type. In England, d'Annunzio would have been a
Churchill; in Italy, Churchill would have been a d'Annunzio.
He is a great student and collector of the literature of Napoleon I, that master adventurer. Before all things, he desires
a dramatic world with villains—and one hero."

In general, the only journals rendered bilious by *The World
Crisis* were those that opposed Churchill politically. The chief
exception was the London *Mercury,* which appeared to be
genuinely discontented with his technique, calling it "ambitious
and crude." The author, it was thought, possessed "no ear, no
fingering, a meagre rhythm, an impoverished imagery," and,
"like the young, he has a fondness of phrases." There was a ray
of hope, however, for even though when "excited with material
and the neighborhood of the engines of war" he is "heavy and
commonplace," at other times "his intelligence wakes and he
writes simply and surely."

The critical tone of these remarks was candid, but the English as a whole are conspicuously frank in their reviews. "It
was one of those books which, once you have set it down, is
almost impossible to pick back up," said a writer not long ago,
dealing with the work of a cherished friend. The give-and-take
spirit is genial, rather unlike that in America, where critics
have been shot down like dogs for challenging a fugitive
comma. But England belongs to an older civilization, in which

all the known insults have been bandied about so persistently
that they have lost their sting. Moreover, the dueling blade has
disappeared, and its modern substitute, the naked subpoena, is
not much of a deterrent to unvarnished speech.

The English reception of *The World Crisis* was, by and
large, that accorded a new and sturdy pretender to immortality
among the nation's great writers. And in America the cheers
were almost undiluted. The St. Louis *Post-Dispatch* called it
"Truly a magnificent work, deeply moving as a story and of
permanent importance as history." In the opinion of the
*Christian Science Monitor,* "Mr. Churchill is a writer of great
power. Though it is full of official data and accurate detail,
his book never loses hold of the tremendous drama which it
treats." And the New York *Herald Tribune* held that "Churchill was alive to his task with every nerve and fiber, and this
aliveness survives and animates *The World Crisis,* making it
the extraordinarily fascinating book that it is."

Faced with reviews like these, Churchill had no reluctance in
undertaking further sweeping works, and he completed, in the
ten-year period of his retirement from public office, his monumental Life of Marlborough. As a direct descendant, he had,
of course, access to all the family papers and lore, so that he
toiled away with uniquely expert advantage. Also, his pro-
pensity for hard labor was so strong that, aside from Marlborough, he had energy left over for a bewildering variety of
other writing. For magazines in England and in America he
spoke up with authority on subjects high and low, but always
at high prices. *Collier's* was the outlet for most of his American articles. He struck some provocative notes. In one issue
he casually predicted the return of silent movies, basing his
stand on the enjoyment he recently had derived from a film of
Charlie Chaplin's. The piece was, in fact, substantially a
minute biography of the comedian, with side lights on panto-
mime, then and now. Churchill gave credit for the art to the
Emperor Augustus, and added that "Nero practiced it, as he

wrote poetry, as a relaxation from the more serious pursuits of lust, incendiarism and gluttony."

Many of *Collier's* readers took the notion, right or wrong, that the great statesman was hitting his ripest vein—a kind of genteel, delayed-fuse chortle—in the pages of the popular weekly. The humor that would seem ill timed in a history of war, or a treatise on his father, often sprang into joyous life in his rapid-fire potboilers. One of his best numbers was entitled "The Shattered Cause of Temperance," a subject for which he had deep sympathy, as evidenced by the warmth and sincerity of his remarks. There were fundamental differences in English and American drinking, Churchill suggested, saying, "It is possible that the dry, bracing, electrical atmosphere of North America makes the use of alcohol less necessary and more potent than does the humid climate of Britain." He spoke at length of his last tour of the United States, during which he had worked hard to observe prohibition from every angle. "I must confess," he said, "that on one occasion I was taken to a speakeasy. I went, of course, in my capacity of a Social Investigator." It was easy to gather from the article that prohibition had caused Churchill suffering on the trip, but his distress was perhaps less acute than he made out. He had omitted to say, in *Collier's,* that his lecture contract had included a paragraph stipulating that his agent must provide him with a bottle of champagne each evening before dinner.

*Collier's* circulation finally got the impression that, at least in a literary way, Churchill could not leave whiskey alone. A short time after his blast at temperance, he came forth with a sprightly item called "How We Carry Liquor." It led off with the astounding statement that "The story of wine is the story of human culture." This unbreakable link between man and the grape assumed the stature of a religious symbol in Churchill's piece, and, to all intents and purposes, established God as the Master Distiller. It was related how Mohammed, after passing a kind of early Volstead Act, saw his thirst-racked followers go half crazy and embark on a world program of murder that was directly traceable to sobriety. Churchill made out a strong case for drinking, but he admitted that the happy medium was not always easy. He divulged how Britishers had learned to swill and stay on their feet, and declared that he, for one, was glad that the days when the English pub advertised "Drunk for a penny; dead drunk for tuppence" were gone. In this piece, as in others of his *Collier's* series, there were cartoon illustrations featuring the author, now holding his belly in lively distress from drinking the barbarous cocktails, now tiptoeing out of a "dry" banquet for a private snifter, again seated at a dining table painfully examining an American hotel menu, which described unspiked orange juice as being worth fifty cents a glass.

It was an opportune time for Churchill to be discussing liquor. As his political impotency gnawed at his vitals, he strove hard for relaxation. Britain's financial plight having worsened after 1931, another National, or Coalition, Government was eventually formed, and Stanley Baldwin, in 1935, was again Prime Minister. But in selecting his Cabinet he passed Churchill over, calling Neville Chamberlain to the springboard ministry of the Exchequer. Churchill burrowed obliviously into his researches on Marlborough and into vacation distraction on the Côte d'Azur. "Yet the life he breathed into the reputation of his long dead ancestor seemed to be at the expense of his own," said *Life* magazine, which was serializing his memoirs and was presumed to be authoritative, several years later. "He turned flatulent and became a conspicuous landmark of the French Riviera. He was the despair of hostesses. There were still flashes of the fine talk that had made a thousand dinner parties famous. But often he sat silent and glowered while the champagne simmered in his stomach. His drinking bouts were the talk of the Empire—a two-bottle man."

Politically, Churchill was in an extraordinary situation in these years. His periodic appearances in Parliament, as a member for Epping, first were objects of curiosity, and some amusement. The prevailing comment was, "Listen to Winston harping away on the same old string." His was the voice in the wilderness, crying hatred of Socialism on the one hand and sounding the dangers of somnolent Conservatism on the other. Essentially he was, as he still is, fighting for the maintenance of empire, for continuing the philosophy of a powerful but benevolent England. He warned against giving away advantage, something that democracies are forever doing out of misplaced shame at having built themselves strong. It is a fatal quirk of men of good will that, once they achieve eminence by thrift and hard labor, they dissipate their police influence by an apologetic urge to elevate all others, including the rogues. In the debates on severing India from Britain, Churchill predicted that an immature withdrawal from the swarming, fanatic land would result in wholesale religious murders and an India set against the Western world. Somewhat more than half of his prediction has now come to pass, and India's frequent siding with Russia gives suspicious validity to the remainder.

Churchill made further enemies among the reorganizers of society when he had the effrontery to point out that both Gandhi and Nehru, the prime exponents of Indian humanitarianism, were die-hard Brahmins, with upper-class viewpoints that would classify as reactionary anywhere in the world. "To abandon India to the rule of the Brahmins would be an act of cruel and wicked negligence," he said in Commons. "It would shame forever those who bore its guilt. These Brahmins who mouth and patter the principles of Western Liberalism, and pose as philosophic and democratic politicians, are the same Brahmins who deny the primary rights of existence to nearly sixty millions of their own fellow countrymen whom they call 'untouchable,' and whom they have by thousands of years of oppression actually taught to accept this sad position."

The extent of Churchill's solitude may be seen from the subsequent action of his old companion Leo Amery, who had patiently backed him at nearly every turn. When the India plea was ended, Amery arose and made the hurtful statement, "Here endeth the last chapter of the Book of the Prophet Jeremiah." He could scarcely have been more wrong. The Prophet, while now without honor in his own country, was slowly gathering both strength and confidence from his lonesome battle. The business of making a clean fight against odds is of incomparable value to the morale, especially if there develop evidences, however slight, of approval. As Churchill hurled his relentless alarms, the House began to fill up with quietly listening members and spectators. The word would go out that Jeremiah was on his way in to read the national tea leaves. The amusement gave way to attention, then to unaffected interest, and, at last, to the crashing rally of support, that awoke only in time to stave off disaster.

But in 1936, when Edward VIII startled the world by trying to make a Queen of the twice-divorced Mrs. Simpson, Churchill's resources were insufficient to turn the tide in the King's favor. Hundreds of columns of newsprint have been devoted to explaining his determined intercession in the case. The popular notion has always been that Churchill's patriotism was simply outraged by any thought of abdication. Some of his friends now feel that there was an extra dimension to his reasoning, that, in Churchill's mind, the polo-playing, night-clubbing Edward was exactly the sort of King that England ought to have. Certainly the two were congenial spirits. Churchill had been present when Edward was made Prince of Wales, at Carnarvon Castle, in 1911, and they had since held lordly wassail together on several occasions, both in England and on the Riviera. A second public misconception, when the crisis arose, was that Churchill had thrust himself all unofficially into the argument. The facts are that Edward invited his counsel and clung to it, as representing the friendliest and sagest voice on the scene, until the bitter end. Just as Churchill considered Edward England's true and rightful King, Edward unquestionably looked upon Churchill as the country's informal Prime Minister.

The romance had flourished for some time, while all of Britain stood in a tacit conspiracy not to bring it into the open. London's editors, stifling their professional instincts, dutifully killed story after story. It was finally the Bishop of Bradford, Dr. A. W. F. Blunt, who spilled the beans during an injured sermon on the first of December. The King had been very naughty, it was implied, and both Dr. Blunt and the Archbishop of Canterbury, resolute guardians of the national weal, were upset. (Bradford was even more upset in 1950 when the House of Lords asked him to explain his exhortations in behalf of the Communist-inspired "Council of Clergy and Ministers for Common Ownership." And one of the pious lights of Canterbury, the notorious "Red Dean," was making somewhat similar news at the time, also in the interest of the "national weal.") The main count against Mrs. Simpson seemed to be that she had trod the matrimonial aisle on two previous occasions. Commoners had at one point or another married into nearly every court of Europe. But the further fact that the lady was an American appeared to clinch her ineligibility in the eyes of the British clergy and Parliament. These various defects could not be expected to offend Churchill too seriously. His mother was an American and, while never divorced, had married three times; in addition, his long-dead kinswoman, Arabella, humble sister of the first John Churchill, had been warmly esteemed by James II, and had borne him four sons in the process. How much these factors affected Churchill's championship of the love-torn King is not known, but they were thought by some to be influential.

As the single-minded Stanley Baldwin applied his by now well-known pressures, the King grew increasingly irritated. Baldwin had a dismal habit of snapping and cracking his knuckles, a mannerism rendered further eccentric, and even slightly dangerous, by an occasional flinging of his right arm past his head, as if he were catching flies. How he rose to political heights in the face of these galvanic exercises remains a mystery, but it is on record that they ruffled Edward VIII. Beyond question, had the age been a few hundred years before,

Baldwin would have found himself snapping and crackling in
the Tower; now he sententiously plodded on with his theory
that a king must on no account be permitted to behave like a
man. A suggested morganatic marriage was denied, Mrs.
Simpson left for the convalescent atmosphere of Cannes, and
the King summoned Winston Churchill, who was preparing
to ask the nation for "time and patience." In his memoirs, *A
King's Story,* Edward has summarized Churchill's status of the
moment:

"It is no doubt somewhat difficult for many of us whose impression of recent history is so dominated by the immeasurable
greatness and prestige of this man to remember, let alone believe, that in 1936, his position in British life, and even more
within his own party, was regarded as anything but immortal.
Throughout the period when the events that are the subject of
this narrative were unfolding he was, in fact, a virtual outcast
from the Conservative party, respected and even feared for his
undoubted intellectual brilliance and audacity but distrusted
by the party leaders, who denied him a place in the Government."

Churchill arrived for a select council of war and dinner at
Edward's sanctuary, The Fort, and delivered a monologue on
the situation. The King and the other guests listened respectfully. "Although I had long admired Mr. Churchill," wrote Edward, "I saw him that evening in his true stature. When Mr.
Baldwin had talked to me about the Monarchy, it had seemed
a dry and lifeless thing. But when Mr. Churchill spoke, it lived,
it grew, it became suffused with light. His argument was simple
and convincing. No constitutional issue had arisen between me
and my Cabinet, and none could arise until Wallis's *decree nisi*
became absolute in April, then nearly five months off."

These facts prompted Churchill to offer a Plan of Action,
which has since been remarked as being typically Churchillian. He advised Edward to go home to Windsor Castle, close
the gates, and leave them guarded by his father's physician,
Lord Dawson of Penn (who was, in point of fact, far too

decrepit for this sort of work), and his own Physician in Ordinary, Lord Horder. Thus an ingress would be denied to all busybodies with clear-cut notions about marriage and the monarchy, presumably including Stanley Baldwin. With his notable zeal for combat, Churchill then advocated a delaying fight that would "allow time for the battalions to march." This would culminate, it appeared, in a monster engagement to see who was stronger—Baldwin or Edward VIII.

The King instead chose abdication, and Churchill, with a splendid bustle of energy, helped him write a suitably eloquent address of farewell. Edward composed the first draft, but Churchill stuck in any number of majestic phrases, and smoothed it all up. When the King broadcast the famous speech, which began, "At long last I am able to say a few words of my own," everybody agreed that it was a noble and emollient effort. Churchill heard it on his radio at Chartwell and modestly commented on the impressive literacy of the King. Then he went up to his workroom, where he resumed his invention of majestic phrases for Marlborough.

III

There followed perhaps Churchill's finest hour, the time of his one-man stand against the Fascists. In repeated parliamentary and journalistic warnings, he had lashed out against any indulgence of the quick and fatal disease. From his obscure corner seat below the gangway—chosen deliberately to accentuate his solitary humor—he thundered, "I predict that the day will come at some point or other, on some issue or other, when you will have to make a stand, and I pray to God that when that day comes we may not find, through an unwise policy, we may have to make that stand alone." His steady hammering at the Germans finally wrung a moving cry of pain from the articulate and rising disciple of brotherly love, Joseph Goebbels, who wrote, "Churchill has painted not landscapes but a picture of the German danger. He is the leader of the implacable haters of Germany in England, and even if he is somewhat less dangerous than those sinister wire-pullers in the half-darkness of the Secret Service and of many ministerial quarters, yet nevertheless he sets in motion those waves of gall which are not to be taken too light-heartedly. His disposition for untenable accusations, Munchausen fairy tales and polemics dates presumably from the time when he was a correspondent of the *Daily Telegraph*."

In these years of British somnolence, the guilt must be shared by nearly everybody except Churchill. The several leaders went on the inexorable record with their views. The aging Lloyd George had pointed with composure to the "magnificent armies of Czechoslovakia and Poland." George Lansbury, while leading the Socialists, declared that the only way to persuade Hitler to disarm was for his neighbors to disarm first. Sir Herbert Samuel, who led the Liberals, a Jew who might be expected to show special alarm over the brutal developments in Germany, took violent umbrage at Churchill's proposal to double the Air Force. "This is rather the language of a Malay running amuck than of a responsible British statesman," said Samuel. "It is rather the language of blind and causeless panic." Somewhat previously, Ramsay MacDonald had announced that "after anxious consideration and much regret" the Navy had been strengthened by the addition of two small cruisers. And in 1935 Stanley Baldwin, cornered by Churchill's vehemence, said proudly, "I give you my word, there will be no great armaments in *this* country."

In a nation afflicted by mass blindness, only Churchill could see. The now familiar events moved rapidly. In 1935 Hitler threw out the Versailles clauses limiting the German Army; shortly afterward he began German conscription. In 1936, as the storm gathered, he established his unholy "Axis" with Mussolini, and only a few weeks later he marched on the Rhineland. Austria received his ministrations in due course. In England these actions were met with decision of a pallid order.

Neville Chamberlain, succeeding Baldwin as Prime Minister, announced early in 1938 that he was assuming personal charge of England's foreign affairs, the Foreign Secretary (Anthony Eden) having resigned for failing to accommodate himself to Hitler's and Mussolini's ambitions. The celebrated umbrella soon came into play and was brandished like a popgun in the face of the Fascist cannons.

Meanwhile Churchill took unofficial and slightly more robust steps. He crossed the Channel for private talks with the political leaders of France, which country he held to be England's principal hope. He obtained the views of the Premier, Monsieur Blum; the War Minister, Monsieur Daladier; and the chief of the General Staff, General Gamelin; and he in turn pounded the table for a close concert of effort. Back in London, he made his report, now that only of an elder statesman, to Lord Halifax, whom Chamberlain had finally appointed to succeed Eden. Afterward, Churchill lumbered into Commons and roared out, *"Arm*—and stand by the Covenant of the League. If the League of Nations has been mishandled and broken we must rebuild it. If the authority in the Covenant is divided we must reinforce it. Here is the practical plan: Britain and France are now united. Together they are an enormous force, which few countries would dare to challenge. I should like to see these two countries go to all the smaller States that are menaced, who are going to be devoured one by one by the Nazi tyranny, and say to them bluntly, 'We are not going to help you if you are not going to help yourselves. What are you going to do about it?' "

His words and his plan were treated precisely as any discredited elder statesman might expect—he was indulgently permitted to close out his address, after which the Members said, in effect, "Hm, ha, to be sure. Now let's get on with the more pressing domestic concerns." As the summer of 1938 faded, the war clouds sailed high overhead, like the advance wisps of a hurricane. The atmosphere, to sensitive and alert persons, was perhaps like that described by Sherlock Holmes in the story dealing with his counterespionage of the First World War. "There's a wind coming from across the channel, Watson," he said, as the friends peered through the darkness at France from their cottage porch on the Sussex downs. "It will be a terrible and destructive wind while it lasts, but we can hope that when it dies down it will leave a cleaner and brighter England."

Hitler's attentions toward Poland and Czechoslovakia became so ugly and forbidding that Chamberlain, umbrella at the ready, made his unsavory visit of propitiation. The foaming maniac at Munich, so like the Kreutze of Churchill's *Savrola,* then promised brief leniency for the rest of humanity if Czechoslovakia should be added to his toll. From the side lines, Churchill arose in terrible wrath. "It is necessary," he shouted, "that the nation should realize the magnitude of the disaster into which we are being led. The partition of Czechoslovakia under Anglo-French pressure amounts to a complete surrender by the Western democracies to the Nazi threat of force. Such a collapse will not bring peace or safety to Great Britain and France. On the contrary, it will bring both countries into a position of ever-increasing weakness and danger."

In a vein reminiscent of his military predictions of the First Great War, he added, "The neutralization of Czechoslovakia alone means the liberation of 25 German divisions to threaten the Western front. The path to the Black Sea will be laid wide open to triumphant Nazi-ism. Acceptance of Herr Hitler's terms involves the prostration of Europe before the Nazi power, of which the fullest advantage will certainly be taken. The menace, therefore, is not to Czechoslovakia, but to the cause of freedom and democracy in every country."

Official Britain's reaction to this was, briefly, "Pooh, pooh." It was similar to that, later, of the military forces in Singapore when a frantic report was rushed in that the Japanese were advancing through the city. One general, momentarily breaking off his connection with a Planter's Punch, was quoted as saying with immense tolerance, "Oh, nonsense—they wouldn't *dare!*"

SARTORIAL STUDIES: *above,* as a horseman in India, 1896, and at a pheasant shoot in Yorkshire, 1910; *below,* as a polo player at Roehampton, and following the hounds at a wild boar hunt in France

MORE COSTUME STUDIES: *above,* in military uniform at the Arc de Triomphe Paris, after having received the Médaille Militaire, and in the ceremonia dress of the Lord Warden of the Cinque Ports; *below,* as artist, dressed in his famous boiler suit and sombrero, selling one of his paintings to a proud purchaser, and in academic robe as Chancellor of Bristol University, 194:

In the years since the war, the heartbroken Chamberlain has been made the popular scapegoat for the deadly and age-old complacency of British officialdom. Churchill, in his account of the struggle that followed, has made it plain that Chamberlain was not much more guilty than his fellows. The public conception of the stringy, corvine minister as a soft, frightened weakling is grossly inaccurate. He was probably several times tougher than any of his detractors, a man who once had lived almost as a savage, on a tiny island owned by his father in the West Indies. ". . . six years of his life were spent in trying to grow sisal in this lonely spot, swept by hurricanes from time to time, living nearly naked, struggling with labor difficulties and every other kind of obstacle, and with the town of Nassau as the only gleam of civilization," Churchill wrote. "He had insisted, he told us [Churchill and his wife], on three months' leave in England each year. He built a small harbor and landing-stage and a short railroad or tramway. He used all the processes of fertilization which were judged suitable to the soil, and generally led a completely open-air existence. But no sisal!"

This last, sad exclamation symbolizes many of Chamberlain's misplaced endeavors. He was a confident, overopinionated man, but his significant traits were more racial than personal. The British, as unyielding as gravity once trouble begins, are reared with an unpunctual awareness of their vulnerability. And it is a tragic mark of democracies in general that they will sacrifice prodigies of manpower and wealth to be impeccably inscribed in the record.

Although Churchill has always been impatient with mulishness, he conceived a genuine respect for Chamberlain. On one occasion early in 1939, according to Beverley Baxter, a well-known Member of Parliament, he even spoke out against a group of young Tories who had (at last) voiced disgust with Chamberlain's weak attitude. "It's all very well for those young fellows," said Churchill to Baxter, "but it's Chamberlain who has to press the button. It's a terrible thing at a time like this to be the one man who has to decide whether the button must be pressed or not."

All too late, Britain awoke to the fact that Churchill, again, had been right from the start. His ten years of unheeded prophecy were drawing to a close. The warnings, the alarms, the many speeches wasted on the desert air of a fatuous Parliament were echoing back with critical importance. At any of a dozen points, say today's experts, Hitler could have been stopped without bloodshed. Churchill had pleaded for action in every case. Now the die was cast. Chamberlain's tardy reversal of policy, involving the proposed alliance with Turkey, the overtures to Russia, and the guarantees to Greece, Poland, and Rumania, was received with understandable scorn in Berlin. The juggernaut was rolling; on the first of September 1939 it rolled with gleaming precision into Poland. On September 3 France and England declared war, and in that evening Churchill was called by the Government to resume his old post at the Admiralty. As the memorable message went out to all units of the fleet, by radio, blinker, and signal flags— "Winston is back"—he arranged his affairs for an extended visit in London. One of his friends says that he moved with calmness and a hint of anticipation. Ever practical, he included several boxes of cigars and a revolver in his luggage. Perhaps because of the gay times in India and the Sudan, Churchill has always seen war as carrying the hopeful chance of personal encounter. "If it comes to hand-to-hand combat," he said, referring to the revolver, "I mean to get one or two before they finish me."

*Part*

# IV

# *Chapter 24*

ENGLAND'S quick reaction once the nation was at war offers an interesting study in psychology. Belatedly aroused, the sentiment in favor of stopping the dictators turned incredibly fierce. Just as a reformed alcoholic makes the most intolerant sort of teetotaler, nobody can be quite as pugnacious as a former pacifist. The nation was united in an immovable zeal to do mayhem to the Hun. In the light of postwar records, it is believable that part of Hitler's sickness was a lifelong sense of inferiority to the British. And in some measure this could be said of his race as a whole. He had often spoken with contempt of the "English public school spirit"; he was now to find it a vexatious and enduring weapon, as tangibly potent as an inventory of tanks and planes. And in the end it proved his undoing.

For England, for the world, this mystic factor was embodied in Churchill. His history of belligerence was noteworthy, but a good percentage of the impact was held to be facial. The arrangement of his features was a continuing setback to tyranny. Experts had searched his countenance and found no suggestion of compromise; they had been obliged to report instead the probability of combat to the death. It was a cheerless prospect. Although Teutonic hysteria is a horrifying urge to destruction, it runs its course like any fever. An insane fighter can perform with superhuman strength, but he seldom triumphs over the stamina of rationality. For Germany, psychiatrists have since recommended the quick, bullying war as

being the safest staple of the nation's martial diet. People close
to Hitler have related that, in his last year, either the sight of
Churchill's photograph or the sound of his voice was enough
to bring a kind of babbling froth to the Fuehrer's lips. Correctly or incorrectly, he had settled on the belief that, except
for Churchill, he could have had his way with Europe.

England's reaction included a flood tide of approval for its
hero of the previous decade. By-passing his last lean years, the
public welcomed him back with shouts of appreciation. During
the formal announcement of war, on Sunday, September 3, he
walked into Parliament to a standing ovation. Both sides of the
House applauded him warmly. Churchill's expression revealed
that this was a congenial improvement: only the week before
they had been denouncing him with gusto. He added a few
words to the tense debate that followed Chamberlain's declaration of Britain's commitment. His statement was, in the
main, a generous acknowledgment of the Prime Minister's
equivocal position. "In this solemn hour," said Churchill, "it is
a consolation to realize and dwell upon our repeated efforts for
peace. All have been ill-starred, but all have been faithful and
sincere. This is of the highest moral value, and not only of
moral value, but of practical value at the present time, because
of the wholehearted concurrence of scores of millions of men
and women whose cooperation is indispensable, whose comradeship and brotherhood is indispensable. That is the only
foundation upon which the trials and tribulations of modern
war can be endured and surmounted.

"This moral conviction alone affords that ever-fresh resili-
ence which renews the strength and energy of peoples in long
and doubtful and dark days. Outside the storms of war may
blow and the land may be lashed with the fury of the gale, but
in our hearts this Sunday morning there is peace. Our hands
may be active but our consciences are at rest."

As the new First Lord of the Admiralty, Churchill put his
own hands to work without delay. On the first day, without the
usual preliminary settling down, he began his routine desk

tasks, calling for the same map upon which he had plotted ship movements in 1914. Curiously enough, it proved to be still on hand, and Churchill picked up his placement of vessels and planes as if the years between 1918 and 1939 had never existed. Also, forgoing union hours, he was on the job until 3 A.M. the night of his appointment. And the next morning he appeared for duty, perfectly fresh, at ten o'clock. Monday, when he took up his official place on the Treasury, or Cabinet, Bench in Parliament, his long banishment was evident in his indecisive actions. Nearly all the important men of the House, those seated on the front benches of Government or Opposition, prop their notes against the jeweled dispatch box that traditionally rests on the broad desk separating the two factions. Churchill, for the first time in the memory of any member, held his notes in his hand. It was thought that the box had been moved slightly and that he preferred not to fumble for it. He arose and gave a straightforward report on the sinking of the *Athenia,* in which many British and American lives had been lost. Simultaneously, in Berlin, Joseph Goebbels was releasing some hotter news on the subject, in which it was disclosed that Churchill himself had ordered the sinking. Lesser German newspapers, obediently taking up the cry, refined this subtle announcement to the point where much of the population actually had the impression that Churchill had personally pulled the switch that released the fatal torpedo. Unfortunately, Goebbels failed to explain Churchill's motive for this baffling act, and Churchill did not volunteer any details.

Logic has never been one of the big guns in the German propaganda arsenal. Throughout the war, Hitler and his subordinate demons wallowed in a morass of non-meshing accounts of Churchill's activities. Their ire was inflamed by his refusal to respond directly to any accusation, defamation, or threat; but they had no sooner cooled down than he released some general blast so ornate and withering that Hitler would spend several days stamping about his costly lair at Berchtesgaden. Chief among the utterances that drove him periodically crazier was Churchill's use of "Corporal Hitler." There is reasonable belief that Shicklgruber, the house painter who changed his name but could hardly disguise his rank, smarted under the stigma of having spent four years fighting a war without advancing to a niche more complimentary than corporal. For an ambitious man, it was an odd failure, and Churchill chose to harp on it. "Corporal Hitler says" and "according to Corporal Hitler" became staples of his wartime reports on losses, progress, and the like. While Churchill could move Hitler to inarticulate frenzy, Hitler inspired Churchill to eloquence. In his postwar account of the struggle, the latter introduced the German leader with a brilliant and memorable stroke: "Thereafter mighty forces were adrift; the void was open, and into that void after a pause there strode a maniac of ferocious genius, the repository and expression of the most virulent hatreds that have ever corroded the human breast— Corporal Hitler."

The contemptuous flinging of the name and rating at the end typifies Churchill's attitude toward his antagonist. The words are those of a member of the upper class—descendant of the Dukes of Marlborough and graduate of the King's Military College—making brief and distasteful mention of an unworthy foe. And they have probably had the usual spinning effect on Hitler's long sleep.

During the eight months that Churchill remained First Lord of the Admiralty, he was able to report comparatively little news of encouragement. It was a bleak hour in English history. The U-boat sinkings, including the catastrophe to the *Royal Oak* at Scapa Flow, the sowing of the magnetic mines, the loss of the *Rawalpindi*—these and similar blows tested British morale in the closing months of 1939. The nation was, of course, ill prepared for war and fighting a holding action until the armament duel could properly be joined. A hoary joke of the British pubs is that the War Office is always preparing for the last war, a *mot* that Churchill has correctly said is also applicable to other departments and to other countries. But numerically inferior though they were in the beginning, his ships fought savagely enough to provide stimulating headlines on several occasions. The first of these on a large scale was the action at the river Plate, on the east coast of South America. It made a thrilling story at a time when the British badly needed a hint that the armed might of the dictators was vulnerable. Searching for raiders, the 8-inch cruisers *Cumberland* and *Exeter* and the smaller cruisers *Ajax* and *Achilles* (the last from the New Zealand Navy) got wind of the Germans' prize pocket battleship, *Graf Spee,* off Montevideo, after she had sunk the merchant vessel *Doric Star.* The *Cumberland* being some distance away, the *Exeter* and the others closed rapidly, at nearly fifty miles an hour. The collision occurred shortly after dawn on December 13. Instead of running for cover, the Nazi Captain Langsdorff (whom Churchill later described as a "high-class person") thought his heavier armament would be conclusive and he elected to turn and fight. It was poor judgment, not inconsistent with the German arrogance of the period.

Taking a terrible battering, *Exeter* doggedly poured salvos into the *Graf Spee,* while *Ajax* and *Achilles* snapped at the enemy like bulldogs. At seven-forty, with the *Exeter's* forward turrets knocked out of action and all their crews killed or wounded, Captain Harwood of the English force withdrew the stricken cruiser and laid down smoke for her consorts, hoping to delay the action until dark, when he could use his torpedoes. All that day the *Spee,* many times hit but not critically damaged, ran toward Montevideo, hounded by *Ajax* and *Achilles.* Intermittent gun flashes from all three ships lit up the ocean. She entered the harbor at midnight.

Beyond the three-mile limit, hopelessly outgunned, *Ajax* and *Achilles* lay in wait, bent on carrying the fight to the death at whatever odds. Luckily, these were soon to improve. The *Cumberland,* in the style of cinema cavalry relieving an MGM garrison, came speeding over the horizon in midmorning, and the *Renown* and *Ark Royal,* near Rio, had signaled their intention of proceeding with all haste.

German documents captured after the war reveal Langsdorff's wire to his Admiralty: "Strategic position off Montevideo. Besides the cruisers and destroyers [this an error on Langsdorff's part] *Ark Royal* and *Renown.* Close blockade at night escape into open sea and break-through to home waters hopeless. . . . Request decision on whether the ship should be scuttled in spite of insufficient depth in the Estuary of the Plate, or whether internment is to be preferred."

At a conference of Hitler and several admirals, it was decided that the best plan was: "Attempt by all means to extend the time in neutral waters . . . fight your way through to Buenos Aires if possible. No internment in Uruguay. Attempt effective destruction if ship is scuttled."

At six-fifteen the evening of the seventeenth, with the population of Montevideo lining the riverbanks and the rest of civilization anxiously awaiting reports, the *Graf Spee* headed toward the sea. A few minutes later, a scout plane from *Ajax* radioed: *"Graf Spee* has blown herself up."

The message was flashed out to all corners of the world, and England took a new lease on the war. Persons then at the British Admiralty say that Churchill danced around the dispatch room like a child, and wrung everybody's hand with uninhibited glee. His excitement persisted until the crews and their three commanders were brought home for congratulations. The celebration, with multiple introductions, went on throughout a gala day and marked one of the few failures on record of one of humanity's great memories. The *Ajax,* *Achilles* and *Exeter* were skippered by, respectively, Captains Woodhouse, Parry and Bell. Churchill first presented the heroes to the King and Queen as Captain Woodhouse of the *Achilles,* Captain Bell of the *Exeter,* and Captain Parry of the *Ajax.* On the next try, for the BBC, he transposed Bell and Parry and left Woodhouse on the quarterdeck of the *Achilles,* a ship he scarcely knew from Adam. That evening, starting a public address and presentation, Churchill relieved Bell of the *Exeter* and gave him Woodhouse's new ship, the *Achilles*. This left Parry aboard the unaccustomed *Ajax*. Trying to settle on a proper command for Woodhouse, possibly Noah's Ark, or the *Graf Spee*, Churchill became so flustered that he stopped and muttered something that sounded to the audience like, "Confound it, I can't keep these men apart. I've been doing this all day. They'll just have to introduce themselves." By this time not only Churchill but the captains were addled, and Woodhouse was believed to have identified himself with the *Exeter*. It was an enjoyable occasion all around.

Nevertheless, a rising dissatisfaction with Chamberlain's ministry came to a head with the subsequent failures in Norway, and he was obliged to face a hostile Opposition in May. Throughout most of the winter, the struggle had slumbered like a hibernating animal, giving rise to the phrase "twilight war" in Britain and "phony war" in some of the impatient, nonparticipating nations. Though slumbering, it was far from phony to Englishmen, who were given periodic accounts of heavy U-boat sinkings and actions at sea in which the men and ships of the Royal Navy were steadily sacrificed. The enemy suffered, too, but the sea war, to the Germans, was never much more than a screen to shield the operations of a prepared and eager land force. As Norway fell and Holland girded for the coming blow, Chamberlain was denounced even by members of his own party. In a stunning speech, Leo Amery, a Conservative wheel horse, a Privy Councilor, and a friend of the Prime Minister, arose and quoted Cromwell's peremptory words to the Long Parliament: "You have sat too long here for any good you have done. Depart, I say, and let us have done with you. In the name of God, go!"

Chamberlain stepped down, and King George sent for Churchill. The culmination of a stormy lifetime of political effort was at last at hand. Years before, during one of his unfavored periods, Churchill had confided to a friend, "I would

quit politics forever if it were not for the possibility that I
might some day become Prime Minister." His perseverance was
now rewarded, in the spring of 1940, with England all but
prostrate. He was asked to form an All-Party, or Coalition,
Government; the Socialists and Liberals agreed to his leadership; and he took office, on the tenth of May, in England's
worst hour of the civilized era. His name was recorded in history beside those of Pitt, Gladstone, Disraeli, and Fox, and he
had, by the simple act of succession, outstripped the fame of
his revered ancestor. As one of his advisers says, "Winston had
finally grown beyond his hero. The line had completed its
cycle." When he stalked away from the ritual of kissing the
King's hand, he wasted no time in exultation but set rapidly to
work. On the following Monday he stood forth with the stirring
address on "blood, sweat and tears." It would be democracy's
theme for the next six years, and an immortal masterpiece
among England's great orations.


## II


The charge has continued to grow in recent years that
Churchill is a warmonger, that he enjoys fighting. It is the
favorite line of Hyde Park speakers, Russian Communists,
American "intellectuals," and additionally consecrated groups.
The subject has been so noisily exploited that it needs an unbiased and authoritative opinion. Victor Gollancz, the English
publisher, a non-Conservative who served on wartime committees with Churchill, feels that he dreads the coming of war
more than any other public figure of modern times, having had
a unique experience of its effect on nations and individuals,
but that once war is declared he has about as much fun as it
is possible to have. Churchill's activities between 1940 and
1946 testify to the accuracy of this view. Warfare has always
provided him with the perfect field for the full employment of
his potential. At such a time, nothing that he does can seem

too bizarre when one reflects that his ultimate aim is the destruction of the enemy.

To be close to the scene, Churchill and his wife moved into the commodious quarters at 10 Downing Street soon after his appointment as Prime Minister. Brendan Bracken, his chief political adviser, and Churchill's brother Jack also occupied rooms on the premises. From this nerve center of executive Britain, and from his office in Whitehall, Churchill bustled around, covering an unbelievable amount of ground, to keep his check on the war. Since the days of the bone-jarring crackups with Captain Scott, he had been wary of flying; now he took it up again, as a passenger. When his physicians advised him that the changing pressures would be unsalutary for a man of his years, he ordered a personal pressure chamber constructed, probably the only one of its kind ever in existence. Shaped like an egg, it was about ten feet long and weighed two tons. The important thing was, it could be hoisted into nearly any plane, while the statesman was inside and occupied at his correspondence. Churchill's eerie compartment was not really home, but it was the next best substitute for its size, with a chair, a built-in couch, a cupboard for bottles, a bookshelf, and numerous ashtrays.

A special train also was rigged up for Churchill—one originally meant for the King and Queen to use during the war. They preferred traveling by auto and insisted that the train be made available to the Prime Minister. It was about the least distinguished-looking piece of railway equipment in Britain, being kept grubby and mud-covered so as to be inconspicuous. Its appearance was a bane to its crew, who were often restrained from smartening it up. They wanted the train bright and shiny for Churchill, but the Government preferred it drab, so as to escape bombs and enemy agents. Churchill established his own staff of stewards aboard; they stocked up with liquors, good foods, boxes of his favorite cigars, and other articles. One of the stewards has said, "Of all the men I ever met, the Prime Minister was the hardest worker. We couldn't get him to stay in the sleeper. He only took cat naps, then he would come down the aisle wearing his bathrobe and smoking a cigar, and get to work on his papers."

People high and low in the government departments became used to having Churchill telephone unexpectedly for information. His requests, either vocal or written, always started out, "Pray tell me," and, as in the first war, contained the stipulation that each report should be confined to one side of one page of foolscap. He gathered round him a staff of experts in every field. The leader of these was Frederick Lindemann, professor of experimental philosophy at Oxford University, whom Churchill employed as a sort of statistical trouble-shooter, paying his salary personally. The two had met at the close of the First World War, when Lindemann, a man of exceptional doggedness, conceived some ideas about airplane "spins" and learned to fly to try them out. Some of the wildest pilots in England stood openmouthed on the ground and watched the sedentary professor go into spins from which test pilots had been incapable of extricating themselves. His theories worked, and he contributed improvements in design that greatly reduced this hazard of flying.

Churchill called his advisers The Team, and they, in turn, referred to him as The Master. Sir Desmond Morton, a military member, had been a crack artillery officer in 1917, the winner of the Military Cross and a man who held the added distinction of having been shot through the heart with comparatively little discomfort. When the second war came along, he was a neighbor of Churchill's at Chartwell; he came to London to carry out assignments for the Prime Minister. Various of Churchill's team—Lieutenant General Sir Henry Pownall, Commodore G. R. G. Allen, Colonel F. W. Deakin, and others—were to remain with him after the war, to act as advisers in the preparation of his gigantic history of the struggle.

Churchill's team tried to act as a buffer between him and the snarls of wartime bureaucracy, but he was a hard man to protect. He insisted on having a special telephone line run from his office to the Censorship Room of the Ministry of Information. The two phones, he decreed, should be red. He scanned the papers acidulously, and the minute he spotted something suspect, he reached for his red phone to complain. People in the Censorship Office dreaded to hear theirs ring. As could be expected of a saint, Churchill was not always in the sweetest humor during the war. He was impatient with any kind of bungling, and he was aggravated by well-wishers who tried to get him into the underground shelters. After a time, nearly everybody gave up urging him, being influenced by the fact that, as one Whitehall worker says, "When the Premier was cooped up in an air raid shelter his blistering temper was far worse than the raid." However, on the few occasions when he did go down, it was agreed that his absolute contempt for the Germans and their bombs did much to impart stout morale to the others. In the room set aside for the War Cabinet, all the seats except Churchill's bore a name card; his had a tiny silver plaque with the inscription, "Please understand that there is no depression in this house and we are not interested in the possibilities of defeat. They do not exist. Victoria R I."

One of Churchill's first acts when war threatened was to recall to duty Sergeant (now Detective Inspector) Thompson, his former bodyguard and all-round helper. Thompson had been long retired from the force and was conducting a peaceful grocery in Norwood when he received a brief telegram— two words under the ten-word limit—from his former boss, who appeared to be in Paris. It read, simply, "Meet me Croydon Aerodrome 4:30 P.M. Wednesday. Churchill." Thompson had grown used to, and even fond of, Churchill's autocratic ways, so with a resigned sigh he rang up a shilling for a can of asparagus, closed the grocery, got out his automatic, and boarded a train to Croydon. Churchill's explanation, when he stepped off the plane, was somewhat less verbose than the telegram. He said, "Hallo, Thompson. Nice to see

you. Get the luggage together and bring it on to Chartwell."
Thompson has since published his serialized reminiscences
of these days, and he has some lively notes on the resumption
of their association. Churchill indicated a willingness to meet
a bodyguard's salary of five pounds a week out of his own
pocket. Thompson made no complaint, although it is presumed that his grocery was netting more than this, unless he
was operating it as a hobby. A number of people noticed that
both Churchill and his wife became less openhanded as the
war went on. His series on Marlborough had failed to find
a popular audience, and his immense earnings from magazines and newspapers were curtailed when he took office.
Meanwhile the vast expenses of Chartwell and his usual high
living rolled on.

Churchill's reasons for needing a bodyguard again were
stated succinctly when they reached home: "Some Frenchmen
told me a bunch of spies were planning to assassinate me.
I was going down to see the Duke of Windsor in Southern
France, but I gave it up. Now, I can look after myself in the
daytime, but I can't have them springing on me when I'm
asleep. Do you wish to borrow a gun?" Thompson and Churchill did considerable bickering about what kind of weapon
was best to carry. The detective had the reasonable notion
that he qualified as an expert on the use of firearms. Churchill
felt qualified, too. "And indeed," Thompson says, "Mr.
Churchill is in fact a first-class shot." Over his charge's objections, Thompson elected to use a Webley .38 in a chamois
shoulder holster of his own devising. Though sympathetic,
Churchill had a subtle attitude of "Aha—you see?" when the
gun slipped out and shot Thompson in both legs.

The relationship between master and employee was in general a curious one. The detective's position was frequently
little more than that of valet; at the same time, he stated his
views positively on matters relating to safety. It was Churchill's custom to argue everything. One time, leaving the private
train, he said, "Clean up these papers and bring them after

me, Thompson." "I will do it gladly," replied the detective, "but I can scarcely guard you outside if I am in here picking up papers." While Churchill tried angrily to stare him down, Thompson stood by with a look of limited deference. Churchill finally stamped out, but he waited on the platform for Thompson before getting off the train.

Like so many others, Thompson had trouble trying to keep Churchill from getting killed by bombs. The fact that he succeeded is a testimonial not only to his patience but to his strength. Once he found Churchill standing in the double doorway at 10 Downing Street enjoying some particularly vivid shrapnel bursts. There was a crash near by and then a number of piercing whistles. "Something is coming this way!" shouted Thompson, and he seized Churchill and flung him inside. The explosion that ensued from the Prime Minister did much to nullify the racket in the street. In Thompson's words, he was "horrified and indignant," and roared, "Don't do that!" His ire was reduced when he found that an employee of the establishment, standing beside him, had been severely hit. Throughout the blitz, Thompson kept referring to No. 10 Downing Street as a "death trap," and Churchill continued to say that he wouldn't alter his mode of living "to suit Hitler." On several occasions he continued to dine in contentment while buildings were crashing down in the immediate neighborhood. Friends of Churchill's have related that he was put in a frightful temper when anecdotes he was relating gave way to concussion. This seemed to be his strongest private reaction to the blitz.

After much persuasion, Churchill finally agreed to remove to a safer building when plane warnings were flashed in from the coast. However, it was his perverse pleasure to wait until the bombs actually started falling; then he would light a cigar, put on his coal-bucket hat, pick up his gold-headed stick, and stroll very leisurely through the barrage to the stronger No. 10 Annex, some thousand yards away. Thompson once sneaked up from behind, removed the hat, and

clapped on a regulation tin helmet. Churchill removed it
without comment and tossed it into the bushes. A few evenings later, strolling along, he vacated a spot that was struck
by a 1000-pound bomb less than five minutes afterward. The
King and Queen came to dine one night and the blitz alarm
sounded shortly after the dessert course. The party quickly
adjourned to the Annex Shelter, but all through the raid
Churchill kept walking outside to look around. The King
stood in the doorway and remonstrated. "I say, Churchill,
hadn't you better join us inside?" he called out three or four
times, but got little more reassurance from his Prime Minister
than an amiable wave.

At length, governmental pressures were exerted to force
Churchill underground. He responded with impatience and
would never have won a gold star for attendance had the roll
been taken. He intensely disliked being cooped up. For one
thing, the guard at the door was obligated to make him throw
down the lighted cigar each time, the rules prohibiting smoking. And no matter how heavy the bombing was, he left
before it was over. The next night, to offset what he considered
his good conduct, he usually went up to the roof of No. 10
Downing Street. "I am sorry to take you into danger, Thompson," he said after an especially foolhardy ascent. "I would not
do it, only I knew how much you like it."

In one way, the trips to the underground were the most
anxious of all for Thompson. Churchill's humor was, as stated,
badly soured by his confinement and he laid about with wrath.
"Although he showed no normal sign of nerves the times
increased when the Old Man wanted to let off steam," the
detective has said in his reminiscences. "Because I was almost
always on the spot I was the scapegoat on many occasions."
After one ferocious tongue-lashing, he complained to General
Ismay that he had been bawled out for absolutely nothing.
The general's reply was, "I get it just the same, Thompson.
If it gives him relief from constant strain, it is well worth it."

Eventually, Churchill's colleagues got together and decided

on an expedient, since it was clear he had no intention of ducking bombs. At Chequers, the country residence for England's Prime Ministers, and at Chartwell—one or another of which he usually visited on week ends—artillery troops and anti-aircraft guns were stationed to fend off low-flying planes. Churchill was delighted. When at Chequers (Chartwell was converted to government offices during the latter part of the war) he made a rite of inspecting his soldiers and their Bofors gun. As a rule he took several guests along, and since these generally included some high-ranking officer, the troops were far from happy. The gun crews had orders that, when a night raid began, Inspector Thompson was to be awakened promptly, so that the business of trying to argue the Prime Minister into the cellar could begin. Churchill countermanded these orders, which had been handed down by the Army Chief of Staff. His program made it clear that he would be awakened only if "my flak" was going into action. The idea was, simply, that he wanted to scamper up onto the parapet and watch the fun.

Eric Ambler, the English author, was a subaltern attached to the gun crew at Chequers; later on he recorded his impression of the duty for the British magazine *Strand*. He was on hand for one of Churchill's birthdays and was invited into the house with his battery captain and two other subalterns. They were ushered into a large, darkened room in which there appeared to be a seated audience of some size. The Prime Minister's favorite entertainment was about to get under way—a film featuring Deanna Durbin. Ambler was shown to a chair on the left of a swaddled figure that he took to be an uncommonly cold-blooded woman, wrapped all around in an eiderdown quilt. When he noticed that, through a tiny aperture resembling the vent in a wigwam, the figure was smoking a cigar, he realized that his neighbor was Churchill. The quilt turned out to be a polychromatic dressing gown of the Premier's own design. The film was *A Hundred Men and a Girl*. No sooner had it started than a low rumble, with

gestures, issued from the figure in the eiderdown. Alarmed,
with visions of a gastric emergency, Ambler leaned forward.
As he did so, the cigar came more plainly into view, held in
one hand and stabbing at the air like punctuation. It finally
dawned upon Ambler that Churchill was rehearsing a speech,
but he was enjoying the movie at the same time, for he broke
into chuckles at exactly the right spots. "The total effect was
curious," says Ambler. 'Mumble mumble mumble, demumble
*mumble* demumble—Ha!—demumble mumble? Er, mumble
de-mumble *mumble* mumble—Cor!—mumble *mumble* de
mumble——' And so on."

After the movie, Churchill disappeared and came back
wearing his siren suit, which was received with restrained
enthusiasm. He met all the officers and invited them again for
the next week, when he was having another Deanna Durbin
film—*Bachelor Mother*. One of the subalterns said, deferen-
tially, "I think the star of *Bachelor Mother* is Ginger Rogers,
sir."

"Deanna Durbin, I'm sure," replied Churchill, bristling
slightly.

The subaltern held fast. "No, sir. Ginger Rogers."

Churchill thrust his jaw out in the familiar expression, then
said, "Well, we shall see." But he wasn't finished. "Exactly
how many rounds of anti-*tank* ammunition does your gun
carry?" he asked sharply, and when the subaltern hesitated,
he gave the correct answer himself, after which he went on to
rattle off every known statistic on the Bofors gun. This done,
he looked as if he had solved the question of *Bachelor Mother*
for once and all. The Prime Minister devoted the rest of that
evening to wrestling noisily with a small black dog. In the
following weeks he was so kindly and genial that the gun
crew began to count itself fortunate. "There could have been
little interest for him in the presence of so undistinguished a
group of junior officers and still less in our conversation,"
said Ambler. "We felt a great affection for him."

Everybody who came into contact with Churchill during

the war felt the strong enigmatic stirring of courage that he stimulated. The effect was almost hypnotic. At the time of Dunkirk, not long after he took office, it was principally his urging that saved the Expeditionary Army. When the treacherous King Leopold of Belgium, whose excellent army was protecting the Allied left flank, suddenly and inexplicably surrendered to the Germans, Churchill wired the British commanders, "March to the North Channel ports. Fight anything that gets in the way." And when the news came from Dunkirk of the quick necessity for evacuation, at 6:30 A.M., May 26, 1940, he sprang out of bed and grabbed for his telephones without putting in his false teeth. He worked throughout the day in this stringhalted condition. What with his natural speech impediment, and the forgotten dentures, Churchill's voice came through in almost unrecognizable form, but there was no mistaking the rolling phrases and impassioned commands to action. While standing in his nightshirt, he put the Admiralty on a crisis footing, and then, still using the telephones, he turned the nation as a whole into a giant Coast Guard station. Somewhat more than 350,000 British and French soldiers were trapped on the beaches, while the enemy was attacking with every available means, bombing the piers, sowing magnetic mines, bringing up artillery, and rushing forward great numbers of troops in fast lorries. In less than an hour the word had been spread, via radio and the newspapers, that "Winnie needs boats." Then the oddest flotilla within the memory of man put out from the ports of England. Altogether the episode provided one of the most gallant chapters in British military annals. First, the Navy headed full tilt for the scene with as many as a thousand ships of all sizes and kinds, from barges and mine sweepers to big warships. But these were only the beginning. Up and down the Thames, and elsewhere, men were jumping into private craft, casting off, and pointing toward Dunkirk. There were million-dollar yachts and fishermen's luggers, racing sailboats and tramps so leaky that only their gunwales were above water. One of the London newspapers carried an item about two moderately drunk night clubbers in evening dress who were stopped while trying to row a dory out of the Thames estuary. "Where the devil do you think you're headed?" came a hail from a Dunkirk-bound ferryboat. "Why, France, as it were," replied one of the men. "Throw us a line—we'll take you aboard," cried the ferry captain, and the roisterers went on to France in safety. From start to finish, the desperate expedition was marked by typically British high spirits. A member of a cruiser unit told of a near-collision in fog and of its signalman's challenge: "What ship are you?"

"H.M.S. *Myrtle T. Bosworth*."

There was a brief silence, then, "What class?"

"Brighton sight-seer—three rifles and a possible hand grenade."

Maintaining a dignified but injured silence, the cruiser continued toward Dunkirk.

In Churchill's words (his report to the House) it was feared that the situation on the French beaches would result in "the greatest military disaster in our long history." But the incredible rescue carried out by the Navy and civilian ships and boats brought 338,000 men across the stormy Channel to England. While the Prime Minister did not minimize the work of the hasty flotilla, he gave the edge of victory to the Royal Air Force, saying, "This was a great trial of strength between the British and German Air Forces. Can you conceive a greater objective for the Germans in the air than to make evacuation from these beaches impossible, and to sink all these ships which were displayed, almost to the extent of thousands? Could there have been an objective of greater military importance and significance for the whole purpose of the war than this? They tried hard, and they were beaten back; they were frustrated in their task. We got the Army away; and they have paid fourfold for any losses which they have inflicted."

Churchill made no attempt to disguise the rescue as a victory. Instead, he painted England's position in dark colors. Just before France fell, he acknowledged that the sacrifices of matériel had been "enormous. We have perhaps lost one-third of the men we lost in the opening days of the battle of 21 March, 1918," he went on, "but we have lost nearly as many guns—nearly 1000 guns—and all our transport, all the armoured vehicles that were with the Army in the North."

Europe was gone, Russia joined the Fascists, and America proclaimed her unshakable neutrality. Churchill called a meeting of his Cabinet, whose members joined in solemn council to hear his dread predictions. They had never found him in better spirits. "Well, gentlemen, we are alone," he told them. "For myself I find it extremely exhilarating."

# *Chapter 25*

I N HIS APPOINTMENTS, the Prime Minister of a Coalition Government must be discreetly impartial. During the war Churchill tried not to show his Tory preferences, but he sometimes failed. Bravely swallowing his distaste for everything Socialistic, he named the Socialist A. V. Alexander First Lord of the Admiralty, and he cut across party lines in many other cases. Clement Attlee, who would later unseat him, was Lord Privy Seal, a post of little importance. Sources close to Churchill say that he has always been contemptuous of Attlee and has seldom missed a chance to heckle him. In one meeting shortly after Dunkirk, when the Prime Minister was being advised against converting shallow underground stations to air raid shelters, Attlee suffered an occupational accident of British politicians. Perhaps because they are compelled to sit bolt upright for years in school, Englishmen perch on their lower spines as much as possible thereafter. Even in Parliament, a formal and ritualistic body, those Members on the front benches, to a man, sit slumped far down and with their feet on the large square desk before them. It makes an odd sight for American visitors: the bewigged Speaker on his elevated stand and below him the scuffed boots of England's greatest names. In the midst of the discussion, Attlee went over backward with a crash. He was badly jarred, in one of the authentic chair-tilting disasters of the political year. Churchill sprang to his feet and cried, "Get up, get up, Lord Privy Seal! This is no time for levity."

Nearly all of his associates felt the sting of Churchill's tongue at one point or another in the war. When Sir John Dill was, for a space, in charge of a branch of Intelligence, he submitted to the importunings of reporters and called a monster press conference. This was all unknown to Churchill, who was rabidly opposed to having war leaders gush out plans and projects for publication. Intending only to be cooperative, Dill blithely reviewed British strategy in fine detail at his meeting. Churchill called him onto the carpet and said, "Dill, I'm told that you're a great general. Now I hear that you've addressed 150 newspapermen. They sat all around you like mice asking for crumbs of cheese, and you had to go and give them a whole damned Stilton!" Also in this period a well-known English scientist had made some strides with an "acoustical rocket," sensitive to sound, and he badgered the Prime Minister and a party to journey to an Oxfordshire farm to see it demonstrated. The season was the dead of winter. The scientist, his wild hair flying in a raw wind, touched off his creation, which rose up a few feet, coughed, emitted a sinister fizzling noise, and then headed pretty rapidly toward Churchill. Displaying a neat burst of speed for a politician past sixty, the latter sprinted for a tree, but as he ran he kept yelling, "Damn the man, damn the man—he can go home in an open car." When they all returned to London, the scientist trailed along behind in a hard-riding jeep, bounced by the rutty roads and exposed to the elements.

At no time did Churchill's colleagues doubt who was in command. He showed genius at reducing bombast in high officials and preventing premature swellings in small ones. Attending one meeting of the Cabinet, he found a somewhat pompous member of the War Office Staff holding a pointer and preparing a large-scale map for a lecture. The man had removed his heavily braided cap and set it upside down on the desk before him. Smoking a cigar, Churchill lumbered by the desk, stopped, fished in his pocket, and tossed a penny into the cap before he went on. The general sat down and Churchill then got the meeting under way. At another Cabinet session, a notoriously self-righteous member of the Ministry of Information balked at some stiff assignment, drawing himself up and crying out, "You should understand that my right hand cannot do two things at once!" Churchill's reply was to thrust his own right thumb into his mouth and set up a vigorous action with all five fingers. "Now have a look at *my* right hand," he said, speaking through the barricade. "It's scratching my teeth and rubbing my nose—both at once!"

Various of Churchill's physicians have decided that his explosions and buffoonery provided part of the recreation he needed so acutely during the war. Customarily he worked as many as sixteen to eighteen hours a day; without fun the strain would have mounted. By good fortune he has always been able to find pleasure in simple things. With the Royal Scots in the first great struggle he had been happy in his tin tub beneath the apple tree, listening to his batman play unpopular records on a scratchy phonograph. Now in the second great struggle he branched out little farther than this. Foremost on his list of diversions was movies. If ones starring Deanna Durbin were not available, he liked sagas of military and political history. He saw *That Hamilton Woman*—a story about Nelson—several times, and there is reason to believe that he identified himself with the hero throughout. In a similar way, Churchill drew much of his relaxation from marching. He is, and has always been, fond of marching as a pastime. He does it by himself, usually with music. Persons of his household have come across him many times prancing the length of his living room, wheeling, retracing his steps, sometimes counting the cadence, occasionally carrying a stick over his shoulder. It is to his credit that he is never abashed when caught at this surprising exercise. Personages of renown have walked in unexpectedly and received nothing more explanatory than a companionable gesture to be seated until the parade is over. Churchill's accompaniments to these maneuvers are easily as bleak as the tunes he favored in his tin tub period. Inspector Thompson, who does not care for marching but had to do a good deal in order to keep the Premier in view, has listed as the leaders: "Run, Rabbit, Run," "Poor Old Joe," "Home, Sweet Home," and "Keep Right on to the End of the Road." There were others, worse. Musically, Churchill has never starred. He has an almost African sense of rhythm, but his appreciation of melodic subtleties is limited. He is known as one of the feeblest whistlers in Kent, and his vocal outbursts in the bath have frightened house guests. "As Winston works he begins to hum," says one of his associates, "and the longer he hums the farther off key he gets. Finally the tune loses its shape altogether and becomes an original. I really think he prefers it that way."

It was probably Churchill's capacity for having fun that won England allies in the war. A Premier with the stolid phlegm of Baldwin, or the involuntary frostiness of Chamberlain, would have had difficulty persuading friends to such a forlorn cause. Churchill's hearty camaraderie drew influential visitors in to listen partly because they were curious about the man. In a way, he acted as a master salesman, one of the greatest who ever lived, never ceasing in his efforts to sell England to whatever part of the world was receptive. And although his line of goods was thin, he opened up some important new territories. Throughout the war years the British capitol was thronged with foreign potentates of every degree. Claridge's Hotel, the swankiest in London, was the headquarters of these powerful gentry, and Churchill wooed them with all the force of his roistering genius. Historic celebrants are born, and cannot be developed by the most anxious tutelage. Those persons around whom guests collect, as if to warm their hands, throw off social calories by an accident of nature rather than by design. From his boyhood, Churchill has seemed to burn increasingly brighter, like raised theater lights, when people gather round to hear him talk. As a war leader he was able to turn his peculair charm on, while pouring a little whiskey into, an Abyssinian medicine man and make him feel like the key figure of the universe. It is a lofty and useful gift; deprived of it, England could easily have perished.

Churchill's sessions with Stalin and Roosevelt are distinguished cases in point. Before their now famous rendezvous in Placentia Bay, to plot the Atlantic Charter, Churchill and Roosevelt had met once before, when the latter visited England during the First World War. They had been members of a dinner party at Gray's Inn. In the course of it, Churchill is said to have remarked of Roosevelt that he had "magnificent presence." Oddly enough, Churchill later professed to have no recollection of the dinner, and Roosevelt was piqued. A good many of Roosevelt's actions were aimed to make various groups and individuals like him, and he smarted under any failure, however reasonable, to score an impression. Churchill, on the other hand, is usually oblivious of the good or bad opinion of persons whom he meets; the Atlantic introduction to Roosevelt was an exception.

In London and in Washington, the conference was viewed as top secret, and the journeys of both President and Prime Minister began in elaborate disguise. The word was given out in official England that Churchill was headed "north" to watch a military operation. An Admiralty train, bearing war leaders, that pulled out of Marylebone Station slowed up for a country stop, where a journalist in the party "saw an excited crowd of people laughing, waving and pointing to someone on the other side." Churchill was standing on the platform, waiting for the train. He had on a nondescript blue serge suit and a yachting cap whose bill was slewed around at an angle, rather in the style of the least fastidious among the Dead End Kids. He was smoking a cigar and appeared to have struck a carnival attitude. Churchill has always reacted favorably to ocean voyages, no matter how solemn their import. H. V. Morton, the English travel writer, who was selected along with novelist Howard Spring to cover the trip, recorded an authoritative report of the Prime Minister's humor:

"He's rather like a boy who's been let out of school suddenly. He says it's the only holiday he's had since the war." It was suggested that another man might envision a voyage through waters dominated by German U-boats as anything but festive.

When the delegation boarded the battleship *Prince of Wales*, Churchill emerged full-blown as an able old salt. Forgoing a valet, he had asked Inspector Thompson to administer to his personal needs, and he instituted a call that went out frequently over the ship's speaker: "Inspector Thompson lay aft to the Prime Minister's cabin." Somebody noted that both the sound and the spirit of this were evocative of Captain Flint's bawling, in one of Churchill's favorite books (*Treasure Island*), "Darby McGraw! Darby McGraw—fetch aft the rum, Darby!" Thompson has told how he was also kept hopping by crew members who wanted Churchill souvenirs—cigar butts, cigar bands that had his name on them, and other articles (including empty bottles, according to a sailor who was aboard and is now risen to be a much-decorated chief petty officer). The crew could never be sure when Churchill was apt to burst in on them. Wearing the characteristic impish grin of his lighter moments, and smoking a cigar, he would clamber down a companionway and make pointed inquiries of a work party. He wished to know how everything was done, down to the last detail. If the group was called to attention, he said, "No, no. Carry on. I want to walk about without interfering. Allow the men to be at ease, so that I can have personal contact with them." In the Warrant Officers' Mess he found the darts in poor condition and presented his hosts with a costly new set he bought from a canteen. Playing at darts, he concentrated just as hard as he afterward seemed to do on the provisions of the Charter.

President Roosevelt's cadaverous agent, Harry Hopkins, was aboard the battleship, having previously visited Churchill at 10 Downing Street. The Prime Minister and this ill but alert ambassador spent a lot of time in conference, bringing closer the meeting of two executive minds that was to form the ful-

crum of the Allied effort. Churchill and Hopkins commonly
got together in the evenings before dinner, and, after dinner,
appeared at the ship's entertainments. At a showing of the
English film, *Pimpernel Smith,* they came into the wardroom
in resplendent condition. Hopkins was smartly dressed in a
dinner jacket, but Churchill had slipped into what seemed
to be part, at least, of the formal costume of the Royal Yacht
Squadron. At each change of reel, he twisted around in his
seat and called out, "Jolly good, what?" or "Splendid," or
another of his pet approbations. Some of the company thought
the movie only passable, but everybody wondered how a man
of such responsibility could sit in perfect detachment while a
great battleship with every gun anxiously manned plowed
through hostile seas. H. V. Morton, in his account of the trip,
tells of running into a violent gale, with the heightened discomfort of having to keep up speed because of U-boats. No
one inexperienced in the sea can foretell the nauseous shock
of smashing into massive mid-ocean combers at twenty-five
or thirty knots. The vibration, the out-of-control pitching
and rolling, the crash and clatter of every object within ear-
shot, the shrieking of wind and water across the decks—all go
to make a sort of Dantesque nightmare of confusion and
despair. At the peak of the gale, around 2 A.M., Churchill, who
had been enjoying himself with C. S. Forester's *Captain
Horatio Hornblower,* rang for a midshipman, who entered
the cabin to find him naked and dancing with rage. The Prime
Minister's quarters were aft, and the propellers were periodically climbing out of water and "waggling the ship's tail." He
put on his siren suit and his black yachting cap and demanded
to be escorted to the admiral's sea cabin on the bridge.

It was quite a stroll. The midshipman, staggering against
the fury of the storm, tried to steer Churchill on an easy, dry
path—out of the way of protruding davits, capstans, and
cables—but only received a reprimand for his pains. "Young
man, do you imagine I have never climbed a ladder in my
life?" the Prime Minister cried at one point, and immediately

afterward clanked his head cruelly on a steel overhang. "But, do you know, the most extraordinary thing happened," said the midshipman later. "I expected a proper mouthful, but— *he never said a word!* I tell you, it was absolutely awe-inspiring."

Approaching Placentia Bay and a personal encounter upon which the entire world hung in large measure, Churchill exhibited a certain degree of unaccustomed tension. When Inspector Thompson remarked that the meeting would be "historic," he replied, "Yes, and more so if I get what I want from him." It was a stirring scene as the gigantic *Prince of Wales* rounded a promontory and entered the mouth of the bay, convoyed by two American destroyers that had made contact at 7:30 A.M. (August 9), an hour and a half ahead of the expected time. The calm gray waters inside the bay were thick with American warships, in formation around the cruiser *Augusta*, which bore President Roosevelt. The day was damp; awnings had been broken out on several decks. The *Prince of Wales* moved slowly by the *Augusta*, which was riding at anchor, and a band of Royal Marines struck up "The Star-Spangled Banner." At the same moment, a band aboard the *Augusta* swung into "God Save the King." Churchill stood at attention on the *Prince of Wales'* quarterdeck, his hand to the bill of his cap; then he took up a pair of binoculars and gazed at the *Augusta*. He commented that President Roosevelt was standing bareheaded beneath a canopy over the forward gun turret and had on a light suit. (The fact was that Roosevelt had been wearing a hat but had removed it to salute the British battleship.) In the same attitude of expectancy, the President was straining for his first sight of Churchill.

When the *Prince of Wales* reached its station and dropped anchor, the waters became alive with small boats; parties of officers were beginning courtesy visits. The British looked on, amazed. "We were a remarkable contrast as we lay anchored side by side," says Morton. "The *Prince of Wales* was camouflaged; her guns protruded from their turrets like rigid pythons. The American ships were uncamouflaged and shone in peace-time grey. We had been in action, and our brass was either painted or tarnished, and our decks were not what they would have been in other days. The American ships were spotless. We admired the beautiful rubber steps of their pinnaces, the gleaming brass, the pine-white woodwork, as those craft lay tossing in our grim shadow. It was almost with a shock that, having lived since 1939 in a country at war, I looked— as over a great gulf of experience—at such evidence of a country at peace."

Churchill and his aides boarded the *Augusta* at 11 A.M. "God Save the King" was played again as he mounted to the deck. He had on his blue serge "semi-naval" suit and his black yachting cap and his expression was at first grave as he walked slowly up to President Roosevelt and took him strongly by the hand. Then he presented a letter from King George, and his face broke into a triumphant grin. The memorable Roosevelt smile, possibly the most winning of modern times—head thrown back and tilted at a cocky angle—greeted the visitor from war-ravaged England. The precise words they exchanged were not heard by anybody except themselves, but the tête-à-tête was plainly one of such instant liking that all the ships' companies relaxed into the mood of genial camaraderie that marked the proceedings of the next four days. After the general introductions, the Prime Minister returned to the *Prince of Wales* and then came back to the *Augusta* for lunch. The function was brilliantly successful. It has always been hard for Churchill to establish himself on a basis of companionable equality with persons of mediocre standing, and Roosevelt, though hailed as the savior of the common man, was distinctly ill at ease with the lower orders. The descendant of the Dukes of Marlborough and the heir of rich Dutch patroons had a community of tastes and interests.

In the afternoon Churchill was pacing the deck of his battleship, thinking over the conference just ended, when a fleet of loaded launches arrived from the American ships. President

Churchill the mason, assisted, in this instance, by his daughter Sarah, who helped him build a house at Chartwell

rtwell Manor, Westerham, Kent

g a roof at Westerham

With Field Marshal Viscount Montgomery and General Eisenhower at Empress Hall, Earl's Court, 1951

*Keystone Pictures Inc.*

Down for the week end at Chartwell in 1950, greeted by his poodle

*Keystone Pictures Inc.*

With President Roosevelt, Madame Chiang Kaishek, and their diplomatic representatives at the three-powers conference in North Africa, 1943

*Topical Press*

Roosevelt was sending gifts to the austerity-hardened British sailors—1500 cardboard cartons each containing an orange, two apples, 200 cigarettes, half a pound of cheese, and a card saying, "The President of the United States of America sends his compliments and best wishes." Obviously it was an occasion of high promise for photographers, who appeared on deck to record the distribution, though with anxious glances at the meditating Premier. Their concern was wasted; his reaction was typically Churchillian. Seeing the preparations, he stepped forward and took complete command, with the tacit hint that he was a photographic master in the classic tradition. "Come over here!" he called to some American sailors who were foolishly listening to instructions of the official photographers, and then, after grouping them, he cried, "Don't take it yet—more tooth." Churchill arranged everything to his satisfaction, and the photographers fell in line with patient sighs.

We are indebted to Inspector Thompson for some intimate scraps of conversations that took place that evening after dinner. The occasion as a whole was so clearly one of the milestones of history that the inspector asked Mike Reilly, of the American Secret Service, to introduce him to President Roosevelt. Overhearing this, Churchill broke in with, "Oh, no. I will perform that introduction myself." The two men turned back into Roosevelt's cabin, and Churchill said, "Inspector Thompson has guarded me faithfully for a period of nearly twenty years. It gives me great pleasure to present him to you." After chatting a few minutes, the President said, "Look after the Prime Minister. He is one of the greatest men in the world." In the small boat going back to the *Prince of Wales,* Churchill told Franklin Roosevelt, Jr., who went along, "Your father is a great man. He has accomplished much. I am glad that our meeting has resulted in such understanding." Young Roosevelt, then a naval ensign, replied that he thought his father had been ennobled by overcoming a crippling affliction through faith and determination. "My

father is really a very religious man," he remarked thoughtfully, and added, "He was talking to me of you, and he said
that Churchill . . ."

"No, no—Winston," interrupted Churchill.

". . . is the greatest statesman the world has ever known."

Churchill and Roosevelt came to have affection and respect
for one another, but they were competitive and did not always
hit it off. After their first meeting, each is supposed to have demanded of his aides, "What did he think of me?" and John
Gunther records that Roosevelt later crowed, "I had thirteen
warships at that meeting and Winston had only two or three."
In the sessions that continued aboard the *Augusta,* there was a
military meeting of minds but a great amount of political bickering. Throughout the war, Roosevelt, under the ceaseless pressures of various groups in the United States, nagged at Churchill to grant independence to India and to renounce the empire
system generally. On one occasion, the Prime Minister was
asked bluntly, "Will you give up Hong Kong?" He was outraged. Roosevelt thought also that Churchill had always been
unduly suspicious and backward about the idealistic new state
of Russia. In consequence, Churchill was talked into making
a number of concessions, at Yalta and elsewhere, that he
thought unwise. At one meeting early in the war, Roosevelt,
backed by Stalin, chivvied Churchill so nastily about establishing a second front according to the Russian demands that several embarrassed onlookers feared that a serious disruption
might result.

Churchill and Roosevelt got together a dozen times in the
course of the war. When news came of the attack on Pearl
Harbor, Churchill was at Chequers. He prepared an immediate
statement for the American people, assuring them that the
British Cabinet would declare war on Japan without delay.
Then he got on the telephone and reaffirmed this in a conversation with Roosevelt. Churchill has always placed strong re-
liance in the personal contact, if the contact involves himself,
and he decided, after England's statement of intentions, to

pack up and visit the White House for Christmas (of 1941). His motives were twofold: in the first place he enjoyed visiting in luxurious houses; second, he was afraid that America might become overly anxious about the war in the Pacific, to the detriment of England's scrap with Hitler. Dozens of cables and telephone messages were exchanged before he left with his large entourage of military personnel. Both the President and the Prime Minister felt that in a homey session of this kind the important questions of what kind of wines to serve, which movies to show, and the like, should be settled beforehand. On the voyage back aboard the *Prince of Wales,* Churchill had been conspicuously entertained by a pair of American films—Donald Duck in *Fox-hunting* and Laurel and Hardy in *Saps at Sea*—and he hoped to have more along those lines.

Persons present at the Christmas visit say that its whole tone was one of good-fellowship. According to Charles J. V. Murphy and John Davenport, writing in *Life,* the pace was set in the beginning by Harry Hopkins, who, as a member of Churchill's party approaching the White House, saw some red-coated British marines standing beside the front entrance. "How the hell did they get in here? The last time we had them around they burnt the place down," Hopkins said. Churchill thought this a prime good hit, and, for a change, allowed himself to be told anecdotes of various kinds for days. He showed a limited partiality for Roosevelt's dialect stories. Under different circumstances, he might have found them trying. Churchill has always been impatient in the presence of garrulity, and he has been known to leave rooms in the middle of "jokes." One of his friends says that "People generally try to tell Winnie shady stories only once—he is quite outspoken about it." Maurice Macmillan, son of the Cabinet minister, describes a wartime appearance of Churchill's at Pratt's, an exclusive London club. A beardless subaltern, excited by drink and the illustrious company, took the floor and sailed into a disreputable account. Churchill stood it for slightly more than a minute; then he got up and left, turning at the door to bellow: "Young man, what you're saying is all a lot of ————. I predict that you will go far—in the wrong direction."

Roosevelt had a predilection for harmlessly off-color stories, and he fed them to Churchill in bulk quantities. So far as is known, the recipient has never handed down a critique of this material, but the chances are that he placed small value on it. However, he did complain, amidst the privacy of his British associates, that Roosevelt seemed to him an unusually talkative man. "He tries to monopolize the conversation," explained the Prime Minister. Roosevelt had an identical view of Churchill. At one war conference, the President remarked to James Byrnes that it would be wonderful if Churchill could refrain from making long speeches, adding that they "hold up business." Byrnes agreed absently and suggested that they were, nevertheless, pretty good speeches. Roosevelt laughed and said, "Winston doesn't make any other kind." Another time, when Churchill arose to rid himself of a few ideas on a trivial subject, Roosevelt wrote "Now we are in for half an hour of it" on a scrap of paper and shoved it across to Edward Stettinius.

For an intensely masculine man, Churchill has always been severe about levity concerning sex. It is a strange quirk. He is by no means modest physically, but rather parades around home with very little on a good part of the time. Roosevelt wheeled himself into Churchill's White House room one morning to find the Prime Minister standing naked before a mirror, shaving. Unperturbed, Churchill made no attempt to cover himself but merely observed that "this is probably the only time in history when the Prime Minister of England has received the head of another great state in the nude." A lady visitor to Chartwell was once being shown about the house by Mrs. Churchill and, to the latter's horror, ran across the great man emerging from the bathroom. He was dressed only in a pair of shorts and was smoking a cigar. Without stopping to chat, he made a courtly bow and went on his way, humming an approximation of a little tune. After the holiday meetings with Roosevelt, Churchill took a villa at Palm Beach for a "rest," during which he worked about fourteen hours a day, interspersing his stints with frequent swims. When the group arrived, Inspector Thompson started in to one of the local shops for a bathing suit and asked the Prime Minister if he would like one too.

"I don't think I need one," Churchill said. "It is entirely private here. Nobody knows I am staying in this place, and I have only to step out of the back door into the sea."

The inspector suggested that he could be seen "through the glasses."

Churchill's reply was, "If they are that much interested it is their own fault what they see."

Shortly afterward he came out on his beach wrapped in a huge white bath towel, and Thompson felt relieved. Approaching the water, however, Churchill yanked the towel free and tossed it to an attendant who was standing near by. Then, naked, he dove into the sea. At this resort, Thompson was impressed, as others have been, with Churchill's odd style of swimming. It has been mentioned that John Pudney, the English poet, was once baffled by Churchill's convolutions in the pool at Chartwell. Inspector Thompson records that the Prime Minister, at Palm Beach, swam out a way and began to turn over and over "like a porpoise," agitating the water so violently that a fifteen-foot shark swam up to see what was going on. The shark's impression was apparently unfavorable, for it got out pretty fast. "My bulk must have frightened him away," Churchill said later.

II

Of Harry Hopkins, arriving in London from a flying trip to Moscow late in 1941, Churchill asked, "How is my pal Joe?" This lightning friendship represented an important turnabout for England's Prime Minister, who had previously thought up such neat phrases about Joe's government as "the foul baboon-

ery of Bolshevism" and "the bestial appetites of Leninism."
Attempting to explain his new stand, Churchill stressed in a
radio address that he did not withdraw his comments on Communism as a philosophy but he welcomed the "glorious warriors" and "mighty heroes" of Russia as comrades-in-arms
against the villain Hitler. Probably no other statesman in the
world could have uttered these joyous transparencies with a
straight face. An English writer also doubted if it would have
been physically feasible to withdraw all the comments within
the space of a single broadcast. Churchill's insight into the
true aspect of Stalin's mind was matched only by his revulsion
from the bloodstained character of Russia's over-all scheme.
His feeling was strong and permanent, and it is creditable
that he was able to take advantage of Soviet power without any
false twinges of conscience. While Churchill's partnership with
Russia was purely one of expediency, many of Roosevelt's advisers saw America's military alliance with Stalin as part of a
greater, nobler union, in which a form of "limited Capitalism"
and an eventually sanctified Socialism would march hand in
hand down the drab corridors of a unilateral world. American
diplomats, innocents abroad, had painted luminous pictures
of the glorious new order; the various missions to Moscow
presented Joseph Stalin as a humanitarian whose sole concern
was equality for all classes, colors and creeds, and, more trag-
ically, as a man who pre-eminently *wanted peace*.

Churchill thought different. If, at the time, he admired anything about the Russian leader at all, it was perhaps his ability
to swill vodka and gorge throughout the night. From the beginning, Churchill and Stalin understood one another perfectly.
The best authorities agree that Stalin knew well enough that
Churchill recognized him as a merciless conspirator to whom
the war was only incidental to Russia's long-range aim of world
conquest. On the other hand, it was plain to Stalin that Churchill's attempted jockeyings, at each conference involving the big
three leaders, had the age-old underlying British motives of
postwar balance of power. The first meeting of Churchill and

Stalin, in Moscow in August of 1942, resembled the head-on collision of two competitive bison. Churchill and Stalin share a few characteristics: each is capable of pursuing an ideal to the bitter death, each has a clairvoyance about the probable course of political events, they are rabidly patriotic in their different ways, they have almost unlimited mutual distrust, and they are gustatory champions in the grand style. For "Moscow No. 1," as the English call the conference, Churchill put on his siren suit (which he had begun to refer to as his "rompers"), and flew to the Russian capital in an R.A.F. bomber.

An observer says that Stalin, a cobbler's son without much distinction in the way of manners, goggled rudely at Churchill's attire at the moment of their first tête-à-tête. Churchill did not appear to be interested in the dictator's dress, which was the familiar gray Russian uniform. They got down to cases promptly. Talking through an interpreter, one Comrade Pavlov, Stalin expressed the opinion that Churchill's North African campaign was trivial and inquired, in effect, when England really planned to get to work and fight. Churchill's diplomatic sang-froid deserted him for a second; he jumped up to speak and pounded the heavy oaken table so hard with his right fist that some glasses at one end danced and rattled. At this point, the enigmatic Stalin got up and announced, through his vocal medium, who was becoming slightly rattled himself, "I don't know what you're saying, but, by God, I like your sentiments!" It was presumed by the English delegation that the Russian Premier approved of Churchill's style of delivery rather than the words expressed. The group then recessed and threw down some vodka. By the second day, Churchill's spirits had revived, and he continued his argument that England was doing her utmost to lift the Russian burden. But by the third day, still stalemated by Stalin's mulish insistence on European landings, Churchill was, for him, badly depressed. He went back to his quarters, and, after a few warming nips of some first-rate brandy he had brought along, went into a distinguished tantrum. According to one member of the party, an

aide tried to quiet him, pointing out that beyond doubt the
room was wired for espionage. Churchill's response was to approach each suspicious fixture in the place—wall lamps, pictures, recessed bric-a-brac—and address them with supremely
eloquent abuse of everything Russian he could call to mind.
The performance went on for several minutes, while the other
occupants of the room were treated to a historic exercise of
one of the world's rich vocabularies. When the Prime Minister
finished, with the Russian situation covered to his satisfaction,
he said, "That will at least make for interesting reading."

The Teheran Conference, in November 1943, with Roosevelt present, was a different story. A closer union of minds was
evident, and the emphasis shifted to celebration. Preliminary
to this meeting of the big three, Churchill and Roosevelt had
met Generalissimo Chiang Kai-shek for a series of talks in
Cairo. The Mena Hotel and a number of surrounding villas
were given over to visitors. Roosevelt's plane was late, and
Churchill wandered around worriedly trying to check on the
reasons why. When it was reported in sight, he said to an associate, "Thank God for that. I am very relieved." The Generalissimo and Madame Chiang Kai-shek, who occupied one
villa, and President Roosevelt, who had another, found
Churchill in one of his most gregarious moods. He seldom
stayed put in his own establishment, but dropped in frequently
on his war partners for informal chats, refreshment and, of
course, business. In the gardens one afternoon, his old bent for
arranging groups to be photographed came to the fore, but he
ran into opposition. Roosevelt also appeared to have pronounced ideas on the subject, and, even more dismaying,
Chiang Kai-shek expressed the most positive opinions of all.
The picture hung up on the question of who was to sit in the
center. Each of the leaders generously tried to arrange one
of the others in this position, and the wrangling went on for an
incredible length of time. The Generalissimo, by exercising his
best military skill, finally had his way, and Roosevelt occupied
the center chair while Churchill was placed on his left. The

Prime Minister later confided to a friend that this was the way he had wanted it all along; his tone suggested that he had neatly outmaneuvered Chiang Kai-shek, general or no general.

At Teheran, Inspector Thompson says, Churchill showed his first anxiety of the war about personal danger. His most rabid enemies (an exceedingly spirited group) have never accused Marlborough's descendant of faintheartedness. When Churchill said, "We have information that German agents have been dropped by parachute to try to assassinate one or all of us," Thompson was gravely concerned. Churchill has always been capable of the heroic gesture—there are too many of these on his record for an accurate count—but in a time of national emergency he takes the practical view. From the airport at Teheran to the British Embassy, he sent the inspector on a "dummy run," making the auto trip alone to see if any hostile bullets were flying about. There was not the slightest hint of cowardice in this act; rather it was the common-sense and even valiant decision of a man who felt that, if somebody had to be assassinated, Thompson was expendable.

The first day's conference was held in the Soviet Embassy amidst an atmosphere of cordiality. In a curious way, President Roosevelt's personality increased Stalin's liking for Churchill. This is not derogatory of Roosevelt; more properly it is complimentary. As one of England's wartime ministers puts it, "Roosevelt had an undisguisably patrician air; Churchill's is feudal: the two are different, and the latter is the more readily assimilable by the peasant mind." John Gunther in his book *Roosevelt in Retrospect* wrote of the relationship among the three: "The President made all-out efforts to win the Soviet dictator's esteem; it pleased him that he and Stalin got along personally better than Churchill and Stalin did. But I have heard from several participants at the conference that Stalin was seemingly perplexed by Roosevelt, though he treated him with great deference. Churchill he could grapple with. Stalin gave the impression that he understood Churchill perfectly, and that there was even a community between them, as be-

tween lusty fellow rogues. But FDR was much more difficult,
a new type of phenomenon puzzling to the glacier-like Russian's mind, nervously elusive, too optimistic, strangely discursive, and perhaps naive."

At the conference table Churchill smoked steadily on a
gigantic black cigar, while Stalin, quite plainly impressed that
anybody could continue to emit such a poisonous vapor and
live, chain-smoked cigarettes in retaliation. Roosevelt smoked
(cigarettes) too, but not with the application of his colleagues.
Spirits were still high on the second day, when Churchill presented the dictator with the Stalingrad sword, a gift of King
George and the British people, in tribute to the stout defense
of the Russian city. For once, Stalin seemed pleased out of his
impassivity. The sword was a beautiful piece of work. Taking
it from the Prime Minister's hands, he tilted it and the blade
slipped out of the scabbard, but he grabbed it up agilely before
it hit the floor. It was then agreed that the next day, November
30, Churchill's sixty-ninth birthday, should be a day of rejoicing. There was a good deal of bickering about who should act
as host. This was made more poignant by the fact that the Shah
of Iran, in whose country the meeting was held, was the nominal host but was so overwhelmed by his visitors that he did
little more than hover in the background like an uncomfortable
busboy. Churchill won out. It was his birthday, he said, and
nothing would do but he should entertain.

The party was remarkable not only for its historic value
but for its important contribution to the annals of carousing.
Stalin warmed up nicely during the preliminary cocktail hour,
when he drank an estimated quart of alcohol. The W.C.T.U.
has never got much of a toehold in Russia. The land is cli-
matically brisk, the national temper is morbid, and excess earnings, if any, have always been expended on hooch. As a
consequence, children of ten and twelve can drink with the best-
trained adults of Kentucky and Arkansas. It is a patriotic skill,
like fire walking in India. Stalin had the bilingual Pavlov at his
side, and together they ranged the great room of the British

Embassy, Pavlov acting as pilot fish. Stalin chatted with animation. Indeed, he went at it so vigorously that Pavlov was running several lengths behind and only a handful of persons ever got the thread of the narrative. The Premier's discourse was punctuated by breezy guffaws, with a good deal of head-waggling, and it was suggested, *sotto voce,* that he was recounting some especially savoured experience, possibly an old purge. Churchill led his thirty-four guests into the dining room, upon whose long, decorated table there rested a birthday cake with sixty-nine candles and, beside it, several presents. President Roosevelt had bought him a blue and white porcelain bowl whose accompanying card read, "For Winston Spencer Churchill, on his 69th birthday at Teheran, Iran, November 30, 1943, with my affection and may we be together for many years."

Nearly all the guests were in exuberant condition by the time they were seated at the table. Churchill arose and announced that the toasts would be drunk Russian fashion, meaning that each toaster would walk around and clink glasses with the toastee. Then everybody began toasting everybody else, and the party moved into that warm, winy wonderland of mutual trust and affection. Churchill pledged Stalin's health with the words, "I sometimes call you Joe, and you can call me Winston if you like, and I like to think of you as my very good friend." Stalin made a rather typically Russian reply in which he said (according to Pavlov), "We want to be friends with Great Britain and America, and if they wish to be friends they can show it by their actions." He proceeded around the table, banged Churchill's glass with his own, and cried, "To my fighting friend!" Anthony Eden got up and proposed a graceful toast to Comrade Molotov and attempted to take a hearty swig, but discovered that he was holding an empty glass. "If I had something to drink, I would give a toast," he told the company. On this trip Churchill had brought along a butler, Frank Sawyer, who now came scurrying out of the shadows with refreshment for Eden. Sawyer was no longer in the first flush of his youth, and his legs seemed about to fold, always the butler's dread on high occasions. In recognition of this, Comrade Stalin collared Sawyer and stood him up at the table and toasted *him*. Then Stalin solemnly began what appeared to be a lengthy tribute to somebody or other only to have it interrupted by a waiter who came flying out of the kitchen and flung a bowl of pudding over him from head to foot. The incident looked very much like something dreamed up by Charlie Chaplin, the more so since the Russian Premier, clawing enough pudding off his face to make speaking physically practical, continued with dignity. Neither did he evince any sign of reproach toward the paralyzed waiter. There was a solid round of applause when he sat down, after a little difficulty finding his chair.

Stalin came out of this birthday party with sincere respect for Churchill the man. In later meetings he always tried to get the Prime Minister apart for private digestive duels. As a rule, Churchill was not loath. People around them, watching this apparent byplay and recognizing its peculiar essentiality to the conduct of the war, conceived a lasting admiration for two of the great constitutions of all time. Many British politicians feel that Churchill made an ally of Stalin by his top performance at the board. It has been conjectured with horror how Stalin would have reacted to, say, Sir Stafford Cripps, the ascetic, who might well have thrown a raw carrot binge and brought the alliance tumbling down with a single stroke. All through the war Churchill matched the Russians flagon for flagon, only pulling leather, as the saying goes, once. In a later meeting in Moscow, Stalin led Churchill out of the dining room at 2 A.M. and said, "Now we will have our own party." The group had just spent five hours running through champagne, several kinds of still wine, brandy, vodka, foot-high mounds of black caviar, nearly every known species of fish, and joints of the customary meats.

Stalin and Churchill went down a long corridor, made frequent turns into other corridors, and at length entered a small but elegant banquet room. On the table was a whole suckling pig. "We shall divide it," said the Russian Premier with satisfaction. Churchill took a glass of vodka and then spoke the words that must have been painful to him. "I am incapable of eating any more at the present time," he told Stalin; whereupon his host sat down and ate the entire pig by himself. There is no reason to believe that Stalin ever held this lapse against Churchill. On the contrary, people who should know feel that the Russian has missed his old drinking companion. They think he will always believe, as he told Bernard Shaw and Lady Astor a few years ago, "You can't shut Churchill out of public life. When the British get into trouble again they will send for their old war horse."

# Chapter 26

THE BURDENS of leadership take an incalculable toll in the passage of six war years, but Churchill seemed never to tire. He traveled thousands of miles, he worked each night until everyone else had gone to bed, and he arose refreshed to hurl the oratorical thunders that rallied a people from despondency and defeat. His physicians and advisers were unable to dissuade him from foolish expenditures of his resources. Before the Normandy invasion, he insisted, in England, on taking General Eisenhower and General Bradley to a range for a three-handed shoot with a carbine. Both officers were honestly amazed at his marksmanship. Against the earnest counsel of his aides, he boarded the destroyer *Kelvin,* after the invasion got under way, and crossed to the French coast. Passing the German artillery positions, he ordered the destroyer captain to "give them a salvo." Several persons on board, including General Smuts and Sir Alan Brooke, thought the captain was going to refuse, and they envisioned a lively ruckus. After a moment's dismayed meditation, the captain turned and gave the command. Churchill expressed chagrin that the Germans had not fired back. Perhaps as compensation, he talked some field officers into conveying him to the Siegfried Line, where he chalked "Hitler, Personally" on a shell and pulled the lanyard of the gun. (He had previously tried to climb into a tank headed for action, but was ejected.)

By the spring of 1945, some of his household thought that Churchill showed signs of emotional wear. He had begun to reminisce about Chartwell. He told Thompson, "If I am able to go to Chartwell, I would like to build some cottages on my land for ex-servicemen to live in." The news of President Roosevelt's death, a few days later, provided undoubtedly his worst moment of the war. Thompson's bell rang at midnight, and he went into the Prime Minister's study to find him weeping and saying, "Terrible, terrible." A few minutes later, Churchill said, "He was a great friend to us. He gave us immeasurable help at a time when we most needed it. I have lost a good friend and one who got things done. We now have to start all over again."

When the end approached in Europe, Churchill kept deploring the fact that Roosevelt could not have lived to see the fruits of their alliance. His sorrow over the President's death was nearly matched by his delight at the belated demise of Premier Mussolini. Churchill announced this latter event to guests in his house by rushing into his dining room and crying, "Ah, the bloody beast is dead!" May 8, 1945, was his, and England's great day of the war; beside it the final coming of victory was a poor anticlimax. The enemy that lay across only twenty miles of water, the Hun that had leveled Europe periodically since the Dark Ages, was again struck down into impotency. The crowds pressed in toward 10 Downing Street as Churchill again commenced a triumphant drive to the House of Commons. By the time the procession reached Parliament Square, he had clambered up on top of the front seat in the open car and was standing bareheaded, grinning and making his sign of victory. At one point he realized that he'd left his cigars behind. "Go to the Annex and get one," he yelled to Thompson. "They expect to see it."

The House was filled to bursting. One Member present has written that, while waiting, "I saw Churchill sitting in the backbench seat he had occupied for ten long years of the 'wilderness.' . . . I saw Churchill, standing at the dispatch box, in good times and bad, grimly telling the nation to expect nothing but hard tidings, jovially congratulating it on successes, urging and encouraging everybody to greater efforts, announcing, with satisfaction and pride, the victories that came our way, without depression the setbacks that came, too. I saw him in good times and bad, cheery and irritable, but always ready with the appropriate word."

When the Prime Minister finally strode in to face the legislators on V-E Day, he was given the most tumultuous ovation in the history of the assembly. Members forsook all attempts to observe the rituals and leaped up on the benches, shouting and waving order papers. Churchill stood at his accustomed place beside the dispatch box. Tears were running down his face, and he was nodding his head, while he waited to exercise his priceless privilege of making the formal announcement of victory.

II

Two months later, on July 26, the British admirably concealed their enthusiasm for their hero when they went to the polls and voted him out of office. The returns of the general election of 1945, midway between the two surrender dates, gave the Labor Party a majority of 146 votes over all other parties. Clement Attlee, the former Lord Privy Seal, succeeded to Britain's highest political post. A great many reasons have been advanced, both in England and in America, for this seeming act of ingratitude. As might be expected, nearly everything recorded on the subject is tinted with each writer's political point of view. In the eyes of the left, Churchill was deposed because he was incapable, by heredity and preference, of correcting the social ills of the underprivileged. According to the right, the British anti-capitalists under the spiritual leadership of the sly and poisonous Harold Laski had fought a hard war undermining the existing form of English society by the propaganda of collectivism. Somewhere between these versions were a few other reasons: the natural wish for change at war's end of a people long chafed by restrictions; the fear of a war government by soldiers and sailors anxious to muster out quickly, and, perhaps of supreme importance, a subconscious desire to obliterate everything closely connected with the memory of the past six years.

As to the claims of the left and right, certain conclusions are now possible in the light of the seven years since 1945. Collectivism has had several bad seasons. The Russian system has become at least ostensibly (and even noisily) unpopular with Americans who formerly cherished it deeply; also, British Socialism has demonstrated its incapacity to survive without fiscal support from the hated capitalists whom it hopes eventually to socialize. This gives rise to an interesting question. In the words of the unpartisan Viennese economist, Dr. Karl Fuerbringer (translated by H. Howard Thurston), "If socialism, a scheme of mediocrities rather than men of proven ability, is financially unworkable, what happens when the United States is at last socialized by confiscatory income taxes and strangulation of industry in the British manner? Without a capitalist nation to produce wealth, civilization may expect chaos [urgemisch]."

More decisively in the British case, it was apparently decided in the general election of 1951 that Socialism did not, after all, provide just that rosy degree of Utopia which had been promised by the advocates of "limited regimentation." There was less food than ever, prices were rising, restrictions hung over the land like spiderwebs, the state-owned railroads stank with filth, money by the hundreds of millions was thrown away in desperation ventures like the one to convert Africa into a peanut farm, the pound was a shrunken and despised currency in the foreign exchange, class hatreds had risen to new heights, the Empire had come apart at the seams, once friendly nations were being exploited by Russia to break off treaties and grab British property, the great and good ally of America was sorely tried by Socialist dealings with enemy Communists, and, through it all, men of enormous incompetence made ignorant and ungrammatical speeches promising sterner times ahead.

The elections of October cast serious reflections on Socialism and its leadership. The British majority decided, as it will always decide in a crisis, that brains are required even to run a government.

### III

As before, Churchill wasted little time in mourning his abrupt repudiation. He had been kicked out so often and so unceremoniously that he had developed an independent set of reflexes to accommodate the shocks. Too, his situation was now subtly different. The hot pangs of ambition were appeased; having been Prime Minister, he had ascended to the topmost rung of the ladder and there was no place else to climb unless he aspired to be King, which situation was already filled. He was content to resume making a living and to settle into a revered but, he hoped, impermanent niche as leader of the Opposition. The government was manned by boobs, and he planned to remove them; in the meantime, his position in British history was secure. To a female Balkan visitor who said, with honest naïveté, "It is terrible—now they will shoot you," he replied, "I have hopes, Madam, that the sentence will be mitigated to a life-term at various forms of hard labor."

He was cool to suggestions of honors. It was generally understood in England that he declined a dukedom. The story was told in the clubs of his answer to an offer of the Garter. "Why should I accept the Garter from His Majesty [it went] when his people have just given me the boot?" When his old constituency of Dundee (which had embraced the waterlogged Scrymgeour) offered to confer on him the freedom of the city, he refused without comment. And he ignored an invitation to speak at Oxford, whose students, before the war, had passed a notorious resolution never to fight for their country. "A curious set of young gentlemen," observed Churchill. "They will not fight and they cannot row."

Certain unofficial honors were pressed on him in the form of gifts. Indeed, a good part of the world-wide indignation at his dismissal was expressed in packages that began arriving at Chartwell soon after the Japanese surrender. Spain led off with a number that stood up well even among the elegant company that followed. It consisted of the stuffed head of a bull that had been born with a startling white "V" on its forehead; the torero Manolete had dedicated the bull to Churchill on D-Day and killed it in his quick, clean style. Jamaica came through with 500 cigars "as a token of appreciation for his services to society," and New Zealand made him a gift of money raised in a "shilling fund." Churchill handed it over to St. Mary's Hospital in Paddington, saying, "They helped everybody—including me—during the war." King Ibn Saud gave him a gold and jeweled sword and dagger and a set of ceremonial robes in a hide case. A man in Portugal got special permission to ship him 116 gallons of a very old port wine, the Stockowners Association of Australia sent him a kangaroo, and a group of Maoris inquired whether he would like a male or female kiwi. An elderly woman living at the Cumberland Hotel mailed him her prize Admiral de Ruyter chair, and, to balance things off, added a dessert service for Mrs. Churchill. Some African farmers sent up a beautiful ebony walking stick because "He was the man who won the war," and Switzerland stepped forward with a rather mysterious "perpetual-motion" clock, bound all around in brass and impossible to wind but "guaranteed to run forever." The French town of Aix-en-Provence, in solemn conclave, officially changed its name to "La Ville Churchill," and Bartlett's *Familiar Quotations,* the helpful volume upon which he had leaned so heavily, came out with a new edition in which there were 60 samples from Churchill himself.

The only mildly sour notes in this orgy of tribute involved a couple of demands that were made on the retiring Premier. Theresa Garnett, the now elderly suffragette, announced that she was opening a Suffragette Museum and asked him if he

would mind returning the whip with which she had once socked
him. And, in Pretoria, a man who had been the prison barber
detailed General Smuts to collect five shillings he said Churchill owed him for a haircut. Churchill had escaped before paying up, the barber related, and he would like to get the account
off the books.

Immediately after the election, Churchill and his wife went
to southern France for a rest. They occupied the Château
Bordaberry, lent him by a Canadian, General Raymond
Brutinel, who for the ten-day visit brought out the furniture
that had been hidden during the German occupation, repaired
all damage to the grounds and gardens, rigged telephone lines,
and installed a new pelota court. Notwithstanding the lavish
surroundings, the Churchills were obliged to subsist on army
rations for most of their stay. Once the war was over, Churchill
elected to space out his work with numerous vacations, most
of which were combined with business in some way. In 1946
he made another trip to the United States, where he accepted
an honorary degree from several colleges, including Columbia
and Westminster College in Fulton, Missouri. He chose the
latter place as the locale of a political blockbuster he dropped
with President Truman sitting on the platform beside him. It
was time for a new alliance, Churchill blandly announced,
cementing together England and America, as an implied buffer
against the growing hostility of Russia. Being the first overt
statement against Russia by a responsible leader of Western
Powers, the speech caused a sensation. Churchill foresaw
trouble with Russia, and said so openly, adding a warning note
that should have been more widely attended: *"I have not always been wrong!"* But Russia was, at the moment, the darling
of the intellectuals, and the former Prime Minister's words were
regarded as heresy of a very reactionary order.

Continuing his travels, he returned to Monte Carlo, the
scene of his former disasters, but this time confined himself
largely to swimming. Churchill seldom packs a bathing suit
for his trips; somebody has to go out and buy him one. Func-

tionaries were sent through the best shops of the principality in a sort of treasure hunt to obtain "the largest pair of trunks in Monte Carlo." Somebody turned up with some crimson ones that had ample material for a good-sized awning. In them he took to the beach. A fair crowd collected, not so much to see Churchill, it was thought, as to have a look at the trunks. He climbed up out of the water, scowled at the onlookers, and was heard to growl, "I'm no bathing beauty." In Switzerland he was lent a house on Lake Geneva by Alfred Kern, the director of the Swiss Bank Corporation. When the mayor of the local village volunteered to serve as butler, Churchill casually signed him on. It made an interesting master-servant relationship: the mayor addressed Churchill as "Your Highness," and Churchill referred to the mayor as "Your Honor." The mayoress came up to fill in as laundrywoman. It was noted, somewhat later in Luxembourg, that Churchill had at last taken cognizance of his faulty French. Preparing to deliver a speech in the Opera House, he led off with, *"Gardez-vous bien—je vous addresse en français."* En route to the city, he had been delayed repeatedly by people who lay down in front of his automobile, to halt the procession and have a look at England's wartime Prime Minister.

Part of the Churchills' reason for wandering at this time was their lack of living quarters at home. Chartwell was being evacuated by the government, and a town house they bought, at 28 Hyde Park Gate, was in the hands of the decorators. When the two establishments were ready for their distinguished occupants, the Churchills returned to England and settled into the pattern of life that they lead today. Twenty-eight Hyde Park Gate is a low, red brick, ivy-covered structure of twenty-five rooms, on a quiet street near the exclusive Park Lane district of London. It has a library and a drawing room and three reception (or living) rooms on the ground floor, and there are ten bedrooms, each with a sitting room, upstairs. The décor of the small reception room nearest the street is built around the handsome, tinted, life-size photograph of his mother. Hyde

Park, where Churchill sometimes strolls when it is sufficiently dark so that he cannot be recognized, is only a few squares away. The other residents of his street are wealthy (or as wealthy as one can be in present-day England) businessmen and a couple of high government officials with tax-exempt expense accounts. Recently, for "office space," he also bought the house next door—at 27 Hyde Park Gate. It was badly blitzed during the war but has several usable rooms. Churchill's neighbors, who almost never see him, were surprised on moving day when he turned up at the curb in a green baize apron and oversaw the uncrating of his books and their removal to the library of his new workshop. He employs six secretaries, most of whom occupy rooms at 28 Hyde Park Gate; various of these accompany him as he moves back and forth between the London house and his Kentish farm home of Chartwell, which is his favorite place on earth.

In a socialized and impoverished country, Chartwell ranks as a magnificent estate. And it is conducted in the baronial manner of the Marlboroughs in their heyday. Besides two hundred acres of farm land, it has eighty acres of garden; in the main residence there are five reception rooms, a great hall, nineteen bedrooms and eight baths, and on the grounds are three separate garages, three cottages, stables, two lakes and the heated, floodlit swimming pool that Churchill built with his own hands. In 1946, a group of his friends bought Chartwell under a financial arrangement whereby he and his family can live in it tax-free for the rest of his life, after which it will go to the National Trust as a memorial of his services to the commonwealth. At the end of the war, too, a London hotel man jubilantly presented Churchill with a mansion at Sevenoaks, near Chartwell, in gratitude for what he had done for the British people. Churchill thanked him and gave it to the British Legion to be used as a convalescent center for wounded veterans.

The tax-free status of Chartwell is handy for Churchill, whose living was for years so luxurious that, despite his large earnings, the outgo threatened his income, a dangerous state of imbalance that Micawber decried eloquently. The servant staffs of both Hyde Park and Chartwell fluctuate, but neither ever has less than a cook, a valet-butler, and two maids. At Chartwell there are, in addition, two gardeners and varying numbers of farm hands and other workmen, and when the six secretaries and Churchill's team of writing experts are added to these, the weekly pay roll is staggering. Expenses are cut down slightly by family contributions of labor. Notwithstanding the leisurely home of her grandmother, the Countess of Airlie, Mrs. Churchill likes to help in the preparation of meals and in general ably fills the position of household steward, while her husband has been known to do the work of two or three laborers. A couple of years ago, he bought some secondhand chicken runs and undertook to repair them himself, climbing up on the roofs and slapping on tar with a big brush. Finished with these, he dug several fishponds and stocked them with carp. A visitor to the farm, several weeks later, thought there was something emphatically ducal about the sight of Churchill sitting on a camp stool beside one of the pools and summoning the fish with imperious gestures and bits of yesterday's sponge-cake. The husband of Churchill's daughter Mary, Captain Christopher Soames, acts as supervisor of agricultural Chartwell. "He hasn't quite put the farm on a pay-as-you-go basis," says one of his friends, "but he does as well as can be expected with his father-in-law so frequently on the scene to give advice." Churchill has a jeep, which he drives himself, and he likes to dash out to the fields and take charge. "He sees himself as a kind of headquarters general co-ordinating his officers in action," believes one of his neighbors. Soames recently acquired a bulldozer, and Churchill was on hand a few minutes after he heard the news. It developed that he was a master tactician with the bulldozer—one of the craftiest bulldozer men on record—and he began to boss Soames and a crew of laborers around with the confidence of his long experience. "Blade up!" he would cry. "Smartly there, my lad—now lower

away and assault that bank. Well done, well done—I couldn't
have improved on it myself." "I do not think that Mr. Churchill knows a great deal about bulldozers," says his head secretary, Miss Sturdee, "but he gave that impression." Off a little
distance, Soames leaned wistfully on a hayrick, perhaps lost in
reflections of the great war, when he had often enjoyed unin-
terrupted command for several hours at a stretch.

All of the Churchills' daughters and their son are, or have
been, married. Their first daughter, Diana, was married in 1932
to John Milner Bailey, the eldest son of Sir Abe Bailey, Bt.,
and was divorced from him three years later. Shortly afterward
she married Duncan Sandys, a young Conservative M.P. As a
lieutenant early in the war, Sandys received a lot of unfair
publicity by asking a parliamentary question that allegedly
violated military security. He was nearly court-martialed but
was finally cleared to everybody's satisfaction. Before the
armistice, Sandys performed valuable services as Financial
Secretary to the War Office. He and Churchill have an area of
compatibility which unfortunately was not the case with the
great man and another son-in-law, the first husband of daughter Sarah. From early childhood, Sarah Churchill has displayed a warm affection for the theater and nearly everything
in it. This included, in 1936, the well-known and much beloved
English comedian, Vic Oliver, to whom she was married on
December 25 of that year. The two had become secretly engaged when they were appearing together in a Cochran revue.
After Sarah's twenty-first birthday, she left by ship for America,
to "think things over," and Randolph, sailing the next day on
the *Queen Mary,* is supposed to have telephoned her in mid-
ocean on instructions from his father. It is generally understood
among Churchill's friends that he was opposed to the union, on
several grounds. There was nothing whatever against Oliver's
character, but a ripe, identifying fragrance lingers over the
music halls and their folk, in the minds of many persons of
traceable lineage. It is possible that Churchill, as he gazed un-
benignly upon Oliver, harked back to the days when sover-

eigns kept a court jester on a leash, and when the Marlboroughs called in troupes of wandering players and tossed them coppers and cold biscuits. In family gatherings, after the wedding, there was at least an undercurrent of collision. Oliver Wendell Holmes' *Autocrat of the Breakfast Table* was a strangled lamb compared to Churchill, who, as noted, prefers to monopolize any conversation in which he participates. Ostensibly, Oliver was a pattern of decorum, but it is in the nature of a comedian to essay levity, or make funny, as the trade term goes. If, midway in a long Churchillian discourse on the probable effects of Phoenician navigation on Cornwall tin mining, Oliver's cheek began to twitch, or he dropped his teaspoon into a bowl of petunias, it was probably involuntary, but Churchill interpreted it as fly-catching, or attempting to steal the audience. There was a sigh of relief all around when Sarah and her husband were divorced, in 1945.

Since the divorce, Oliver has refused to capitalize on his association with Britain's foremost figure. England is no less keen than America about books and magazines of the stripe of *I Shook Down the White House Furnace* and *My Three Years with Capone,* but Oliver has turned a deaf ear to all such offers. It must be said in fairness that Churchill, on his side, has never produced a book about Oliver, although he has written volubly about others of his family whose popularity scarcely comes up to that of the comedian. Only recently Oliver declined to be interviewed by the highly rated British researchist, Ruth Phillips, who was helping collect notes for an American biography of Churchill. In a letter of explanation, Oliver said that he was very sorry not to be able to comply with her wishes as he had made it a strict personal rule never to speak about his ex-father-in-law. He went on to give this added poignancy by disclosing that he had been offered ten thousand dollars from an American publishing company to write five thousand words for a story about Churchill and had flatly refused this offer. He could not, he said, betray confidences of which he had happened to partake during his personal association with the Churchill family. Though separated from Oliver, Sarah has not separated herself from the theater. She has appeared in several plays and movies, both in England and America, and has lately become available by the week to American followers of the jangling new medium of video.

Associates of Churchill say that he has issued a kind of papal bull to the effect that members of the family are not to discuss him for literary purposes. Captain Soames once wrote a biographer that "nearly every event in Mr. Churchill's life has been made public, and all that we [Soames and his wife, Mary] could add would be purely private matters, which we would certainly not take it upon ourselves to do." This prohibition even extends to Mrs. Churchill and their son Randolph. The wartime Prime Minister has let it be known emphatically that whatever writing about him is done for pecuniary gain he intends to do himself, if possible. Randolph has collected his father's speeches but has thus far resisted any desire to write the definitive biography, as Churchill himself immortalized Lord Randolph.

It is common knowledge in England that Churchill remains hopeful about his son, who, at forty-one, has not come up to the exhausting standards of accomplishment set by the brilliant parent. Randolph is an affable, prematurely gray man with an exceptional agility at club life and a capacity for continuous labor that his father might call indifferent. "Randy has inherited the old man's gift for frequent celebration," one of his fellow club members puts it. However, another feels that "A juxtaposition to Winston for so many years could be quite sapping to a chap's energies, particularly without a decent allowance and all that sort of thing." Churchill has never believed in setting his children up with financial recklessness. Diana once explained to a group at a country house that she was an inexpert equestrienne because she had "never been able to afford a thorough course of riding lessons." Randolph has earned considerable money from journalistic efforts on general subjects and in 1940 won a seat in Parliament. (He lost a contest in the recent general election.) Churchill construed his son's maiden address as lacking in force and gave him a mild tongue-lashing about it, crying, "Haven't you learned yet that I put something more than whiskey into my speeches?" In the course of numberless conversations with Churchill, an English publisher has heard him mention Randolph only once. On that occasion, apropos of some remark or other about his son, Churchill said, "Oh, yes, he's gone to New Zealand to fight a libel action. I rather think that he will lose it."

On the whole, Churchill has been very fortunate as a family man. The peccadilloes of offspring in the public eye are of course given heightened conspicuousness. In addition, it is unhappily true that the twigs often tend to bend in a direction opposite to that of the parent tree. Churchill's children have been neither more saintly nor more damned than the average, and Randolph's career is a source of inspiration when set against the colorful moneygrubbing of several political progeny in America. And, finally, in Mrs. Churchill the statesman has been blessed with a wife of perfect quality for a man of his temperament. Mrs. Churchill manages to perform the difficult task of providing a handsome and efficient backdrop for her husband's career without effacing her own individuality. She is an intelligent, athletic, still beautiful woman whose political tastes, some feel, are not necessarily identical to Churchill's at this point. Her excitement was only moderate when he returned to the Conservative Party. Her leaning is Liberal, but it is perhaps a clubwoman's affection for charitable causes rather than any profound devotion to the ideals of strictly political liberalism. Indeed, a few newspapermen in London believe that Mrs. Churchill has only a cloudy grasp of what her energetic husband is up to professionally at any time, and that she is concerned principally with seeing that he gets his daily staple of roast beef. During the war, she occupied herself in campaigning for the Y.W.C.A. and serving as chairman of the Aid to Russia Appeal Fund, which drummed up medicine and other supplies for Moscow. Also, she founded and promoted into a

successful enterprise the Fulmer Chase Maternity Home, a sizable establishment in Buckinghamshire whose resources were
meant in the beginning for the pregnant wives of low-salaried
junior officers. In connection with these activities, she scurried
around with a bustle that matched her husband's, dropping into
canteens, inspecting, making talks at rallies, and keeping her
eye on the smallest details of operation. She had a special
preference for appearing suddenly in some kitchen or other and
tasting everything. If a dish seemed out of joint, she never
hesitated to say so.

To Mrs. Churchill is imputed the admirable thrift that is
characteristic of her Scottish countrymen. She has never been
considered a lavish tipper; also, she believes in paying servants
what they are worth. She plays a cautious, rather Hibernian
game of croquet, strategically sound and skillful enough in its
execution to inflict occasional defeats on Noel Coward, one of
her frequent adversaries, whose game ranks among the best in
England. Her tennis has always been in the expert class, and
she acquits herself creditably, but not greedily, in sessions of
six-pack bezique with Churchill, who likes to win. Mrs. Churchill speaks French flawlessly, and, with a wonderfully straight
face, encourages her husband when he insists on conversing in
that language. There has never been any doubt as to who is the
leading spirit in the Churchill home. Notwithstanding the
Y.W.C.A., the Maternity Home, and her other interests, Mrs.
Churchill never allows anything to interfere with the progress
of Winston Churchill the statesman. Persons are to be found in
England who think, with some justification, that both she and
Randolph are better extemporaneous speakers than the Premier.
But she is his most faithful audience and is always to be found
in the Ladies' Gallery when he arises for a set address in the
House of Commons. It is his custom to look up briefly before
he starts, at which time she gives him a little wave and a smile
of encouragement.

In an age of increasing moral decay, when it is considered
backward in a few circles to be steadfastly married, it is heart-

ening to know that Churchill, in his backward way, has never as much as lifted an eyebrow at any woman besides his wife. He is undoubtedly the least flirtatious of history's important men. The fact is that his anger over any kind of moral laxness borders on a complex. An anecdote from the days when he was Chancellor of the Exchequer has to do with Lady Houston's going to him with a voluntary payment of a million and a half pounds as death duties on her husband's estate. When she had written the check, she offered her cheek and said, "Now that I've done it don't you think that I deserve a——"

"A pat on the back?" cried Churchill with alarm, and giving her a masculine whack, he beat a hasty retreat.

The Churchills seldom see each other before luncheon. ". . . my wife and I tried two or three times in the last forty years to have breakfast together, but it was so disagreeable we had to stop, or our marriage would have been wrecked," he once wrote in a letter to an acquaintance. Nevertheless there has been an abundance of pleasant and even exhilarated family life. Visitors present at gatherings of the clan just before the war tell of the three girls ragging Churchill with a sort of guessing game about his political opponents. "Who is it that's tall and stringy, carries an umbrella and has an Adam's apple like a turkey?" one of them would say, and the others would seek further clues in a mock-serious effort to identify Chamberlain: "Is he just a *little* dried up, or am I on the wrong track?" etc. Occasionally Churchill would complain that they were being disrespectful; later, at the radio in the library, as they all listened to a Chamberlain speech, he would keep up a rumbling chorus of criticism. "Ah, ha, another split infinitive!" he said at one point, and again, "That remark meant absolutely nothing at all."

Since the war, overnight guests at Chartwell have been few. Neither do the Churchills visit much in other houses. Once a year he went for a short stay with the King and Queen, but one of his admirers feels that he probably did this "chiefly in the interest of picking up copy for his works." Churchill's labors have increased in recent years. Luncheon and dinner guests at Chartwell are mostly members of his writing staff or persons connected in some other way with his publications. Walter Graebner, who has acted with great diplomacy as liaison man between *Life* magazine and Churchill since 1937, has seldom known Anthony Eden, for example, to stop overnight at Churchill's farm home. When Graebner, who lives in London, makes one of his frequent business trips down to the estate, he drives back the same day, or night, a total distance of about fifty miles. Churchill's staff say that he is fond of Graebner; not long ago, he gave him a handsome set of his books, expensively bound in red leather.

Mrs. Churchill is much closer to her children than are most English mothers. Mollie Panter-Downes, the English correspondent, once commented, in an article on Mrs. Churchill for *Collier's*, that "The children have always been her companions, even at an age when most English families at a corresponding social level keep them well apart in the nursery or the schoolroom. The hairdresser who used to do her hair for many years recollects that her room was pretty certain to be full of babies crawling between his legs as he got to work." Churchill, who is not the most accommodating man in the world, sometimes puts himself out surprisingly for his daughters or his son. Once, several years ago, Diana unexpectedly found herself alone for the evening and felt very downcast. When her father asked what she would like to do, she brightened up in normal feminine style and said she'd greatly enjoy dropping into a night club. Churchill recoiled slightly; then, with the kind of fortitude that had made him a standout in debate and battle, he put on his evening clothes and took her into London. As might be expected, he saluted the occasion with full honors, dancing nearly every dance and staying until just before the place closed.

Churchill is at his best at dinner, conversationally fluent, able to trace the large course of human events and capable, at the same time, of turning aside to explore topics of surprising obscurity. Just as, long ago at the French front, he entertained his officers with an erudite sermon on lice, he is posted on a bewildering variety of other small concerns. Churchill has adequate weapons for repelling competition at dinner. Being slightly deaf, he uses the blessed infirmity as one tunes a radio, weeding out the rot and admitting the infrequent gems. While bores have shouted in his ear with embarrassing clamor and found him immovable, a whisper from the other side about one of his books will engage his instant attention. For bumptious youngsters, Churchill leans on his special technique, which is very efficacious. He will listen to a sentence or two of immature babble, then bawl out, "How's that? Speak up!" The talker is usually so rattled that he subsides. A mysterious fact is that, once in a long while, Churchill will sit huddled in apparent deep dejection, neither speaking nor replying. It is a Hamlet-like brooding, not brought on by alcohol but rather the result, a few think, of getting one of his intuitive glimpses of the probable future and mourning the human follies to come.

After-dinner entertainment is apt to consist of television or movies. These are Churchill's staples. With his wife he goes occasionally to the theater, but it is apparent that he prefers to sit down in his own house, with a glass at hand, and be amused without the fuss of dressing up. Also, he has never pretended to the dubious eminence of intellectualism. On the contrary, he has often described himself as merely a hard worker and a man with common sense rather than an exquisite brain. The theater's affectations, its fopperies, its flimsy and continuous bleating about social inequality, have perhaps made him wary. He likes films of sprightly tone. He wants to be entertained and not instructed. His favorite theme still is the extolling of England; his favorite actor was the late Leslie Howard, whose death in an airplane accident Churchill publicly deplored. There was some talk that Howard, smoking a cigar, had been mistaken for the Prime Minister when climbing aboard the plane and that the Germans had marked the craft for destruction. Both Chartwell and the London house are equipped with television; the former has a comfortably heated projection room for movies in the basement, with seats for forty persons. Each week the newest releases are flown down from London, and on Sunday evening the best of these are shown as a regular ritual. The audience is made up of family, domestics, other employees, Churchill's writing assistants, and dinner guests. A local projectionist comes in for the showing. Upstairs, the lord of the manor waits until everyone else is seated. Then, with his glass and his cigar, he makes an entrance, going down to an upholstered seat in the front. The servants rise, and even the others make a rustling gesture of courtesy. Marlborough at his peak, movieless, in an unheated castle, lacking even a small-screen television set, never lived half so well.

# Chapter 27

Painting may no longer be considered wholly recreational with Churchill. His skill as an artist has reached the point where any word except "professional" would be an unjustified description of his success. In the beginning, however, he hoped only to develop a therapeutic hobby. At one time or another he had tried various outlets. It is not widely known that Churchill, in a period of political crisis, once bought a cheap violin and essayed to prepare himself for the concert stage. The fancy passed. Unlike bricklaying, the musical art was tougher than it looked. About all he got out of it was a witticism from Philip Snowden, a government opponent, who said, "I understand that Winston has taken up a new pastime—fiddling, and very appropriate, too."

When, in the First World War, Churchill blossomed out as Charles Morin, at a Parisian exhibit, his work did not go unnoticed. He sold one picture for $150, and a critic, in the inimitable fashion of the guild, wrote that "This man has fugue." Morin is still trying to figure out what it means; he has asked several artist friends, members of the Royal Academy, but has got little or no satisfaction. As producing workmen, they are not privy to the secret profundities of artistic oracles. In any case, when one has fugue he may expect to retain it indefinitely, for Churchill's painting has increased in stature through good days and thin.

Sir John Lavery, the English artist who taught Churchill to take his first small but unhesitant steps, continued to look after

the budding pupil. The two remained close friends in after
years. Churchill enjoyed getting together with Lavery at somebody's country house, where they painted each other's portraits. "I think it appealed to Winnie's sense of competition,
and at the same time there was coming into existence quite a
store of Lavery Churchills," says an acquaintance of both men.
Lord Charles Beresford, one of the clique that had repudiated
the First Lord after Gallipoli, later came across Churchill and
Sir John beneath some trees at Lady Paget's house, engaged at
their usual occupation of exchanging portraits. "Hello, Winston, when did you begin this game?" asked Beresford. Without
turning his head, Churchill replied equably, "The day you
kicked me out of the Admiralty, my lord." "Ah, well," said
Beresford, "perhaps I may have saved a great master." Along
the line of competition, Churchill finally jockeyed Lavery into
painting a landscape he had just done; then he entered both
pictures anonymously in a contest. Churchill's was adjudged to
be superior to that of Lavery, who, when he learned of this
extraordinary decision, took it calmly. Churchill did not appear triumphant; neither did he seem downcast. He is sensibly
able to absorb all possible tutelage without feeling overween-
ingly beholden to anybody.

Soon after the First World War Churchill went on a holiday
to Cannes, where several British statesmen were attending a
conference with the French over German reparations. Painting at nearby Roquefort and Grasse, he encountered and
worked with Sir William Orpen, a member of the Royal
Academy, who had been named official artist to the conference.
A few days later, Lord Curzon, who fancied himself as an art
critic, saw Churchill walking along a street in Cannes carrying
a canvas under his arm. "What's that you've got there, Winston?" cried Curzon in a condescending tone.

"Oh, just a picture," said Churchill.

"May I see it?"

Churchill propped the picture up on the sidewalk and
Curzon looked it over through a monocle. "Well," he said at

length, "the landscape part is passable, quite passable indeed, but I don't much care for the figures in the foreground."

Churchill removed a cigar from his mouth and said with concern, "I'm really very sorry to hear that, for I got Orpen to paint them in for me."

He has always liked to watch good artists at work, and he has no hesitation in getting them on the job if the occasion warrants it. When, in France, he was visited by Paul Maze, Simon Lavy, and Vuillard Segonzac, three of the country's best, he was delighted. "I have a rather large canvas under way here and I would be much obliged if you would help me finish it," he told the visitors. Then he laid out the assignments, giving one man the trees, another the sky, and the third the water, according to the way he saw their gifts. Completing the picture, he asked them to sign their names, and had, as one of his friends says, "A collector's item worth a great deal of money should any future Churchill find himself pinched for cash."

Churchill began the custom of taking his easel and other artists' materials along wherever he went. He visited Egypt and had the misfortune to suffer a nasty fall from a camel while attempting to paint the Pyramids. He had been warned that the project was risky—a camel's work habits are known as bohemian—but he insisted that there was no finer movable studio in existence. The precise cause of the upheaval was open to surmise, but the camel suddenly faced Mecca and saluted the Christian world with its rear heels. Churchill, thrown heavily to the sand, was badly smeared with the paint that he'd intended for a pyramid. He clambered up without reportable comment and for once did not press for a return engagement. The incident is cherished in artistic circles, being the only near-serious professional fall from a camel ever recorded by an artist of renown.

Curiously for him, Churchill has always been shy about showing his pictures. He has sent them to exhibits under various pseudonyms but has not, in recent years, made any attempt to sell them. Most of his best products are hung in a

specially adapted cottage on the grounds at Chartwell. If some
guest evinces a genuine interest, the master will take him on a
conducted tour of the gallery. In 1947, for the first time,
Churchill submitted a few of his works to the Royal Academy,
using the name "Mr. Winter." Two were selected for hanging.
By the next year, however, his fame had so far progressed that
the Academy elected him Honorary Academician Extraordinary; the Society of British Artists, too, made him an honorary member. And in 1949, six of his pictures were shown at
the Royal Academy's exhibition.

Paul Maze has said of Churchill, "He paints joyfully—alas,
he has taken hints from others and lost some of his spon-
taneity." An influence of Cézanne has been found in his landscapes, and his figures, conspicuously weak in his repertory,
are impressionistic. He is a bold colorist, a reflection of his
character, which is one of bright and positive hues rather than
shadowy grays and melancholy browns. Picasso, whose political background would not necessarily tend to make him
generous toward Churchill, once said, "If that man were a
painter by profession he'd have no trouble in earning a good
living." A lot of fine English and French artists have added
personally to Churchill's tutelage and complimented his work.
At one time or another, Walter Sickert and Sir William Nicholson helped him, the latter functioning for a while as a kind of
unofficial painting master to the Prime Minister, as music
masters were appointed to the children of nobility. Of Churchill's landscapes, Eric Newton has commented that "They are
by no means inconsiderable. They would have been worth
looking at had the name they bore been far less illustrious."
And perhaps the best index to the commercial value of the
statesman's art is provided by the director of London's most
famous gallery, who says, "Were they by an unknown they
would be worth 150 guineas [$450] each. Signed by Churchill
—any sum he chose to ask, and for as many pictures as he had
to sell."

Churchill reluctantly allowed one of his larger paintings to be auctioned off at a recent Y.W.C.A. benefit. A rich Brazilian admirer, Senhor Chateaubriand, known in South American circles as "the newspaper king," came to the function prepared to acquire the item for as high as thirteen thousand pounds. What was his surprise, and embarrassment, when the bidding began to expire in the vicinity of a thousand pounds and he finally got the prize for the peculiar sum of £1310.10s. The game but pauperized British present had already expended their carefully saved capital for fat-free foods and taxes for multiplying government bureaus. Though not inclined to sell the actual pictures, Churchill has been lenient in the matter of certain reproduction rights. In his realistic way, he struck a neat bargain with Joyce C. Hall, the American greeting-card magnate. Hall bought the greeting rights to sixteen of the statesman's oils and told the press, "He is a wonderful artist whom few people in America know. He is too modest about his paintings. Our cards will insure that he gets the notice he deserves." He quoted Churchill as favoring the plunge "in order to encourage amateur painters." While the price for this artistic wedding was not advertised, it was said to be substantial. The Soho Galleries in London have the British right to publish Christmas card reproductions of his pictures. In three years, says the management, the sales have run to six figures (in pounds). The fact that Churchill is backward about selling his work does not mean that he holds it cheaply. When *Life* magazine imported eighteen of his paintings to be reproduced in color, he had them insured for three hundred thousand dollars.

John Rothenstein, the director of London's Tate Gallery, has described his impressions of Churchill at work, by means of an article in the *Sunday Times,* beginning with Delacroix's observation after calling on Corot: "To know a painter you must see him in his studio." Rothenstein found Churchill (at Chartwell) wearing a siren suit, a very wide-brimmed "painting hat," and a pair of black slippers with his initials worked on them in gold. Before getting the session under way, the artist gave his guest a bottle of champagne and some lunch, and then sang him a music hall ballad he'd learned from Walter Sickert. Offered a cigar, Rothenstein refused, with the rather sententious remark that "Every man should have one virtue"—his was not smoking. Churchill instantly picked this up, saying, "There is no such thing as a negative virtue. If I have been of any service to my fellow men, it has never been by self-repression, but always by self-expression."

In the studio, Churchill begged his visitor to "Speak, I pray, with absolute frankness." Warmed by champagne, Rothenstein fired off a few small guns at one of the landscapes. He stuck pretty close to the special parlance of career appraisal and said, in effect, that the shore was too pale and lightly modeled to support the weight of the heavy trees, with their dense, dark foliage. "Instead of growing up out of the earth, they weigh it down," he added. "Oh, but I can put that right at once," cried Churchill, springing toward his easel. "It will take less than a quarter of an hour."

Rothenstein was horrified.

"But this painting must certainly be among your earliest?"

"I did it about twenty years ago," replied Churchill, lighting a fresh cigar.

"Well, then," said Rothenstein with finality, "surely it's impossible for you to recapture the mood in which you painted it, or indeed your whole outlook of those days."

Grumbling, Churchill gave the idea up. It was plain that he felt he could recapture the mood with ease, or even the whole outlook, but he capitulated to criticism.

"Mr. Churchill," Rothenstein wrote, "has set himself to cultivate the restricted possibilities open to him with the utmost assiduity and discernment. He is, therefore, able to do much more than enjoy himself in the sunlight. By the skilful choice of subjects within his range but to which he can respond ardently, he is able to paint pictures of real merit which bear a direct and intimate relation to his outlook on life.

"In these pictures there comes bubbling irrepressibly up his sheer enjoyment of the simple beauties of nature—water, whether still or ruffled by wind; snow, immaculate and crisp; trees, dark with the density of their foliage or dappled with sunlight; fresh flowers and distant mountains; and, above all, sunlight at its most intense.

"The highest peaks of his achievement are, in my opinion, 'The Goldfish Pool at Chartwell' (1948), 'The Loup River, Quebec' (1947), 'Chartwell under Snow' (1947), and 'Cannes Harbour, Evening' (1923). These express with insight and candour his vivid and voracious enjoyment of living."

Churchill wrote a little book entitled *Painting as a Pastime* in 1948 and illustrated it with good color reproductions of his favorite canvases. The text throws some intense sunlight on his attitude toward art as practiced by himself. Clearly enough, he still sees his painting as relaxation rather than a serious expression of his creative force. "Change is the master key," he says. "A man can wear out a particular part of his mind by continually using it and tiring it, just in the same way as he can wear out the elbows of his coat." At a time when he was past forty, Churchill suddenly realized that he was wearing out the elbows of his mind and decided that "The cultivation of a hobby and new forms of interest is therefore a policy of first importance to a public man."

His account of his actual start differs somewhat from that once given by Sir John Lavery, and must therefore be presented: "Some experiments one Sunday in the country with the children's paint-box led me to procure the next morning a complete outfit for painting in oils.

"Having bought the colours, an easel, and a canvas, the next step was *to begin*. But what a step to take! The palette gleamed with beads of colour; fair and white rose the canvas; the empty brush hung poised, heavy with destiny, irresolute in the air. My hand seemed arrested by a silent veto. But after all the sky on this occasion was unquestionably blue, and a pale blue at that. There could be no doubt that blue paint mixed with white should be put on the top part of the canvas. One really does not need to have had an artist's training to see that. It is a starting-point open to all. So very gingerly I mixed a little blue paint on the palette with a very small brush, and then with infinite precaution made a mark about as big as a bean upon the affronted snow-white shield. It was a challenge, a deliberate challenge; but so subdued, so halting, indeed so cataleptic, that it deserved no response. At that moment the loud approaching sound of a motor-car was heard in the drive. From this chariot there stepped swiftly and lightly none other than the gifted wife of Sir John Lavery. 'Painting! But what are you hesitating about? Let me have a brush—the big one.' Splash into the turpentine, wallop into the blue and the white, frantic flourish on the palette—clean no longer—and then several large, fierce strokes and slashes of blue on the absolutely cowering canvas. Anyone could see that it could not hit back. No evil fate avenged the jaunty violence. The canvas grinned in helplessness before me. The spell was broken. The sickly inhibitions rolled away. I seized the largest brush and fell upon my victim with berserk fury. I have never felt any awe of a canvas since."

Sooner or later in his book, it was to be expected that Churchill would see art from a military viewpoint. The blood of Marlborough runs strong in his veins, and the gay times in India and the Sudan did nothing to curb a natural enthusiasm. Several other well-known persons have the same tendency. Ernest Hemingway, as he walks through life, with his flanks protected, appraises each shifting scene in terms of a passage at arms. "In all battles," writes Churchill, "two things are usually required of the Commander-in-Chief: to make a good plan for his army and, secondly, to keep a strong reserve. Both these are also obligatory upon the painter." Artistic reserves, to Churchill, signify a landscape well stocked with vivid objects. "I must say I like bright colours," he says. "I agree with Ruskin in his denunciation of that school of painting who eat 'slate-pencil and chalk, and assure everybody that they are nicer and purer than strawberries and plums.' I cannot pretend to feel impartial about the colours. I rejoice with the brilliant ones, and am genuinely sorry for the poor browns. When I get to heaven I mean to spend a considerable portion of my first million years in painting, and so get to the bottom of the subject. But then I shall require a still gayer palette than I get here below. I expect orange and vermillion will be the darkest, dullest colours upon it, and beyond them there will be a whole range of wonderful new colours which will delight the celestial eye."

Here below, Churchill's selection of places in which to paint reflects his love of color. The titles of his pictures tell the over-all story of his artistic travels. There are: "St. Jean, Cap Ferrat," this spot a long finger of land thrust out into the Mediterranean between Villefranche and Monte Carlo; "By Lake Lugane," a cobalt body of ice water in the Swiss Alps; "The Mediterranean Near Genoa," "The Mill, Saint-Georges-Motel, Normandy," "Near Antibes" on the Riviera, "Desert Scene" at Marrakech in North Africa, "Village Near Lugano," also in Switzerland, and, using perhaps the brightest of England's color impressions, "The Weald of Kent under Snow."

Churchill has impressed people with the lordly and precise bustle which it takes to get him set up for work. His costume is extravagant, with a broad, limp hat, a white, shoe-length smock that looks like an Arabian burnous, a dead cigar in his mouth, spectacles perched far down on his nose, a whacking large easel on oversize stilts, and, frequently, a bucket of frosted champagne at his feet. In a hot place, he instructs a servant to set up an umbrella on a long pole, or, if the sod is rocky, to stand by his side and hold it. On several occasions in troubled periods, Inspector Thompson has been numbered among the unvivid objects in the immediate landscape—revolver at the ready, alerted for assassins or hysterical art critics. Hundreds of strollers have come upon Churchill thus accoutered, and have gone away happy and refreshed.

The statesman's general appearance has also proved of interest to other artists. In 1948 the United States Artists' League found his face "among the ten most provocative in the world," and a great many fine painters and sculptors have essayed to immortalize it. Walter Sickert once did a head and shoulders (working, for some reason, from a photograph) which gave the subject such a pugnacious look that Mrs. Churchill objected. Churchill likes it. In newsreels he has a horror of looking soft or effeminate and insists that no make-up shall be applied. It is difficult to pose him. His cousin, Clare Sheridan, a sculptress, modeled his head in 1942; she sat in a corner of his study at No. 10 Downing Street while he worked on dispatches. It was a fractious job, frequently hanging up on the business of his cigar. Churchill declined to remove it. At long last, with the connivance of Mrs. Churchill, Miss Sheridan persuaded him to forgo the cigar for an hour. Then she quickly modeled his mouth, put on the other finishing touches, and shipped the work to the Royal Academy, which refused it with the dispatch for which the group is noted. Another bust, by Sir William Reid Dick, was later presented to the Royal Academy by Churchill's parish of Westerham. This one was accepted.

The R.A.F. Club in Piccadilly has recently hung a painting of Churchill by Charles Julian Orde, breaking a precedent by having the club's first likeness of a living person on its walls. In one way or another, Churchill has opened several artistic vistas. His physiognomy affects people curiously. Several years ago, some zestful Australians built a gigantic head of him from wood and adorned it with an eight-foot bamboo cigar. The assembly, *in toto,* is the sole landmark along the thousand-mile highway between Alice Springs and Darwin. In a similar vein, a Mr. Marsh, of Margate, proposed to erect a statue of Churchill on the cliffs at Dover, so large that it could be seen on a clear day by art lovers in France. For the cigar motif, Marsh designed one that would be illuminated by a big red light bulb in the end. He got an organization together, stimulated an American branch, and began soliciting funds. But it all fell through.

Churchill likes three portraits of him that were done during the war by Frank Salisbury, who caught him in military moods.

Churchill's favorite is in a standing pose and now hangs in the Constitutional Club. When Mrs. Churchill saw it, she said, "It has a very fierce expression and one that I would not have chosen." She told him afterward, "It will make everyone terrified of you." The Prime Minister was agreeably affected, saying, "Surely, in wartime, that is all to the good." Salisbury is entertaining on the subject of the three works. To begin the first one, he was told to enter the House of Commons, crouch behind the Speaker's chair, and make sketches during a Churchill address. Soon after this, an aide of the Premier rang Salisbury to say that the subject would shortly visit the artist's studio. Then the aide rang back to fix the probable time of arrival at 6 P.M. He kept ringing with frequent bulletins. At five fifty-five: "The P.M.'s car is at the door of No. 10"; at six twenty-three: "There is a bustle in the hallway"; at six fifty-five: "He is about to enter the car"; and at seven thirty: "Should be there any minute now."

Churchill turned up a few minutes before eight, abruptly took a seat, got out some notes to peruse, and in total silence waved Salisbury to his labors. The silence continued for an hour, at the end of which Churchill arose, stopped briefly by the picture, said, "I do landscapes myself," and left. A few days later, Salisbury was summoned during an air raid to Churchill's dugout, where he found the Prime Minister in bed. "I have a fancy for one in battle dress," the artist was informed. Churchill had slipped into a battle jacket and retained the lower part of his pajamas. The painting turned out successfully; it hangs today in the home of the statesman's daughter, Mrs. Duncan Sandys, where he often stops to admire it.

In *Painting as a Pastime,* Churchill wrote, "To be really happy and safe, one ought to have at least two or three hobbies, and they must all be real." Hobby-wise, art has remained his first love, but he has faithfully tried to branch out. In 1949 he bought his first race horse, Colonist II. Harking back to his art phase, he selected a jockey's costume featuring a pink jacket with chocolate-colored sleeves and cap. Bernard Baruch, hearing the news, sent him over a complete set of fine racing silks, and the horse carried them to good advantage when it won its first race. Before very long it was apparent that Churchill was more at home as a race-horse owner than as a player of roulette at Monte Carlo. By now, Colonist II has won nearly thirty thousand dollars, stimulating a sizable expansion of its owner's stable. Churchill in 1950 had nine horses, seven of them in training. Altogether, his stable properties are worth about a hundred thousand dollars. Both jockeys and trainers wonder at his luck. They think it may have something to do with his pre-race ritual. With a good deal of ceremony, he goes down to give the horse a talking-to. This continues for several minutes. One of the Premier's friends says, "It might be an exaggeration to describe the horse's face as apprehensive, but I noticed the same look from sluggish ministers after a wartime Cabinet meeting. In any case, the horse gets into motion pretty fast and keeps glancing back over its shoulder. Winston's oratory has been producing that same effect throughout the animal kingdom for more than fifty years."

# Chapter 28

T o produce the speeches and books that have enriched the world's store of important ideas, Churchill begins his work day about 10 A.M. He has breakfast in bed, a nourishing meal consisting, perhaps, of half a cold partridge, several rashers of bacon fried into a curl, a boiled egg, toast and marmalade, and buttered scones and tea—the whole washed down by a bottle of light white wine. Dr. G. A. Goolden, the ship's surgeon aboard one of the transports on which Churchill made a wartime voyage, says that the Prime Minister's staple breakfast, that trip, was curried chicken, ham, beef, and a bottle of sauterne. The doctor was impressed by Churchill's high temper at the slightest sign of muddleheadedness on the part of anybody. The morning repast disposed of, he gets out a writing board that he built himself and sets about making notes. The board is somewhat out of the ordinary, having two felt-covered bricks at either end, where Churchill rests his elbows. He lights up a big cigar when he starts—one of the cigars he imports wholesale from dealer John M. Rushbrook in New York[1]—and allows the fire to expire soon afterward. For his cigars, Churchill designed, and an artisan fashioned, an ingenious device that might have commercial value,

[1]Author's note: Churchill is not regarded as a cigar connoisseur by some of his friends. His favorite blend is half Havana and half Virginia tobaccos. However, he once cabled Rushbrook, "Kindly send another 1000 with slight variations at your discretion." He smokes about sixteen cigars a day but actually consumes only a fraction of each.

although he has never tried to market it. His name for the invention is a "fender," but it could more properly be called a saliva-collector, being, in fact, a sort of spit valve, like that on a trombone. As Churchill chews away on his dead cigar, there is an inevitable overflow and the fender gathers it up. He changes fenders (which look like paper collars) when one fills its office, and his butler, William Greenshields, carries the discardee away to the incinerator on a gold-plated tray.

Churchill calls for his first whiskey and soda of the day when he gets his cigar going. Contrary to many published reports, he does not gulp this down, nor swill a succession of morning whiskeys, but rather sips along very slowly, scarcely finishing the drink by noon. On rare occasions he will have two before the lunch hour. Now and then he grants a brief business conference in the morning. He never gets out of bed; it seems doubtful, acquaintances think, that he would make more than a gesture of arising should the King appear. One of his publishers has visited Churchill several times in the morning. For nearly twenty years, Churchill has been "in process of completing" his epochal *History of the English Speaking Peoples*. The coming of war, with its rich opportunity for producing a multivolume chronology of those anxious but exciting events, interrupted Churchill's *History*. Not long ago, he handed over the material he had finished and said, "Well, there it is, 450,-000 words. I'll be glad to see it published."

The statesman was asked, respectfully, "Upon what note have you ended it, Mr. Churchill?"

"Why, I've brought it up to the death of Lincoln. That seems a capital place to wind it up," Churchill replied.

"Our contract provides that the *History* be brought up to the present," he was told. "The death of Lincoln occurred quite some time ago."

Churchill grumbled and fumed, and squared the account in various ways. He seldom answered business letters, necessitating frequent trips by the heads of various concerns to Chartwell or to 28 Hyde Park Gate. Several of these people have expressed interest in the way Churchill husbands his cigars. "He keeps several grades on hand," one visitor says, "and gives them to people in accordance with the standing they are in at the moment." The day of the above conversation about the contract, Churchill gave the publishing representative what the latter describes as "a filthy Mexican weed that almost killed me." An hour or so later, perhaps out of penitence, Churchill offered him a drink and invited him to stay to lunch.

In the period of social hubbub preceding lunch, Churchill will have another whiskey and soda, and during the meal he is apt to drink a bottle or two of champagne or some good still wine, depending on the food served. Under this stimulation, he talks with enthusiasm, drawing out the midday meal to more than two hours, as is the fashion everywhere in upper-class England. Immediately after lunch, he retires to his room, undresses completely, puts on his pajamas, and turns in for a two-hour nap. There are various accounts as to the origin of this habit of Churchill's. Some feel that he acquired it long ago, when, as a supernumerary attached to the Spanish Army in Cuba, he followed the local custom of stretching out beneath a tree to avoid the heat of the day. One story has it that he got the idea from Edison, whose life he admired and who never had an ordinary night's sleep but took naps whenever he sensed an energy lag. Perhaps the best bet is that he picked up the habit from his former secretary, Sir Edward Marsh, who once advised Churchill that he could greatly prolong the working day by sleeping in the afternoon.

When he arises, Churchill digs into his labors. He has made notes in the morning; now he begins to dictate. This may take one of several forms. As in his First World War days, he is keen on bathing, and he may crawl into the tub, station a secretary outside his bathroom door, then, amidst happy splashes and snatches of disconnected song, start bawling out the lively sonorities with which the political world will be entertained. Some days his urge for baths is stronger than others; for example, he appears more bathtub-prone at Chartwell than at

Hyde Park Gate. At either place, however, he may take several
baths in a row, breaking off only to dry himself and put on a
robe. For a lot of his dictation, Churchill has a large and, by
now, workable dictaphone in his study. Attached to it is a
microphone of the sort used with public address systems. This
stands on the floor at the edge of a strip of carpeting which has
a deep groove worn down the middle. While dictating, he
walks back and forth on the carpet, whose placement is such
that, if he steps off, his voice will no longer be audible in the
mike. In addition to his dictaphone, his six secretaries, and his
"work team," or high-flown helpers, everything about Churchill's labors is elaborate and costly. In the preparation of his
currently appearing series, a personal narrative of the Second
World War, he makes the rough drafts himself, allocates each
section to the indicated team-member expert, and then, when
they've finished, puts it all together and slicks it into his final,
characteristic wording. At his own expense, he has the material
printed at the Chiswick Press (near Chartwell) in large folio
form, each folio measuring about twelve by eighteen inches,
enclosed in attractive boxes, and, at last, conveyed up to Cas-
sell's, the publishing house that is bringing it out in England.
After that comes the business of rereading to make it editorially
impeccable. Churchill is fanatic on the subject of literary and
factual perfection. He will keep his entire staff up till 4 A.M.,
if need be, to remove a shadow of doubt from any tiny point of
reference. Despite his long hours with his white-collar workers,
he guards the schedules of his domestics, once halting his butler
in the midst of a shoe-cleaning operation. "But you can't go to
Parliament with one boot shined and the other muddy," ex-
claimed the butler. "Oh, yes, I can," replied Churchill, and he
snatched up his hat and stick and set off, to attract a great
many interested glances.

The heavy work of his day comes in the long hours after
dinner. The evening meal is his time for serious drinking. Before dinner he may have several whiskey and sodas, and he
downs a hearty quantity of champagne before the dessert,

cigars, and brandy arrive. In the period after the ladies with-draw, Churchill's consumption of fine old French brandy has been praised by virtuosi at the tippler's art. One of his strongest admirers is Stalin, who, though able to outeat any Britisher on record, probably including Henry VIII, was never able to match Churchill glass for glass. All through the rest of his waking hours—and he works himself and his staff until one, or two, or three o'clock in the morning—Churchill has a glass of brandy and soda close at hand. During these stints, a week of which would hospitalize the average ox, he functions with bril-liance while all around him lesser men are falling from exhaus-tion. In going over a manuscript with Churchill, an editor once said, "You have certainly done prodigious work on these volumes." Churchill replied, "Yes, and I've drunk more pro-digious quantities of whiskey in doing them than perhaps any other man in the world could have done."

His industry at his speeches, and in general with the party, is equally conscientious. Gerald O'Brien, who as public relations director for the Conservatives has worked with Churchill for years, finds the assignment a pretty sure method for growing old in a hurry. The business of political campaigning hinges on clockwork appointments. When people assemble for a meeting or an address, they expect to be met or addressed. It is Church-ill's pleasure to start from half an hour to two hours late for nearly all dates and try to make up this time on the road. Often he travels by special train, but he prefers to go in his own car, a black Humber driven by a harried chauffeur named Tom. It is axiomatic that Churchill's campaign weather will be fine. Nevertheless, O'Brien has frequent nightmares about several of the trips. A typical start will see Churchill and one or two others pile into the Humber around five thirty for a seven o'clock speech at a point a hundred miles distant. Churchill, or his valet-butler, is carrying a supply of emergency brandy. As his chauffeur swings into the high road, Churchill crouches, with a flask, on the edge of the back seat and urges him to greater speeds. "But the machine is traveling at eighty-five miles per hour now, Mr. Churchill," the chauffeur will protest. "Faster! Whip it up a bit!" comes the answer.

The car is overhauled by police with regularity. On a recent trip, it was doing eighty around a slight curve when one of the rear tires blew out. There was nothing for Tom to do but pull up. Almost the instant he did, a van full of irate constables screeched to a halt alongside. They had been trying to catch the runaway for miles. Their equanimity was restored as soon as they identified their distinguished quarry; they even helped fix his tire. Churchill stood off to one side of the road, serenely puffing at a cigar. He made no sign of apology but only got in and cried "Drive off!" when the tire was fixed. The constables saluted humbly. On another such occasion he transferred to the police car, whose driver had offered to rush him ahead, and spent the rest of the ride egging on the policemen exactly as he had been doing Tom. For a campaign trip to Cardiff, Churchill started so late that O'Brien was in a pitiable state of nerves. Mrs. Churchill accompanied the group. In one of his blandest humors, Churchill became immersed in his conversational gift and passed the brandy back and forth with such frequency that his wife got annoyed. She was also outraged at the reckless bursts of speed to which her husband had succeeded in exhorting Tom. Finally she cried, "Please let me out. I refuse to continue this ride." With the utmost courtesy, Churchill drew up at a country railroad station and escorted her to the platform. Then he climbed back into the car and, plying the brandy bottle, lit out down the road like a bat out of hell for Cardiff. By the time they arrived, what with the brandy and his nerves, O'Brien was done up—out practically cold. Churchill supervised the laying out of his public relations officer on a table in the rear of the hall. Then he went ahead and made a rouser of a speech. Afterward, returning to the rear, he appeared confused about the origin of O'Brien's trouble, and expressed the opinion that it was "probably something he ate."

O'Brien has always had trouble trying to get Churchill to

prepare a speech on time. When pressed about its possible contents, the statesman is apt to be vague. Advance copies for the papers quite often are not forthcoming. Nevertheless, Churchill attends carefully to his remarks. He either writes out the speeches in longhand, or dictates them to a secretary; then he has notes typed up on pieces of white cardboard, each about four by six inches in size. His arrangement of the notes on these is undoubtedly unique; nobody seems to know why he does it. The top line of type runs full length across the card, but the second is shorter, and the third shorter yet, until, in the bottom line, only one or two words remain:

> It painful to me see as
> have seen in journeys
> about country small
> British house
> or business
> smashed

Regardless of the notes, he memorizes his speeches and has always done so, except for one short-lived experiment. Moreover, he rehearses them before a mirror, studying his gestures, and records them on a machine, which enables him to play them back and edit them for clarity, voice inflection, tone quality, and general structure. Churchill worries a good deal about people going to sleep during his speeches—he himself has enjoyed some grand naps while bores droned on—and he keeps saying, as he works, "Now we'd better have some comic relief here—I'd better drop in a joke to wake them up." One of his most effective customs is to insert local allusions, for which he has a freak memory. He will mention casually some hero of the area, or one of its cherished events, and raise a wild storm of applause. As a rule, he can summon such references without aids, but he has his staff check each one to be sure. O'Brien has never yet run across an error of so much as a word in any of them. "What would you do if you lost your notes, Mr. Churchill?" the publicity director once asked. Churchill's reply was, "I do not take out fire insurance on my house because I feel very strongly that there's going to be a fire."

Conservative leaders feel that, if he lost his notes and his memory failed, an address by Churchill would hardly come up to scratch. Actually, he is a poor speaker extemporaneously and will invent the most ingenious excuses to avoid being thus trapped. He needs time to build the balanced edifice of his message. This is in singular contrast to his firecracker wit in the cut and thrust of parliamentary debate. When suddenly confronted by newsreel cameras and microphones, he will choose his words with almost painful deliberation. His voice is considered "classless" in England, having no identifying accent of school or university, caste or locality. The old trouble with the lisp is still occasionally noticeable, but he contrives his sentences with such skill that nearly all sibilants are avoided. Although Churchill dislikes being cornered for impromptu remarks, he never worries about approaching deadlines for speeches. Once, on a train with O'Brien, he had not yet written a single word, and everyone was apprehensive. However, their fears were groundless, since the candidate began to talk at about the midway point in their trip and talked the whole speech out before he finished. The final product, when delivered that evening, was a verbatim repetition of Churchill's conversation on the train. "With identically the same gestures," says O'Brien.

A B.B.C. engineer who worked with Churchill on broadcasts during the war thinks that he at first had great contempt for radio speaking, because of the absence of gestures. It often took persuasion to keep him from hammering on the table with his fist, giving rise to an earsplitting racket over the air. He also objected to the announcements preceding his talks. "Surely everyone knows I'm going to speak," he kept saying. The people in the broadcasting studio felt that, of the two microphones before him, he identified the one on his left as Hitler and the other as Mussolini. He would turn his head to snarl his insults at these two liberators at the appropriate times, dividing his attention fairly. Churchill liked to wear his siren suit to the broadcasts, and he sat in a relaxed posture far back in a chair as he spoke. He never missed a cue, lost his place, or stumbled in any way. "In twenty-six years I have never seen anyone so massively composed at the microphone," the engineer says.

Even though everybody else in his vicinity is going to pieces, Churchill remains unbothered in political crises. There are frequent signs of temper but never any hint that he is rattled. He also keeps his own counsel despite the heaviest pressures. On the pivotal campaign trips by train, he is about the only member of the company never dismayed by mishaps, delays, misplaced documents, and the like. On one trip to the north of England, when nobody could find the advance copies of an important speech which had been promised to reporters riding in the next car, Churchill sat reading *Huckleberry Finn,* having a calm and conspicuously detached good time. This was despite the fact that the reporters were clamoring, in the emergency, to be permitted to approach him for personal notes. Churchill has never been co-operative with the press. On the contrary, he is probably the least accommodating public figure within the memory of man. Walter Graebner, whose job in London with *Life* is more managerial than journalistic, said that he had never, in ten years, been able to get a *Time* or *Life* correspondent in to see Churchill. Many reporters in London for the American newspapers, such as the New York *Times* and the *Herald Tribune,* have never been able to wangle an interview with the statesman at any time during their stay abroad. This gives rise to a certain amount of natural annoyance. Raymond Daniell, the well-known chief of the *Times'* London bureau, tried to approach Churchill when one of the latter's recent books appeared, to get an autographed copy for Arthur Hays Sulzberger, the owner of the paper. Daniell was able to reach him at last, by telephone, and found him affably disposed, perhaps because the *Times,* together with the London *Daily Telegraph* and *Life,* has been serializing *The Second World War* for a total sum somewhat in excess of a million dollars. In a sudden burst of friendliness, Churchill said, "No doubt you would like me to autograph one for you, too?"

Daniell was able to say, "I'm sorry, but I haven't bought a copy."

There was a brief silence, and then the conversation was ended in formal tones.

Aboard the campaign train, Churchill never speaks to the reporters, English or American; O'Brien does not think that he knows any of their names. Neither, as head of the state for years, did he hold press conferences in the fashion of American Presidents. Except for brief shipboard sessions when he came to America for aid, he held himself aloof from journalists. The reason for this apparent rudeness is that Churchill decided, long ago, that he himself would exploit whatever literary material lay in his remarks. He has often growled to secretaries, "They [reporters] can easily follow what I do by listening to my speeches and reading the papers," a statement that certainly contains a remarkable incongruity, as an American writer recently pointed out: "It's difficult for a reporter to catch up on Churchill in the papers without first catching him to have something to put in the papers." The statesman is also uncooperative with biographers and magazine contributors. This, too, among his circle, is understood to be based on an eagerness to continue making money himself in sufficient quantities to support his family in style. At a recent lunch in London, an American biographer was asked by Lord ————, a naval officer high in the Admiralty, "Tell me, have you found Winston helpful?" When told no, he said, perhaps facetiously, "Now, then, why don't you offer him a hundred pounds?"

Churchill feels entitled to his privacy, and is probably one of the few great men of history with courage enough to protect it. His reasons for sequestering himself are ample, and even grudgingly respected by many of those most anxious to see him. He has been able to do a lot of valuable work in the time he might have allotted to well-meaning reporters. However, some journalists in London believe, maybe with justification, that a political servant has no right to insist on a writing monopoly concerning his acts in behalf of the public. Like nearly every other in the world, the argument has two indisputable sides. When he thinks that people have written rashly about him, Churchill uses effective arguments, many of them presented by lawyers. He is quick to sue, as the late Louis Adamic, author and whilom liberal, found out. In Adamic's book, *Dinner at the White House*, there were several passages criticizing Churchill's conduct of the war and containing a footnote that said, "As Drew Pearson revealed in one of his columns in 1945, the motives for the British policy in Greece were at least partly linked up with the fact that Hambros Bank of London, the chief British creditors of Greece (they gave up to 17 percent on their loans which the leftist or E.A.M. Greeks wished to scale down to 5 percent) had bailed Churchill out of bankruptcy in 1912." In a British High Court, the statement was proved to be untrue; the publisher (Harper and Brothers, in England and America) made a public retraction; and Churchill was awarded damages against the publisher and author of five thousand pounds, together with three hundred pounds in costs.

Paradoxically, Churchill can be the soul of condescension. Nobody ever knows exactly what reaction to expect from him. During the war, the British had in America a comparatively obscure member of the embassy office named Isaiah Berlin, whose reports on various conditions and trends came to be read in London with deep respect. They were polished models of careful research and both precise and witty analysis. Before the war was over, Churchill was reading them with amused satisfaction. And when he saw in a London paper an announcement that Mr. I. Berlin had arrived from America, he roared to his staff, "I must have that fellow to lunch *today!*" The Berlin mentioned in the dispatch, Irving Berlin, of New York, turned up in answer to the invitation with pleasure somewhat tempered by astonishment. As he and his host started the meal, Churchill said, "You have written some wonderful things. I have admired them greatly. Now tell me, of all that you have written, which one do you think was the best?"

Berlin thought a moment, then replied, "Well, Mr. Prime Minister, I hardly know, but I guess I would say, 'Alexander's Ragtime Band.' "

Churchill laughed without restraint, feeling that this was political wit at its peak. Then he essayed a feeler on the American presidential campaign, asking, "What will happen in that election over there?"

Not wishing to give a snap judgment, Berlin weighed the question and said cautiously, "A lot of people think Roosevelt will lose."

"Ha! Do they, now?" cried Churchill, keenly interested.

"And again, quite a number think that he will win."

Churchill said, "Excuse me a moment," and went out to find one of his secretaries, to whom he shouted, "Will you please tell me who that is in there?"

"Why, Mr. Irving Berlin, the composer, Mr. Churchill," answered the secretary. It was feared that the Premier was on the verge of an embarrassing eruption, but he returned to the lunch and made himself agreeable, chatting with Berlin on a variety of subjects and complimenting him on the fine songs he had written.

The criticism has been raised, amidst the Tories, that Churchill's autocratic ways have occasionally hampered the success of the party. This seems untenable in view of the October election, which was widely acclaimed as a personal victory. In a long-term sense, however, the towering majesty of such a gigantic oak possibly tends to stifle the growth of nearby political saplings. It may be unfortunate for the party, and for Churchill, that any organization which he heads is soon reduced to the status of a one-man machine. Churchill has an inborn compulsion to run things with a high hand, and this trait was thought by many to have influenced his defeat after the war. The British, it is said, had tired of being driven on such a tight rein. If this is true, it would appear that Churchill's basic force, his enduring desire to lead, is simultaneously a weakness, if a too disregardful exercise of it has periodically deprived the British, and the world, of his guiding genius. His relationship with Lord Woolton, the party chairman, is a source of entertainment to party subordinates. Churchill selected Woolton, who had formerly organized a chain of successful stores and has a brisk and commanding manner, and treats him with paternal firmness. Many people in the party are rendered half paralyzed by Woolton's imperious presence; Churchill calls him "Uncle Fred" and sends him hopping on errands. Once, when both were traveling by auto to a campaign meeting, somebody asked Woolton what he planned to discuss. The chairman, who was perched up in front with the chauffeur, turned around and replied a little pettishly, "Oh, it doesn't matter what I'm going to say; Winston is speaking, you know." Bundled up in the rear seat, Churchill replied easily, in his modest way, "That's right, Uncle Fred. That's right."

Around the House of Commons, Churchill is accorded the sort of deference that was given an eighteenth-century monarch. He usually arrives for sessions a little late, in his chauffeur-driven Humber; he gets out ponderously, chewing on a cigar, and goes into the smoking room. For all his public appearances, he "times" his cigars, to be sure they are not smoked down comically short. In the chamber, a special black leather chair is set aside for his personal use, and lackeys, watching carefully, rush him drinks when he raises one hand with a slight, regal gesture. He has never demanded servility, but the English, of both parties, take such pride in his record of accomplishment that they proffer it spontaneously. Simon Worthington-Digby, the Tory whip, says that Churchill is not necessarily approachable as he sits brooding in the smoking room. He does not encourage windbags to interrupt his thoughts, though he has never, to date, gone to the lengths of his father in hiring a House waiter to listen to the end of somebody's anecdote.

For years, Churchill has refused to take the stipend provided for His Majesty's Members of Parliament. Herbert Morrison, the former Labor Minister, was once sufficiently incautious, in a speech outside the House, to attack Churchill on the ground of absenteeism, "despite the fact," he said, "that the Opposition Leader still draws his pay." In making this statement, Morrison unwittingly called down upon his head some rare Churchillian thunder. Not only did he *not* accept his two thousand pounds a year as a Member, replied the patriarch, but he had never even taken the annual two thousand pounds to which he was entitled as a former Prime Minister. Morrison sent him an instant apology, in an open letter beginning, "My dear Churchill——" He received an unruffled answer from the accused, starting off, "Dear Lord President of the Council——"

In the venerable assembly, Churchill no longer provides the catalysis for Tory debate but leaves this strenuous job to his first lieutenant, Anthony Eden. During nearly any speech by the Opposition, Eden is up and down like a jack-in-the-box, quizzing, challenging, trapping the speaker. The Foreign Minister's fiery actions belie his languid appearance that Americans have come to know from newsreels. It is regrettable, think several Tories, that Eden is content to accept his formal speeches from the hands of press workers in the party. Although Churchill composes and memorizes each address, Eden often delivers a vital statement while reading it for the first time himself. But in the debates he is the personification of energy, with a gift for caustic rejoinder. Alongside him on the front bench, Churchill sits listening, with a hand cupped to an ear, sometimes smiling, often growling, occasionally even chiming in without observing the rite of arising. There is nothing very ritualistic about Churchill. It is a custom for Members leaving the room to get up, walk away from the Speaker (presiding officer), and then turn and bow before disappearing. Churchill generally gets up and shambles out without a backward look, and as likely as not will have a cigar in his mouth before he reaches the door. With the other front benchers on both sides, he frequently sits on the base of his spine and puts his feet on the desk before him. At these times it is to be noted that he has a fondness for zipper shoes, ones that he created himself. In periods of disfavor, he has been known to doodle artistically, drawing designs and caricatures of his colleagues, and even making paper airplanes and sailing them into a hat.

A gauge of his popularity may be taken on the fete days, the sessions of unpartisan pride, of national rejoicing, when Englishmen band together to hail a good thing that is simply English. Churchill's birthday may be counted as one of these. As he forges on past his biblical threescore and ten, bringing further honors to England, his birthdays become times of increasing acclaim. They are, perhaps, the only state birthdays ever informally evolved of a man still living. Then he is at his best in Parliament. The chamber is filled—with his allies and comrades and with men who the day before were attacking him without stint. Before he goes to the House, his habit is to enter Westminster Abbey, across the yard, where England's mighty are buried. Beneath the banners of the dukes and princes, near the grave of the Unknown Soldier, not far from Pitt's sepulcher, he says a private prayer. His appearance in the House, in the formal attire that he always wears there, brings a standing storm of applause and shouts of "Hear, hear!" Churchill tries to make his expression fierce, the look of the boy warrior of Malakand and Omdurman, the face of a fighter *à outrance* for more than half a century. But he is easily moved to emotion, and the tears roll down his cheeks as he bobs his head like a schoolboy.

England continues to cry hail to her man of heroic size, the last of the great statesmen, a giant among pygmies. In the words of his compatriot from Avon, "When comes such another?"